THE POLYTECHNIC OF WALES LIBRARY

TREFOREST
Llantwit Road, Treforest, Pontypridd.

SIGN LANGUAGE OF THE DEAF

Psychological, Linguistic,
and Sociological Perspectives

PERSPECTIVES IN
NEUROLINGUISTICS and PSYCHOLINGUISTICS

Harry A. Whitaker, Series Editor
DEPARTMENT OF PSYCHOLOGY
THE UNIVERSITY OF ROCHESTER
ROCHESTER, NEW YORK

SIGN LANGUAGE OF THE DEAF

Psychological, Linguistic, and Sociological Perspectives

Edited by

I. M. SCHLESINGER

Department of Psychology
The Hebrew University of Jerusalem
Jerusalem, Israel
and
The Israel Institute of Applied Social Research
Jerusalem, Israel

LILA NAMIR

Department of Psychology
The Hebrew University of Jerusalem
Jerusalem, Israel

ACADEMIC PRESS   New York   San Francisco   London   1978

A Subsidiary of Harcourt Brace Jovanovich, Publishers

159. 912.8:801

SIG

419

SIG

COPYRIGHT © 1978, BY ACADEMIC PRESS, INC.
ALL RIGHTS RESERVED.
NO PART OF THIS PUBLICATION MAY BE REPRODUCED OR
TRANSMITTED IN ANY FORM OR BY ANY MEANS, ELECTRONIC
OR MECHANICAL, INCLUDING PHOTOCOPY, RECORDING, OR ANY
INFORMATION STORAGE AND RETRIEVAL SYSTEM, WITHOUT
PERMISSION IN WRITING FROM THE PUBLISHER.

ACADEMIC PRESS, INC.
111 Fifth Avenue, New York, New York 10003

United Kingdom Edition published by
ACADEMIC PRESS, INC. (LONDON) LTD.
24/28 Oval Road, London NW1   7DX

Library of Congress Cataloging in Publication Data
Main entry under title:

Sign language of the deaf.

    (Perspectives in neurolinguistics and psycholinguis-
tics)
    Includes bibliographies.
    1.   Sign language—Addresses, essays, lectures.
I.   Schlesinger, I. M.   II.   Namir, Lila.
[DNLM: 1.   Deafness.   2.   Manual communication.
HV2474   S342s]
HV2474.S55   001.56   77-16767
ISBN 0-12-625150-9

PRINTED IN THE UNITED STATES OF AMERICA

235917

102/92

Contents

PART IV METHODOLOGICAL PROBLEMS

List of Contributors

Numbers in parentheses indicate the pages on which the authors' contributions begin.

RICHARD L. BLANTON (243), Department of Psychology, Vanderbilt University, Nashville, Tennessee

HARRY BORNSTEIN (333), Department of Psychology, Gallaudet College, Kendall Green, Washington, D. C.

PENELOPE H. BROOKS (243), Psychology Department, George Peabody College for Teachers, Nashville, Tennessee

AARON V. CICOUREL (271), Department of Sociology, University of California, San Diego, San Diego, California

ELMA CRAIG (141), Department of Linguistic Science, University of Reading, Reading, England

DAVID CRYSTAL (141), Department of Linguistic Science, University of Reading, Reading, England

GORDON W. HEWES (11), Department of Anthropology, University of Colorado, Boulder, Colorado

LILA NAMIR (1, 97), Department of Psychology, The Hebrew University of Jerusalem, Jerusalem, Israel

HILDE S. SCHLESINGER (57), Mental Health Services for the Deaf, Langley Porter Neuropsychiatric Institute, University of California, San Francisco, California

I. M. SCHLESINGER (1, 97), Department of Psychology, The Hebrew University of Jerusalem, Jerusalem, Israel, and The Israel Institute of Applied Social Research, Jerusalem, Israel

WILLIAM C. STOKOE (365), Linguistics Research Laboratory, Gallaudet College, Kendall Green, Washington, D.C.

BERNARD T. TERVOORT (169), Institute of General Linguistics, University of Amsterdam, Amsterdam, The Netherlands,

LARS VON DER LIETH (315), Audiologopedic Research Group, University of Copenhagen, Copenhagen, Denmark

Preface

Recent years have seen a burgeoning interest in the sign language of the deaf. After an almost complete neglect of the field in previous decades, researchers in various countries are beginning to find this nonvocal language a fascinating subject of study. There is already a considerable amount of research on the linguistic, psychological, social, and educational aspects of sign language. A major volume is very much needed to provide a background for the researcher, the student, and the educator.

This book presents a state-of-the-art report. It was first contemplated by Thomas A. Sebeok, who approached the editors with the challenge of compiling a survey of this rapidly expanding field. Throughout the planning stages he provided us with invaluable guidance. But for his expertise and the help of his wife, Donna Jean Umiker-Sebeok, this volume would not have been possible. We take pleasure in acknowledging their contribution and thanking them for their cooperation.

The first chapter, "The Phylogeny of Sign Language" by Gordon Hewes, is intended to present sign language against its evolutionary background and offers an impressive array of data marshaled to defend the author's thesis, which will surely interest many readers other than students of sign language. It is symptomatic of the immature state of the field of sign language studies that such a wide coverage is quite out of the question for the other chapters in the volume.

Hewes's chapter is followed by that of Hilde Schlesinger, who presents a fascinating account of sign language acquisition by small children. This may also serve as an excellent introduction to newcomers in the field giving them a feeling of what sign language is like.

The second section of the book, on linguistic aspects of sign language, contains our paper on the grammar of sign language, followed by that of David Crystal and Elma Craig, who discuss the linguistic status of natural and contrived sign languages. A chapter by Bernard Tervoort completes this part of the book. Its title, "Bilingual Interference," does not fully indicate its wide scope, for in discussing bilingual interference Tervoort amply documents many peculiarities of the lexicon and grammar of sign language, and its profound differences in such respects from oral language.

While the second part of the volume is devoted to linguistic aspects, the third part attempts to link sign language research with various other disciplines. Richard Blanton and Penelope Brooks view sign language from the angle of psycholinguistics. Their chapter also includes an interesting discussion of Wilhelm Wundt's writings on the subject. The authors raise several important questions for which, as they rightly point out, only the most tentative answers are available to date. Their chapter makes us acutely aware of the need for more research on sign language. The vicissitudes of research in this field are brought home to us in the next chapter, by Aaron Cicourel, which presents a sociolinguistic point of view. Reporting on his own experiences in studying communication in sign language, Cicourel allows us insights regarding what occurs when signers communicate between themselves and what the investigator of this problem lets himself in for. That sign language may be important for the psychosocial adjustments of the deaf is convincingly argued by Lars von der Lieth. His chapter presents among other things, valuable material, partly of a historical nature, on the use of sign language. The final chapter in this part is also of an applied nature. Harry Bornstein discusses the educational implications of the use of sign language. For generations a heated controversy has been going on concerning the place of sign language in education, the opposing factions—the "oralists" and the "manualists"—becoming deeply entrenched in their respective views. What each faction defends is dogma rather than rationally supported views, and it is important that this volume include a scholar's sober presentation of what is going on in this field today.

We hope that this volume succeeds in demonstrating the great theoretical and practical importance of research on sign language to its readers. If this relatively young field is to prosper, a sound methodology will have to be developed. While several of the chapters touch on methodological problems (notably those by Cicourel and by Blanton and Brooks), it was found appropriate to conclude the volume with a chapter devoted wholly to methodology. The choice here fell on William Stokoe, the pioneer of sign language research, who, more than most of us, is in a position to take a synoptic view in discussing this subject, and to present the methodological lessons to be learned from his long experience in the field. We hope that there will be many readers who become as dedicated to sign language research as he is.

When we set out to compile a list of possible contributors we realized that there were more than we could possibly accommodate within one volume. To avoid too much overlap we had, therefore, to choose between alternatives—a choice which was not always easy to make. In some respects, the coverage in this volume remains incomplete, partly because the pressure of time and other circumstances compelled some of the prospective contributors to withdraw. Among the lacunae we should mention the important work going on at the Salk Institute under Bellugi, Klima, and their associates, to whose work, unfortunately, we have not been able to do sufficient justice in this volume; methods of notation for sign languages; and work underway in the USSR and the Far East. We believe that in spite of these gaps the present volume gives a view from many angles of a new and vigorously developing field of research.

We should like to express our thanks to the editor of this series, Harry A. Whitaker, for all his interest and encouragement, and to the various contributors to this volume for their cooperative attitude which greatly eased our task.

Introduction

I. M. SCHLESINGER
LILA NAMIR

Sign language is a form of manual communication which is used in every community of deaf persons and seems to be invented anew by them whenever such a form has not been previously established. It consists largely of stable, conventional hand movements and postures each of which conveys concepts, reminiscent of pantomime but in fact far from being simply this. Unlike finger spelling, where different handshapes represent letters of the alphabet, and which is thus a letter-by-letter translation of spoken language, sign language is on the whole independent of spoken language.

One of the characteristics of sign language is that many of the signs are iconic (i.e., their forms resemble in some way what they denote). Although this is not always clearly apparent in signs, on closer inspection we can often trace their iconic origin. There are, however, also signs for function words in the language. To get a fuller picture of the structure of sign language, the reader is referred especially to the chapters by Namir and Schlesinger, by Hilde Schlesinger, and by Tervoort.

The answer to where sign language originated or who invented it is twofold. The springing up of some sort of sign language in every deaf community is attested to in numerous works and revealingly described, for instance, in an autobiographical work by the postlingually deafened British poet David Wright (1969). There have also been a number of attempts at creating systematic sign languages, based on those in use among deaf communities—notably the work of l'Abbé de l'Epée. The

1

history of these efforts has been reviewed by a number of authors, including Wright.

One of the questions typically asked us when we lecture about how signs depict objects and imitate actions is: Is the language, then, international? The answer to this is: Not necessarily so—although sign languages often seem to resemble one another across communities and countries to a striking degree, and far more so than do spoken languages. The reasons for the differences are many: There are different ways of signing the same thing iconically, and no special reason for signers in different places to converge on the same sign form. Then, not all concepts can be directly described iconically. In such cases a sign often describes something related to the concept instead. This transfer of meaning (from a concept directly described to what it is intended to denote) greatly increases the choices open. Signs may also be compounded, very much as words are in spoken languages, and this possibility greatly increases the range of alternatives available.

Where a sign language has been allowed to develop over time, being used in a well-established signing community (as has happened, for example, in parts of America and in Scandinavia), spoken language sometimes intrudes into the sign language via systems such as finger spelling. This factor again contributes to widening the differences between sign languages. Within the same country, too, there may be various dialects differing among themselves in degree of intrusion of spoken language. This is discussed in the chapter by Bornstein. Other chapters in this volume frequently make reference to different versions of sign language, using a considerable variety of different terms. We have made no attempt here to standardize the use of terminology, preferring instead to expose the reader to the proliferation of terms in current use. These are explained in the contexts in which they occur.

Further, sign languages have often been subjected to deliberate attempts at intervention on the part of educators of the deaf. These are almost always hearing persons who have acquired sign language as adults, who, with the welfare of deaf users in mind, attempt to make sign language more like spoken language, or use it in the interest of spoken language. One of the results of the various efforts to "improve" and develop sign language is, for instance, that today American sign language of the "high" variety is not well understood elsewhere.[1] When watching the users of this variety communicate among themselves, Israeli deaf

[1]The terms "high" and "low" used in reference to sign language are not intended, of course, to imply any value judgment.

cannot understand them, although they do seem to find it easier to understand certain European varieties of sign language—which, perhaps, have been subject to less systematic intervention. American signers, then, if they wish to make themselves understood by nonusers, will have to resort to versions of sign language which are "lower," i.e., which include more pantomime, are less close to English in terms of the systematic introduction of function-word signs, have fewer finger-spelled elements, and so on. Finger spelling is not known in Israel, and thus the language used there—although it would be untrue to say it has been "unsullied" by spoken language—has undoubtedly been influenced by it less than, for instance, has the American sign language.

In conclusion, while sign language is clearly not an international language, the "lower" varieties are to some extent mutually intelligible. This was brought home to us when, after the reunification of Jerusalem, which had been split in two for close to 20 years, a group of deaf Arabs from East Jerusalem came to visit the center for the deaf in West Jerusalem, and apparently at once "found a common language."

Let us review now briefly some of the problems discussed by the authors of the various chapters in this book. We refer here to what Mackay (1970) calls "integration of codes." This he distinguishes from "interference of messages," which occurs when the grammatical structure and vocabulary of one of the languages spoken by a person intrude on another language also spoken by him. Many deaf persons know both how to speak and how to sign (although their proficiency in one mode as opposed to the other may differ) and their use of each mode may be expected to show some trace of influence of the other mode. This phenomenon of bilingual interference between spoken languages has been amply documented and studied. In sign language there is an additional peculiarity facilitating such intrusion: namely, that sign and spoken languages can be performed simultaneously. This is amply demonstrated in Tervoort's chapter, and additional examples are also found in that by Hilde Schlesinger.

As Mackay points out in discussing spoken languages, when such intrusions become common, they may ultimately be assimilated into the code itself, and become "integration of codes." As far as sign language is concerned, there is also a sociolinguistic factor at work. Given that even proficient signers seem to accord the use of spoken language higher status than that of sign language (see, for example, the chapters by Hilde Schlesinger and by Bornstein), the prospect exists that the structure of spontaneous sign language will converge more and more with that of spoken language, and that this sign language will gradually become extinct. It would be a great loss if this were to occur before any "original" sign language were to be adequately described, for it seems to us to possess great theoretical importance for linguistics.

That a study of the structure of sign language may throw light on linguistic theory in general is suggested in Hewes's chapter, which makes a case for spoken language to have developed out of gesturing. In fact, the theoretical importance of sign language was long ago recognized. At the turn of the century Wundt (1900/1973) devoted an entire section to sign language in his *Völkerpsychologie*—recently reissued and now available to English readers. Interest in the phenomenon later abated until very recently, for a variety of factors discussed in the chapter by Blanton and Brooks. Of the great linguists in this century, neither Bloomfield nor Sapir seems to have had firsthand knowledge of sign language; both dismissed it cursorily as no more than a derivative of spoken language—which better acquaintance with the language shows is not so. Other linguists followed their lead in largely ignoring sign language.

That sign language is important for the theory of language presupposes the claim that it is indeed a language. This very claim, however, was once the subject for heated debate, and it seems the controversy is not dead yet. In the past, such debates were often tinged with emotionally charged attitudes in favor of or against the use of sign language. It should be evident, however, that the problem of the linguistic status of sign language is not intrinsically tied to any value judgment. Different opinions on the subject are implied or stated explicitly by various contributors to this volume. Views range from Stokoe's definite affirmation to the cautious, even skeptical, approach of Tervoort—who suggests we await the results of further research before taking a final stand—to the preference of Crystal and Craig to relegate sign language, at least for the time being, to the status of "a system."

It seems to us, however, that to a large extent this issue itself is a terminological rather than a substantive one. This is because the question "Is sign language a language?" can be understood in two ways, and the facts which are relevant to answering it will differ accordingly. Crystal approaches this question by setting up a list of criteria for judging whether a given system of communication is a language, and then goes on to examine the extent to which different systems (including sign language) meet each of these criteria. However, since the criteria are based mainly on an analysis of spoken language characteristics, his comparison really deals with the question in what respects sign language is like a **spoken** language. His qualified answer is that it is unlike it in some respects—whereas in others the matter is left open, pending further investigation.

Some readers may maintain that whatever its divergence from spoken language, sign language still qualifies as a language. This claim, of course, is based on a different definition of language. Investigators espousing this approach may not all have an identical notion of language. Some may hold that **any** system of communication might validly be regarded as a language, while others may impose additional constraints and restrictions, such as using the term "language" only for fairly elaborate systems of communication. Thus, according to one conception criticized by Crystal, any system which functions like spoken language in everyday give-and-take **is** a language. This includes sign language, but leaves open the question of whether systems of more restricted function (such as the radio, or television, or tic-tac signs mentioned by Crystal) can also be termed languages. It must be admitted that as it stands this definition is not sharp enough (see Crystal's footnote 6); in any case this approach to defining language differs from Crystal's in that it takes a single characteristic of spoken language—its social function, in this case—and sets it up as a criterion for what is to count as a language. Crystal, on the other hand, sets up a number of such criteria.

We feel, after all, that the conflicting answers to the question of whether sign language is a language are really answers to different questions. After the dust settles on this terminological issue, little, if any, difference of opinion may remain. The labeling is in the end not very important so long as it does not engender confusion or spurious disagreement. It seems to us to matter little whether one opts for Crystal's fastidious nomenclature— which accords to sign language only the term "system"—or plunges wholeheartedly into the indiscriminate labeling of divers' signs, and so on, as "languages." Rather, what **is** important is to describe the characteristics of each system. It is in this task that the criteria proposed by Crystal may be expected to prove their usefulness.

By focusing analysis on spoken languages, however, as did Crystal, it appears that some of the fruitful criteria may be overlooked. For instance, the fact of "nonsimultaneity" is certainly not a characteristic one would think of in describing spoken languages, but the characteristic of "simultaneity" is an interesting feature of sign language which does distinguish it (and perhaps certain other systems) from spoken language. It is suggested, therefore, that a further analysis of the various systems may lead to a still more detailed comparison.

One of the more important questions about sign language, which is central to its linguistic status, is whether or not it has a "grammar." Our chapter in this volume attempts to deal with this question. Regularities in expressing grammatical relations have been observed by a number of writers, but, as we point out, it appears that these regularities are to a large extent due to the influence of the spoken language, and the sequence of signs used by a signer tends to follow the word order used in his predominant spoken language. Moreover, some sign languages have imported from the spoken language the notion of inflections, which they incorporate into the signing sequence in some conventionalized form such as finger spelling (i.e., via direct translation from the spoken language). In our view, however, the really interesting question concerns the state of sign language **before** spoken language leaves its imprint on sign language grammar. So far as we could see, this original language too observes a few regularities in the sequence of signs. Does this justify our "dignifying" it with the name "grammar"? Crystal has raised some doubts, for the following reasons. First, as he points out in his chapter, one may wonder whether regularities which seem to be based on cognitive tendencies (like the sign for the attribute following that for the thing it describes) merit the name grammar. Second, it is questionable whether a few isolated constraints on sign order can be treated as of the same ilk as the complex system of rules that governs spoken languages. Again, in line with our previous argument, it seems far less a matter for concern whether or not we call the rules operating on sign language by the name grammar than it does to be clear about what **are** the differences and similarities between spoken and sign language in respect to the regularities observed.

Questions of linguistic status do not detract from the practical importance of sign language, for instance, in education—where it is unfortunate indeed that heated controversy for so long obscured the real issues at stake. These issues are discussed in the chapters by Bornstein and by Blanton and Brooks. The deeply ingrained attitudes of some educators are dramatically exemplified in Cicourel's chapter, and both he and von der Lieth discuss the very important psychological and motivational, as well as social, consequences of using sign language.

In trying to determine the educational potentialities of sign language, a crucial question, so far only cursorily investigated, is whether there are limitations inherent in sign language. Those who maintain that sign language is potentially limited, both as a means of communication and as a vehicle for cognitive processes, have postulated varying reasons for this claim. But even if they are proved correct, the question still stands whether sign language, as it is today, is impoverished **because** it was never called on to meet the demands of more advanced pursuits. If this is indeed the case, it can surely be rectified by amplifying the language. As we saw above, the grammar appears to be rather sparse, and in addition signers seem to have a very limited vocabulary. On the other hand, important experiments on the expansion of the vocabulary have been carried out, for example at Gallaudet College under Bornstein.

As for the arguments regarding possible inherent cognitive limitations,

Blanton and Brooks discuss in their chapter the question of the cognitive effects of sign language use per se, and this matter seems of such importance that there is undoubtedly a need for further psycholinguistic research. Further, it has often been claimed that sign language is not phonetic, and this is seen as a potentially limiting factor—by Crystal, for example. One could, however, argue against this that perhaps sign language should rather be viewed as a combination of simultaneous phonemes. Certainly it has been possible to describe signs analytically, using a restricted alphabet of symbols.[2] The question remains, however, to what extent this analytical alphabet is operative psychologically, or just imposed by the investigator.

Another possibly limiting factor which has been suggested by Crystal is connected with the sensory modality in which sign language is perceived. Crystal doubts whether it is possible to make as many fine distinctions in the visual mode as in the acoustic mode of spoken language. This question is still open to investigation. We have a suspicion that the discriminability of signs in principle may be much larger than is sometimes thought. It is common knowledge, for instance, that a person can distinguish an enormous number of human faces from one another, these appearing to us as more dissimilar than other stimuli (and incidentally one of the reasons why faces are used in banknotes so often—as a deterrent to easy forgery). Perhaps for proficient signers signs may become as discriminable as faces seem to be to almost all of us. Moreover, even should there prove to be an upper limit to perceptual discriminability of signs, we suggest that this might be overcome to a large extent by transfer of meaning, compounding, and so on.

We are convinced that sign language needs much more research, both from the linguistic viewpoint and from that of practical considerations such as those raised by Blanton and Brooks, von der Lieth, Cicourel, and others. We ourselves are acutely aware of the enormous difficulty of research into this language, where, unlike in general linguistics, there is no established methodology to fall back on. Stokoe, the pioneer of modern sign language research, makes some suggestions in his chapter to make up for this lack. That we cannot copy general psycholinguistic methods in investigation of problems which arise in connection with sign language use becomes clear from the papers of Blanton and Brooks and of Cicourel. Researchers in sign language will have to find their own way. In fact, the work reviewed in the present volume seems to suggest that they are already finding it.

[2]For a discussion of this see E. Cohen, L. Namir, and I. M. Schlesinger, *A new dictionary of sign language* (The Hague: Mouton, 1977).

REFERENCES

Mackay, W. F. 1970. Interference, integration and the synchronic fallacy. In J. E. Alatis
    (Ed.), *Report of the twenty-first annual round table meeting on linguistics and lan-
    guage studies*. Washington, D.C.: Georgetown Univ. Press.
Wright, D. 1969. *Deafness: A personal account*. London: Allen Lane.
Wundt, W. 1973. *The language of gestures*. The Hague: Mouton. [Originally published
    1900.]

Part I

PHYLOGENY AND ONTOGENY

1

The Phylogeny of
Sign Language

GORDON W. HEWES

A **phylogenetic model** is a construct which seeks to provide an evolutionary précis for the origin and development of some group of biological organisms, or of some organs or functions of such a group of organs, over a substantial period of time. Similar developmental models can be built for inorganic systems, from galaxies to terrestrial land masses or oceans. That such models have contributed immensely to the advancement of science cannot be gainsaid. Linguists dealing with a domain which cannot cover more than a very few million years have usually demanded more from would-be model builders than have astrophysicists, geologists, or paleontologists, whose schemata often extend over millions or even billions of years. Such events were unwitnessed by human eyes, and can only be reconstructed through elaborate chains of circumstantial evidence and much conjecture. Viertel (1966) refers to "theories of [language] origin involving unobservable geneses," as if almost all geneses with which science is concerned were not similarly afflicted. Vetter (1969, Chap. 14) likewise apologizes for the absence of "first-hand" knowledge about language origins. This chapter rests on the premise that "language, like every other part of culture, has had an evolutionary career [Harris, 1964, pp. 174–175]," and on Lenneberg's somewhat more cautious observation that "the roots of language may be as deeply grounded in our biological constitutions as for instance our predisposition to use our hands [1960, p. 869]," although Lenneberg failed to pursue his own suggestion linking language and the hands in his later *Biological Foundations of Language* (1967). Fortunately there are linguists and psycholinguists who do not consider serious glottogonic model building to be beyond the bounds of scientific propriety (cf. Fillenbaum, 1971, pp. 256–262; Jakobson, 1970, pp. 444–445; Mounin, 1967, p. 22; Olschewsky, 1969, p. 734; and many others to be cited below).

Willingness to reopen the question of language origins (Wescott, 1967; 1974) soon leads one to recognize that this topic involves much more than recent research literature (Hewes, 1977, pp. 3–53). It happens to be one of the most venerable problems in intellectual history, and some of the basic issues were already being argued by Plato and his contemporaries in rather sophisticated fashion (cf. Plato, 1921, *Cratylus*; Aarsleff, in Harnad *et al.*, 1976, pp. 4–13). The problem of sign language soon became a part of the discussion which, with occasional lapses, has been continuing for the last 2300 years (Stam, 1976). By the eighteenth century, when interest in glottogenesis reached one of its peaks, sign language held a central position in much of the theoretical argumentation. The *idéologues* who carried some of the spirit of the Enlightenment into the Napoleonic Era, in their short-lived Société des Observateurs de l'Homme (the world's first anthropological organization) hoped to make the study of language origins and of the sign language a major part of their scientific program (Degérando, 1969; Jauffret, 1909, p. 485). In the nineteenth century such eminent figures as Alfred Russel Wallace, who, like Darwin, had promoted what came to be known as the Darwinian revolution, and Edward B. Tylor, considered in the English-speaking world as "the father of anthropology," were supporters of the gestural theory of language origin.

The exclusion or inclusion of sign language in definitions of language can be followed through a bulky literature, where the matter has been debated by the upholders of a narrow oral criterion for "true language," and by those, in the author's view theoretically more sophisticated, who find no difficulty in detaching the notion of language from its sensory medium (Jakobson, 1964, p. 217; Mead, 1956, p. 175; Morris, 1946, p. 38) and can see it in a broader semiotic frame. Part of the confusion arises from the current widespread use of the term "nonverbal communication" to cover gestural or sign-language communication, as if **words** are in any ultimate sense **vocal**. The literature on so-called nonverbal communication makes it very clear that some of the topics covered are nonvocal, albeit verbal, whereas others are nonverbal, but vocal communication (Duncan, 1969; Ekman & Friesen, 1969, p. 63; Greimas, 1968; Kristeva & Lacoste, 1968; Wiener, Devoe, Rubinow & Geller, 1972).

For sign language communication in particular, the literature is concentrated on two major systems: (1) that developed for the instruction of the deaf in the late eighteenth century by the Abbé de l'Épeé, and carried to the United States early in the nineteenth century by Thomas Hopkins Gallaudet, where it became ASL (American Sign Language); and (2) the sign language of the Indians of the North American Plains. Part I of La Mont West's dissertation (1960) is a lengthy analysis of the North American Indian sign language, but in Part II West presents what is so far the most comprehensive survey of sign languages in the rest of the world, with statistical charts showing the extent of their morphological overlapping. Unfortunately, West's dissertation is available only in microfilm or photocopies of the original typescript, and has therefore received almost no critical comment.

THE QUESTION OF ANIMAL LANGUAGE

For Descartes, man and beast were separated by an impassable cognitive gulf, with creative reason and language on our side, and automaton-like behavior on the other. The Cartesian view of man and language continues to affect much thinking in this field, recently and most explicitly in the work of Chomsky (1966, pp. 3–6; Englefield, 1977). Although Chomsky's revival of seventeenth-century views about language was seen as something of a recent revolution in linguistics, the fact is that the vast majority of the structural linguists whose work Chomsky attacked held the very same Cartesian position without so labeling it, and confidently supported the position that language was a species-specific human monopoly, thanks to cerebral properties they were not in the least interested in investigating. Even the "materialist" Soviet psycholinguists, still following in the footsteps of Pavlov, seem unwilling to accept the import of the recent language research with chimpanzees, since, apparently by definition, nonhuman animals cannot learn to handle the "second signaling system." Thus, while Zhinkin (1971) states that the roots of language lie "deep in the layers of the evolution of animal life," we find A. A. Leontiev (1970) suggesting that semiotics has "become lately a sort of signal that the author on principle does not qualitatively demarcate different types of sign systems, and in particular communicative systems of animals and human language [p. 122]."

ANTHROPOID APE COMMUNICATION

That other animal species than man have systems of communication is something our species has probably known from the beginning of hominization. Indeed, the popular wisdom has attributed full-fledged language capacity to other animals in myth and fable, often postulating an era "when animals talked." It has taken critical minds a long time to distinguish communication from language, particularly when a few birds, at least, have exhibited startling ability to produce fairly acceptable imitations of human speech. Augustine acknowledged that beasts "have certain signs among themselves," but was not sure that they used them for the express purpose of signification to others (1952, p. 637). With the growth of anatomical knowledge, the question of why at least certain animals did not speak became more acute, and this was a point raised about monkeys as they became more familiar to Europeans as a result of trade with tropical Africa and South America. Perrault (1676) was struck by the general similarity of the larynx and other vocal tract parts in monkeys he dissected to the corresponding anatomy of man (Vartanian, in La Mettrie, 1960, p. 215). Tyson, who dissected a young chimpanzee in 1699, was even more puzzled, since he found that the ape's brain, as well as its vocal organs, differed only in size and a few other particulars from human brains and larynges. This may have stimulated La Mettrie's (1960) proposal in 1747, that an ape (chimpanzee or orangutan) be taught language by someone who had had experience in teaching the human deaf— that is, starting by means of signs. La Mettrie (1960) had, in fact, deliberately turned the Cartesian principle on its head in *L'Homme Machine*. It was not until the 1960s that this pregnant suggestion was independently fulfilled by the Gardners and by Premack (using a somewhat different approach).

Edward Sapir (1933) was out of step with the crypto-Cartesian behaviorists of his day in expressing confidence that studies of the higher apes "will help supply some idea of the genesis of speech [p. 158]." Charles Darwin had been less sanguine, holding in *The Descent of Man* (1888, p. 91) that apes lack language because they lack sufficient intelligence, but Romanes, a younger Darwinian, was so impressed with the intelligent behavior of a London zoo chimpanzee that he felt she was about equivalent to a human child "just before it begins to speak [Romanes, 1888, pp. 125–126]." Romanes claimed that chimpanzees frequently employed conventional gestures themselves, and that if somehow brought to speak, they could use words, even if they could not form propositions (1888, pp. 127–128). There is thus a solid tradition, in spite of decades of neglect by linguists, in favor of determining continuities between apes and man in the matter of symbolic communication (Eisenberg, 1973, p. 233). Further, this tradition has often viewed sign language or gesture as the most likely bridge over which higher primate social communication moved into human language (cf. Hinde, 1972; Dingwall, 1977; Andrew, 1972, for reviews of animal social communication). Eisenberg

(1973, pp. 235–236) notes that mammalian ethograms[1] (many of them involving social communication) average around 70 to 100 items, and that there is not as much difference between mammalian orders or genera as might be supposed. Asiatic elephants, for example, though limited as to facial expression displays, may have at their disposal some 200 different combinations of signals based on trunk positions, ear movements, and vocalizations. Our notions about the simplicity of anthropoid ape communication under natural conditions arise from counting only distinguishable vocal calls. If these are considered in combination with a range of facial expressions, hand and arm signals, plus body postures and movements (cf. Stokoe, 1974; in Harnad *et al.*, 1976, pp. 505–513), the situation becomes complex.

Nevertheless, earlier writers often exaggerated the gestural propensities of monkeys. Jaeger, writing in 1867, said that monkeys possess a "perfectly developed gestural system [Fano, 1962]." Mallery, who studied North American Indian SL, believed that "monkeys have gestural abilities nearly equal to our own [1881, p. 275]," and he likened children's gestures to those of apes (1881, p. 276). Recent fieldwork has deflated these views. Social communication in primates is multimodal, but visual signals other than hand or arm gestures predominate: eye movements, flicking the eyelids, facial and mouth displays, piloerection, genital displays, body postures, and body movements are much more evident than patterned hand and arm signals. Vocalizations are important, but secondary, with olfactory signals playing a role only in close interaction, mostly connected with sexual behavior. Good surveys of primate social communication can be found in Altmann (1968), Bertrand (1971), Diebold (1968), Ploog (1972), and Shafton (1976). There are now several excellent studies on social communication in particular primate species (e.g., Poirier, 1970, on the Nilgiri langur). All of these studies stress the overwhelming affective or emotional nature of primate signaling, and the minimal amount of environmental referential information which is transmitted. Only a few signals serve, in some species, to differentiate terrestrial from airborne predator approaches, or to warn conspecifics of danger from snakes. Much of the social communication in nonhuman primates seems to involve social hierarchy maintenance rather than external dangers or attractions (D'Aquili, 1972, pp. 14–16; Shafton, 1976).

The principal role of the primate hands is in feeding, or food-related exploration of the immediate environment, in social or personal grooming, and holding or grasping others, including infants. The primate hand constantly tests objects for their possible food value by picking up or

[1]Ethogram: the total behavioral scheme of an animal species.

plucking them, bringing them to the nose, and then to the mouth for tasting. The mouth–hand linkage is thus very marked in primates (Leroi-Gourhan, 1965, p. 38), but except in some of the pongids and in man, less conspicuous as a part of the social communication apparatus.

We may now focus on the pongids (great apes, chimpanzees, gorilla, orangutan), since these are closest biologically. There is evidence that terrestrial life in primates has promoted both greater general intelligence, and some changes in signaling behavior. Rumbaugh and Gill (1973), after using a battery of tests, found not only good fit between the broad taxonomic ordering of primates from prosimians[2] to pongids and intelligence, which comes as no surprise, but also a positive relationship between ground-dwelling habits and higher intelligence. Gibbons, although ranked as low-grade anthropoid apes, seem less intelligent than macaques. The other arboreal–terrestrial division is between the mostly discrete vocal calls of tree-dwelling monkeys, and the more graded vocalizations of ground-dwelling species, along with a tendency to employ sounds of lower pitch on the ground (Marler, 1965). While we are less concerned here with vocal communication, these observations suggest that the character of primate communication has been significantly molded by habitat factors—a necessary part of the sign language phylogeny model we shall be employing.

We may now focus on the great apes, chimpanzee, gorilla, and orangutan, since the pongids are closest biologically to *Homo sapiens* on all counts—anatomically, physiologically, serologically, socially, and intellectually—and hence approach more closely than any other animals the status of the earliest hominids, according to the overwhelming consensus of modern scientists. Here at least we find some manual and arm gesture which several observers regard as manlike, even if not part of a structured sign language system (Goodall, 1968b, p. 291; Kainz, 1961, pp. 102–107, 193; Kortlandt, 1967, 1973; Rumbaugh, Savage-Rumbaugh, & Gill, 1977). The other reason for concentrating on pongids is that so far it is only in these animals that a way has been found to break the Cartesian barrier (cf. R. A. & B. T. Gardner, 1971). R. L. Garner went to West Africa with primitive wax-cylinder phonographic equipment and set himself up in a cage listening post in the tropical rain forest in order to study the "language" of monkeys and apes (1900, pp. 114–115). Later fieldworkers have found nothing to substantiate Garner's enthusiastic reports. Kortlandt, who regards the pongids, and the chimpanzee in particular, as

---

[2]Prosimians: the primate suborder containing lemurs and tarsiers, considered to be the most primitive in an evolutionary sense.

having been forced back into marginal habitats by the rise of the hominids, and is willing to see protocultural behavior among chimpanzees on a broader scale than most fieldworkers, is forced to agree that the "manipulatory potential of the chimpanzee hand is far from fully exploited in their expressive behavior [1967, p. 100, 1973, p. 14]." In the natural environments occupied by the extant pongids, there is little incentive for developing ways of conveying information to others about distant stimuli, except by looking toward the stimulus, with or without body alignment, or by starting to move toward it (Menzel, 1973). Lip pointing in chimpanzees seems to have some locative function with respect to startling stimuli in the immediate environment. In captivity, chimpanzees learn to respond appropriately to human pointing gestures, and under the conditions of the Washoe study, may of course acquire the use of manual gestures to refer to distant and unseen stimuli, such as a dog barking in the night. In any case, referential signs are few (Andrew, 1963, p. 1040; Reynolds, 1970, pp. 388–389; Wind, 1970, pp. 79–80).

Work with the pygmy chimpanzee, *Pan paniscus*, however, indicates that this species may have a more elaborate manual gestural repertoire than *Pan troglodytes* (reported by Sue Savage-Rumbaugh, in Rumbaugh *et al.*, 1977).

Most of the data on chimpanzee signing comes from the work of a few investigators, notably van Lawick-Goodall and her colleagues at the Gombe Stream, Nishida and others working in the Mahali Mountains and other areas not far from Gombe, and Kortlandt working in West Africa (Goodall, 1968a, 1968b, 1971, 1973; Kortlandt, 1967, 1973; Nishida, 1970). Most of the gestures recorded relate to close interpersonal interaction, such as greetings, reassurance, begging, and the like. More interesting are gestures supposed to mean "May I pass?" "Come with me," "You are welcome," and "Halt!" reported by Kortlandt (1965, 1967, pp. 88–100; cf. Dröscher, 1971, pp. 212–213). The "halt" signal consists of a display of the sole of the foot to those following behind the leader on a trail (Kortlandt, 1967, p. 94 and Fig. 12). Kortlandt also notes an arm and extended finger gesture which seems to serve as a snake warning signal (1965). All are holophrastic, and none have been reported to occur in combinations, much less in anything resembling multiword sentences. Some of these gestures are found to vary from one group of chimpanzees to another, strongly suggesting that social learning rather than innateness is involved (Goodall, 1973, pp. 163, 166–167; Stephenson, 1973, pp. 201–202). Menzel observed the spread of a new gesture from one individual to the rest of his experimental colony (1973, p. 38). A further problem is that all of these reports have been collected under conditions which do not permit sufficient controls to be really confident of their meanings. On the other hand, captive chimpanzees may pick up human gestures (cf. Hayes & Hayes, 1951; Kellogg, 1969).

Gorillas are generally less expressive than chimpanzees, although they possess one stereotyped sequence (the well-known charge display with its chest slappings, tearing up of vegetation, ground thumping, etc.) which chimpanzees do not match (Schaller, 1963, p. 116). Schaller notes gorilla locative stances, head shaking which he says signifies "I mean no harm," and some gestures which may be idiosyncratic. Practically nothing has been reported on orangutan gesturing under natural living conditions.

This brief mention of the material on pongid signing should not lead us to forget that much pongid communication is multimodal, and that these hand, arm, and foot gestures are usually accompanied by significant facial expressions, glances, body positions, and body movements. Vision has turned out to be the proper vehicle for apes to acquire language, to the surprise of few primatologists (cf. May, 1974). Pongid vision is practically identical to man's, with one very interesting exception. Rumbaugh, Gill, and Wright have recently shown (1973) that the apes are more easily distracted visually by objects in the immediate foreground than are human subjects. Preadaptation to life in open-country environments may have been involved in hominid use of gestures made beyond the usual close range of pongid arm and hand signaling. With this seemingly minor exception, the repertoire of pongid motor actions corresponds almost perfectly with the roster of "empirically valid cultural units" of behavior which Marvin Harris (1964, pp. 46–52) calls **actones**. If we exclude the special characteristics of human vocal communication, this raises the question of whether there are any specific abilities, including mental ones, underlying the human use of language which cannot be attributed also to apes (Krashen, 1973). The difference may lie more in the asymmetries of human brain function, or cerebral lateralization, rather than in any specific behavioral elements. Human beings are overwhelmingly lopsided with respect to preferences for both hand functions and language functions (Eisenson, 1972). I have elsewhere suggested that gestural communication was localized on the left cerebral hemisphere along with right-handedness before the emergence of spoken language, which was then likewise controlled from the left hemisphere (Kimura, 1977; Levy in Harnad et al., 1976, pp. 810–820; cf. D'Agostino, 1974, who considers cerebral lateralization to be the "key mutation" underlying man's skilled tool using and language). W. O. Dingwall disagrees with this position (Dingwall, 1977). Much research in neurology and related areas will be required to determine the plausibility of these assumptions. Bryan Robinson reminds us that human vocalization rests on two quite different neural systems (1967, p. 353), whereas that of nonhuman primates, overwhelmingly affective in character and nonreferential, is limbic or involuntary. This is not to say that ape calls are not used for distant signaling: Some can be heard well at 1.5 kilometers or more (Reynolds, 1970, p. 385). The point is that apes do not use their voices "to bring about events [Eisenson, 1972, p. 2]," although novel vocal signals may be invented, as can happen with gestures (Fleischman, 1968, pp. 278-280). Young chimpanzees, around the age they start to crawl about, are conspicuously silent, which Kortlandt says may be a protection from predators such as leopards (1973); this, at least, has no human counterpart.

Studies of the manipulatory abilities of primate hands, ranging from those of lemurs and New World monkeys to pongids, conform to about the expectations from the taxonomic scale (Parker, 1972), though in a few tasks lemurs surpassed gibbons and macaques, and guenons did little better than lemurs in nearly all tests. Gorillas and chimpanzees were closely matched, with orangutans in third position. Primate hand activity has been studied almost wholly from the standpoint of their grasping and manipulatory behavior in locomotion, feeding, grooming, and so on, or with an eye to human tool-handling performances, but not, as far as I know, with respect to manual gesturing abilities. Chimpanzees, and probably gorillas and orangutans, seem to be able to approximate human manual gesturing skills used in ASL (American Sign Language of the Deaf), although they might be deficient in finger spelling, which involves some rather small and precise finger positions.

Bruner (1972, pp. 699-702) sees language emerging initially in support of and loosely linked with action, and by this he means especially manual action. His perspective is close to that of the Piagetians. Referring to ontogeny, Bruner (1972) writes, "At the onset of speech, then, language is virtually an outgrowth of the mastery of skilled action and perceptual discrimination [p. 700]." Turned into a phylogenetic statement, it seems quite relevant to this discussion of ape behavior. Years before there was much evidence about social communication in pongids, Sapir (1933) wrote that the roots of language "probably lie in the power of the higher apes to solve specific problems by abstracting general forms or schemata from the details of given situations," and he went on to say that in early mankind, symbolic interpretation of events arose from significant action accompanied by "largely useless or supplemental vocal behavior [p. 159]." As we have seen, apes under natural conditions do not put either their gestures or vocal calls into sentencelike strings, even though under human tutelage they can acquire this skill. However, they very definitely do exhibit sequential stringing of significant bits of action in play, various social encounters, and in their use of tools in subsistence and other behaviors (cf. Reynolds, 1968, pp. 304–305). One could view this as a kind of preadaptation to syntax in language. Sign languages lend themselves to order-rules (Hill, 1973a, p. 10; Peters, 1972; Peters & Mech, 1973; but cf. Schlesinger, 1970, for some apparent exceptions). That order rather than complex inflection was primitive was a view held by many nineteenth-century philologists concerned with language typology. It was not until later that Jespersen and others came to regard English and Chinese with their marked dependence on word order as elegant and progressive rather than archaic or degenerate. All the chimpanzee language experiments so far have been undertaken by English-speaking investigators who have not inflicted on their subjects the tricky grammars of German, Russian, or (Heaven forbid) something like Navaho.

Chimpanzees can cope with experimental problems involving something very much like syntax, even without the prolonged training connected with teaching them ASL or some other form of visible language. Rensch (1967, p. 55) reports experiments by Crawford and by Dohl in which successive locked boxes, etc., had to be opened with special keys or other tools, in a fixed sequence, in order to obtain rewards. Successful solution of such tasks seems to require syntagmatic abilities of a fairly high order, which, if disturbed, would be termed apraxia in human patients (de Renzi, Pieczuro, & Vignolo, 1968). A. R. Luria (1973, pp. 15–16) distinguishes two basic kinds of aphasia, each with different left hemisphere cortical representation, one of which he calls paradigmatic, the other syntagmatic. Though apes lack speech, I suspect that there is a cortical area, probably in about the same location, which permits apes to solve locked-box problems, and also has something to do with pongid ability to acquire sign language or other visible language. However, unlike the situation in man, this function may not be lateralized, so that injury to just the left hemisphere area would not produce apraxia or syntagmatic disruption.

G. H. Mead (1956, p. 168) and many others believed that nonhuman animals, although conscious of feelings and sensations, "gesture" only on an unconscious level, and without language could not achieve anything like human self-consciousness (cf. Eccles, 1973). However, anthropoid apes can be shown to recognize themselves, and not merely some other ape, in a mirror image (Gallup, McClure, Hill, & Bundy, 1971). Mirrors are artifacts of civilization, to be sure, and their natural counterparts, such as reflecting ponds, are not as likely to provoke the kinds of testing that both apes and monkeys do when confronted with mirror images. Chimpanzees and other higher primates appear to distinguish individuals, mostly visually, unlike members of other mammalian orders who seem to use mainly smell. Count (1974) notes that higher primates regularly equate their own body parts with the corresponding body parts of human beings, putting spectacles properly over their eyes, and hats on their heads, which strongly suggests possession of vivid body schemata, which, like self-awareness, may play a role in glottogenesis. This would have been particularly important in the genesis of a sign language system incorporating reference to body parts and functions, but also, perhaps at a much later stage, using body and body-part metaphors, which are of course also present in all spoken languages (a head of land, brow of a hill, foot of a mountain, eye of a spring, the tooth of an implement, mouth of a cave, etc.).

Primate play has been considered preadaptive for language (Rensch, 1972; Reynolds, 1972; Reynolds, in Harnad *et al.*, 1976, pp. 150–166), since it is coordinated by often complex signals, and as we have noted, has a syntactic quality. Van Lawick-Goodall, discussing diffusion of new behavioral traits within or between chimpanzee communities, notes that there is apparently less play between young chimpanzees than there seems to be among macaques and baboons. If, as the present phylogenetic model for sign language holds, new signs had to be invented and socially transmitted, the prevalence of play among juveniles might have had a considerable influence on language diffusion. In captivity, where so much more seems to happen to demonstrate the behavioral potentiality of chimpanzees, play among juveniles can be quite elaborate, and some instances of imaginative play have been reported. According to Hayes and Hayes (1951), Viki pulled around an imaginary toy on an equally imaginary string. Lucky, another chimpanzee, (Fleming, 1974, p. 38) has been observed using ASL to a kitten which she treats as a kind of baby doll. Children begin to engage in this kind of play between 19 and 26 months, with some preliminary foreshadowing as early as 16 months (Sinclair, 1970, p. 123).

Hunting occurs among chimpanzees, but not, it seems, to any significant extent among either gorillas or orangutans (Montagu, in Harnad *et al.*, 1976, pp. 266–274). Compared to baboon hunting, it is more complex, and is often followed by food-sharing sessions (Teleki, 1973a, 1973b; cf. Goodall, 1971, 1973) in which begging and other gestures are prominent. Perhaps equally important, chimpanzees hunt in silence. Combining some suggestions of Kortlandt and mine, P. H. Stephenson (1974) regards this controlled vocal silence as a major factor in language emergence, paving the way for the inhibition of vocal sounds which rapid articulate speech demands. I would see the maintenance of silence during hunting as a possibly important selective pressure toward the use of gestural signals, especially as hunting became more and more of a tactical or strategic exercise. Bertrand (1971, p. 471), unaccountably, I think, sees chimpanzee silent hunting as an argument against a correlation of hunting and language emergence.

That apes might be taught to speak, or at least to acquire some sign language, is an old idea, quite apart from the worldwide mythic attribution of language to animals. Aside from Samuel Pepys' casual mention of it in his celebrated diary, we have seen that La Mettrie took the idea quite seriously (in *L'Homme machine*, 1747). Vartanian, the editor of the critical edition of that work, regarded the proposal as "curious, ill-advised, and not really in keeping with modern thinking [LaMettrie, 1960, p. 27]," which also shows how dangerous it is to be dogmatic about anything. R. M. Yerkes' suggestion that chimpanzees might be able to acquire the sign language of the deaf (1925) was noted by Paget (1963), who wrote that if a deaf-mute were to rear a baby chimpanzee, then the initiation of the chimpanzee into sign language would very likely succeed. E. Critchley added (1967, pp. 23–24) that he did not consider the notion at all eccentric. Yerkes and Nissen tried some low-level sign-related experiments with chimpanzees in 1939, with little result. The Hayeses devoted considerable effort to trying to get their chimpanzee Viki to speak (Hayes & Hayes, 1951; Kellogg, 1969, p. 385), and found somewhat to their dismay that she used and understood gestures without any explicit training. Kohts-Ladygina (1935) reported that her young chimpanzee Joni acquired a few gestures which she said resembled some also used by her own son. Kellogg's chimpanzee Gua developed a gesture indicating a wish to urinate or defecate. Hayes has informed me (personal communication, July 23, 1951) that the use of sign language with Viki had been considered but rejected because of their interest in getting her to handle spoken words.

The Gardners are reporting in much greater detail on their own and other chimpanzee language projects, but we should add here that the first responses of the child language acquisition experts to the protocols of Washoe's sign language were that Washoe did not exhibit some of the characteristics of human children in the early stages of language development. I have objected to Brown's criticism (1970) on what I think is the valid ground that he compared the language progress of Washoe, who was learning ASL, with that of children learning to speak English—that is, another language, using a different sensory and motor modality. The proper basis for comparison would have been between Washoe and a hearing child who was brought up to use ASL; failing that unlikely situation, the next best comparison would be between the ASL-using chimpanzee and a deaf child starting to learn ASL at about the same age. I found only one usable reported case (Hewes, 1973a), but Bellugi and her colleagues by now have ample materials for better comparisons of this sort (Bellugi & Siple, 1971; Bellugi, Siple, & Klima, 1972; Bellugi, Siple, & Fischer, 1973; Bellugi & Klima, in Harnad *et al.*, 1976, pp. 514–538). Morris (1946), apropos of language capacities in nonhuman species, advised us not to reject the possibility out of hand, but to wait for empirical evidence. In my opinion that is what we now have, in increasing quantity. My response to the reports of the Gardners and Premack was to incorporate their findings in a glottogonic model in which gesture, as in many previous speculations, had preceded speech, and had provided, so to speak, a ready-made grammatical and lexical foundation for it (Hewes, 1973b, 1973c). That Washoe, other chimpanzees, and a gorilla, have acquired some competence in a modern, sophisticated sign language largely used by the deaf does not weaken my version of the old gestural hypothesis (cf. Bertrand, 1971, p. 469; Cicourel & Boese, 1972a, p. 231; Patterson, 1977; Stokoe, 1973; Stokoe in Harnad *et al.*, 1976: 505–513), since it was not suggested that a primordial gestural language would have resembled any extant sign language at all closely. There are still some last-ditch defenders of the uniqueness of man's language capacity, apart from the vocal aspects of it. Healy (1973) wonders if apes could ever acquire a "phonemic" language, which in sign language terms would presumably be something like finger spelling, since she apparently be-lieves ASL to be mostly iconic, and the plastic token language used by Premack to be likewise not composed of discrete and arbitrary elements. The "Yerkish" visible language being read by Lana, in the experiment of Rumbaugh *et al.* (Rumbaugh & Gill, 1973; Rumbaugh (Ed.), 1977), does consist of superimposed combinations of geometric symbols, color coded for various semantic domains. Neither the colors nor the geometric sym-bols have any iconic relation to their referents. Finally on this point, it is quite clear that none of the pongid language studies was designed to see what an ape might do with a simulated hominid protolanguage, nor has there been the slightest effort to approximate either modern natural living conditions of great apes or the supposed environments of early mankind. The artifacts and foods, etc., employed in all these studies have been those of contemporary Western civilization, and not replicas of Oldowan (pebble) technology.

   In presenting a resume of gestural or sign language theories below, I should make it clear that my own version of language phylogeny is eclectic and multifactorial, and that I do not conceive of sign language and then spoken language as the outcome of one or a few grand principles or evolutionary processes. My view resembles the kind of model presented by Wind (1970, Fig. 30, p. 80; an even more detailed presentation by Wind has since been prepared, 1974), although his aim was to account for the morphology and functions of the human larynx, which, as he notes (1974), does not appear to play the central part in the emergence and evolution of speech.

THEORIES ABOUT GESTURE AND LANGUAGE—SEVENTEENTH AND EIGHTEENTH CENTURIES

Although interest in gesture in relation to language can be traced back to Classical Antiquity, and to the writings of the Church fathers and many others, we have to go to the seventeenth and eighteenth centuries for more significant thoughts on the matter. Vossius (seventeenth century) regretted that gesture "had been replaced by speech," so that we do not now enjoy a "universal and self-evident system of signs and pantomimic expression [quoted by Farrar, 1873, p. 67]." Mandeville, in *The Fable of the Bees* (1728) thought early man could have made himself well understood with "dumb signs." Man, he said, was initially unfitted for speech, feeling no need for it. Children isolated in the wilderness would make themselves intelligible by means of signs and gestures, before attempting to do so with sounds (Kaye, 1924). Kaye suggests that both Condillac and Herder derived their ideas about a primordial gesture language from Mandeville (1924, p. 140).

The Abbé Etienne Bonnot de Condillac (1715–1780) was a prominent advocate of the serviceability of sign language for early mankind, although he was careful as a cleric to soothe possible ecclesiastical critics by offering his hypothesis simply as a philosophical exercise about how language might have arisen in an isolated pair of children, whereas everyone knew that Adam had acquired language in the Garden of Eden by divine inspiration. Basically, his aim was to show that man could have acquired language unassisted, and like Mandeville, he imagines a pair of children in the wilderness who employ the "language of action" (i.e., gesture), using the voice merely to call attention to the motor signs (cf. Kuehner, 1944). We need not be concerned here with the eventual growth of speech, and the favorite eighteenth-century guesses about the order in which the various parts of speech might have appeared.

Vico had similar ideas of mute early man's communicating in signs (Leroy, 1965, p. 173; Stam, 1976, pp. 9–19). Rousseau's (1754) glottogonic theory began with "simple cries of nature" which were combined with gestures, "which are in their own nature more expressive, and depend less for their meaning on a prior demonstration." Practically the same views were held by Diderot (1713–1784), Maupertuis (1698–1759), and Helvétius (1715–1771), who considered man's hands as the original vehicle for communication (Sayce, 1880). Dufief, writing in 1804, said that the original language was gestural, "for pointing out things, and the ideas conceived in those objects."

EARLY NINETEENTH-CENTURY
GESTURAL THEORIES OF LANGUAGE ORIGIN

The Abbé Sicard, successor to the Abbé de l'Epeé at the Institut des Sourds-muets, was a member of the circle of idéologues mentioned earlier which flourished between 1799 and 1805. There was disagreement over whether gestures were mainly innate or instinctive in character, or learned, but acquired more readily than spoken words because of their iconic appropriateness. Dugald Stewart (1829, vol. 3, Chap. 1) asserted that there was an instinctively based "natural language of signs" which had certain limitations that led in time to the formation of languages of "artificial signs"—i.e., speech. Stewart refers to North American Indian sign language as a "mute lingua franca," comparable to the sign language of the deaf. Alexander Murray (1775–1813) also postulated a primordial gesture language with vocal accompaniment—the latter consisting of precisely nine separate syllables, a notion not too different from that of N. Ja. Marr early in the twentieth century (cf. Thomas, 1957, p. 97).

In nearly all of these formulations, sign language, which admitted to be more logically related to its referents, was considered crude, uncouth, and inherently limited in comparison to spoken language, which therefore took its place. At the same time, gesture could be graceful and elegant, as in rhetoric and drama, when refined into an art form.

The explosive growth of philology which followed the demonstration that Sanskrit was related to various European languages had several effects on glottogonic speculation in the nineteenth century (Stam, 1976, pp. 216–241). The concept of "roots" was especially linked to the gestural origin hypothesis, since a large proportion of the reconstructed roots of both Indo-European and Semitic referred to simple motor actions. Thus Fiske (1863, pp. 448–449) supported the gestural theory, adding that natural selection would have tended to associate certain root sounds with particular gestures and external objects; a few years later Fiske (1869) spoke of a "language of manual signs which may have preceded and then ushered in the language of articulate words [p. 366]." Vocalizations occurring casually at the moment of pointing out or otherwise referring to things by signs would eventually replace the gestures. Jäger envisaged in

1867 an evolutionary sequence in gestures and "perceptual sounds" that
would become refined in signifying elements, then into "air picture imitations," replaced still later by "sound pictures [Rosenkranz, 1961; Sommerfelt, 1954, p. 889]." Modern sign languages for Jäger contained rem-
nants of the *Ursprache*. Jäger also envisaged a dramatic impetus to
language evolution when a "microcephalic ape" mother gave birth to the
first "macrocephalic human baby" possessing a greatly enlarged
language-learning capacity. This genetic and obstetrical miracle is still
part of some otherwise scientific glottogonic theories. More plausibly,
Rémi Valade (1866), whose practical acquaintance with the SL of the deaf
came from his position at the Institut des Sourds-muets, wrote a vivid
account of how gestural language would have functioned for early man.
He observes that only by such signing would the analytic faculty of the
human mind have developed. Farrar (1873) and Upham (1869, p. 504)
follow the same line. Upham cites some of the earlier reports on feral
children, but omits the case of Victor, the wild boy of Aveyron, reported
by Itard (1801/1962), certainly the best documented case until that time.
However, no clear-cut effort to teach Victor by means of a sign language
appears in Itard's account. Lazarus Geiger also believed that "grimace
and gesture" preceded speech (cf. Kainz, 1962, vol. 2, p. 580; Romanes,
1889, p. 366). For Marty (1875; cf. Stein, 1949, p. 158), gesture and sound
communication were closely intertwined, forming a single medium of
communication, with miming to make the sounds meaningful. A. H.
Sayce (1880) adhered to a gestural origin theory, but Mallery (1881, p. 273
ff.) disagreed somewhat, noting that both gesture and sound have always
been available. Still others in general support of gestural theory at this
time were Rambosson (1880, p. 382), and Hermann Paul (Fano, 1962, p.
279; Sommerfelt, 1954, p. 891). Romanes was a Darwinist who wrote very
intelligently on the emergence of man's cognitive powers (1888). For him
too gesture preceded speech, later subsiding into ancillary status (1888,
pp. 152–153). He exhibits much interest in the problem of glottogenesis,
and includes a classification of signs, expressing ideas about the interplay
between gesture and speech in terms we would now describe as feedback
(1888, p. 88, table; Chap. xvi, pp. 360–431).

Whitney (1885) proposed a gestural beginning for language: "It is altogether probable that gesture at first performed the principal part, even
to such an extent that the earliest human language may be said to have
been a language of gesture-signs [p. 767]." Voice superseded gesture
through a process of natural selection. These views were seconded by
George H. Darwin (1874), who rebuked F. Max Müller for his objections
to the gestural hypothesis, saying that there could be no doubt that a

"society of dumb men would soon elaborate a language of great complexity [p. 897]." Jastrow (1886, p. 556) advocated the priority of gesture, partly on the ground that its signs are "more general and uniform" than those of speech.

Edward B. Tylor, in anthropology, pursued the topic of language origins through all of his books (e.g., 1909, 1964), advocating the priority of sign language. Tylor visited schools for the deaf in Great Britain, and also paid a visit to the institution for the deaf in Berlin, acknowledging personal help from Heymann Steinthal who had written on deaf SL in 1851. Tylor clearly perceived that the crux of the problem in glottogenesis was determining how ideas could become linked to arbitrary signs; in the case of manual gestures, this connection had "hardly ever been broken, or even lost sight of for a moment [1964, p. 51]." Tylor realized that early hominids were not mute, and the vocal communication of emotion had accompanied mankind throughout evolution. Romanes, discussing some of Tylor's work on sign language and glottogenesis, pointed out, however, that modern deaf people inherit, in their brains, the "physiological structures" built up for speech, so that their sign-making facility rests in part on built-in adaptations for vocal language (1888, p. 113).

Ludwig Noiré is best known for his labor theory of language origin, that is, that vocal utterances emitted during cooperative work gave rise to speech (the *yo-he-ho* theory). However, he too believed that man had communicated by gesture prior to this. Noiré was also interested in the relationships of tools to language (1917, pp. 11–12).

CONTEMPORARY GESTURAL THEORIES OF LANGUAGE ORIGIN

At the turn of the century, additional support for the gestural theory came from Cesare Lombroso, W. T. Preyer, and Charles Aubert (1901), whose sketch of prehistoric gesture language reads almost like an eyewitness account. More influential were the views of the psychologist Wilhelm Wundt, whose work on gesture is now (1974) being reissued. Wundt's writings on glottogenesis were numerous, and very perceptive, as G. H. Mead recognized (1904, pp. 380–381). In the beginning, gesture was mainly emotional in function, and grammatical structure was negligible (Wundt, 1916, p. 64). Gesture became speech through mouth gesture, much as Alfred Russel Wallace had suggested. Articulation of speech sounds arose from mimetic and pantomimic activity, with the resulting sound at first merely incidental (cf. Hickerson, 1973, p. 3). Despite the formidable reputation of Wundt, later psychologists neglected his ideas, and he had almost no impact on linguistics.

Ernest Thompson Seton, neither a linguist nor a psychologist, but a writer on outdoor life and prototypical boy scout, had a lifelong interest in sign language, as well as in woodsman's trail signs and other nonverbal communication. Seton's *Sign Talk* (1918) includes a statement of the gestural theory of language origin: "The word had, perforce, to be arbitrary, but the gesture was logical [pp. xv–xvi]." Seton compared the communicative effectiveness of a "mere squeak in a concealed pipe" (the vocal tract) to manual gestures with their graphic, free-moving, externally visible parts utilizing all the dimensions of space, speed, motion, form, and action. Three other writers at about the same time also supported the gestural theory: Willis (1919, p. 18), Solomonson (1922), and the brain specialist Tilney (quoted in Paget, 1963, p. 133).

N. Ja. Marr (d. 1934) later dramatically attacked by none other than J. V. Stalin, was a leading language theoretician of the early Soviet period (cf. Thomas, 1957, p. 97 ff.). Marr believed that man's earliest language was gestural, and had developed into an effective medium, fully satisfying the social needs of early man. Marr wrote with some knowledge of sign languages, since they were still in use among certain Caucasus mountain villagers (cf. West, 1960). Marr believed that speech had come very late, starting with tribal rallying cries, and in conjunction with magico-religious activities of a privileged class of shamans. Marr reconstructed speech to four primordial syllables, similar to Alexander Murray's nine root syllables of 1823. It is interesting that in the wave of posthumous criticism of Marr, starting with Stalin's heavy barrage, one of the fantasies Marr was accused of related to the "head spinning" suggestion that language in gestural form might go back as much as 900,000 years. The present (1974) glottogonic conservatism of Soviet writers may be related to the withering onslaught on Marr's views many years after his demise.

Marcel Jousse, active around the same time as Marr, developed a devoted following for his theories about gesture and mimesis (1969; cf. Fano, 1962; Kristeva & Lacoste, 1968, p. 134), mainly expressed in lectures at the Ecole d'Anthropologie in Paris. Jousse accepted the priority of gestural language over speech, and often protested that language studies had too long been fixated on sound and speech phenomena (1936, p. 202). He followed the reports of work with anthropoid apes with great interest (1936, pp. 201–203). His position is exemplified by his remark (1936): "Endowed with his essential mimism and intelligence, the first *anthropos* expressed himself as spontaneously in gestures as he walked on his legs [p. 215]." Space is insufficient to expound the whole range of Jousse's views about sign language communication. He is little known outside of France, perhaps in part because his prose resembles that of Claude Lévi-Strauss.

Drexel (1951, pp. 63–64) suggested that Lower Paleolithic man used gestures, or else nonarticulate vocal sounds, such as continuants, to which, during the Middle Paleolithic, dentals were added. Oakley (1953, pp. 264–267) also favored the gestural hypothesis, and drew on the mouth–gesture theories of Paget (1963) and Jóhannesson (1952) for the shift from gesture to articulate speech. These two investigators had worked quite independently, until they discovered each other's work in the World War II era.

Haldane (1955, p. 398) believed that acoustic signals as used by man could have been derived from visual ones, adding the interesting suggestion that the domestication of the dog in late prehistoric times could have enhanced the role of speech, since dogs have better hearing than sight. Others at the time who propounded the primacy of gesture include Entwhistle (1953, p. 17) and Ammer (cf. Rosenkranz, 1961, pp. 41–42), who placed the advent of speech around 20,000 B.C. Stuart Robertson also accepted the gestural hypothesis, but considered that it had rather low communicational efficiency compared to speech (1958, pp. 2–3).

Raymond A. Dart, discoverer of the first australopithecine, wondered whether they had language (1959, p. 156 ff.). He leaned toward a gestural language for these and still later hominids, and thought it likely that articulate language did not emerge until Upper Paleolithic and Mesolithic men adopted a marsh-fishing way of life. A. S. Diamond (1960, pp. 265–269) favored a gestural protolanguage, although he considered it unlikely that sound was not also utilized to indicate emotional states.

Jacques van Ginneken's model for glottogenesis was, if anything, more bizarre than Marr's. He claimed that articulate speech came after the invention of writing, prior to which language was mostly gestural, followed by a stage of click sounds similar to those of the Khoisan languages (cf. Fano, 1962, p. 286; Przyluski, 1941, pp. 31–32; Stopa, 1973a, 1973b). The shift from click language to modern kinds of consonants did not occur until after picture language had appeared.

Thorndike (1943, pp. 95–98) derived spoken language from infant babbling which was reinforced, but he postulated a preoral stage in which gesture was used, with gestures disposing others to attend to vocal utterances. About this time, Sturtevant composed several scenarios to suggest how gestures or vocal sounds could have acquired meanings and entered into a protolanguage system (1947, pp. 47–50; cf. Rosenkranz, 1961, pp. 117–118). Assirelli dealt with glottogenesis in several papers, rejecting a simple gestural origin for language (1948, pp. 95–96), but conceding that gestures are more iconic, and that they may have prevailed during a long "visual-hieroglyphic" phase of glottogenesis. Stein (1949, p. 83) attributed gesture language to pithecanthropus (*Homo erectus*), apparently without any careful examination of the evidence.

Langer (1960, pp. 127–128) said that the visual complex, rather than the auditory–vocal channel, was decisive in early language, since visual images are particularly prone to conversion into symbols (1960, p. 129). However, she did not set forth a clear-cut gestural model for glottogenesis, becoming involved at this point in her argument with how the vocal organs could have been "moved to register the occurrence of an image [p. 133]."

Fano (1962, p. 290), after an extensive review of glottogonic theories, concluded that the gestural hypothesis was the sole likely solution to this "vexatious problem." In the beginning, language was a mimetic–pictographic system, rather than one of agreed-upon phonetic signs. Hallowell (1963, p. 450) conceived of protocultural human communication resting on other than the speech mode, but he was evidently reluctant to be more precise than that. Von Eickstedt (1963, vol. 3, p. 2040), adopting the gestural hypothesis, adds that it was not until spoken language had emerged that "inner speech," with its extremely important cognitive byproducts, became feasible. Edmund Critchley saw a long era of gesture language, which may have survived several abortive developments of spoken language (1967, p. 36) before the advantages of speech prevailed.

Bruner, although not much interested in advancing one glottogonic theory against others, nevertheless marshals much evidence that can be used in support of the gestural model. He chides psychologists for not exploring hand and language skills more completely (1968, pp. 60–61), and views predication, with topic and comment, as analogous to the differential roles of the hands in holding and manipulating (1968, pp. 62–63). For Bruner (1968), "the origin of the uniquely human **form** of language remains very much a mystery. I have proposed that it is a refinement of human skill as exhibited in the attentional system and motor system as represented by man's clever hands [pp. 63–64]." Bruner's sequence of behaviors in the young child—enactive, iconic, and symbolic—could be applied to the phylogeny of hominid behavior with little strain.

For Collinder (1965, p. 22), gesture was accompanied by significant facial expression, with voice as a subordinate factor in communication (cf. Shafton, 1976). McBride (1968, p. 15) notes the formation of autonomous sign languages in every institution for the deaf, which he thinks would make sense if speech had evolved through long periods of signing and miming.

Trân Dûc Thâo's papers on the genesis of language from deictic gesture

(1969a, 1969b, 1970) speak of the liberation of the brain through language and consciousness. Zhinkin (1971, p. 84), without explicitly accepting a gestural predecessor of oral language, suggests that early man, encountering some terrifying stimulus, would run to his fellows, and pointing to the fearful object would involuntarily imitate the state of fear with vocalization, which after a long time ("a few millennia") might become a word, now deprived of its original affective content. That hominid vocal cries had somehow to be decontextualized or rendered affectively neutral is a widely expressed notion. Lieberman's general glottogonic model follows most of the foregoing scenarios, except that he pays closer attention to the problems of turning a prearticulate vocal code into one resembling modern articulate speech (1972, pp. 86–91). Cicourel's (1974) outline of language emergence is similar. Hockett had rejected the gestural path to language in his earlier speculations, but more recently (1973, p. 384) admits that the critical steps toward modern language need not have occurred in the vocal–auditory channel, but might have involved visible body motions, with the definitive switch to a concentration on mouth and ear coming later.

Several glottogonic models involving a gestural phase or a preponderant role for gesture in the early stages of glottogenesis have been offered recently. May (1974) postulated a developed gestural language as a preadaptation for speech, based on "pre-speech" foci in the Broca and Wernicke areas of the left cerebral hemisphere. By the close of the australopithecine era, May assumed that a grammatically ordered sign language system was in use. Other scenarios along these general lines have been proposed by Jaynes, Lamendella, and Steklis and Harnad (all in Harnad et al., 1976), by Shafton (1976), and Dingwall (1977), differing in details but agreeing in the attribution of an early preponderance of manual gesture in language evolution.

Whereas spoken languages with accurate pronunciation are acquired slowly, and only in childhood, gesture languages, which are visible and more or less iconic rather than arbitrary, should be easier to learn at all ages, and thus might have greater diffusional potential. It is possible that early oral languages served in part for boundary marking, as is the case with many bird calls, while a gestural language could be used as a regional lingua franca.

In modern times, sign languages have occasionally emerged to fulfill the communication needs of one or a few profoundly deaf members in larger hearing communities (Farb, 1974; Gajdusek & Garruto, 1973; Kakamasu, 1968; and Kuschel, 1974). If blindness were as frequent as deafness in early human groups, vocal substitutes for gesture might likewise have arisen.

A recurrent issue in glottogonic discussions, whether in the gestural or vocal mode, has been duality of patterning or double articulation, that is, the coexistence in modern spoken languages of a small set of meaningless phonemic units, and a larger set of units having semantic value. Several linguists have insisted that this duality or double articulation is the essence of true language, whereas it is by no means clear that all sign languages necessarily have such duality. Duality in articulate, spoken languages seems to me to be the result of having to handle comparatively large lexicons. It is not necessary to assume that the biograms[3] of the australopithecines or even *Homo erectus* required lexicons exceeding a thousand terms, and even that may be an overestimate. On this thorny issue see Chafe (1967, p. 60), Bidwell (1968, p. 8), Hockett (1960a, 1960b, 1973), Dingwall (1977, p. 33), and for American Sign Language, Stokoe (1972a, 1972b, 1973).

"EQUAL TIME" THEORIES: GESTURAL AND VOCAL LANGUAGES DEVELOPED TOGETHER

While most of the sources we have quoted above adhere to some version of the gestural theory, we may now consider some who adopt a kind of "equal time" approach, in which signing and vocal language arose together. Among supporters of this notion, one of the earliest was Warburton (1698–1779), who thought that the primal language was a mixture of spoken words and actions (Aarsleff, 1967, p. 22). Others were Blair (1718–1800), Charles Darwin (1888, p. 184), Hyde Clarke (1881), and more recently, Przyluski (1941, pp. 32–33), who said that a rudimentary spoken language would not have been understandable except with accompanying signs. Similar views in favor of a kind of tandem growth of the two modalities have been expressed by Kainz (1962 vol. 2, p. 580), Grace de Laguna (1963, p. 6), Rule (1967, p. 160), and Goggin (1973, p. 175). Even Lieberman has criticized the writer for possible overemphasis on the gestural side of the language-origin scenario (1973, p. 60).

Opponents of the gestural thesis include several well-known figures. DeBrosses disagreed with Condillac's view of the priority of the "language of action" and argued that man had spoken from the beginning, which is of course in accordance with the Old Testament account (Kuehner, 1944, p. 37). For Herder, voice was just as basic and natural as

---

[3]Biogram: the total behavioral pattern, or repertoire, of a given animal species; the biologically based life program of an animal species (or, for that matter, a plant species, to the extent that plants exhibit "behavior").

expressive movement, though he conceded that the earliest language would have been simpler than present-day languages (cf. Viertel, 1966, pp. 121–124). F. Max Müller's rejection of gestural origin theory was more complete, and he showed little or no interest in sign languages "with their less perfect symbols [Whitney, 1874, p. 70]." Lord Monboddo (1714–1799) ruled out a nonvocal origin for language, "such as our dumb persons use [Aarsleff, 1967, p. 38]." Vendryès (1925, pp. 7–9) said that early man had settled on the vocal channel because his limbs were too busily engaged in other kinds of useful activities, whereas the vocal–auditory tract would have been "idle" most of the time, and so available for communication. Géza Révész wrote a major book on language origins (1959), in which he saw no reason to adopt a gestural model, partly because many other animals already use vocal communication. For Révész, human language was vocal from the start, and he explicitly denied that anything in the cognitive development of children provided any support for any other conclusion. Kainz (1962) regarded the gestural theory as "clearly false [vol. 2, p. 580]." Other rejectors of sign language as the forerunner of speech include Geschwind (in Salzinger & Salzinger, 1967, p. 31), Bateson (1968, pp. 618–619), Lenneberg (1967), Kristeva (1968, p. 53), Zhinkin (1971, p. 88), and in her 1972 paper, Hill (p. 5). For Washburn, gesture played no more role in the emergence of human language than it now does in pongid social communication (1973). Bunak's glottogonic model is phonetic, and does not mention gesture (1958). Pätsch, writing within an explicit Marxian framework, considered gestural theories "anti-evolutionary [1955]." Fischer (1974), at a language origins symposium, considered vocal sounds the essence of language. Count (1974) is somewhat skeptical of the writer's version of glottogenesis via the gestural path.

GLOTTOGENESIS AND TOOLS

Many recent language origin schemes incorporate ideas about the relationship of tools or toolmaking to glottogenesis (cf. Montagu, pp. 266–274, Isaac, pp. 275–288, and Marshack, pp. 308–309, all in Harnad et al., 1976). Progressive changes in stone implements furnish almost the only evidence we have concerning hominid cognitive evolution until the Middle Paleolithic, where deliberate burial first appears, or the Upper Paleolithic, with its cave art and proliferation of complex lithic toolmaking traditions. Semënov (1959, pp. 37–39) has vividly illustrated the connections between lithic tool manufacture and the elaboration of mental programs required to handle it. Yakimov (1973, p. 8) concurs. Leroi-Gourhan

(1964, 1965, p. 41) has explored these relationships very thoroughly and their relation to language. Marshack's studies of graphic markings (1971, 1972, in Harnad *et al.*, 1976, pp. 288–311) which may represent Upper Paleolithic tally keeping, or even calendrical notation, have also suggested some connection with language elaboration. Other recent treatments of the language–toolmaking problem are by E. Critchley (1967, pp. 72–73), Oakley (1951, p. 72), and Holloway (1972, p. 199; in Harnad *et al.*, 1976, p. 346). Holloway believes that the imposition of arbitrary form on the environment, as in toolmaking, indicates a capacity to create language in which arbitrary symbols are "imposed" on reality. However, early tools may not have been entirely arbitrary in form, and protolanguage may have had a very strong iconic component, even though the ape language experiments indicate that these animals are capable of handling arbitrary signs (cf. Premack, 1971a, 1971b, 1972; R. A. Gardner & B. T. Gardner, 1969; Rumbaugh *et al.*, 1973; Rumbaugh *et al.*,1977; and Fouts, 1973).

Trân Dûc Thâo (1969a, p. 25), Masters (1970, p. 309), and Bronowski (1967) all assert that toolmaking is close to whatever underlies the ability to manipulate verbal symbols. Bronowski sees language really emerging with the achievement of "master tools," that is, tools used to make other tools, which he believes began to appear around the time fire was regularly used, conservatively placed by him about 300,000 years ago. Recent French finds date the first use of fire as far back as 750,000, at the L'Escale site.

On the other hand, MacIver (1961, p. 8) argues that the amount of language needed in order to make tools has been exaggerated, a point on which I agree, while not denying a significant relation between tools and language. It is worth noting that another sphere of activity with language analogies is etiquette, or formalized patterns of social interaction (cf. Tsiviane, 1970), which, like tool manufacture, involves programmed action sequences with a predetermined order.

If the earliest language(s) utilized the gestural mode, the tool–language connection must have been especially close, since the actions of actually using or making tools are practically identical to the gestures used to symbolize such actions (Kaplan, 1968). I have already observed that existing evolutionary studies of the human hand emphasize the role of toolmaking and tool manipulation but fail to consider whether the evolution of the hand has had anything to do with hominid social communication.

Clark (1970, pp. 143–147), looking at the diversification of tool kits from the Middle Paleolithic onward, suggests that man was passing into a new cognitive sphere based on speech during this time (cf. Isaac, in Harnad *et al.*, 1976, pp. 275–288). However, only one study seems to have focused on the effect of verbal mediation on toolmaking (Bernard, 1971), in which a modern flint-knapper demonstrated, but without speech, the methods of producing various kinds of tools to one group of learners, and supplemented his demonstration with verbal explanations to another group. It was found that the verbal mediation had little effect on the making of Oldowan (pebble) tools, but affected the learnability positively in the case of Upper Paleolithic type implements.

The relative learnability of visual signals, such as gestures, and sounds is relevant here. Jakobson (1965, p. 217) has observed that visual indexes are more readily discriminated than auditory ones. Auditory "icons" are poorly recognized, as sound-effects experts were aware in the days of radio theater. But even with manual gestures, some are harder to master than others. Fouts (1972) showed that there was a very great range in learnability of manual gestures for chimpanzees. A more basic aspect of manual gestures, of course, has to do with their discriminability at various distances, or under different conditions of illumination, or background contrast (cf. Moser, O'Neill, Oyer, Abernathy, & Showe, 1961). I have suggested (Hewes, in Harnad *et al.*, 1976, pp. 498–499) that in darkly pigmented human populations, the lighter pigmentation of the volar skin (palms of the hands, soles of the feet) and beneath the nails may have been adaptive for manual communication, if this had been a major means of hominid language for a long enough time to allow natural selective forces to operate.

HUNTING AND GLOTTOGENESIS

Along with tools, hominid hunting has figured in glottogonic speculation as well as in possible preadaptations for language among chimpanzees, as I have already noted. But, as P. Reynolds cautions us, it is not enough to say that early hominid hunting was facilitated by some sort of language, when animals like timberwolves hunt quite successfully without it (personal communication, March, 1969). It must be shown how human hunting really differs from hunting by wolves or other specialized carnivores. To begin with, hominid hunters are at several disadvantages, compared with the Carnivora. Excellent higher primate vision does not offset a rather feeble sense of smell; nails instead of claws, and diminished canine teeth are also nonadaptive for killing thick-skinned herbivores, and so on. Effective entry into the predator or even the scavenger niche by hominids obviously depends on engagement of superior cognitive powers, coupled with extrasomatic weapons and/or butchering tools. Cooperative hunting is the preferred model for early hominid hunting, but several genuine carnivores have achieved this. Chimpanzee hunting (Teleki, 1973a, 1973b) is collaborative, but weaponless, and the prey are smaller in size than the predators. Peters and Mech (1973, pp. 25–29) discussing cooperative hunting in the light of timberwolf data, suggest that cognitive terrain mapping is extremely important (cf. Premack, in Harnad *et al.*, 1976, pp. 547–550; Menzel & Johnson, in Harnad *et al.*, 1976, pp. 131–142). Presumably, vegetable food foragers have cognitive maps of some sort, but their territories tend to be small, at least among primates.

De Laguna (1963) sketched some of the aspects of early human hunting in relation to language emergence. Using much fuller data, Clark (1970, pp. 71–72, 102–103) has considered the role of language and other factors in early hunting, concluding that **vocal** language may not have been critically necessary. Lancaster (1968, p. 456) also discusses these matters, and although she adopts a vocal model for glottogenesis, shows how a language system providing for environmental reference enhances hominid exploitation for food resources in a given territory. Finding the way back to base camping places, to distant water holes, or to isolated stands of food-bearing plants, requires good cognitive maps, involving the use of visible landmarks in a species not equipped with superior olfaction.

Trân Dûc Thâo (1969a, p. 33) suggests ways in which australopithecine hunters would find deictic gestures advantageous for pursuing game moving out of sight behind environmental obstacles such as hills or thick vegetation. Peters (1972) has shown how topic and comment messages would have served an early hominid hunter–scavenger. Integration of information about terrain, patterns of movement of game over regular trails, etc., amount to "strategic" planning. At some stage in hominization, our ancestors surpassed competing predators in this respect, quite apart from the advantages of superior weaponry. While it is fairly easy to advance plausible ways in which emerging language capacities, and gesture in particular, would have contributed to a "deviation amplifying cybernetic system," Washburn (1973) warns that we are entering an era in which guessing about the behavioral aspects of hominization has rapidly rising requirements for expertise.[4]

Hill (1973b) has provided a long and well-argued paper on language and early hominid population structure, which goes beyond the hunt as such, in which she has skillfully woven ideas about group size, social communication, geographical factors, and plant collecting as well as hunting or

---

[4]The writer's qualifications for speculating about early hominid behavior in environments resembling those of modern African savannas are very slight, but do include short firsthand experience in game reserves in Kenya, Tanzania, South Africa, and Nigeria.

scavenging. It is worth noting that there was only the briefest mention of language in the volume edited by Lee and DeVore, *Man the Hunter* (1968, pp. 231–234).

The utility of arm or hand pointing in spotting game is most marked when the potential prey are at a considerable distance. Whereas Menzel's chimpanzees, in a football field-sized outdoor enclosure, could be directed toward hidden rewards by glance or body position on the part of the experimenters (Menzel, 1973, 1974) such generalized pointing probably would not suffice for directing the attention of others in one's hunting party to animals one or more kilometers away, across tree or brush-encumbered landscape. Modern hunters (or spotters of enemy positions in warfare, etc.) usually supplement arm- or hand-indicated bearings with verbal information: "You see that tall tree [pointing toward it]? Now move a little to the left, between there and the low bush. . . ." But gesture can supply many other kinds of useful information besides simple location. It is highly effective for transmitting information about direction and relative speed of movement, or even the gait of distant animals. As has been noted for chimpanzee hunting, its silence has further advantages for human stalkers, such as avoidance of starting up birds which may lie in the vegetation along the route. There are additional factors which I think have been overlooked in connection with early hominid hunting. Successful tracking of game by recent hunters involves the skillful "reading" of many kinds of trail signs, whether in the form of hoofprints, droppings, or of bruised or broken or partly consumed plants. These skills are chiefly visual, though smell (and even heat sensing, in order to determine the recency of a dropping) and the sounds made by the prey or other creatures may be involved as well. The ability to identify particular game animals by their hoofmarks, to determine their numbers, whether they were moving slowly and securely or rapidly and warily, seems to me analogous both to reading and to the decoding of gestural signs. G. H. Mead once observed that the footprints of bears could be read as "symbols" (1956, p. 183), adding that being able to decipher such a mark was what "we mean when we speak of a human being thinking a thing out, or having a mind." Like so many gestural signs, animal tracks are only parts of larger and rather different wholes. As far as I know, only human hunters inspect hoofprints **visually** for guidance; other mammalian predators simply sniff at them.

Related to the hunt, at least among modern hunter–gatherers, are hunting dances or rituals, in which important animals may be skillfully imitated, by mime and gesture, but also of course by onomatopoeic sounds. McBride (1973, p. 15) has related such hunting performances, before or after the actual hunt and kill, to language development. Fischer, discussing such mimicry in relation to hunting, has noted the importance of being able to imitate animal calls. Such animal calls (and bird-song imitations especially) still play a role in human communication in both hunting and warfare, where stealth is important. Cue summation, in which signals on more than one channel occur, has been shown to enhance information transmission (Cushman, 1973). It has been suggested that one of the pathways from sign language to speech might have been via a combination of iconic gestures and "diacritical" sound approximations.

P. C. Reynolds (1972) speaks of "ecology and semantics" in connection with the growth of meanings in early human communication systems. In 1908 Scott (p. liii) had already suggested that early human groups possessing superior protolanguage would have enjoyed a selective advantage, owing to improved capacities for organizing defense or attack. However, it is also probable that any such communicational advantages would not be long in spreading from one group to another, as has regularly happened with superior weaponry. To be sure, any hominid with a decided genetic incapacity to handle more efficient language would perhaps be at a fatal disadvantage—a notion which on more than one occasion has been put forth to help explain the seemingly rapid disappearance of the Neanderthal populations.

From another standpoint, a gestural protolanguage could have promoted the successful expansion of its users into new and varied environments, where survival would be enhanced by rapid formation of cognitive maps based on a shared toponymic system, and generic topographical terminology for recurrent landscape features. To be sure, many introduced species (such as rabbits in Australia!) have multiplied horrendously without the aid of language, or very sophisticated cognitive maps.

Emphasis on hunting activities may unintentionally minimize the usefulness of a gestural protolanguage in vegetal subsistence behavior. Just as the ability to use topic and comment to refer to rendezvous localities benefits hunters or scavengers, plant collectors can profit from superior intelligence concerning places where particular wild fruits, shoots, roots, and the like, may be harvested. Again, one could object that other foraging animals manage without language to secure a livelihood. The point is that language and language-labeled cognitive maps should improve such foraging activities. Despite the glamor and "male chauvinism" associated with hunting, early man probably derived more of his food resources from plants (or other relatively stationary organisms, such as shellfish) than from stalking or pursuit of herbivores. The postulated foraging parties of mainly females and their young would become more productive not only if edible plants could be discerned at greater distances and named, but perhaps even more important, if the approximate times or seasons of their availability could somehow be discussed. A significant element in both hunting and plant collecting has to do with rough calculation of the time required to reach particular places or landmarks en route, and of course, to return safely before nightfall. Many migratory animals appear to use solar positions as diurnal indicators of both direction and the passage of time, and it has even been suggested that some migratory birds employ the configurations of constellations for nighttime guidance. How long the hominids utilized such direction and time markers we do not know, but several ethnographic accounts refer to people without clocks pointing to the sun and its apparent course in the daytime sky to denote segments of time, and hence the distance which could be covered in such an amount of time. Indicating the passage of whole nights is commonly signed by a sleeping gesture (tilting the head and closing the eyes). Tallying moons (Marshack, 1971) may have been a later procedure. My point is that these very useful kinds of messages could have been quite effectively developed in a prevocal sign language system.

The Middle Paleolithic, which was the age of Neanderthal man and Mousterian Culture in the central-western Old World, seems also to have been the first epoch for which we have unambiguous evidence of symbolic behavior, beyond manufacture of tools to a pattern. Middle Paleolithic mankind buried his dead deliberately, at least in some areas, and with "offerings" ranging from animal bones to red ochre and wildflowers, with the latter two suggesting body ornament (cf. Constable, 1973, p. 81). In the realm of pure guesswork, life in cave mouths or rock shelters, which seems to have become more frequent in some areas in those times, might have led to the discovery that manual gestures could be projected on cave walls by firelight.

Lieberman and his colleagues, carefully reconstructing the vocal tracts of several fossil men, and comparing the results of the computer-based simulations of speech sound parameters producible in these tracts with those of known vocal parameters of chimpanzee, macaque, newborn human infant, and modern human adult, found that articulate speech sounds were out of the question not only for modern apes and monkeys, but also for the fossil australopithecines and *Homo erectus* (Lieberman, 1972, 1973, 1975; Lieberman, Crelin, & Klatt, 1972). Articulate speech, they claim, might have been possible in Steinheim Man, about 300,000 years ago, and in Rhodesian man, considerably later. Neanderthal man, represented by the La Chapelle-aux-Saints specimen, would have had a peculiarly nasal vocal quality, and may not have been able to produce the critical "calibration" vowels, /i/, /a/, and /u/, which enable speakers of all modern languages to correct for the wide differences in the sizes of vocal tracts in children, and between males and females. Their findings support the writer's position as to the late appearance of articulate speech, and indirectly at least, suggest that if the australopithecines or *Homo erectus* had some sort of language, it may not have been vocal, but gestural.

LANGUAGE AND THE MEDIATION OF THOUGHT

Advanced toolmaking or tool using seems to be linked to cerebral lateralization, and both are thus possibly tied to language (cf. D'Agostino, 1974; Critchley, 1953, pp. 326–353). While speech is now usually mainly handled in the left cortex, gestural language is also, whereas the right hemisphere mainly serves to integrate spatial information, environmental sounds instead of human speech sounds, and, more generally, according to Semmes (1968), integration of "dissimilar units," requiring multimodal coordination (cf. Levy, in Harnad *et al.*, 1976, pp. 812–820). Each hemisphere seems to retain low-level capacities much more fully represented in the other. We thus return to Bruner's comment on the "topic and comment" functions of the left and right hands, respectively. Cushing long ago had noted that the Zuni Indians call the right hand "the taker," and the left, "the holder [1892, p. 290]." Cobb (1944) adds that the more skilled hand would be more frequently used to display objects to others, while attention-getting sounds were uttered: "Here began primitive speech, expletive at first, but later combining with signs of the leading hand to symbolize something [p. 32]." Brain-injured individuals, by the way, exhibit sharp differences in their ability to replicate the hand gestures of others (Kimura & Archibald, 1973), with left cortex damage often producing marked deficiency, while right cortex damage usually did not impair this function.

We are without direct evidence of when or under what conditions language mediation of thinking became internalized. At some stage, in the cognitive evolution of our species, people learned how to suppress vocal communication, while "talking to themselves." The deaf do the same with internalized signing. The performance of complex manual skills can be improved with internalized verbalization; more experimental data are needed to determine if internalized manual gesture is less effective than internalized vocal language with highly complex manual activity related to crafts, tool using, etc.

COGNITIVE DEMANDS ON THE HUMAN BRAIN

Modern human thinking seems to be based on interactions between the "verbal" coding system, which of course has been mostly the spoken language, until the recent importance of reading, and the imaginal or pictorial code, derived from experience with objects in the external world (Atwood, 1971, p. 290). The human brain can evidently store an immense number of visual patterns (1971, p. 347) in long-term memory, but far less in the short-term auditory memory system. Worden (1971, pp. 25–26) provides some details about the differences between the visual and auditory channels. The human primary visual cortex contains around 538 million neurons, whereas the auditory cortex has only about 100 million. The optic nerve contains about a million fibers, compared to the mere 30,000 in the cochlear nerve. These figures may help to explain why duality of patterning or "double articulation" may have become a necessity for a language in the vocal–auditory channel, but might not be so urgent in a visually based system. The marked enlargement of the hominid braincase (approximately threefold between the australopithecines and the Neanderthalers and modern man) could not have been a casual biological "accident," since such a hypertrophied brain is biologically extremely expensive (cf. D'Aquili, 1972, pp. 17–23; Holloway, 1973; Pilbeam, 1972, p. 122; Tobias, 1973; Yakimov, 1973). A great many specialists on human evolution agree that cognitive demands, and probably language, or language-retrievable visual memory, somehow account for the relatively rapid expansion of the brain. A very modest language skill obviously does not require a big brain; as Lenneberg has pointed out for "bird-headed" human dwarfs, and some other microcephalics, simple speech is often present, and the various ape language-acquisition studies demonstrate this for sign language (Lenneberg, 1967, 1971). The changing volume of the hominid cranium could fit equally well a vocal or sign language model for early language development (cf. Jerison, in Harnad *et al.*, 1976, pp. 370–382).

THE ANTIQUITY OF SPOKEN LANGUAGE

If we reassemble these notions, our model may indicate that the capacities required for spoken language were not much developed prior to about 300,000 years ago, but that there are good reasons to postulate a gestural language before that time, perhaps going back to the australopithecine hominids. The writer agrees with May (1974) that such a model provides the most elegant way to explain how speech could emerge, since it eliminates the theoretical need to account simultaneously for the beginnings of either lexicon or syntax, but only a transformation from one channel to another. That the latter transformation involves matters of great complexity, especially with respect to the formation of speech sound processors or decoders, to say nothing of rearrangements to permit vocal language production, is fully acknowledged, but the gestural origin hypothesis greatly simplifies this step or stage in glottogenesis. Krantz also agrees with this model, with the suggestion that even Neanderthal man may have been mainly dependent on gesture language (1973, p. 14). Krantz then explains the rapid changeover to the *Homo sapiens* cranial and facial configuration—prominent chin, canine fossae, large mastoids, thinner-walled cranium, etc., as correlates of the diffusion of fully articulate speech and the genetic material underlying its achievement. Except for the head, face, and vocal tract features associated with the new form of language, Krantz suggests that other gene pool factors responsible for the various geographic adaptations we usually call "racial" need not have been much affected, thus agreeing in principle with Carleton S. Coon's "sapiensization" model which attracted so much adverse criticism. Postulating a rapid spread of articulate language in the Upper Paleolithic runs somewhat counter to my earlier notion that speech lends itself especially well to the formation of local social boundaries, in contrast to the more universally decodable gestural languages. However, if "babelization" was somehow culturally advantageous, we might be able to reconcile these seemingly contradictory positions. An analogue in the recent history of our species is the rapid, worldwide diffusion of the exclusive national state pattern of political organization. Livingstone's assumptions about the possible relation of language development, incest taboos, and institutionalized local exogamy are relevant here (1969, p. 48). Speech may be peculiarly useful for the maintenance of small band or tribal social units (cf. Birdsell, 1968); "dialects" and even different languages of course exist in sign language, but it is questionable whether one can equate the mechanisms which produce these differences and those which can support spoken-language differences in adjacent populations for centuries and millennia.

Several linguists, working from different premises, agree that all existing spoken languages go back to a common "vanishing point" between about 35,000 and 40,000 years ago (Foster, 1969, 1970, 1971; Jaynes, in Harnad *et al.*, 1976, pp. 315–316; Swadesh, 1966, 1971; cf. Washburn & McCown, 1972), although such views have not gone unchallenged (Bender, 1972). Hockett (1973) is in substantial agreement, placing the birth of modern spoken language around 50,000 years ago, while not precluding a much longer era of vocal languages of a different character. These suggestions, unverifiable save by glotto-statistical extrapolations, nevertheless roughly fit the model derived from vocal tract reconstructions by Lieberman (1975), and inferences based on the cultural efflorescence of the Upper Paleolithic.

LANGUAGE AFTER THE SHIFT TO SPEECH

Our phylogenetic model for sign language has now been brought to the point where the major burden of human language had shifted to speech, and it only remains to sketch very briefly what happened to sign language thereafter. The Upper Paleolithic, as we have noted, witnessed some remarkable cultural advances, not only in graphic or plastic "art" (whatever was its social function), but in technology—in stone, bone, antler, and presumably in wood, skin working, basketry, canoe building, garment making—to say nothing of inferred elaborations in social structure, ritual, folklore, etc. Marshack has recently demonstrated that this period also saw advances in counting or notation, including possibly lunar calendar keeping (Marshack, in Harnad *et al.*, 1976, pp. 289–311). From certain ethnographic groups we are also led to suggest that late Upper Paleolithic or Mesolithic peoples may have developed graphic symbolism in perishable sand, clay, or soil media, such as the Walbiri (and other groups) in Australia carry on today (cf. Munn, 1973). Such graphics, as Leroi-Gourhan reminds us, are "frozen" manual gestures—gestures made in more permanent media than air. We need not go so far as to insist that the frequent representations of hands in the prehistoric art of parts of Europe provides a direct record of manual sign language (Leroi-Gourhan, 1967), although the idea is provocative, and perhaps just as valid as the idea that the handprints and hand outlines, which often lack fingers, are records of actual finger mutilation. Martí (1971) has assembled an impressive volume on human hands in art, particularly in Mesoamerica.

The earliest forms of writing tend to contradict the assumption that writing is everywhere and always a mere back formation from speech (Englefield, 1977, pp. 64–77). Both in Egyptian hieroglyphic writing (Gardiner, 1957, pp. 442–458) and in the early stages of Chinese writing (Kümmel, 1969; Wieger, 1965), there is considerable evidence of the influence of hand and arm gestures, along with other kinds of visual symbolism. Basso and Anderson (1973) have described a recent Apache Indian invention of a ritual script which also weakens the notion that writing invariably emerges from efforts to represent speech. That counting and computation are visually and spatially based, rather than rooted in the vocal–auditory mode, seems even clearer. Swadesh (1966) suggests the finger-name origins of many numeral words. Computation in the Classical Mediterranean world was very much a matter of manual and digital gesture, and such techniques survived into Medieval and later times, probably stimulating the development of finger spelling (Bechtel, 1909; Richardson, 1916; Sanford, 1928; Smith, 1925; such a system of finger computation persisted until at least the nineteenth century in Persia, according to Palmer, 1869).

In the nineteenth century, the interest in the reconstructed roots of primordial Indo-European and Semitic led to the suggestion that many of them represented transformation from manual gestures or other action signs, either through the process of "mouth gesture" (Jóhannesson, 1944, 1952; Paget, 1944, 1951, 1963; c. Handel *et al.*, 1968), or otherwise (Dart, 1959, pp. 161–163). Wherever linguists have tried to explicate reconstructed roots, most of the glosses turn out to refer to very basic actions, which might very easily be represented in sign language. Jóhannesson claimed that 85% of reconstructed Indo-European roots, and 80% of those in Hebrew, were derivable from "mouth gesture," which, according to his theory, had manual gestural antecedents (cf. E. Critchley, 1967, p. 37; Jousse, 1925, pp. 44–46). Brown, Black, & Horowitz (1955) say that "it is possible, however, that the origin of speech in gestural imitation and physiognomic languages has left a residue of roughly translatable words in all languages [p. 393]," on the basis of their study of sound symbolism in Czech, Hindi, and Chinese, and that of Allport in Magyar, and Rich in Japanese and English.

While European monastic sign languages, the complex gesture languages of South Indian dance drama (Kathakali), the various sign languages in use around the world in tribal and other societies, and the modern sign languages of the deaf, of workers in specialized occupations, etc., occupy only a tiny fraction of the time span here considered in our phylogenetic model, their study should obviously illuminate much of what is now very imperfectly known about the properties and capacities of such communication systems. The demonstration, beginning in the late 1960s, that chimpanzees (and other pongids) can acquire gestural and other forms of visible language should be a powerful stimulus for the serious consideration of the hypothesis that a long period of manual signing preceded articulate speech.

Appendix

Approximate dating[a] (number of years ago)	Cultural periods	Fossil hominid remains	Some significant cultural features (first appearance)
10,000	Metal Ages Neolithic Mesolithic	All classified as *Homo sapiens sapiens*	Recent and modern cultures
35,000	Upper Paleolithic	Early *Homo sapiens sapiens* (Cro-Magnon, etc.) Niah Cave man	Development of Cave "art"; regional blade tool industries
100,000	Middle Paleolithic (Mousterian, and other traditions)	*Homo sapiens neanderthalensis* and other archaic sapiens groups	Burials with offerings Flake tools predominate in many areas. Probable use of skins in cold regions
300,000	Late Lower Paleolithic; emergence of Levallois technique (prepared cores) Acheulean	"Pre-Neanderthalers": Steinheim, Swanscombe, Rhodesian Saldanha Tautavel? Fontechevade	Highly finished handaxes (in some areas)
500,000	Chellean (or early Acheulean)	*Homo erectus:* Peking	Crude handaxes in some areas, choppers, chopping tools in others
		Vertészöllös, Ternifine, Lantian, Olduvai, Heidelberg, Java (Trinil, Sangiran)	Use of fire
10^6	Late Oldowan		
2×10^6 3×10^6	Earliest Oldowan industries	Various Australo-pithecines (extending back to 5 $\times 10^6$?) *East Rudolf* = KNM-ER 1470 [at 2,900,000 years ago]; *Hadar (Ethiopia)*	Very crude stone and possibly bone, tooth, and horn implements

[a] The approximate dates are based on physical determinations, such as potassium–argon, fission-track, and for the last 50,000 years, carbon 14.

REFERENCES

Aarsleff, H. 1967. *The study of language in England, 1780–1860.* Princeton, New Jersey: Princeton Univ. Press.

Altmann, S. A. 1968. Primates. In T. A. Sebeok (Ed.), *Animal communication: Techniques of study and results of research.* Bloomington: Indiana Univ. Press. Pp. 466–522.

Andrew, R. J. 1963. Evolution of facial expression. *Science, 142,* 1034–1041.

Andrew, R. J. 1972. The information potentially available in mammal displays. In R. A. Hinde (Ed.), *Non-verbal communication.* New York: Cambridge Univ. Press.

Assirelli, O. 1948. La première langue de la humanité. *Scientia, 83,* 95–105.

Atwood, G. 1971. An experimental study of visual imagination and memory. *Cognitive Psychology, 2,* 290–299.

Aubert, Charles. 1901. *L'art mimique.* Paris. [*The Art of Pantomime,* E. Sears, trans., 1927]. London: G. Allen and Unwin.

Augustine. 1952. On Christian doctrine. In *Great books of the Western world.* Vol. 18. Chicago: Encyclopaedia Britannica.

Basso, K., & Anderson, N. 1973. A Western Apache writing system: The symbols of Silas John. *Science, 180,* 1013–1022.

Bateson, G. 1968. Redundancy and coding. In T. A. Sebeok (Ed.), *Animal communication: Techniques of study and results of research.* Bloomington: Indiana Univ. Press. Pp. 614–626.

Bechtel, E. A. 1909. Finger-counting among the Romans in the fourth century. *Classical Philology, 4,* 25–31.

Bellugi, U., & Siple, P. 1971. Remembering with and without words. Current Problems in Psycholinguistics Colloquium, Centre National de Recherche Scientifique, Paris.

Bellugi, U., Siple, P., & Fischer, S. 1973. A comparison of sign language and spoken language. *Cognition,* 173–200.

Bellugi, U., Siple, P., & Klima, E. 1972. The roots of language in the sign talk of the deaf. *Psychology Today, 6* (1), 60–64, 76.

Bender, M. L. 1972. Linguistic indeterminacy, or why you cannot reconstruct "Proto-human." Unpublished manuscript, Dept. of Anthropology, Southern Illinois Univ., Carbondale.

Bernard, H. R. 1971. The influence of language on stone tool making. Paper presented at the Symposium in honor of Charles Friedrich Voegelin, annual meeting, American Anthropological Association, New York.

Bertrand, M. 1971. La communication chez les primates supérieurs de l'Ancien Monde. *Journal de psychologie normale et pathologique,* Année *68,* 3/4, 451–474.

Bidwell, C. 1968. Some typological considerations bearing upon language prehistory. *Linguistics, 44,* 5–10.

Birdsell, J. B. 1968. Some predictions for the Pleistocene based on equilibrium systems among recent hunter–gatherers. In R. B. Lee & I. DeVore (Eds.), *Man the hunter.* Chicago: Aldine. Pp. 229–240.

Bronowski, J. 1967. Human and animal languages. In *To honor Roman Jakobson, Essays on the occasion of his seventieth birthday.* The Hague: Mouton. Pp. 374–394.

Brown, R. 1970. The first sentences of child and chimpanzee. In *Psycholinguistics: Selected Papers.* New York: Free Press. Pp. 208–231.

Brown, R., Black, H., & Horowitz, A. 1955. Phonetic symbolism in natural languages. *Journal of Abnormal and Social Psychology, 50,* 388–393.

Bruner, J. S. 1968. *Processes of cognitive growth: In infancy.* Worcester, Massachusetts: Clark Univ. Press.

Bruner, J. S. 1972. Nature and uses of immaturity. *American Psychologist, 27* (8): 687–708.
Bunak, V. V. 1958. L'origine du langage. In *Colloques Internationaux du Centre National de la Recherche Scientifique, Les processus de l'hominisation*. Paris: Centre National de la Recherche Scientifique.
Chafe, W. L. 1967. Language as symbolization. *Language, 43* (1), 57–91.
Chomsky, N. 1966. *Cartesian linguistics: A chapter in the history of rationalist thought*. New York: Harper.
Cicourel, A. V. 1974. Gestural sign language and the study of non-verbal communication. *Sign Language Studies, 4*, 35–76.
Cicourel, A. V., & Boese, R. J. 1972a. The acquisition of manual sign language and generative semantics. *Semiotica, 5* (3), 225–256.
Clark, J. D. 1970. *The prehistory of Africa*. London: Thames and Hudson.
Clarke, H. 1881. Mr. Wallace and the organs of speech. *Nature, 24* (617), 380–381.
Cobb, S. 1944. *Borderlands of psychiatry*. Cambridge, Massachusetts: Harvard Univ. Press.
Collinder, B. 1965. Remarks on the origin of speech. In J. B. Bessinger, Jr., & R. P. Creed (Eds.), *Franciplegius, medieval and linguistic studies in honor of Francis Peabody Magoun, Jr*. New York: New York Univ. Press.
Condillac, E. B. de. 1971. *An essay on the origin of human knowledge; Being a supplement to Mr. Locke's Essay on the human understanding*. T. Nugent, translator. Gainesville, Florida: Scholars' Facsimiles and Reprints.
Constable, G. 1973. *The Neanderthals*. New York: Time–Life Books.
Count, E. W. 1974. On the phylogenesis of the speech function. *Current Anthropology, 15* (1), 81–88.
Critchley, E. 1967. *Speech origins and development*. Springfield, Illinois: C. C Thomas.
Critchley, M. 1953. *The parietal lobes*. New York: Hafner.
Cushing, F. H. 1892. Manual concepts: A study of the influence of hand usage on culture growth. *American Anthropologist, 5*, 289–317.
Cushman, D. R. 1973. The cue summation theory tested with meaningful verbal information. *Visible Language, 7* (3), 247–260.
D'Agostino, A. 1974. Lateral asymmetry: A key mutation in human evolution. Unpublished manuscript.
D'Aquili, E. 1972. *The biopsychological determinants of culture*. Reading, Massachusetts: Addison-Wesley.
Dart, R. A. 1959. On the evolution of language and articulate speech. *Homo, 10*, 154–165.
Darwin, C. R. 1888. *The descent of man and selection in relation to sex*. (2nd ed.) New York: Appleton.
Darwin, G. H. 1874. Professor Whitney on the origin of language. *The Contemporary Review, 24*, 894–904.
Degérando, Joseph-Marie. 1969. *The observation of savage peoples*. (F. C. T. Moore, Ed. and trans.). Los Angeles: Univ. of California Press.
Diamond, A. S. 1960. *The history and origin of language*. London: Methuen.
Diebold, A. R., Jr. 1968. Anthropological perspectives: Anthropology and the comparative psychology of communicative behavior. In T. A. Sebeok (Ed.), *Animal communication: Techniques of study and results of research*. Bloomington: Indiana Univ. Press. Pp. 525–571.
Dingwall, W. O. 1977. The evolution of human communication systems. In H. Avakian-Whitaker & H. A. Whitaker (Eds.). *Studies in Neurolinguistics*, vol. 4. New York: Academic Press.
Drexel, A. 1951. *Ursprung und Wesen der Sprache*. Zurich: Akademie-Verlag.

Dröscher, V. B. 1971. *Le langage secret des animaux*. Verviers, Bibliothèque Marabout N. 224.

Duncan, S., Jr. 1969. Nonverbal communication. *Psychological Bulletin, 72* (2), 118–137.

Eccles, J. C. 1973. Brain, speech and consciousness. *Naturwissenschaften, 60*, 167–176.

Eickstedt, E. F. von. 1963. *Die Forschung am Menschen*. Stuttgart: F. Enke Verlag.

Eisenberg, J. F. 1973. Mammalian social systems: Are primate social systems unique? In E. Menzel, Jr. (Ed.), *Precultural primate behavior*. Basel: S. Karger.

Eisenson, J. 1972. Language, the chimpanzee and the developing differentiated brain. Unpublished manuscript.

Ekman, P., & Friesen, W. V. 1969. The repertoire of nonverbal behavior: Categories, origins, usage, and coding. *Semiotica, 1* (1), 49–98.

Englefield, R. 1977. Language: its origin and relation to thought. In G. A. Wells & D. R. Oppenheimer (Eds.) London: Elek/Pemberton.

Entwhistle, W. J. 1953. *Aspects of language*. London: Faber and Faber.

Fano, G. 1962. Saggio sulle origini del linguaggio. Con una storia critica delle dottrine glottogoniche. In G. E. Torino (Ed.).

Farb, P. 1974. *Word play: What happens when people talk*. New York: Knopf.

Farrar, F. W. 1873. *Chapters on language*. London: Longmans, Green.

Fillenbaum, S. 1971. Psycholinguistics. *Annual Review of Psychology*, 167–255.

Fischer, J. L., 1974. Comments, Symposium on the origins of language. In Roger Wescott (Ed.), *Language origins*, Silver Spring, Maryland: Linstok Press.

Fiske, J. 1863. The evolution of language. *North American Review, 97*, 411–450.

Fiske, J. 1869. The genesis of language. *North American Review, 109*, 305–367.

Fleischman, M. L. 1968. Vocalizations of chimpanzees. *Primates, 9*, 273–282.

Fleming, J. D. 1974. The state of the apes. *Psychology Today, 7* (8), 31–38, 43–46.

Foster, M. L. 1969. Ten postulates for primordial language construction. Paper presented at the annual meeting, American Anthropological Association, New Orleans.

Foster, M. L. 1970. Explorations in semantic phylogeny. Paper presented at the annual meeting, American Anthropological Association, San Diego.

Foster, M. L. 1971. American Indian and Old World languages: A model for reconstruction. Paper presented at the annual meeting, American Anthropological Association, New York.

Fouts, R. S. 1972. The acquisition and testing of gestural signs in four young chimpanzees. (Pan troglodytes). Annual meeting, Animal Behavior Society, Reno.

Fouts, R. S. 1977 i.p. Capacities for language in great apes. In S. Tax (Ed.), *World Anthropology*. The Hague: Mouton; Chicago: Aldine.

Gajdusek, D. C., & Garruto, R. M. 1973. The focus of hyperendemic goiter, cretinism and associated deaf-mutism in western New Guinea. *Proceedings, IXth International Congress of Anthropological and Ethnological Sciences*, Chicago.

Gallup, G. C., Jr., McClure, M. K., Hill, S. D., & Bundy, R. A. 1971. Capacity for self-recognition in differentially reared chimpanzees. *The Psychological Record, 21*, 69–74.

Gardiner, A. 1957. *Egyptian grammar*. London: Oxford Univ. Press.

Gardner, B. T., & Gardner, R. A. 1971. Two-way communication with an infant chimpanzee. In A. M. Schrier & F. Stollnitz (Eds.), *Behavior of non-human primates: Modern research trends*. New York: Academic Press. Vol. 4, pp. 117–183.

Gardner, H. 1973. The contribution of operativity to naming capacity in aphasic patients. *Neuropsychologia, 11*, 213–220.

Gardner, R. A., & Gardner, B. T. 1969. Teaching sign language to a chimpanzee. *Science, 165*, 664–672.

Garner, R. L. 1900. *Apes and monkeys, their life and language*. Boston: Ginn.

Geschwind, N. 1970. The organization of language and the brain. *Science, 1970*, 940–944.

Goggin, J. E. 1973. An evolutionary analysis and theoretical account of the discontinuous nature of human language. *Journal of Communication, 23*, 169–186.

Goodall, J. van Lawick-. 1968a. A preliminary report on expressive movements and communication in the Gombe Stream chimpanzees. In P. Jay (Ed.), *Primates: Studies in adaptation and variability*. New York: Holt. Pp. 313–374.

Goodall, J. van Lawick-. 1968b. The behaviour of free-living chimpanzees in the Gombe Stream Reserve. *Animal Behaviour Monographs, 1*, 165–311.

Goodall, J. van Lawick-. 1971. *In the shadow of man*. Boston: Houghton-Mifflin.

Goodall, J. van Lawick-. 1973. Cultural elements in a chimpanzee community. Pp. 144–184. In E. W. Menzel, Jr. (Ed.), *Precultural primate behavior*, IVth International Congress of Primatology. Basel: S. Karger.

Greimas, A. J. 1968. Conditions d'une sémiotique du monde naturel. *Langages, 10*, 3–35.

Haldane, J. B. S. 1955. Animal communication and the origin of human language. *Science Progress, 43* (171), 385–401.

Hallowell, A. I. 1963. Factors in behavioral evolution. In S. Koch (Ed.), *Psychology: A study of a science*. New York: McGraw-Hill.

Handel, S., DeSoto, C. B., & London, M. 1968. Reasoning and spatial representation. *Journal of Verbal Learning and Verbal Behavior, 7*, 351–357.

Harnad, S., H. D. Steklis, & J. Lancaster, Eds. 1976. *Origins and evolution of language & speech. Annals of the New York Academy of Sciences*, vol. 280.

Harris, M. 1964. *The nature of cultural things*. New York: Random House.

Hayes, K. J., & Hayes, C. 1951. The intellectual development of a home-raised chimpanzee. *Proceedings of the American Philosophical Society, 95* (2), 105–109.

Healy, A. F. 1973. Can chimpanzees learn a phonemic language? *Journal of Psycholinguistic Research, 2* (2), 167–170.

Hewes, G. W. 1973a. Pongid capacity for language acquisition. In E. W. Menzel, Jr. (Ed.), *Precultural primate behavior*. IVth International Congress of Primatology. Basel: S. Karger.

Hewes, G. W. 1973b. An explicit formulation of the relationship between tool-using, tool-making, and the emergence of language. *Visible Language, 7* (2), 101–127.

Hewes, G. W. 1973c. Primate communication and the gestural origin of language. *Current Anthropology, 14* (1/2), 5–24.

Hewes, G. W. 1977. Language origin theories. In Duane M. Rumbaugh (Ed.), *Language learning by a chimpanzee*. New York: Academic Press.

Hickerson, N. 1973. Wilhelm Wundt's contribution to an evolutionist linguistics. Texas Tech Univ. Duplicated.

Hill, J. H. 1974. On the possibility of continuity theories of language. *Language, 50*, 134–150.

Hill, J. H. 1973a. Discussion: On the possible contribution of ambiguity of expression to the development of proto-linguistic performance, by Charles R. Peters. American Anthropological Association, Symposium on language origins, Annual Meeting, 1972.

Hill, J. H. 1973b. Language acquisition and ancient human population structures. Unpublished manuscript, Wayne State Univ.

Hinde, R. A. (Ed.) 1972. *Non-verbal communication*. New York: Cambridge Univ. Press.

Hockett, C. F. 1960a. The origin of speech. *Scientific American, 203*, 88–96.

Hockett, C. F. 1960b. Logical considerations in the study of animal communication. In W. E. Lanyon & W. N. Tavolga (Eds.), *Animal sounds and communication*. Washington, D.C.: American Institute of Biological Science, Publication No. 7.

Hockett, C. F. 1973. *Man's place in nature*. New York: McGraw-Hill.
Holloway, R. L. 1972. Australopithecine endocasts, brain evolution in the Hominoidea, and a model of Hominid evolution. In R. Tuttle (Ed.), *The functional and evolutionary biology of primates*. Chicago: Aldine–Atherton. Pp. 185–203.
Holloway, R. L. 1973. Early hominid endocasts: Volumes, morphology, and significance for hominid evolution. Paper presented at the IXth International Congress of Anthropological and Ethnological Sciences, Chicago.
Itard, Jean-Marc-Gaspard. 1962. *The wild boy of Aveyron*. (English translation by G. Humphrey & M. Humphrey.) New York: Appleton. [Originally published 1801.]
Jakobson, R. 1964. On visual and auditory signs. *Phonetica, 11*, 216–220.
Jakobson, R. 1965. Quest for the essence of language. *Diogenes, 51*, 2–57.
Jakobson, R. 1970. Linguistics. In *Main trends of research in the social and human sciences*. The Hague: Mouton. Pp. 419–463.
Jastrow, J. 1886. The evolution of language. *Science, 7*, 555–557.
Jauffret, Louis-François. 1909. Introduction aux Mémoires de la Société des Observateurs de l'Homme, 18 messidor, An IX. Aperçu des Travaux qui doivent occuper la Société des Observateurs de l'Homme. Société d'Anthropologie de Paris, Bulletins et Mémoires, Série 5, *10*, 473–487.
Jóhannesson, A. 1944. Gesture origin of Indo-European languages. *Nature, 153*, 171–172.
Jóhannesson, A. 1952. Gestural origin of language. Reykjavik and Oxford: H. F. Leiftur & B. H. Blackwell.
Jousse, M. 1925. Etudes de psychologie linguistique. *Archives de Philosophie 2* (4), 1–241.
Jousse, M. 1936. Le mimisme humain et l'anthropologie du langage. *Revue Anthropologique, 46*, 201–215.
Jousse, M. 1969. *L'Anthropologie du geste*. Paris: Editions Resma.
Kainz, F. 1962. *Psychologie der Sprache*. (3rd ed.) Stuttgart: Ferdinand Enke.
Kainz, F. 1961. *Die "Sprache" der Tiere: Tatsachen, Problemschau, Theorie*. Stuttgart: Ferdinand Enke.
Kakamasu, J. 1968. Urubú sign language. *International Journal of American Linguistics, 34*, 275–281.
Kaplan, E. F. 1968. *Gestural representation of implement usage: An organismic-developmental model*. (Ph.D. dissertation, Clark Univ.) Ann Arbor, Michigan: University Microfilms. No. 68-17, 231.
Kaye, F. B. 1924. Mandeville on the origin of language. *Modern Language Notes, 39*, 136–142.
Kellogg, W. N. 1969. Research on the home-raised chimpanzee. In G. H. Bourne (Ed.), *The chimpanzee: Anatomy, behavior, and diseases of chimpanzees*. Basel: S. Karger.
Kimura, D. 1977. The neural basis of language qua gesture. In H. Avakian-Whitaker & H. A. Whitaker (Eds.). *Studies in Neurolinguistics*, vol. 4. New York: Academic Press.
Kimura, D., & Archibald, Y. 1973. Motor functions of the left hemisphere. London, Ontario, Univ. of Western Ontario, Dept. of Psychology, Research Bulletin No. 266.
Kohts-Ladygina, Nadia. 1935. Ditya shimpanze i ditya cheloveka. Moscow, Museum Darwinianum, *Scientific Memoirs, 31*.
Kortlandt, A. 1965. On the essential morphological basis for human culture. *Current Anthropology, 6* (3), 320–326.
Kortlandt, A. 1967. Handgebrauch bei freilebenden Schimpanzsen. In B. Rensch (Ed.), *Handgebrauch und Verständigung bei Affen und Frühmenschen, im Hinblick auf die menschliche Kulturentwicklung*. Stuttgart: Verlag Hans Huber. Pp. 59–102.
Kortlandt, A. 1973. Comment, on G. W. Hewes, Primate communication and the gestural origin of language. *Current Anthropology, 14*, 14–15.

Krantz, G. S. 1973. Comment, on G. W. Hewes, Primate communication and the gestural origin of language. *Current Anthropology, 14*, 14–15.

Krashen, S. D. 1973. Mental abilities underlying linguistic and non-linguistic functions. *Linguistics, 115*, 39–55.

Kristeva, J. 1968. Le geste, pratique ou communication? *Langages, 10*, 48–64.

Kristeva, J., & Lacoste, M. 1968. Bibliographie [on gesture]. *Langages, 10*, 132–149.

Kuehner, P. 1944. Theories on the origin and formation of language in the eighteenth century in France. Unpublished Ph.D. dissertation, Univ. of Pennsylvania.

Kümmel, P. 1969. *Struktur und Funktion sichtbarer Zeichen*. Quickborn: Verlag Schnelle.

Kuschel, R. 1974. The silent inventor: The creation of a sign language by the only deaf-mute on a Polynesian island. *Sign Language Studies*.

Laguna, G. A. de. 1963. *Speech, its function and development*. Bloomington: Indiana Univ. Press.

La Mettrie, J. O. de. 1960. La Mettrie's "L'Homme machine": A study in the origins of an idea. Critical ed., A. Vartanian (Ed.). Princeton, New Jersey: Princeton Univ. Press.

Lancaster, J. B. 1968. Primate communication systems and the emergence of human language. In P. Jay (Ed.), *Primates: Studies in adaptation and variability*. New York: Holt.

Langer, S. K. 1960. The origins of speech and its communicative function. *The Quarterly Journal of Speech, 46*, 121–134.

Lee, R. B., & DeVore, I. (Eds.). 1968. *Man the hunter*. Chicago: Aldine.

Lenneberg, E. H. 1960. Language, evolution, and purposive behavior. In S. Diamond (Ed.), *Culture in history. Essays in honor of Paul Radin*. New York: Columbia Univ. Press. Pp. 869–893.

Lenneberg, E. H. 1967. *Biological foundations of language*. New York: Wiley.

Lenneberg, E. H. 1971. Of language knowledge, apes, and brains. *Journal of Psycholinguistic Research, 1* (1), 1–29.

Leontiev, A. A. 1970. Social and natural in semiotics. In J. Morton (Ed.), *Biological and social factors in psycholinguistics*. Urbana: Univ. of Illinois Press. Pp. 122–130.

Leroi-Gourhan, A. 1964. *Le geste et la parole. Technique et langage. Sciences d'aujourd'hui*. Paris: Editions Albin Michel.

Leroi-Gourhan, A. 1965. *Le geste et la parole: La mémoire et les rythmes*. Paris: Editions Albin Michel.

Leroi-Gourhan, A. 1967. Les mains de Gargas. Essai pour une étude d'ensemble. *Bulletin de la Société Préhistorique Française, 64*, 107–122.

Leroy, M. 1965. Individualist tendencies in linguistics. *Diogenes, 51*, 168–185.

Lieberman, P. 1972. *The speech of primates*. The Hague: Mouton.

Lieberman, P. 1973. On the evolution of language: A unified view. *Cognition, International Journal of Cognitive Psychology, 2* (1), 59–94.

Lieberman, P. 1975. *On the origins of language: an introduction to the evolution of human speech*. New York: Macmillan.

Lieberman, P., Crelin, E. W., & Klatt, D. H. 1972. Phonetic ability and the related anatomy of the newborn and adult human, Neanderthal Man, and the chimpanzee. *American Anthropologist, 74* (3), 287–307.

Livingstone, F. B. 1969. Genetics, ecology, and the origins of incest and exogamy. *Current Anthropology, 10* (1), 45–61.

Luria, A. R. 1973. Two basic kinds of aphasic disorders. *Linguistics, 115*, 57–66.

MacIver, A. M. 1961. The instrumentality of language. *The Aristotelian Society, 62*, 1–20.

Mallery, G. 1881. Sign language among North American Indians compared with that among other peoples and deaf-mutes. *U.S. Bureau of American Ethnology, Annual Report, 1*, 263–552.

52   Gordon W. Hewes

Marler, P. 1965. Communication in monkeys and apes. In I. DeVore (Ed.), *Primate behavior: Field studies of monkeys and apes*. New York: Holt. Pp. 544–584.

Marshack, A. 1971. Upper Paleolithic notation and symbol. Paper presented at VIII Congrès International des Sciences Préhistoriques et Protohistoriques, Beograd.

Marshack, A. 1972. Cognitive aspects of Upper Paleolithic engraving. *Current Anthropology, 13*, 445–478.

Martí, S. 1971. *Manos simbólicos: Mudrā en Asia y América*. México, D. F.: Litexa, S. A.

Marty, A. 1875. *Über den Ursprung der Sprache*. Würzburg, Germany: A. Stubers Buchhandlung.

Masters, R. D. 1970. Genes, language, and evolution. *Semiotica, 2* (4), 295–320.

May, R. C. 1974. An hypothesis concerning the evolution of human language. Unpublished manuscript.

McBride, G. 1968. On the evolution of language. *Social Science Information, 7* (5), 81–85.

McBride, G. 1973. Comment, on G. W. Hewes, Primate communication and the gestural origin of language. *Current Anthropology, 14*, 15.

Mead, G. H. 1904. The relations of psychology and philology. *Psychological Bulletin, 1* (11), 375–391.

Mead, G. H. 1956. *On social psychology*. Selected Papers. Chicago: Univ. of Chicago Press.

Menzel, E. W., Jr. 1973. Leadership and communication in young chimpanzees. In E. W. Menzel, Jr. (Ed.), *Precultural primate behavior*. IVth International Congress of Primatology. Basel: S. Karger. Pp. 192–225.

Menzel, E. W. 1974. A group of young chimpanzees in a one-acre field. In A. M. Schrier & F. Stollnitz (Eds.), *Behavior of nonhuman primates*, vol. 5. New York: Academic Press.

Morris, C. 1946. *Signs, language and behavior*. New York: Prentice-Hall.

Moser, H. M., O'Neill, J. J., Oyer, H., Abernathy, E., & Showe, B. M., Jr. 1961. Distance and finger-spelling. *Journal of Speech and Hearing Research, 4*, 61–71.

Mounin, G. 1967. Histoire de la linguistique des origines au vingtième siècle. Paris: Presses Universitaires de France.

Munn, N. D. 1973. *Walbiri iconography: Graphic representation and cultural symbolism in a Central Australian society*. Ithaca, New York: Cornell Univ. Press.

Nishida, T. 1970. Social behavior and relationship among wild chimpanzees. *Primates, 11*, 47–87.

Noiré, L. 1917. The origin and philosophy of language. Chicago: Open Court Publishing.

Oakley, K. 1951. A definition of man. *Science News, 20*, 69–81.

Oakley, K. 1953. Origin of language. In S. Tax (Ed.), *An appraisal of Anthropology Today*. Chicago: Univ. of Chicago Press. Pp. 264–267.

Olschewsky, T. M. 1969. Problems in the philosophy of language. New York: Holt, Rinehart and Winston.

Paget, R. A. S. 1944. The origin of language. *Science, 99*, 14–15.

Paget, R. A. S. 1951. The origin of language. *Science News, 20*, 82–94.

Paget, R. A. S. 1963. *Human speech: Some observations, experiments, and conclusions as to the nature, origin, purpose and possible improvement of human speech*. London: Routledge and Kegan Paul.

Palmer, E. H. 1869. Explanation of a difficult passage in Firdausi. *Journal of Philology, 2*, 247–252.

Parker, C. E. 1972. A summary of the superordinate categories of a behavioral taxonomy for primate manipulation. Paper presented at the IVth International Congress of Primatology, Portland.

Pätsch, G. 1955. *Grundfragen der Sprachtheorie*. Halle (Saale): Veb. Max Niemeyer Verlag.

Patterson, F. 1977. Linguistic capabilities of a young lowland gorilla. Paper presented at a

Symposium, "An account of the visual mode: man versus ape." American Association for the Advancement of Science, Annual Meeting, Denver, February 21, 1977.

Paul, H. 1891. *Principles of the history of language*. London: Longmans, Green.

Peters, C. R. 1972. On the possible contribution of ambiguity of expression to the development of proto-linguistic performance. Paper presented at the American Anthropological Association, Symposium on Language Origins.

Peters, R., & Mech, L. D. 1973. Behavioral and intellectual adaptation of selected mammalian predators to the problem of hunting large animals. Paper presented at the IXth International Congress of Anthropological and Ethnological Sciences, Chicago.

Pilbeam, D. 1972. Adaptive response of Hominids to their environment as ascertained by fossil evidence. *Social Biology, 19* (2), 115–127.

Plato. 1921. *Cratylus*. (H. N. Fowler, Ed. and trans.). Loeb Classical Library. Cambridge, Massachusetts: Harvard Univ. Press.

Ploog, D. 1972. Kommunikation in Affengesellschaften und deren Bedeutung für die Verständigungsweisen des Menschen. In H. Gadamer & P. Vogler (Eds.), *Neue Anthropologie, II*. Biologische Anthropologie. Stuttgart: Georg Thieme Verlag.

Poirier, F. E. 1970. The communication matrix of the Nilgiri langur (*Presbytis johnii*) of South India. *Folia Primatologica, 13*, 92–136.

Premack, A. J., & Premack, D. 1972. Teaching language to an ape. *Scientific American, 227*, 92–99.

Premack, D. 1971a. Language in chimpanzees? *Science, 172*, 808–822.

Premack, D. 1971b. On the assessment of language competence in the chimpanzee. In A. M. Schrier and F. Stollnitz (Eds.), *Behavior of non-human primates: Modern research trends*. New York: Academic Press. Vol. 4. Pp. 185–228.

Przyluski, J. 1941. Le langage, la langue et la parole. *Journal de Psychologie Normale et Pathologique, 37*, 29–38.

Rambosson, J. 1880. Origine de la parole et du langage parlé. *Académie des Sciences Morales et Politiques: Revue des travaux et comptes-rendus, 114*, n.s. 14–15 (115), 106–132, 374–400.

Rensch, B. 1967. The evolution of brain achievements. In T. Dobzhansky, M. K. Hecht, & C. Steere (Eds.), *Evolutionary biology*. New York: Appleton. Pp. 26–68.

Rensch, B. 1972. Art, play and related phenomena in apes and monkeys. Paper presented at the IVth International Congress of Primatology, Portland, Oregon.

Renzi, E. de, Pieczuro, A., & Vignolo, L. A. 1968. Ideational apraxia: A quantitative study. *Neuropsychologia, 6*, 41–52.

Révész, G. 1959. *Origine et préhistoire du langage*. Paris: Payot.

Reynolds, P. C. 1968. Evolution of primate vocal–auditory communication systems. *American Anthropologist, 70* (2), 300–308.

Reynolds, P. C. 1970. Social communication in the chimpanzee: A review. In G. H. Bourne (Ed.), *The chimpanzee*. Basel: S. Karger.

Reynolds, P. C. 1972. Play, language and human evolution. Papter presented at the Annual Meeting, American Association for the Advancement of Science, Washington, D.C.

Richardson, L. J. 1916. Digital reckoning among the ancients. *American Mathematical Monthly, 23*, 7–13.

Robinson, B. W. 1967. Vocalization evoked from forebrain in Macaca mulata. *Physiology and Behavior, 2*, 345–354.

Robertson, S. 1958. *The development of modern English* (2nd ed., rev.). Englewood Cliffs, New Jersey: Prentice-Hall.

Romanes, G. J. 1888. *Mental evolution in man: Origin of human faculty*. New York: Appleton.

Rosenkranz, B. 1961. *Der Ursprung der Sprache: ein linguistisch–anthropologischer Versuch*. Heidelberg: Carl Winter, Universitätsverlag.

Rousseau, J. J. 1754. What is the origin of inequality among men, and is it authorized by natural law? Great Books of the Western World, Vol. 38. Chicago: Encyclopedia Britannica.

Rule, C. 1967. A theory of human behavior based on studies of non-human primates. *Perspectives in Biology and Medicine, 10*, 153–176.

Rumbaugh, D. M. 1973. The learning and symbolizing capacities of apes and monkeys. Paper presented at the IXth International Congress of Anthropological and Ethnological Sciences, Chicago.

Rumbaugh, D. M., Ed. 1977. *Language learning by a chimpanzee: the Lana Project*. New York: Academic Press.

Rumbaugh, D. M., & Gill, T. V. 1973. The learning skills of great apes. *Journal of Human Evolution, 2*, 171–179.

Rumbaugh, D. M., Gill, T. V., Brown, J. V., von Glasersfeld, E. C., Warner, H., & Bell, C. 1973. A computer-controlled language training system for investigating the language skills of young apes. *Behavior Research Methods and Instruments, 5* (5), 385–392.

Rumbaugh, D. M., Gill, T. V., & Wright, S. C. 1973. Readiness to attend to visual foreground cues. *Journal of Human Evolution, 2*, 181–188.

Rumbaugh, D. M., Savage-Rumbaugh, S.,and Gill, T. V. 1977. Language skills, cognition, and the chimpanzee. Paper presented at Symposium, "An account of the visual mode: Man versus ape", American Association for the Advancement of Science, Annual Meeting, Denver, February 21, 1977.

Salzinger, K., & Salzinger, S. (Eds.). 1967. *Research in verbal behavior and some neurological implications*. New York: Academic Press.

Sanford, E. M. 1928. De loquela digitorum. *Classical Journal, 23* (8), 588–593.

Sapir, E. 1927. Language as a form of human behavior. *The English Journal, 16*, 421–433.

Sapir, E. 1933. "Language." *Encyclopedia of the Social Sciences, 9*, 155–169.

Sayce, A. H. (1880). *Introduction to the science of language* (4th ed.). London: Kegan Paul.

Schaller, G. B. 1963. *The mountain gorilla. Ecology and behavior*. Chicago: Univ. of Chicago Press.

Schlesinger, I. M. 1970. The grammar of sign language and the problems of language universals. In J. Morton (Ed.), *Biological and social factors in psycholinguistics*. Urbana: Univ. of Illinois Press. Pp. 98–121.

Scott, F. N. 1908. The genesis of speech. Publications of the Modern Language Association, *Proceedings for 1907, 23*, xxvi + liv.

Semënov, S. A. 1959. Znachenie truda dlya razvitiya intellekta v antropogeneze. *Sovetskaya Antropologiya, 2*, 31–49.

Semmes, J. 1968. Hemispheric specialization: A possible clue to mechanism. *Neuropsychologia, 6*, 11–26.

Seton, E. T. 1918. *Sign talk*. Garden City, New York: Doubleday.

Shafton, A. 1976. *Conditions of awareness—subjective factors in the social adaptations of man and other primates*. Portland, Oregon: Riverstone Press.

Sinclair, H. 1970. The transition from sensory motor behavior to symbolic activity. *Interchange, 1* (3), 119–126.

Smith, D. E. 1925. *History of mathematics*. Boston: Ginn.

Solomonson, F. 1922. The genesis of language. *Quarterly Journal of Speech Education, 8*, 372–379.

Sommerfelt, A. 1954. The origin of language. *Journal of World History, 1*, 885–902.

Stam, J. H. 1976. *Inquiries into the origin of language: The fate of a question*. New York: Harper and Row.

Stein, L. 1949. *The infancy of speech and the speech of infancy*. London: Methuen.

Stephenson, G. R. 1973. Testing for group specific communication patterns in Japanese macaques. In E. W. Menzel, Jr. (Ed.), *Precultural primate behavior*. IVth International Congress of Primatology. Basel: S. Karger. Pp. 51–75.

Stephenson, P. H. 1974. On the possible significance of silence for the origin of speech. *Current Anthropology, 15* (3), 324–326.

Stewart, D. 1829. *The works of Dugald Stewart*. Cambridge, England: Hilliard and Brown.

Stokoe, W. C., Jr. 1972a. *Semiotics and human sign language*. The Hague: Mouton.

Stokoe, W. C., Jr. 1972b. Classification and description of sign languages. *Current Trends in Linguistics*, vol. *12*, 345–370. The Hague: Mouton.

Stokoe, W. C., Jr. 1974. Motor signs as the first form of language. In R. W. Wescott, G. W. Hewes, & W. C. Stokoe, Jr. (Eds.), *Language Origins*. Silver Spring, Maryland: Linstok Press.

Stopa, R. 1973a. The origin of language. Accademia Nazionale dei Lincei, 370, Problemi attuali di scienza di cultura, Quaderno No. 182, Atti del Colloquio Internazionale sul Tema, L'origine dell'uomo. Pp. 295–315.

Stopa, R. 1973b. Hominization. *Journal of Human Evolution, 2*, 371–378.

Sturtevant, E. J. 1947. *An introduction to linguistic science*. New Haven, Connecticut: Yale Univ. Press.

Swadesh, M. 1966. Linguistic overview. In J. D. Jennings & E. Norbeck (Eds.), *Prehistoric man in the New World*. Chicago: Univ. of Chicago Press.

Swadesh, M. 1971. *The origin and diversification of language*. J. Sherzer (Ed.). Chicago: Aldine.

Teleki, G. 1973a. The omnivorous chimpanzee. *Scientific American, 228* (1), 32–47.

Teleki, G. 1973b. The predatory behavior of chimpanzees in Eastern Africa. Paper presented at the American Anthropological Association, Annual Meeting, New Orleans.

Thomas, L. 1957. The linguistic theories of N. Ja. Marr. *University of California Publications in Linguistics, 14*, 1–176.

Thorndike, E. L. 1943. *Man and his works*. Cambridge, Massachusetts: Harvard Univ. Press.

Tobias, P. V. 1973. Implications of the new age estimates of the early South American hominids. *Nature, 246*, 79–83.

Trân Dûc Thâo. 1966. Le mouvement de l'indication comme forme originaire de la conscience. *La Pensée, 128*, 3–24.

Trân Dûc Thâo. 1969a. Du geste de l'index à l'image typique. *La Pensée, 147*, 3–46.

Trân Dûc Thâo. 1969b. Du geste de l'index à l'image typique: La naissance du langage. *La Pensée, 148*, 71–111.

Trân Dûc Thâo. 1970. L'alvéole de la dialectique de la connaissance. Introduction à la fonction de la phrase. *La Pensée, 149*, 93–106.

Tsiviane, T. 1970. Contribution à l'étude de certains systèmes sémiotiques simples. In A. J. Greimas (and others), *Sign–language–culture*. The Hague: Mouton. Pp. 390–400.

Tylor, E. B. 1904. *Anthropology: An introduction to the study of man and civilization*. New York: J. A. Hill. [Originally published, 1881.]

Tylor, E. B. 1964. *Researches into the early history of mankind and the development of civilization*. Chicago: Univ. of Chicago Press. [Originally published, 1865.]

Upham, T. C. 1869. *Mental philosophy: Embracing the three departments of the intellect, sensibilities and will*. New York: Harper.

Valade, R. 1866. *De l'origine du langage et de l'influence que les signes naturels ont exercée sur sa formation. Discours prononcé à la distribution solennelle des prix.* Paris: Boucquin.

Vendryès, J. 1925. *Language: A linguistic introduction to history.* New York: Knopf.

Vetter, H. J. 1969. *Language behavior and communication: An introduction.* Itasca, Illinois: Peabody.

Viertel, J. 1966. Concepts of language underlying the 18th century controversy about the origin of language. Georgetown Univ., *Monograph Series on Languages and Linguistics, 19,* 109–132.

Wallace, A. R. 1895. The expressiveness of speech, or, mouth–gesture as a factor in the origin of language. *The Fortnightly Review, 64,* 528–543.

Washburn, S. L. 1973. Comment, on G. W. Hewes, Primate communication and the gestural origin of language. *Current Anthropology, 14,* 18.

Washburn, S. L., & McCown, E. R. 1972. Evolution of human behavior. *Social Biology, 19* (2), 163–170.

Wescott, R. W. 1967. The evolution of language: Re-opening a closed subject. *Studies in Linguistics, 19,* 67–82.

Wescott, R. W., Ed. 1974. *Language origins.* Silver Spring, Maryland: Linstok Press.

West, L., Jr. 1960. *The sign language: An analysis* (Ph. D. dissertation, Univ. of Indiana). Ann Arbor, Michigan: University Microfilms.

Whitney, W. D. 1874. Darwinism and language. *North American Review, 119,* 61–88.

Whitney, W. D. 1885. "Philology." *Encyclopedia Britannica* (9th ed.). Vol. 18, pp. 765–780.

Wieger, L. 1965. *Chinese characters, their origin, etymology, history, classification and signification.* New York: Dover.

Wiener, M., Devoe, S., Rubinow, S, & Geller, J. 1972. Nonverbal behavior and nonverbal communication. *Psychological Review, 79* (3), 185–214.

Willis, G. 1919. *The philosophy of speech.* London: Allen and Unwin.

Wind, J. 1970. *On the phylogeny and ontogeny of the human larynx: A morphological and functional study.* Groningen, The Netherlands: Wolters-Noordhoof.

Wind, J. 1974. Speech emergence during primate evolution. Unpublished manuscript.

Worden, F. G. 1971. Hearing and the neural detection of acoustic patterns. *Behavioral Science, 16,* 20–30.

Wundt, W. 1901. The origin of language. *Wolkerpsychologie, 1* (2), 544–614.

Wundt, W. 1916. *Elements of folk psychology: Outlines of a psychological history of the development of mankind.* New York: Macmillan.

Wundt, W. 1974. *The language of gestures. Approaches to Semiotics, 6.* The Hague: Mouton.

Yakimov, V. P. 1973. Traits of discontinuity in human evolution. Paper presented at the IXth International Congress of Anthropological and Ethnological Sciences, Chicago.

Yerkes, R. M. 1925. *Almost human.* New York, London: Century.

Zhinkin, N. I. 1971. Semiotic aspects of communication in animal and man. *Semiotica, 4* (1), 75–93.

2

The Acquisition of
Bimodal Language [1]

HILDE S. SCHLESINGER

There is a relatively small number of deaf children who occupy a unique place in the research on cognitive and linguistic development. Owing to irreversible nerve damage before language acquisition, they clearly have an inadequate auditory contact with the environment. They do not fully partake of the exciting state of resonance (Lenneberg, 1967) during which the sounds heard by the normally hearing infant acquire peculiar prominence permitting selective attention for meaning. These deaf youngsters, although not totally devoid of sound (as is frequently stated), perceive it in such a diminished or distorted form as to make the linguistic blocks immensely difficult to encode, to process, and therefore to reproduce.

Most youngsters with inadequate auditory contact with the environment are born to hearing parents. They look and sound like normal infants; their defect is invisible; their early vocal behavior is normal. Early diagnosis depends on the severity of the hearing loss, the shape of the hearing loss, the parental perspicacity—which is admiringly high (according to Fellendorf & Harrow, 1970)—and the professional support of the parental suspicions—which is disappointingly low (Meadow, 1968b; Schlesinger & Meadow, 1972). Perspicacity of the parents is more severely stressed with increasing ability of the infant to hear. Some youngsters' hearing loss will not be noticeable until there is nonoccurrence of

[1]This research was supported by grants from the Maternal and Child Health Research Program and the Office of Education, Handicapped Children's Early Education Program.

expected speech, an increasing lack of intelligibility in the speech, or even only an eerie absence of consonants.

The linguistic prognosis of early deafness depends on the onset, the severity, the shape of the loss, and optimal intervention techniques. Educators and other experts have disagreed as to optimal intervention but have, with Pygmalion-like certainty and tenacity, attempted to shape the language more successfully. There is a general but vague acceptance of Hunt's (1961) paradigm that the deaf child should hear and see more. There has been a modicum of agreement as to the theoretical value of early, consistent, and appropriate amplification. Indeed, with modern advances in audiology and hearing aids, the auditory contact with the environment can be increased for most, if not all, deaf children, and they will hear more. Depending on the pattern and severity of the hearing loss, some youngsters will learn to appreciate environmental sounds; some will learn to discriminate between speech and environmental sounds, between female and male voices, between cheerful and angry voices; and some will eventually be able to repeat words—even unfamiliar ones—with good approximation. We are accumulating data that indicate that the optimal implementation of auditory help occurs only too rarely. Incomplete audiological workups couched in nonstandard units and esoteric language often lead to inadequately prescribed hearing aids which are only too frequently in poor repair. Some hearing aids have been so powerful in some frequencies—usually the lower ones—as actually to produce nerve damage leading to additional hearing loss.

The attempts to help the deaf child "see more" are also disputed. There are only a few professionals who feel that lipreading is a sufficient vehicle for language acquisition; most recommend it as a tool for reading an already learned language. Until recently, the attempts to help the child see more through an alternate visual language system have been vigorously opposed.

Even with early diagnosis and early auditory intervention there remain a large number of deaf youngsters who do not acquire even the rudiments of the first stage of language, and even larger numbers who acquire some of the rudiments but not the finer modulations of their native language, spoken English, during their preschool years. School starts early for deaf children, and the elements of spoken language are drilled unceasingly in many classes. Knowledge of the typical "errors" in the language of the adult deaf is widespread. A number of relatively ineffectual techniques have been elaborated to overcome these errors. Unfortunately, the drills are largely unsuccessful. Educational achievement studies continue to indicate that there is a 3- to 4-year language gap; the average deaf person reads at a fifth-grade level or below; only 12% are said to achieve linguistic competence. Only 4% are proficient speech readers or speakers, and there are no studies to indicate any causal relationship to intelligence (Furth, 1966). Thus most deaf children born to hearing parents do not become proficient in the phonology, semantics, or syntax of their "maternal language," spoken English.

Most deaf adults do, however, acquire mastery of language, that "most momentous and at the same time most mysterious product of the human mind [Langer, 1948, p. 94]." It is, however, a language in another modality replacing the auditory–vocal channel by the visual–motoric one. Others before us have demonstrated that American Sign Language (Ameslan), the language used by the large majority of deaf American adults, is a language with its own morphology, semantics, and syntax (Stokoe, Casterline, & Croneberg, 1965). Others have plotted its transformational grammar (McCall, 1965), and some are looking into its early acquisition (Bellugi & Klima, 1972; Klima & Bellugi, 1972). Still others are involved in describing and inventing several sign systems designed to represent or parallel English (Bornstein, 1973).

DESIGN FEATURES IN SPEECH AND SIGN

We have found Hockett's (1960) article helpful in focusing on some inherent differences between aural–vocal and visual–motor languages, especially as they affect the crucial areas of language acquisition and early parent–child communication. Let us start with his 13 design features characterizing human spoken language.

Vocal Auditory Channel, Rapid Fading, Broadcast Transmission and Directional Reception, Interchangeability, and Total Feedback

These first five features all deal with the primacy of the auditory–vocal components for most human languages. In our case, the auditory–vocal channel is replaced or supplemented by the visual–motoric channel. There is less fading quality to visual signals as compared to auditory ones. There is some fading quality since most signs do depend on rapid movements of hands and fingers held in front of the body, especially head and trunk. A very few visual signs can remain indefinitely as if frozen or sculptured. The broadcast transmission and directional reception existing for the auditory–vocal channel are totally absent, and the radiolike reception of spoken language is replaced by a silent television monitor which must be attentively watched.

Interchangeability and total feedback are similarly affected. We have previously stated that most deaf youngsters have some auditory contact with the environment. In proportion to the amount of sound received, we would expect and do find that some of the auditory–vocal aspects of spoken English remain intact for them. Nevertheless, most deaf individuals cannot automatically reproduce through vocalization an utterance whose meaning they can understand. Ruth, for example, at 5 years, 9 months (5:9), finger-spells Y-O-S-E-M-I-T-E but pronounces it "Yosmite," demonstrating that her linguistic utterance is not phonetically interchangeable with that of her maternal input. The visual–motoric aspects of language show only a partial feature of interchangeability in that the hand configuration is clearly interchangeable, but the sign reproduced is inverted 180° from the sign seen. An individual using sign language must reproduce a cross-lateral mirrorlike image of his own input. This complex series of steps may account for the fact that young sign language learners have been noted to invert signs to themselves (Gardner & Gardner, 1973; Schlesinger & Meadow, 1972). The feedback mechanism predominantly absent for the acoustic components of language does appear to exist for the visual–motoric components in terms of kinesthetic proprioceptive feedback systems. We have observed innumerable children and adults who almost imperceptibly move their fingers as they read, think, or otherwise perform cognitive activities. There is also some experimental evidence that hand muscle potentials are present during cerebral activities of deaf individuals (Max, 1935).

The next eight design features all apply, although with some modifications, to any version of American sign language.

Specialization, Semanticity, and Arbitrariness

We share these features with other primates. Specialization refers to the fact that the motoric representation of a sign serves no function except that of a signal. Some mammals make sounds or motions (panting or the cat's back arching) which may have a side effect of transmitting information to others of their species but have a primarily biological function.

The next design feature is that of semanticity, referring to the fact that words or signs have a specific meaning, and label a set of relational principles instead of being labels of specific objects (Lenneberg, 1973, p. 1211). Actually, sign language has some semantic markers which English lacks. For example, state verbs are usually made close to the body. Action verbs are usually signed several inches from the body. Feeling signs usually involve the middle fingers of both hands. Femaleness and maleness in terms of family members are distributed differentially on the face. The next design feature, arbitrariness, needs considerable modification to apply to sign languages. In spoken language, for most words (except for onomatopoeic ones), the ties between the meaningful message elements and their meaning is arbitrary. In sign languages, however, many signs are said to be iconic (pictorial) and to have a history or to have legends. This iconic or ideographic quality of sign language has been used to deny its place in the nation of human languages. However, from a study of sign language acquisition of a deaf youngster, we noted the following:

> Many signs bear no obvious relation to their origin, even for adults; e.g., *America* is represented by both hands with fingers interlaced moving in small circles—allegedly because such a hand construction resembles Lincoln's log house. Certainly, when we study Ann's total sign vocabulary of 117 signs at age 19 months, it is difficult to imagine that even with her intelligence she was able to pursue the etymology of such signs as *milk* (hands as in movement of milking cow), *girl* (thumb stroking cheek as for tying a bonnet string), *water* (with index, middle, and ring fingers stretched out, as for letter W^2 and held to chin), *smart* (index finger to forehead moving upwards and out), or *funny* (index and middle fingers touching tip of nose and moving outward). She might, however, have had enough experience with life to reason out the signs such as *dog* (palm of hand tapping knee), *ice cream* (hand held to mouth with slight licking protrusion of tongue), or *rain* (both hands held above head with fingers moving individually and downwards). Even giving Ann credit for remarkable etymological talent at 18 months, at least half of her sign repertoire can have no ideographic meaning to her at that age [Schlesinger & Meadow, 1972, p. 59].

Discreteness

This next design feature refers to the fact that although human vocal organs can produce a huge variety of sound, only 40 sounds are used for meaningful speech in English, and the differences between them are functionally absolute. For example, the English words "pin" and "bin" are different to the ear only at one point.[3]

The human hand can also produce a large variety of gestures. Birdwhistell (1970) finds it necessary to use 94 symbols and their permutations in

---

[2]Finger-spelled letters refer to the American manual alphabet.

[3]Occasionally special accommodations must be made so that semantically different words are perceived as different words. For example, for some reason the phonological system of the inhabitants of Saxony differs radically from that of other speakers of German. They do not phonologically differentiate between /b/ and /p/, /d/ and /t/, and other consonant systems. (They clarify their understanding by referring to soft and hard consonant systems even to each other.) The noun "Peter" can otherwise not be differentiated from the word "Baeder" (meaning baths).

order to describe his system of nonverbal communication. Stokoe *et al.*
(1965) decrease the number of symbols necessary for writing the American Sign Language to 55. Very discrete changes in hand position, movement, and placement in relationship to the body can vary the meaning
markedly. For example, "vote" and "tea," semantically very different
words, are represented by both hands in which index finger and thumb
touch, whereas the other three fingers are spread out. The sign *vote* is
made by just barely entering the hollow circle of the thumb and index of
the left hand, while *tea* is made by a slight circular movement in the same
space. The T hand, made by the thumb in the enclosed fist between index
and middle finger, palm outward, refers to *toilet* when the hand is slightly
shaking. It refers to *Tuesday* when the hand is slightly circling.

Displacement

This is said to characterize man (and Washoe, the sign learning chimpanzee) uniquely—for the ability to talk about things that are remote in
time or space or both. It provides freedom from immediacy. In this
regard, we noted (Schlesinger, 1972) that freedom from immediacy is not
usually available to most deaf youngsters. When we compared 20 hearing
children with 40 deaf children during a 7-minute segment of mother–child
interaction, we noted that 95% of the deaf children and their parents
limited communication to topics with a visual reference point: Both of the
exceptions had a high level of communicative competence, one because
of a greater use of residual hearing and the other because of early bimodal
linguistic input. On the other hand, 45% of the hearing group made at least
a passing comment concerned with nonvisual reference, while 15% of this
group had prolonged conversations on some topic without visual reference.

Productivity

This is the capacity to say (sign) things that have never been heard (or
seen) before and to be understood by other speakers or signers of that
language.

We shall now introduce some of our linguistic youngsters who will be
described at greater length later in the chapter. Ruth, at 2 years, 10
months (2:10), signs and states, *"I want some cookies and juice and
please."* She appears to be productively and creatively using a soft
imperative but in a form rarely, if ever, heard before. Elsbeth, at age 3:9,
fearful of an examination, reassures herself by asking in signs, *It au-
diologist? No doctor, no medicine, no shot, yes?* Elsbeth has the most

profound hearing loss of all of our linguistic youngsters. As auditory contact in the speech range has not yet been established, her speech acquisition is more delayed, and her vocalizations during her signing are mostly unintelligible. Nevertheless, she was surely understood by signers, although speakers may have seen only a fearful youngster.

Duality of Patterning

Hockett (1960) refers to the fact that "tack," "cat," and "act" are totally distinct in meaning but are composed of just three basic, meaningless sounds in different permutations. Again, identical hand configurations (Dez) moved differently (Sig) or held in a different position (Tab) can dramatically change the meaning of a sign. Clawlike index and middle finger, for example, moving from elbow toward wrist mean *steal*; the same configuration held at the eyes means *blind*.

Traditional Transmission—Linguistic Socialization and Sign Language Acquisition

This last design feature needs a subtitle because of its most crucial differences as compared to the transmission of all vocal languages. Traditional transmission refers to the detailed conventions of language by learning and teaching, in contradistinction or in supplementation to the postulated biological foundations. We alluded earlier to the fact that most deaf children do not appear to learn their maternal language successfully, nor do most learn Ameslan early. Only a very small percentage of deaf children acquire language through traditional transmission. These are the deaf children of deaf parents, who will be referred to in greater detail later.

Most deaf adults can be said to be to some extent bilingual, bimodal, and diglossic, and to share some of the advantages and disadvantages of these states. Bilingualism usually refers to the coexistence of two languages which differ radically in most linguistic features with only minimal sharing of vocabulary items (the Alpenstock, le stress, der Hamburger), minimal resemblances in some aspects of grammar, and varying degrees of phonological similarities. Ferguson (1959) forged a new term— Diglossia—to refer to two or more varieties of the same language used by the same speaker under different conditions. Stokoe (1969–1970) expanded the concept of Diglossia to explain some of the vagaries of sign language acquisition and use. Diglossic utterances apparently share more vocabulary items, more grammatical constructions, and even more phonology than do bilingual utterances, and yet they differ. Unfortunately, neither term is sufficient to adequately describe language as used by the deaf community since both terms include the root "tongue" and thus primarily refer to spoken languages. "Bimodalism" may contribute to resolving this vexing problem. This term occurred to the author fortuitously when perusing one of Drs. Klima and Bellugi's (1972) papers and coming upon the term language in another modality. This other modality refers to uttering language in a codified system of signs with the hands, rather than a codified system of sounds through the voice.

The encompassing term "sign language" can refer to English gestemically (gesturally) uttered and understood instead of phonemically (Stokoe, 1970), or it can refer to American Sign Language also gestemically uttered and understood but with less sharing of vocabulary and grammar. The differences inherent in the bilingual, diglossic, and bimodal features of language as used by the deaf individual are illustrated in Table 2.1.

The table may be of potential linguistic importance, but it seems to the author to be most relevant to psycholinguistics. All the terms used share the ubiquitous ethnocentric bias "thou who makes utterances different from mine makes inferior utterances." Bilingualism is a well-known word used with pleasure by some and with disdain by others. Languages are not protected from the human propensity to attach value labels to all observable differences, be they chronological, sexual, religious, tribal, or linguistic. Most bilinguals in America have been exposed to some prejudice and attempts at suppression, at least from World War I until very recently (John & Horner, 1971). There appears, however, to be increasing evidence that there might be distinct cognitive advantages to bilingualism (Lambert & Peal, 1962), but that the native colloquial language must be genuinely respected in order to facilitate the learning of any other form or system (Bernstein, 1961, 1970; Diebold, 1965, 1966; John & Horner, 1971), and that the bilingual child can easily switch codes depending upon the abilities and desires of his or her communicators (Brown, 1973; Schlesinger & Meadow, 1972; Stokoe, personal communication, 1973).

The ethnocentric fate of Diglossia and bimodalism is similar to that of bilingualism. One of the varieties of Diglossia has always been more prestigious than the other without sufficient attention paid to the usefulness of knowing more than one way of "glossing" about the world. Bimodalism points out the ethnocentric bias even more forcefully: "To utter with the hands" has been unacceptable in Anglo-Saxon countries whether the gestures were ethnic or linguistic as in sign language. But cognitive and psychological advantages have been described for the deaf child who can utter with his hands early (Schlesinger & Meadow, 1972, and others later in the chapter). It is to be hoped that more intensive

TABLE 2.1

Billingualism and Bimodalism in Deaf Individuals with Categories Borrowed from Diglossia

Features	Bilingual (or diglossic) Bimodal		Monolingual Bimodal
Nomenclature	American Sign Language	Visual English	Spoken English
Prestige	L-low even by many deaf people	H-high by most deaf and hearing individuals	H+-held in even higher regard except for few exceptions
Acquisition	By immersion without explicit discussions	Formal, prescriptive with rules and norms to be imitated	Laboriously and frequently unsuccessfully
At homeness	Up	Down	Further down
Place of usage	Home, family "insiders"	School, employment "outsiders"	"The hearing world"
Stability	Needs further study	Parallel to changes in spoken English	
Linguistic modulations indicated by	Location in space of signer or sign Other modulations still under study	As in English but gestemically	Inflectional systems, articles prepositions, copulas, etc.
Vocabulary item	Generally shared	Shared but higher number of lexical items from English	
Transfer vocabulary	Borrows from H	Excludes L	
Gestemic system	More flowing	More "refined" More precise[a]	

[a] An even more precise rendition of English is possible when each word is finger-spelled into the air. This system is used only as an educational technique and is rarely seen as an adult system of interpersonal communication, although finger spelling supplements signing in most sign systems.

studies of sign language can diminish the human propensity to judge and will contribute to a broader acceptance of all human differences.

NONTRADITIONAL LANGUAGE ACQUISITION

How do deaf individuals acquire the bilingual, bimodal features which characterize them? Only a very small percentage learn either language or modality through traditional transmission. We have discussed previously the fragmented, incomplete acquisition of spoken English for a large variety of deaf children. Most deaf adults have acquired sign language surreptitiously from peers rather than adults, sometimes early in adolescence. (We have not encountered a deaf child over the age of 11 who has not indicated some rudimentary acquaintance of sign language.) The language was, however, known to be taboo to most children. Most parents had been strongly prejudiced against it. The youngsters who had labored long and unsuccessfully to learn spoken language came upon sign language in a variety of ways with a variety of reactions. Unfortunately, no scientific study exists about language acquisition at this age level, but anecdotal reports and case histories reveal that some of the youngsters are able to acquire sign language with a maximum of speed and a minimum of trauma, while others learn it slowly or not at all.

TRADITIONAL TRANSMISSION—DEAF CHILDREN OF DEAF PARENTS

There is a small number of deaf youngsters who do grow up with relatively traditional transmission of maternal language. Ten percent of deaf children have deaf parents, of whom a large proportion use sign language early in their childrearing.

In our generally psychiatrically–behaviorally oriented work with deaf children and adults, we noted, as other investigators had noted before us, that deaf children of deaf parents do better both academically and psychologically as compared with deaf children of hearing parents (Brill, 1960, 1969; Meadow, 1968a, 1969; Quigley & Frisina, 1961; Vernon & Kohl, 1970). One of the reasons has been postulated to be a greater acceptance of deafness, a greater and more realistic expectation of a deaf individual, and a consequently greater acceptance of the child as he or she is. The other main reason has been postulated to be the early use of sign language between parent and child. This second reason is the focus of the present chapter and is an attempt to describe more microscopically the linguistic events between mother and child which appear to lead to greater meaning and enjoyment. It may be that deaf parents have a partial way to govern the encounters their children have with their environments, to foster both an optimal rate of rapid intellectual development and a satisfying life (Hunt, 1961, p. 363).

Our initial interest in the communication patterns of deaf youngsters and their parents was primarily psychiatric in focus. Having noted repeatedly that "normal" youngsters in our longitudinal study (Schlesinger & Meadow, 1972) and our young psychiatric patients and their parents were beset with linguistic retardation and "disturbed communication," we were curious to see if early, reciprocal, meaningful, and joyful communication between parents and their deaf youngsters could alleviate linguistic retardation and provide more access to successful communication in terms of feedback, appropriacy, efficiency, and flexibility (Ruesch, 1957). Having noted that deaf children of deaf parents do approximate successful communication more frequently, we wanted to know if a new pioneer group of hearing parents and their deaf youngsters could give us further clues as to early linguistic events and their influence on cognitive, affective, and linguistic development.

CONNIE'S CHILDREN

"I Think I Have to Dance with Connie"[4]

Our pioneer lingustic parents are dissimilar in many ways: They are deaf, they are hearing; they are highly educated, they have limited education; they live in bustling cities, on army posts, on isolated ranches. They are similar in many ways: They are all young, intelligent, and appear to be more able than many parents to place deafness in a realistic perspective, not needing the rose-colored glasses of denial, or the dark-colored glasses of despair. They were all vitally interested in the traditional transmission of their culture to their children.

Transmission of culture invariably entails transmission of language. Since most of our parents are hearing, the vehicle of expressing the maternal language is spoken English. However, they were all willing to

[4]The speaker is Ruth (4:4). Most groups of children studied for their language acquisition have been identified by the city of their respective studies. Our children live in many cities, but many of them have had some contact with Connie Yannacone, one of the pioneer teachers of bimodal or "total communication." Her skill and sensitivity have contributed greatly to the ability of parents and children to use bimodal language competently and joyfully.

learn a new language modality in order to enhance the development of their children. We had postulated from the inception of our studies that bimodal input would favor accelerated language acquisition and the production of speech. Early in our work we had provided an operational definition of optimal bimodal input which stated that "Sign language is generally considered to be helpful in the development of deaf children when it is used with positive affect, without conflict, is accompanied by speech and auditory training, and is used early before a feeling of communicative impotence occurs between parent and child."

The Process of Learning Bimodal Language

As we shall see more fully later, perceptual salience plays a role in the acquisition of formal linguistic markers. In terms of the more or less bimodal language acquisition of our deaf infants, we must consider both the auditory and visual perceptual systems. The input language must be accessible to the infant perceptually, environmentally, and psychologically, and for a sufficiently long time to become encoded. The encoded symbols must be reproducible by the infant. There must be some feedback mechanism, and the expressive language of the infant must be met with some minimal acceptance. However, for these deaf infants both the visual and auditory systems have marked interference on either the perceptual, environmental, or psychological levels (see Table 2.2).

In order to optimize language acquisition, we attempted to influence perceptual, environmental, and psychological factors so as to increase the accessibility of the auditory and visual linguistic building blocks.

Acoustically, we tried to implement the optimal version of modern auditory techniques. Visually, we attempted to provide the parents with a system of communication which they could use comfortably and competently. This was not easily done; the parents had to choose among innumerable proponents of innumerable sign language systems. Was it to be Ameslan or one of the new sign systems? Most of the parents elected to use one of the newer versions of sign language, one more closely resembling English in terms of word order, prefixes, suffixes, tenses, etc. Their choice appears to have been influenced by the following: a strong desire for English language and speech acquisition (more easily accomplished by simultaneous bimodal input), a greater ease in their own acquisition of a new modality of English rather than a sign language with its own syntax, and a paucity of child-oriented signs in Ameslan. All the parents have, however, expressed an acceptance of Ameslan, and most expect their children to learn it from their peers and deaf adults.

Subsequent to their decision to use sign language, and to use a particu-

TABLE 2.2
Effect of Deafness on the Accessibility and Reproduction of Bimodal Language (with the Processing Mechanism Intact)

Accessibility	Reproduction
(Input)	(Output)
Accessibility of *acoustic* signals	*Decreased by lack of auditory feedback*
Decreased by severity of loss	
shape of loss	*Decreased* by felt prejudice against deaf speech
early onset of loss	
Increased by optimal auditory intervention	*Decreased* because of low communicative value to child
hearing aids	
auditory training	
Accessibility of *visual* signals–signs	
Decreased by taboo mechanisms	
Increased by maternal acceptance	*Increased* by kinesthetic proprioceptive feedback system
competence	
frequency of use	

Note: We postulated early in our work that increasing the accessibility of both auditory and visual symbols would increase the reproduction of both speech and sign language.

lar variety of it, the parents were further burdened by the fact that the new signs created by different groups varied from teacher to teacher and from time to time. The children were not similarly distressed; they quite easily incorporated the changes and occasionally used two different signs in the same sentence. The parental choice to use sign language created further problems. Some schools frowned on the choice and precipitated the parents into a conflict. The linguistic superiority of the youngsters who started bimodal language early brought on yet another crisis because no adequate school placement could be found. When feasible, we worked with the teachers to diminish the conflict or help change the curriculum.

We postulated that youngsters with varying degrees of hearing loss, but with the optimal linguistic input described above, would be able to narrow the ubiquitous linguistic chasm and learn to assert, deny, request, order, and so forth, in the same sequence and at almost the same rate as any children learning any language. We further postulated that the youngsters could learn language with a high level of complexity and could do so joyfully and confidently.

We proceeded to observe a series of youngsters via monthly videotape sessions in a number of natural settings: home, school, zoo, market. We recorded the visual and the auditory components—the modalities—of the language systems used by the children and parents (see Table 2.3).

We are now pleasantly submerged in reams of videotape, replete with sound and sign. The sounds range from vague approximations of English, to intelligibly pronounced English words, to strings of words in sentences. The signs vary from random motions in space, to approximations of adult signs, to adult signs, and to strings of signs. The motoric expression of language has generally undergone more analysis than the phonetic–vocal mode.

Our bimodal transcripts will be coded as follows:

word	=	sign alone
"word"	=	spoken word alone
"word"	=	sign and spoken word produced simultaneously
". . ."		will be used when meaningful elements are clear enough to be recognized after several trials.
A–B–C	=	finger spelling

The First Signs—Ann, Otto, Elsbeth, and Ruth

We met two infants with deaf parents using sign language. We met them before the infants reproduced meaningful signs and long before they reproduced them in strings of meaningful utterances. Their early receptive understanding remains unknown to us, but productively they seemed to us to use their hands as if they were signing more frequently and discretely than other infants. We knew these children, however, when the motoric expression of a meaningful sign was mature enough to be understood by the mother (and research assistants).

Ann, the deaf infant of deaf parents, often saw the sign *pretty* as used by her mother (an open hand palm inwards sweeping gracefully in a circle over the face). At 12 months, Ann reproduced the sign to the great delight of the mother who reproduced it on Ann's face and said *"pretty."* We described the acquisition of Ann's one sign utterances more fully in *Sound and Sign: Childhood Deafness and Mental Health* (Schlesinger & Meadow, 1972).

We also observed Otto, the 10-month-old hearing infant of deaf parents, during one of his first productions of the sign *milk*. The mother was patiently standing in front of Otto's high chair repeating the sign for *milk* (right hand closing and opening rapidly as in the milking motion), while holding a full baby bottle in her left hand. Otto signed *milk* only upon

TABLE 2.3

Recorded Language Samples and Modalities

	Age visual–motoric language initiated	Observation period	Hours of observation	Parental input	
Otto	Birth[a]	4 mos.–2:1	9½	Ameslan	monolingual, monomodal[b]
Ann	Birth[a]	8 mos.–2:10	12	Ameslan English	bilingual; bimodal
Elsbeth	20 mos.	1:10–3:10	11	Bimodal English	
Carlos	Birth[a]	1:10–3	6½	Ameslan English	bilingual; bimodal
Sergei	2:6	2:5–4:5	7	Bimodal English	
Ruth	17 mos.	2:10–6:3	37	Bimodal English	
Marie	3:1	3:4–5:10	12	Ameslan English	bilingual; bimodal
Karen	17 mos.[a]	3:4–6:7	6¼	Bimodal English	
Josette	2:9	4:3–6:4	17	Bimodal English	
Jessica	20 mos.	1:8–3:3	4½	Bimodal English	
Roberto	13 mos.	1:7–2:3	3½	Bimodal English	

[a] Deaf parents.
[b] Hearing child with bimodal English input during infancy through educational intervention.

having the cherished substance available to him when the bottle was relinquished by his mother and placed in his mouth. The author wonders whether Otto, in his receptive language stage which preceded this expression, reacted physiologically by sucking movements or salivation to the sign *milk,* not accompanied by milk.

Elsbeth, the deaf child of hearing parents, started sign language at 19 months. Three months later, she spontaneously used a repertory of 53 signs. At 26 months, we observed her leafing through a book labeling pictures with signs. *Carrot* eluded her, and with a partial semantic understanding—"something to eat"—she labeled it *apple.* She was able to reproduce the new sign correctly immediately upon watching her mother's modeling. All of the youngsters observed in their early sign language acquisition used baby versions of signs (see Schlesinger & Meadow, 1972, p. 65).

When we met the youngsters at a later date, they did indeed combine two or more signs. The number of word–morpheme or sign–morpheme averaged over 100 consecutive utterances has been called mean length of utterance or MLU.

Ruth: Started sign language at 17 months

MLU	Chronological age
1.4	34 months
1.45	36 months
1.5	37 months
2.7	44 months
3.0	48 months
4.68	52 months

When Ruth's MLU is plotted against her chronological age, the resulting slope looks very much like those of the famous Adam and Sarah. Eve's slope, however, is more rapidly ascending (Brown, 1973).

These early signs were combined meaningfully to express certain semantic notions. Semantic notions depend on cognitive development, but cognitive development and linguistic development do not run off in unison. The child must find linguistic means to express his intentions. Slobin (1973) notes that "the rate and order of development of the semantic notions expressed by language are fairly constant across languages, regardless of the formal means of expression employed [p. 183]." The formal means of any language, however, can be easily accessible as, for example, the Hungarian locative, or quite inaccessible as, for example, the Finnish yes–no questions, or the Arabic noun plurals. These last two inaccessible linguistic markers are apparently so difficult that young Finnish children simply do not ask yes–no questions, and Arabic youngsters up to 15 do not use noun plurals. What makes a given linguistic means of expression more or less accessible to the child? It probably varies from language to language as determined by the psycholinguistic complexity of the formal means used by any language to express the semantic intention under consideration (Slobin, 1973). Slobin has also charmingly organized his framework of linguistic universals in terms of self-instructing mottoes, in which the child gives himself advice to bear upon the task of organizing and storing language. We shall attempt to use and follow his framework by utilizing examples of utterances analyzed from the output of our youngsters, and to emphasize crucial similarities and differences to spoken languages.

Word–Sign Order—Otto, Ann, and Josette

Slobin's operating word order principle (1973, p. 197) reads, "Pay attention to the order of words and morphemes." We would like to add: And render unto each sender the word order which you receive from him.

How well do our youngsters follow that basic instruction? There is one major difference observable in the modality of sign representation. Although two spoken words cannot be said at the same time, two signs can be produced at the same time with both left and right hand busy at expression. This has been noted in terms of pointing (Hoffmeister & Moores, 1973), in terms of ostensive or demonstrative utterances, and has been observed in our youngsters.

Jessica, at 2:6, while wanting something of both her parents, signed *father* and *mother* simultaneously. Roberto, at 20 months, signed *candy* and *donkey* simultaneously. Janet at 15 months singned *more* with one hand and *blocks* with the other with both hands touching in the midline.

However, these examples remain rare, and most youngsters follow word order. Ruth, whose input was monolingual but bimodal, clearly indicated that she followed the instruction to the letter. Her earliest sign–spoken utterances (which occurred between 2:10 and 3:1) can be analyzed in any of the schemata described by linguists. We have chosen I. M. Schlesinger's (1971) schema for position rules in two-word utterances.

Schlesinger (1971) proposes a performance model consisting of I-markers representing universal semantic relations and realization rules which are language specific. He then converts these I-markers into utterances. If a semantic notion contains agent and action, the linguistic positional rule results in **agent + action.**

Examples: *"girl wait"*

"J-S (Josette) *cry"*

"J-S wait"

"kitty-cat running"

The semantic notion of action and direct object has a positional rule of **action + direct object**

"help you"

"get Indian book"

The semantic notion of agent and direct object has the positional rule of action + direct object. We have no two-sign utterances, but at 2:11, we have:

agent + action + direct object

"I want some paper."

"I want some cookies and juice and please."

When one word of the utterance modifies the other, the modifier precedes. This positional rule of child language creates the following structure:

modifier + head

"old man"

"Smith mommy"

"little juice"

"yellow airplane

"yellow window"

"swimming girl"

"bad wolf"

Ruth has three examples in which the modifier follows the noun, but it is postulated that these examples represent condensed adult sentences:

"pear better"

"Michele sick"

"watch dirty"

All of these utterances could contain the copula "is" and be perfectly adult sentences.

Unlike the relations discussed above, negation does not hold between two elements but "operates on one element." The position rule specifies the order:

negation + X

"Don't move" (don't is one
morpheme in sign language)

The word indicating to whom something is given, thrown, said, etc., is the dative. The position rule is:

X + dative

"Show me"

"Show you"

"Give me"

Ostensive sentences are used for utterances used to identify names, objects, etc. They usually include "here," "there," "see" as introducers:

introducer + X

"Here home"

The word indicating where something is located or where the action takes place is usually placed in the second position. The rule produces:

X + locative

"I tree"

"Come camera"

"Come here"

"Bye bye store" (going store)

Stokoe has kindly given us permission to quote from an unpublished paper (personal communication, 1973) that describes the language of a charming youngster, 3:1, whose input was both bilingual and bimodal. It would appear that the father usually communicated to her in Ameslan, whereas the mother's imput was signed English. The youngster promptly paid attention to word order in both languages and rewarded each parent accordingly:

To father:	To mother:
doll pretty	*pretty pink doll*
motel sleep	*sleep motel*
write me	*I want to write,* etc.

The word order for youngsters exposed to Ameslan is an interesting question. Fant (1974) postulates that three-sign utterances in Ameslan do not have a fixed order. Stokoe (1969–70) indicates that as recently as 1955 noun + modifier was "correct" word order in Ameslan and chuckles at the similarity to French. He also notes that youngsters raised in Ameslan quickly dispelled this notion of correctness.[5]

We furthermore have two examples of youngsters whose input was bilingual and bimodal but with one language considerably less rich in input. The author is not labeling any languages rich versus not rich, but only stating that any language can be used richly or poorly in the child's environment.

[5]The author, who is a Francophile, has always enjoyed the French flair that she encountered in both the deaf subculture and the American Sign Language.

Thus we have Krista, the hearing daughter of a hearing mother and a deaf father with excellent bimodal facility. Both parents spoke to the girl richly and her output at 19 months included:

"Hello sun jabber out please" ("jabber out" probably meaning "come out").

Her signing input was almost holophrastic on the parents' part, and was also returned in single holophrastic signs.

OTTO

We also find Otto, a hearing child exposed to Ameslan from his parents and to spoken English from nursery school peers and teachers. The maternal input as observed is usually limited to one- or two-sign utterances, although the mother has been observed to communicate much more complexly to deaf adults. Otto signs with an upper bound of two.

At 2:4, Otto indicates to:

Mother:	Hearing people:
want candy	"I want to get up there"
sit	"Otto sit down?"

Otto typifies a felicitous outcome of a potential tragedy. At first he was believed to be deaf. It took the presence of a sensitive teacher to reverse that diagnosis. The medical experts, unacquainted with deafness at first, thought to remove Otto from his parents in order to give him a "normal" environment. Fortunately, that possibility was squelched rapidly. However, the hearing experts continued to feel that Otto needed more contact with human speech, and the deaf mother was generally in agreement with this solution. She had learned, as we have, that hearing infants of deaf parents can indeed have some speech difficulties in their early years, and she did not wish that fate for Otto. So an alliance was formed between two devoted women interested in fostering Otto's well-being—his mother and his teacher.

The teacher communicates with the mother in sign language. She sensitively describes her successful resolution of the potential pitfalls of the varied sign languages now in existence:

There is a difference between Mother and myself. Mother is Ameslan and I am SEE or whatever I've picked up, wherever I've picked it up. Some of my signs come from the parents, others from a different state, so some signs are different, and we have reached the agreement that her sign is the right sign for Otto. . . . She and her husband and two daughters are in an established language with which they're comfortable. . . . Therefore, the language they use is the language that's right for Otto. And she corrects me if I use an inappropriate sign for her house. . . . In other words, there is a sign for truck, but she has no sign for truck; therefore, it's right for her to fingerspell truck and tell Otto, "No, they aren't all cars. Some of them are trucks." [The teacher spells out T-R-U-C-K imitating the mother.] "Some of them are buses." [The teacher again imitates the mother, B-U-S-E-S, then again, V-A-N-S, and so on.]

We noted earlier that Otto uses more complex sentence structure in his spoken English than in his sign language output. However, the actual number of lexical items in his sign language vocabulary may well be larger than that in his spoken vocabulary. This is why the teacher felt "that Otto needed some English meals so that his lexical items for spoken food would increase."

One more anecdote of interest. We mentioned earlier that first sign utterance precedes the first spoken utterance in all children exposed to sign language, be they hearing or deaf (Schlesinger & Meadow, 1972). It may well be that the motoric expression of new lexical items is easier initially than the vocal reproduction. This is corroborated by the following:

Otto was playing with an electric toy that would not function. He discovered by palpation that it contained batteries and pointed to them. The following dialogue occurred:

Teacher: *"give me the"* $\Big\langle$ B-A-T-T-E-R-I-E-S
"batteries"

The simultaneous finger spelling and saying of "batteries" occurred three more times, whereupon Otto found another toy which needed batteries and came to the teacher and said:

Otto: *"give me the"* B-A-T

with no attempt to vocalize any portion of the word.

ANN

Unfortunately, we do not have ongoing observational data on youngsters who are exposed to rich, ongoing communication with Ameslan (such as Stokoe's youngster had been). Karen, first analyzed in *Sound and Sign: Childhood Deafness and Mental Health* (Schlesinger & Meadow, 1972), was primarily exposed to visual English. Ann, also described in *Sound and Sign*, might have been such a youngster had she not moved away at an early age, however, her first sign uttterances at 17 months indicate that there may have been a beginning of Ameslan syntax. Her action + object order was as in English:

eat cracker

However, her modifier + noun:

dirty dog

interchanged with noun + modifier:

girl funny

She was also found to sign:

good finish

which is an Ameslan way of indicating the semantic opposite of "now." Several similar versions are found in Stokoe's mimeographed paper.

JOSETTE

Josette developed quick facility with determiner + noun categories, as can be seen in the following:

"White shirt. Where, where is my white shirt?"

"Get in orange car."

"No, the yellow horse is eat brown hay."

"The man is under the brown car. The man is under her car. Daddy is pull in the white car."

"M-C (Michelle) had a new rocking horse like my horse."

"Michelle has a white horse."

"Me have a beautiful rocking short horse like J-E-R-Y's horse. Right? yes."

"And last night me ride the orange horse outside there."

She also invested *"fireplace wall shelf"* for mantelpiece. It can be seen there is no doubt in her mind that determiners precede nouns in a specific order. There are two interesting examples where she is experiencing marked difficulties. Having learned that determiners precede nouns, what does one do when the proper noun is Black? Josette's first attempt:

"I went to Dr. Far and black and black Dr. black."

Mother:	*"You get mixed up. Only Dr. Far first."*
Josette:	*"F-A-R is name. Were fix my ear. And me went to in other her doctor. Right? Yes."*

Connie's question: *"You went to a black doctor?"*

(Mother explains: *"Dr. Black is the doctor."*)

Josette's attempt: *"Dr. Black is name. Is the doctor black is friend the F-A-R."*

The next example occurs in the same linguistic sample when Josette was 4:8. Connie and Josette are looking at the book "Little Red Riding Hood" in sign language. Josette is answering a series of complicated questions and finally develops a struggle over the word order of Little Red Riding Hood. For example:

Josette: *"Mother. Riding. Little Riding Hood told the wolf. What you had. What you had big eye."*

Some intervening discussion.

"The wolf will eat the ride hood. The wolf will go to catch the ride. Little ride hood."

Further intervening short versions of "adult" "Little Red Riding Hood," but Josette again:

"Wolf will go T-O-Y. The ride. Little ride hood."

Numerous utterances later, and a triumphant but still confused version occurs:

"Little and ride red. Little ride. Red. Ride hood is. And woman is grandmother. Were go to eat her breakfast."

The Ends of Words–Signs

One of Slobin's (1973) important and richly documented operating principles is: "Pay attention to the ends of words." There is evidence from studies in acoustic phonetics (e.g., final syllable lengthening) that gives additional support for the argument that word endings attract the child's attention (1973, p. 189). Evidence from studies of cross-cultural acquisition of spoken languages indicates that the child learns to express his or her semantic intentions more quickly in inflectional systems which follow rather than precede the content words. Bulgarian articles are suffixes and appear early. German and English articles precede nouns and appear relatively late. Hungarian locatives which are expressed inflectionally are in advance of Serbo-Croatian prepositional locatives in a bilingual child. The example from English which best corroborates the above principle occurs in the acquisition of the English present progressive, which, in its earliest forms, is represented by the child by the verbal inflection "ing" in the absence of a preverbal auxiliary.

We have some tentative data which appear to indicate that this universal principle may be directly related to the acoustic properties of the language and may show important differences when the main channel is visual. Our data can be subdivided into two main observational studies.

THE "ING" PHENOMENON AND THE PRESENT PROGRESSIVE

The present progressive as acquired by English-speaking children is a fascinating phenomenon. Grammatically it occurs first as just indicated—the "ing" in the absence of a preverbal auxiliary. It is acquired as the first of a series of morphemes which modulate early English grammar. Its order of acquisition is not related to parental frequency of usage (Brown, 1973). Its semanticity is principled (in contradistinction to most other English grammatical markers which are purely arbitrary). It refers to a process, named by a verb, that is in progress at the time of speaking, but only temporarily so. It is further subdivided semantically in that action verbs can always take the progressive state while state verbs need the further distinction of volition. Thus, state verbs declared to be involuntary, such as "want," "need," "know," and "like," "see," and "hear," never take the progressive while state verbs, like "look," "listen," and "sleep," which have a large voluntary component, do take the progressive. Children appear to learn this principle early. It is noted that children who frequently use the involuntary state verbs above never use them incorrectly. However, numerous errors such as "I knowed" and "two sheeps" occur in the acquisition of arbitrary grammatical morphemes. Children learning spoken English thus follow Slobin's principle of "Pay attention to the ends of words" and pick up the inflection before they pick up the auxiliary.

What can the study of our deaf youngsters add to the "ing" phenomenon? The "ing" suffix of a sign is a new invention and does not exist in American Sign Language. It is represented by the I hand twisting slightly downward and to the right and is used like the spoken "ing" both in the gerundive, as in "stop crying," or in present participles used as modifiers ("sleeping bag"). It is generally considered important by parents and incorporated quickly following the first exposure to it. Very young children can represent it motorically.[6]

Although "ing" in the gerundive or present participle is not usually

---

[6]Actually, most signs and finger spelling appear to teach us that very young children may have greater manual dexterity than that usually assumed in child development textbooks.

coded as part of the acquisition of the present progressive, we shall combine the two features because of our focus on perceptual salience (see Figure 2.1). We have noted that the perceptual salience to any one individual youngster seems to depend on at least two variables: the youngster's residual hearing, which permits him or her to "hear" some phonetic component of the inflection, and the mother's precision in its use. Brown (1973, p. 375) refers to the fact that some spoken inflections are likely to be touched very lightly in moving from one word to another (e.g., mommy's girl) and may partially contribute to the relatively late acquisition of the possessive. Motorically, "ing" is usually attached to a verb sign placed in front of the body and may perceptually fuse into the main sign. The light vocal touch of the possessive may be found again in

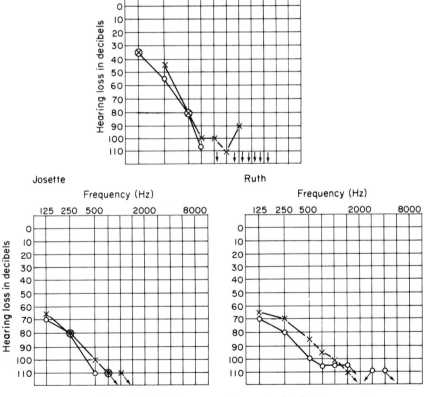

Figure 2.1 Audiograms and perceptual salience.

the light touch from the content word to the morpheme. On the other
hand, the motoric auxiliaries *is*, *are*, etc. (the I or R hand touching the
chin and moving outward) are perceptually very distinct and probably do
not fuse for the child.

We first noted Ruth's acquisition of "ing" at:

> 2:10   *"swimming"*
> 2:11   *"kitty cat running"*
> 3:1   "crying" *crying going home, yes*

The next transcript at 3:8 contains some complicated grammatical transformation but no form of progressives. The example

> "C-I" *is* "dropped her slipper"

seems to be an occurrence of a past regular and is seen as a semantic
correction on Ruth's part rather than as a new acquisition of the auxiliary.

> At 4:4   *"We are going to the tree farm"*
> At 4:6   *"I'm going to help Roger say that tape"*
> *"she said, she said yes, she is saying to me that she*
> *is on the telephone"*
> *"when I was swimming with my sunglasses with*
> *my old book"*
> "she is talking to her teacher, she is coming home
> from school"
> "I'm putting on my boots"
> *"because, because we are coming back to*
> *America"*
> *"when we were in Hawaii then I am going to have*
> *a new friend"*
> "what are you doing?" "where are you going?"
> *"what is doing?"*
> *"Connie is peeking a car and she was in a*
> *accident"*
> At 5:8   *"No, Jackie is going to be in the hospital for ten*
> *weeks. C-A-S-P-A-R will be here in 2 weeks. He*
> *stays in the. . . ."*

There are only two examples at ages 2:11 and 3:1 where the auxiliary is
missing, followed by one transcript in which it was not used at all. This
was immediately followed by the consistent use of adult forms. The adult
forms exist both in the spoken and the sign version. It is to be noted that
Ruth probably has sufficient hearing to hear some portion of the "ing"

inflection. Furthermore, Ruth's mother tends to be quite precise in both her spoken and sign inflections.

Ends of Words–Signs and Perceptual Salience—Josette and Serjei

JOSETTE

One of our other youngsters, Josette, is particularly fascinating. Just as Brown (1973) describes Eve as a "harried executive [p. 318]," because of her frequent usage of "hafta" (have to), Josette appears to approach the world as if all actions were taking place at the exact moment of utterance and at her volition. She appears to be incessantly and voluntarily in action. No involuntary state verbs for her! Let us look at some examples of her "ing." We first see Josette at 4:1, following 1 year and 3 months of sign language with her parents and in the school system.

> *"Write R-U* (Ruth) *is write."*
> *"Wash, wash you is wash."*
> *"Mama. Doll are run away."*
> *"You don't. Oh, doll are drop. Bad."*
> *"He sleeping and O.K."*

One month later:

> *"The tree is fall there."*
> *"No, Daddy is jump over the wood for the tree. The yellow*
>   *horse is eat."*

Josette points to the barn and says, *"sleeping"* in response to questions of where the horse sleeps, but continues:

> *"The yellow horse is sleep in ground."*
> *"Yellow horse sleeping there."*
> *"No, the yellow horse is eat brown hay."*
> *"Mama is run."*
> *"Yellow horse is went sleeping in hay."*
> *"Yellow horse is running away."*
> *"Yellow horse is jump. Yellow horse is fall down on the*
>   *sand."*

A month later, she is excitedly describing an accident:

> *"The man crashed her the red car in the other. Fire man is*
>   *hose her water in the other. A sick, yes. Mama's house."*
> *"Daddy is help her yellow car safe."*
> *"Daddy is pull in the white car."*

> *"Policeman is H-I me."*
> *"Yellow horse is wait now and run."*
> *"J-O-S-E-T-T-E is ride, ride the horse. Yellow horse."*
> *"Many, many people are watch the many cow horse."*
> *"No, I am cowboy. Ride the yellow horse and rope the cow."*

At 4:8, we still find occasional:

> *"She is run away"*

or

> *"The ghost went to sleeping and the Santa Claus will do come here?"*

Also:

> *"I'm go to be teacher. Wait and me to go wait for teacher."*

At 4:8, she overgeneralizes interestingly:

> *"T-S-Y is hearing me calling. Yes. Calling. You want some chocolate? Hot chocolate? Okay now?"*

Brown indicates that involuntary verbs such as "seeing" and "hearing" are not used in the present progressive, and that children tend not to overgeneralize. Shall we postulate that "hearing" for Josette is not an involuntary activity owing to the state of deafness? Furthermore, it might appear that she is correcting herself and changes it to "calling," which is, of course, a voluntary action verb. At 5 years, many examples switch back and forth, such as in response to:

> *"What have you been doing?"*
> *"Ride yellow horse."*
> *"She is staying a no. Doll is stay. A-T gramma B-A-R-B-A house."*
> *"She is seeing Mama again."*
> *"He is cry."*
> *"She is laugh. She is laughing a Connie."*
> *"She is sleeping. He is feeling so hot, hot, hot."*
> *"She is cry. Because Mama is swim again. Car driving away."*
> *"I not going to wait anymore. You have to go by yourself. You will put on your hearing aid and you will be swim with you."*
> *"Baby is sleeping. He not eat. Daddy is cut by the turkey again."*

And in answer to "How are you?":

"Feeling fine."

In most of her examples, especially the early ones, the present progressive includes the auxiliary and omits the inflection. Auditorily, this youngster is less likely to perceive the "ing" than Ruth. Visually, we need further analysis of the maternal input for the present progressive. One of our staff members believes that Josette's mother is quite precise and consistent in making the sign, although I would imagine that she does it with somewhat less than military precision.

Having noted this potentially significant difference, we were anxious to videotape Serjei, a youngster with considerably more hearing than either Josette or Ruth and with a relatively precisely speaking and signing mother.

SERJEI—A YOUNGSTER WITH MORE HEARING

We theorized that both the inflection and the auxiliary would be clearly accessible to Serjei and that he would produce both early. However, we noted another interesting feature in his utterances. The maternal linguistic input is relatively identical in both modes, although we have found instances where the mother modulates her spoken English while her sign modality leaves out articles, prepositions, copulas, and auxiliaries, as well as inflections. Transcribing a bimodal linguistic sample is most complex. We shall attempt to represent it by two lines with the:

$$\begin{cases} top\ line & = \text{sign} \\ \text{"bottom line"} & = \text{spoken word} \end{cases}$$

Thus Serjei's mother:

"Shawn" $\begin{cases} play \\ \text{"played"} \end{cases}$ *"in the snow yesterday"*

Do E-R-I-C *"sleep in the snow?"*
"Did Eric"

"Oh Elsbeth" $\begin{cases} sleep \\ \text{"slept"} \end{cases}$ *"in a"* $\begin{cases} sleep \\ \text{"sleeping"} \end{cases}$ *"bag on vacation"*

"Is Connie" $\begin{cases} have \\ \text{"having"} \end{cases}$ *"girl or boy baby?"*

"Are you" $\begin{cases} feel \\ \text{"feeling"} \end{cases}$ *"sick? You not* $\begin{cases} talk \\ \text{"talking"} \end{cases}$
                          "You're"

Although these are exceptions rather than the rule, it does appear that Serjei's linguistic modulations in sign and spoken English are most consistent with his input and its accessibility to him. Serjei himself uses a simultaneous bimodal output. He regularly omits the "ing" morpheme and auxiliaries when signing, but uses them in his spoken utterances. Note some of his linguistic output. (Again, upper line is signed, lower line is spoken when the simultaneous versions of grammatical modulations differ.)

Age 4:6:

$$\text{``Serjei''} \left\{ {go \atop \text{``going''}} \right\} \text{``Lake Tahoe''}$$

"Daddy working *for people* over *there*."
"*Serjei's* (pronounced z) *going far away*."
"*Going to the hamburger store*."

$$\text{``Me and you''} \left\{ {play \atop \text{``playing''}} \right\}$$

$$\left\{ {Dream \atop \text{``Dreaming of''}} \right\} \text{``Candy''}$$

$$\text{``No, no Daddy''} \left\{ {work \atop \text{``working''}} \right\} \text{on the firehouse.''}$$

Although an exact phonetic transcription of Serjei's utterances has not yet been completed, there are instances which indicate that there are similar differences between his sign and spoken modulations as far as tenses:

$$\text{``I''} \left\{ {forget \atop \text{``forgot''}} \right\} \text{``the pie.''}$$

Third person singular:

$$\text{``Serjei''} \left\{ {want \atop \text{``wants''}} \right\} \text{``chocolate milkshake.''}$$

Copula:

$$\left\{ {Where \atop \text{``Where's''}} \right\} \text{``another chair?''}$$

His possessive, which we hope will immortalize Connie's baby, was noted in speech only:

"Connie's tummy's fat."

A careful perusal of Serjei's linguistic utterances will show that there are no instances of signing alone and frequent instances of both bimodal utterances or purely spoken utterances. Bimodal ones continue to rivet our interest. Another feature of interest must be noted. Serjei's mother decided when he was 2:6 to use bimodal total communication. Serjei had received early, consistent, and relatively successful amplification, and the degree and shape of the hearing loss was such that his initial vocalizations were not too deviant. Indeed, his imitations of individual vowel sounds at 2 were excellent, and Serjei represents the type of hearing loss in which deafness is frequently missed in the early stages. However, when consonants occurred, his hearing frequently failed him. Furthermore, when individual sounds became combined into words, the intelligibility of his speech decreased further. Since the outset of bimodal communication, Serjei's intelligibility has increased, and his receptive understanding has considerably increased. Serjei demonstrates that clearly accessible bimodal input accelerates language acquisition in speech and signs.

Perceptual Salience and Other Morphemes

One of Slobin's operating principles reads: "Underlying semantic relations should be marked overtly and clearly." Hearing children scan adult spoken utterances for clues to meaning and are aided by overt, morphological markers which are regular and perceptually salient. Such markers probably play a similar role in production, helping the child keep track of where he is in the transition from thought to utterance. Children apparently prefer that grammatical functors be not only present whenever possible, but also that they be marked clearly acoustically or, in our cases, visually. Brown (1973, p. 398) summarizes the acquisition of 14 morphemes and finds that a detailed study of the grammar and semantics of the morphemes suggests that the order of acquisition is dependent upon relative complexity—grammatical or semantic—but is not related to the frequency of morphemes in parental speech. Perceptual salience, broken down into such variables as amount of phonetic substance, stress level, and usual serial position in the sentence, is probably a more important variable (p. 409).

How are deaf children helped to scan adult spoken and signed utterances? Which morphological markers to them are regular and perceptually salient? The new English morpheme markers in signs may vary in interesting ways in their perceptibility for deaf children. Although we have not scored the 14 morphemes to Brown's criterion, we have observed the order and frequency of their initial occurrence, noting their position (Tab), hand configuration (Dez), and motion (Sig). We have some observations which suggest that visual perceptual salience plays an important role in the acquisition of sign grammatical modulations. Two of our youngsters, for example, handle the articles "a," "the," and "some" long before their acquisition of plurals and possessives. Some of the grammatical, motoric morphemes are in such close proximity to the content words that they might fuse into the content word. Others differ and have a greater visual lag either in terms of distance, time, or location in space between the content word and any of the motoric morphemes.

The articles "a" and "the" are produced in the neutral zone (somewhere in front of the body) with the A or T hand moving to the right. All the nouns modified by the articles require very distinct movements, either to the midline at the chin, as in *a little juice*, or to the midline in front of the body, as in *the box* or *the living room*. The article "some" is represented by the left hand lying palm up in front of the body with the right open hand perpendicular to it and moving toward the body. We saw that sign preceding *juice*, which is made at the chin, some distance from the neutral zone of the body.

Plurals and possessives are both represented by an S hand at the shoulder. The plural marking is stationary; the possessive marking moves from a palm out to a palm in location. However, parental observations indicate that although the hand position and the movement of the hand are as above, the usual shoulder position is changed to somewhere in front of the body, usually in close conjunction to the sign transformed. Either S thus may become imperceptible to the child even while attentively watching.

The past regular, as well as early past irregulars noted, has two features which might contribute to early acquisition. The sign is clearly visible, the palm of the open hand facing the body at the right shoulder and flipping backwards; another version suggests a D hand flipping backwards. Both versions are some distance from the action verbs most frequently used by the youngsters, verbs which are usually signed in front of and away from the trunk, such as *drop* and *push*. The tense marker itself contains a semantic marker in that the hand indicates visually "something behind me" as the *will* indicates "something yet in front of me." We are thus postulating that some of the visual representations of the morphemes are more likely to be perceived at earlier stages than others. Some of the bimodal examples also suggest that perceptual salience plays an important role and varies for different children. Thus we have Ruth saying:

$$\text{"J-S}\ \left\{ \begin{array}{l} \textit{fought} \\ \text{"fight"} \end{array} \right. \text{with Ruth yesterday."}$$

or Josette:

$$\text{``I''} \left\{ \begin{array}{l} had \\ \text{``have''} \end{array} \right. \text{``a new hat.''}$$

or Serjei:

$$\left\{ \begin{array}{l} go \\ \text{``going''} \end{array} \right.$$

$$\left\{ \begin{array}{l} dream \\ \text{``dreaming of} \end{array} \right. candy$$

Ruth and Josette, with their greater extent of hearing loss, are clearly noting the more adult morphemes first in sign rather than in speech. Serjei, having more hearing with a maternal input which occasionally leaves out the sign modality, also indicates that he is using the more adult morphemes in the modality which is more frequently and more clearly accessible to him. We intend to pursue more ardously the bimodal maternal language and the child's expressive language in Serjei's case.

Overgeneralizations

Slobin (1973, p. 204) notes that the most widely noted aspect of children's speech has been their tendency to overregularize or overgeneralize, and so do our youngsters. Thus Elsbeth is found to sign:

"My" sleeping, bagging tent. My sleeping camping.

And Josette is found to sign:

*"We have to found her teacher to dance dancely like you
and me."*
"She is coffeeing coffee."
"The wolf will go to die-d-y." (i.e., the wolf will die)

(She placed the D for past tense plus the y to make it adverbial.)
And finally, Ruth stating:

"What is that noisy?"
"Fastly" (instead of quickly)

The Interest in Initiating Communication

One of the most striking observations about our linguistic youngsters is their delightful communicative confidence. Many deaf youngsters are symbolically silent, attentively watching adults who appear to pour language into inert receptacles; the youngsters themselves rarely initiate verbal communication with either adults or peers. Brown (1973) comments on the achievements of the two "linguistic" primates—Washoe with sign language and Sarah with token language. He carefully describes their "language" acquisition as compared to that of human children. We shall not for the moment discuss their achievements per se, but focus instead on one major difference between the two:

> A . . . slightly odd feature is the failure of Sarah to take up her token language as a medium of communication. She is always the respondent who solves problems when the experimenter sets them. She has almost never initiated communication. When the tokens have been left in her cage, she has either ignored them, or, once or twice, repeated some recent exercise. In this respect, Sarah is quite unlike Washoe and, of course, unlike human children. Washoe constantly uses Sign to initiate interaction to get what she wants, to comment on events. . . . An interest in initiating communication does not appear on any list of linguistic universals I know of, but when it is absent, we notice how unhuman the performance is [p. 44].

It is chilling to realize that the above description of Sarah may resemble the linguistic interaction frequently noted with "unsuccessful" deaf children. These youngsters demonstrate normal intellectual potential, mastery of many of the cognitive tasks described by Furth (1966), but show marked linguistic retardation. They are noted to reply monosyllabically, and only when parents request communication. They themselves almost never initiate communication. Some of these youngsters are known to have had rigorous language "training" with a paucity of "linguistic immersion." We are presently investigating the optimal linguistic input for deaf youngsters. We have previously described the genesis of communicative competence in deaf children and found it to be significantly correlated with a quality of joyfulness or pleasure in themselves and their mothers (Schlesinger, 1972; Schlesinger & Meadow, 1972). We have also focused on the importance of "meaning" in early communicative events. Meaning and enjoyment are hard to achieve, and their absence may also lead to communicative silence rather than to initiative. Our bimodal linguistic youngsters do show a felicitous linguistic environment.[7]

Successful initiation of communication might be expected to promote question formation usually delayed in the language acquisition of deaf youngsters (Quigley et al., 1973). An ongoing grammatical study of Ruth's questions shows accelerated "question" acquisition and illustrates the range of her interests.

---

[7]We are studying other "successful" linguistic youngsters who were not exposed to early bimodal language. Evidence thus far tends to indicate that their success is highly correlated to residual hearing.

3:8   *"May I have" little bit?*
      "What's that?"
      "Where is prince?"
      "See, may I see?"
4:4   *"Do you want more questions?"*
      "Why am I in the videotape?"
4:6   "What is that noisy?"
      "Who's on the telephone?"
      "Who's that on the telephone?"
      "D-I-D you have a good time at my house?"
      "Do you, Marsha, want a blue telephone"
      "Do you want to talk to my mommy?"
5:0   *"What happened to you?"*
5:8   *"Where is* S-A-L-I-N-A-S?
      "What is the sign for" E-N-V-I-R-O-N-M-E-N-T?
6:2   *"How do you spell S-Y-M-B?"* (Symbionese)

Ruth asks questions, comments on the world and its contents, and does so with adults and children. Furthermore, she does so in different modalities depending on the abilities of her communicators. She is fully aware of who is deaf and who is hearing, who has minimal knowledge of signs and who has good competency in signs. She has invented an imaginary play-mate C-A-S-P-A-R and complains that:

> *"He does not understand what long things are. He understands little short things."*

We reported previously that over a period of time Ruth increased her use of speech alone and decreased her use of signs alone, whereas the combined mode of speech and signs remained relatively stable (Schlesinger & Meadow, 1972). Our ongoing work 3 years later further corroborates this trend.

We have presented fragments of bimodal linguistic utterances to illustrate some language universals. Bimodal language acquisition appears to share many of the known facts of spoken language acquisition. We have described the first sign utterance and the growth of sign vocabulary. We gave examples of the two-term utterance and its adherence to word–sign order. We suggested that the bimodal, perceptual salience affects the order of morpheme acquisition. We noted some special features of bimodalism and bilingualism. We were delighted by the psychological concomitants of early meaningful communication. Our children differ in many ways, but they are all acquiring the languages of their mothers. Our hearing parents have demonstrated that language in another modality can be learned in adulthood. Our deaf youngsters have demonstrated their capacity to learn one language in two modalities or even two languages in two modalities. We expect to demonstrate our gratitude to them in our ongoing psychiatric linguistic study.

REFERENCES

Bernstein, B. 1961. Social class and linguistic development: A theory of social learning. In A. H. Halsey *et al.* (Eds.), *Education, economy and society.* New York: Free Press.

Bernstein, B. 1970. A sociolinguistic approach to socialization, with some references to educability. In F. Williams (Ed.), *Language and poverty.* Chicago: Markham. Pp. 25–61.

Birdwhistell, R. L. 1970. *Kinesics and context: Essays on body motion communication.* Philadelphia: Univ. of Pennsylvania Press.

Bornstein, H. 1973. A description of some current sign systems designed to represent English. *American Annals of the Deaf, 118,* 454–463.

Brill, R. G. 1960. A study in adjustment of three groups of deaf children. *Exceptional Children, 26,* 464–466.

Brill, R. G. 1969. The superior I.Q.'s of deaf children of deaf parents. *The California Palms,* 1–4.

Brown, R. 1973. *A first language, the early stages.* Cambridge, Massachusetts: Harvard Univ. Press.

Diebold, A. R., Jr. 1965. A survey of psycholinguistic research, 1954–1964, with a survey of theory and research problems. In C. W. Osgood & T. A. Sebeok (Eds.), *Psycholinguistics.* Bloomington, Indiana: Indiana Univ. Press.

Diebold, A. R., Jr. 1966. The consequences of early bilingualism in cognitive development and personality formation. Paper prepared for the symposium, The Study of Personality: An Interdisciplinary Appraisal. Rice Univ., Houston, Texas, mimeographed.

Fant, L. J., Jr. 1974. Workshop in Ameslan. California State University, Hayward.

Fellendorf, G. W., & Harrow, I. 1970. Parent counseling 1961–1968. *Volta Review, 72,* 51–57.

Ferguson, C. A. 1959. Diglossia. *Word, 15,* 325–349.

Furth, H. G. 1966. *Thinking without language: Psychological implications of deafness.* New York: Free Press.

Gardner, A., & Gardner, B. 1973. Teaching sign language to the chimpanzee, Washoe. The text of the soundtrack of the film which has been edited for distribution by The Psychological Cinema Register, Audio Visual Services, The Pennsylvania State Univ.

Hockett, C. F. 1960. The origin of speech. *Scientific American, 203,* 88–96.

Hoffmeister, R. J., & Moores, D. F. 1973. *The acquisition of specific reference in the linguistic system of a deaf child of deaf parents.* Research report No. 53, Project No. 332189, Grant No. OI-09-332189-4533 (032), Department of Health, Education and Welfare, U. S. Office of Education, Bureau of Education for the Handicapped.

Hunt, J. M. 1961. *Intelligence and experience.* New York: Ronald Press.

John, V. P., & Horner, V. M. 1971. *Early childhood bilingual education.* New York: Materials Center MLA-ACTFL.

Klima, E. S., & Bellugi, U. 1972. The signs of language in child and chimpanzee. In T. Alloway, L. Krames, & P. Pliner (Eds.), *Communication and affect*: A comparative approach, New York: Academic Press.

Lambert, W. E., & Peal, E. 1962. The relation of bilingualism to intelligence. *Psychological Monograph, 76*.

Langer, S. K. 1948. *Philosophy in a new key*. New York: Mentor Books.

Lenneberg, E. H. 1967. *Biological foundations of language*. New York: Wiley.

Lenneberg, E. H. 1973. On explaining language. In L. J. Stone, H. T. Smith, & L. B. Murphy (Eds.), *The competent infant*. New York: Basic Books.

Max, L. W. 1935. An experimental study of the motor theory of consciousness. 111. Action-current responses in deaf-mutes during sleep, sensory stimulation and dreams. *Journal of Comparative Psychology, 19*, 469–486.

McCall, E. 1965. A generative grammar of signs. Unpublished master's thesis, Univ. of Iowa.

Meadow, K. P. 1968a. Early manual communication in relation to the deaf child's intellectual, social, and communicative functioning. *American Annals of the Deaf, 113*, 29–41.

Meadow, K. P. 1968b. Parental responses to the medical ambiguities of deafness. *Journal of Health and Social Behavior, 9*, 299–309.

Meadow, K. P. 1969. Self-image, family climate, and deafness. *Social Forces, 47*, 428–438.

Quigley, S. P., & Frisina, R. 1961. Institutionalization and psycho-educational development of deaf children. *Council for Exceptional Children Research Monograph, A, 3*.

Quigley, S. P., Wilbur, R. B., & Montanelli, D. S. 1973. Development of question-formation in the written language of deaf students. Paper read at the Society for Research and Child Development, March.

Ruesch, J. 1957. *Disturbed communication*. New York: Norton.

Schlesinger, H. S. 1972. Meaning and enjoyment: Language acquisition of deaf children. In T. J. O'Rourke (Ed.), *Psycholinguistics and total communication: The state of the art*. Washington, D.C.: American Annals of the Deaf.

Schlesinger, H. S., & Meadow, K. P. 1972. *Sound and sign. Childhood Deafness and Mental Health*. Berkeley: Univ. of California Press.

Schlesinger, I. M. 1971. Production of utterances and language acquisition. In D. I. Slobin (Ed.), *The Ontogenesis of grammar*. New York: Academic Press.

Slobin, D. I. 1973. Cognitive prerequisites for the development of grammar. In C. A. Ferguson & D. I. Slobin (Eds.), *Studies of child language development*. New York: Holt. Pp. 175–221.

Stokoe, W. C. 1969–1970. Sign language diglossia. *Studies in Linguistics, 21*, 27–40.

Stokoe, W. C. 1973. Personal communication.

Stokoe, W. C., Jr., Casterline, D. C., & Croneberg, C. G. 1965. *A dictionary of American Sign Language on linguistic principles*. Washington, D.C.: Gallaudet College Press.

Vernon, M., & Kohl, S. D. 1970. Early manual communication and deaf children's achievement. *American Annals of the Deaf, 115*, 527–536.

Part II

LINGUISTIC ASPECTS

3

The Grammar of
Sign Language

LILA NAMIR
I. M. SCHLESINGER

The discussion of Sign Language grammar in this chapter is based mainly on our research on the sign language of the deaf in Israel (henceforward: ISL).[1] In addition, material concerning other sign languages has been culled from the literature in the field.

There can be no doubt that the sign languages of the deaf, the American Indian Sign Language, and the sign languages used by some monastic orders are all different languages; and even the Sign Language used by the deaf in one country may at times be in part incomprehensible to those in another one. On the other hand, the various sign languages also have many features in common, particularly in comparison to spoken languages. It will often be convenient, therefore, to treat of all these languages as if they were one language, and we will accordingly (following the usage of several other writers) refer to Sign Language (or SL) and discuss its characteristics.

[1] This research was carried out under Project No. VRA-ISR-32-67 of the U.S. Department of Health, Education and Welfare: Social and Rehabilitation Service, carried out at the Hebrew University, Jerusalem, in cooperation with the Association of the Deaf in Israel and the Helen Keller House (I. M. Schlesinger and J. Shunary, principal investigators).

THE PROBLEM OF SIGN LANGUAGE GRAMMAR

Sign Language has for a long time been regarded as a somewhat disreputable poor relation of spoken language. The great linguist Sapir (1921, p. 21) dismissed it briefly as a derivative of spoken language, and later Bloomfield (1935, p. 144) stated the same view, listing "deaf-and-dumb" language alongside writing and telegraphy. Bloomfield claims that "many and all complicated or not immediately intelligible gestures are based on the conventions of ordinary speech [p. 39]," the reason being that gesture has "so long played a secondary role under the dominance of language that it has lost all traces of independent character." Both Sapir and Bloomfield deal with Sign Language only in passing and do not cite any evidence for their judgments. It seems, however, that these were influenced partly by statements in the literature to the effect that Sign Language has little or no grammar. If this were so one might question any claim of Sign Language to the full status of a language. But—what are the facts?

Inflections

As most writers have pointed out, sign languages appear to be almost entirely devoid of the usual type of inflection. Apparently, being a basically iconic language, Sign Language did not naturally create suffixes and prefixes, which do not convey isolable bits of meaning but typically modulate the meaning of other lexical items. Only in those sign languages which have been modified by outside influences are such bound morphemes to be found frequently. Thus, in the "High" variety of the American Sign Language there are affixes translated from spoken language, and usually derived from finger spelling. Stokoe (1972, p. 85) reports an affixed sign which corresponds to the English agentive -er suffix. Hirsch (1961) also reports that different vocalizations are used by deaf German signers to distinguish between genders. But, so far as we know, as long as Sign Language is left to itself, it does not develop an inflectional system of the kind familiar from spoken language.

Parts of Speech

Closely related to this is the absence in Sign Language of what one might properly call parts of speech. In many spoken languages grammatical categories such as noun, verb, and adjective are distinguished morphologically. As has been maintained, Sign Language—at least in its unadulterated form—is not given to inflectional trimmings. Frequently, therefore, the same sign will be used for both the noun and the related verb (or more properly, for what in spoken language would be referred to as a noun and a verb, respectively), e.g., in ISL, for *tailor* and *to sew,* for *fisherman* and *to fish,* for *food* and *to eat.* Such functional changes are, of course, also to be found in spoken languages (cf. English "fish"—"to fish," "contact"—"to contact," etc), but they seem ubiquitous in SL.

Omissions

Another characteristic of SL emerges by comparing signed utterances with their English translations: Many words in the English sentence do not have a corresponding sign. The pronoun "I" is often omitted when the speaker is the subject of the sentence, and so, also, are other pronouns when they function as objects (but see the discussion of directionality below). There is no sign in ISL for the word "and." Signs for function words, like "if" and "because," are also frequently omitted. Thus, a signer may sign:

I lose I club here never

to say that if he loses (i.e., the elections) he will never again come to the club.

Not only function words but also various predicates may be omitted: "come," "do," "be," "show," "see," etc. For instance, an ISL signer signed:

Tuesday H . . . R . . .

by which he meant: On Tuesday H . . . and R . . . will come. In McCall's (1965) corpus of American SL there are examples like the following:

John (i.e., John eats)

cannot funeral cannot (i.e., cannot go to the funeral)
and omissions of prepositions like:

skinny broom (i.e., skinny as a broom)

McCall attempts to write a generative grammar for her corpus, and to accommodate such eliptical utterances she must make generous use of deletion transformations.

The lack of inflections and classification of signs into grammatical categories, taken together with the paucity of function words and with other omissions, serve to give SL a somewhat "telegraphic" appearance. The following is a short excerpt from McCall's corpus [pp. 88–89]:

Two children. One marry. Two grandchildren. Work close
frat building. One still school. Mother gone. My aunt true
me phone. Sorry can't funeral. Me work. Me awful cry.
Come night.

It seems little wonder that such staccato utterances should have made SL appear to be devoid, or almost devoid, of grammar. Writing about the sign language used by the North American Plains Indians (a hearing community using SL alongside their extremely diverse verbal languages for intertribal communication and ceremonial occasions, as well as for communication with white men), Mallery (1880) observed almost a century ago that there is no organized sentence form in Sign Language, no articles, particles, case, gender, verbs, subject or predicate "The sign radicals, without being any of our parts of speech, may be all of them in turn [p. 359]." This characterization appears to be appropriate to most sign languages.

The Status of Sign Language

In considering SL sequences such as the above, one is also reminded of utterances of young children who have not yet learned to speak grammatically, an impression further reinforced by the great repetitiveness which signers often indulge in, as seen in the following excerpt, also from McCall (1965, p. 89):

Wife drive. Me sleep backseat. Drive. Me sleep. Yes. Yes.
New. Have new. Yes. Yes. Me lie=on backseat.[2] *Me*
lie=on backseat. Wife wife have drive.

These repetitions may be functional in the same way that they are functional in child language. As Raffler-Engel (1970, p. 30) has observed, by repeating words the child introduces redundancy into his utterances, which makes things easier both for the hearer and for himself. As soon as he begins to use function words, these repetitions largely disappear. Sign Language, it will be remembered, has few function words.

Gestures are in fact inextricably intertwined with the development of verbal language in the child, as several investigators have pointed out (e.g., Bruner, 1975; Dewey, 1971). Some scholars, notably Wundt (1904), also believe gestures to lie at the root of the phylogenesis of language (p. 633 ff.; cf. also Paget, 1944). From here it is only one step to the specula-

---

[2]Here and elsewhere a double hyphen (=) is used to indicate that two words translate the same sign.

tion that the peculiarities of sign language are due to its being of fairly recent origin. Neumann (1968, pp. 20–21) observes that only since the first schools of the deaf were founded, around 200 years ago, could a sign language as a conventional means of communication develop. This is because the young do not have any opportunity to form a community unless brought together within an institutional framework: Most deaf children grow up in families of hearing persons. Hence, he argues, Sign Language has all the weaknesses of a young language: it has few lexical items, most of which are imitative or describe a characteristic of the referent, and there are no grammatical categories or function words—in fact, he claims, no syntax in the sense of commonly known languages.

So much for the debit side. It seems, however, that there must be something wrong with this picture of an emaciated microlanguage which emerges from the above citations from several writers on the subject. No one who has observed deaf persons conversing in Sign Language can avoid quite the contrary impression—that Sign Language is a full-blooded language, capable of serving the needs of the deaf in their everyday give-and-take (Schlesinger, 1971). Granted that SL is indeed a young language—but even a young language must be fairly complex to survive as an independent means of communication, which it undoubtedly is.

The above characterizations of SL would appear to be one-sided, and partly based on incomplete information. SL may be in many respects unlike spoken language, but it has its own peculiar resources, which may largely make up for those grammatical devices which it lacks. As Sapir and Swadesh (1946) have pointed out (speaking of spoken languages): "It would be naive to imagine that any analysis of experience is dependent on pattern expressed in language. Any concept, whether or not it forms part of the system of grammatical categories, can be conveyed in any language [p. 111]."

Take, for instance, the lack of inflection in SL. There is no reason why this should be at all debilitating. Notions which in certain spoken languages are expressed by inflections may be expressed by special signs in SL. Thus, to the extent that persons are referred to, gender can be indicated in SL by the addition of the sign for *man, male,* or *woman, female* (cf. English "she-wolf," "man-servant," etc.). And although there is no inflection for tense, the future and past can be indicated by special signs (which describe forward and backward movements, respectively, in ISL as well as in various other sign languages). If it is pointed out that an action or event takes place in the present, this can be done by using the sign *now* (in ISL, pointing to the ground by the signer's feet). Here it should be noted that spoken languages also differ in the extent to

which they make use of inflections, and that, according to some authorities, inflections actually developed out of auxiliaries, or other function words (cf. Jespersen, 1922, pp. 422–425, for a discussion of this issue).

Inflectionlike Phenomena

Another device taking the place of inflection is used in Sign Language to indicate the plural: reduplication of the sign. Sapir (1921, p. 60) informs us that this is also the way the plural is formed in Nass, a (spoken) language of British Columbia.

Contrary to the sweeping generalizations made by some writers, inflections are really not totally absent in SL. The phenomenon we have described under the term *directionality* (Cohen, Namir, & Schlesinger, 1977) may really be viewed as a kind of inflection. Some signs may be modified by changing the direction of the movement. Usually these are signs denoting actions, and the direction indicates the "source" of the action and/or its "endpoint", i.e., the actor and the patient, or goal. Thus, in ISL we have *help me,* with the movement toward the speaker, and *help you,* where the direction of the movement is toward the person addressed, and we can similarly distinguish between *I ask you, you ask me, I ask him,* etc. Similarly, *must* (be obliged to) differs from *I must,* in the direction in which the movement is made. The same phenomenon has been reported for American Sign Language (Friedman, 1975, 1976).

Directionality, thus, is a device which may take the place of inflection for person. The device consists of a modulation of the radical (*help, ask,* and *must,* in the above examples) which modifies the meaning. Similar modulations are explored at length in La Mont West's (1960) unpublished Ph.D. dissertation on Indian Sign Language. West makes a distinction between major and minor morphemes. The former are a large-membership class (roughly comparable to that of content words), whereas the latter are a low-membership class with relatively high text frequency. Minor morphemes include prefixes, suffixes, and suprafixes (i.e., affixes in temporal contiguity), and "repetition" (p. 110). Examples are: "hither" (performed by a straight movement toward self which participates in signs like *arrive, heart, owl,* and *me*); plural or dual, which participates in signs like *spouse, walk, frog*; duplicative (performed by repetition): alternative (two hands alternately repeating what is signed): and "across" (straight movement to left). The internal morphological structure of the sign thus looks after the expression of various grammatical functions. There are opportunities for such morphological structuring which are unique to SL: It is possible to perform two signs simultaneously (cf. Cohen *et al.*, 1977), as, for instance, in West's suprafixes.

Paralinguistic Features

Certain grammatical functions in SL are taken over by facial mimicry and posture. As will be seen later on, these may be involved in the signing of negation, questions, and degree. They are the counterpart of intonation and other paralinguistic features in spoken language. Transcriptions into spoken language (as in the short excerpt quoted above) cannot convey the full effect of these, and as a result the impression gained by them is of a language much more impoverished than it appears to its users. It does not seem legitimate to characterize SL as spoken language minus certain grammatical devices, as writers in the field have so often done. The way SL functions is so different from spoken language that the task of comparing them must be approached with the greatest caution.

Take the "telegraphic" character of SL utterances commented on above. If, in reading a transcript of SL, one imagines the words being spoken at a regular speech rate, one cannot help feeling that it poses unduly severe demands on the "listener." However, the rate of signing is always much slower than the rate of speaking. (In a filmed sample of spontaneous signing, we found signers to form, on the average, 1.25 signs per second, and never more than 2 signs per second. For American Indian Sign Language, West [1960] found signing rate to range from .45 signs per second—which gives the impression of hesitancy—to 1.25 signs per second—which, he reports, gives the impression of great speed.) This gives the person addressed more time to deal with the incoming message and fill in the missing links. The relative paucity of function words is therefore far less disturbing than a casual perusal of transcripts might lead us to think. Thus there may be a mutual balance between rate and redundancy: the fewer the number of items, the slower the intake of individual items has to be; and conversely, the faster the rate of transmitting, the more redundant the message must be to be understood.

Further, the sparsity of function words may be partly counterbalanced by a certain type of redundancy: Signers are usually very repetitive (see above). These repetitions of course slow down the flow of information still further. Add to this such features as juncture and facial mimicry, which are usually profusely used by signers (but difficult to classify and transcribe), and pantomime, with which signing is often interspersed, and one ends up with a totally different picture. Here is a language whose means of communicating differ very much from those of spoken language. Little is gained by taking a list of grammatical features of spoken language and checking off those which are to be found in SL and those which are not.

The thing to do, then, is to approach the problem of SL grammar from the contents to be expressed. One may take a semantic notion and ask how SL deals with it: How does SL distinguish between one and many of the same kind (plurality)? How does it distinguish between things that happened in the past and those about to happen in the future? It is questions of this type to which we address ourselves in the last part of this chapter. But first we want to discuss a problem which has been a central concern of investigators of SL, including ourselves.

The Problem of Sign Order

One of the first questions we asked ourselves when we began studying ISL was how this language expresses the major grammatical relations, i.e., the subject, verb, object. Or, stated in more appropriate semantic terms, how does ISL distinguish between agent, action, and goal (patient). These notions are not expressed by any kind of inflections. Taking our cue from inflectionless languages, which use word order to signal these relations, we reasoned that in ISL the order of signs should serve to make these communicatively important distinctions. To our surprise, however, we found sign order to be rather free.

This presented a problem. An inflectionless language without a fixed order of morphemes seemed to be an anomaly, for it appeared to be lacking the means to express relations one would assume as essential to efficient communication. We therefore decided to look into the question of sign order more deeply. The results of our study are described in the next section. It turned out (as was the case with the issue of inflections, which cannot be dismissed summarily by stating that they are absent in SL) that the problem of relative position of signs is much more complex than one might at first expect.

RELATIVE POSITION OF SIGNS

> "Do cats eat bats? . . . and sometimes: Do
> bats eat cats? . . . As she couldn't
> answer either question, it didn't matter
> much which way she put it."
> —*Alice in Wonderland*

Previous Research

Several writers have remarked that SL lacks a fixed sign order. West (1960), who—as we have seen—argues that there is a rigid morphological structure in the signs of Indian SL, believes sign order to be "in most cases a redundant, non-obligatory, stylistic matter [p. 90]." Similar claims have been made about the SL of the deaf by many writers (e.g., Fusfeld, 1958).

Apparently dissenting evidence comes from one of the rare attempts at a systematic analysis of SL syntax, which was made by McCall (1965). Her data were collected on American deaf people filmed at gatherings where "sign was the predominant means of communication." She took as her framework Chomsky's earlier version of transformational grammar (Chomsky, 1957). (Cf. Stokoe, 1972, for a discussion of the problem of writing a grammar of SL.) She postulated rewrite rules which generate phrase structures on which (optional or nonoptional) transformations may be applied. Thus, one of the structures generated by her rules is what she calls an "adverb of emphasis" followed by a noun phrase, a predicate, and a time marker. All of these, except for the predicate, are optional (as indicated in the following by parentheses):

$$(Adv_e) \ (NP) \ Pred \ (T)$$

This can result in such sequences as:

(Maybe) *(John)* *help* *(tomorrow)*

The order of these elements can, however, be permuted by transformations. The fact that McCall succeeds in describing sign sequences by a generative grammar seems at first blush to run counter to the claims that there is no fixed sign order in SL. Note, however, that her grammar allows for many transformations permuting sign order. Since there are no constraints on the use of these transformations and they can be applied as liberally as one wishes, her grammar in effect does not bear evidence to any binding regularities in sign order.

There is one observation of McCall, however, which does support the claim that the SL investigated has rules of sign order. She writes: "Those conversant with Sign often are able to indicate whether or not a given construction is typical of manualism [p. 6]." Such judgments of grammaticality are possible only where there is a grammar. It should be borne in mind that McCall studied American SL, and apparently that of the High variety. Users of this language have much contact with English, and there is undoubtedly much bilingual interference from spoken language. McCall goes on to argue that the American sign language has constructions dissimilar from those of English, but no data are given as to how firmly these are entrenched, or to what extent signers' judgments of grammaticality pertain to these as well. Even if it should turn out that this brand of SL has a relatively fixed sign order, there is still no guarantee that this is true also of other sign languages which have remained relatively uninfluenced by spoken language. One such language is ISL, whose history is rather short. It has, until very recently, led only a clandestine existence, its legitimacy not being recognized in the schools for the deaf; and it is a merger of the indigenous language which was formed spontaneously in the deaf community with dialects imported by deaf immigrants from various countries (cf. Sella, 1969; Shunary, 1969). Hence, one would not expect an overwhelming influence of Hebrew, or for that matter, of any other spoken language. The question is, does this relatively unadulterated sign language have a fixed sign order?

Consider what a negative answer to this question would imply. In English, the difference between "man bites dog" and "dog bites man" is one of word order. If sign order is not semantically relevant in ISL, and there are not any other grammatical means, such as inflection or prepositions, to express such relationships, the user of ISL will presumably perform the signs for "man," "dog," and "bite," and rely on the speech partner to infer the intended relationship between the signs from his knowledge of the world. Should he intend the less probable message that it was a man who bit a dog, then, in the absence of other grammatical expedients, he would be obliged to supply additional verbal context to make himself understood (e.g., he might add that the dog was hurt, or ran away.) One need not assume any great degree of sophistication on the signer's part to impute to him such a manner of "short-circuiting" grammar. Informal observations of ISL suggested that just this technique of supplying additional context was often resorted to by signers.

For everyday give-and-take the above means of conveying grammatical relations may be perfectly sufficient because of the great degree of redundancy inherent in such discourse. Where the situation imposes greater demands of the communicants, however, it is a different matter. Specifically, this problem may be expected to arise in instruction, guidance, and counseling—or wherever there may be greater novelty in the context communicated, greater abstraction, or a need for greater precision than is the case with ordinary conversation.

The question of interest to us, therefore, was whether ISL has grammatical means at its disposal which the signer can fall back on in situations such as the above—and which are perhaps disregarded in those situations where the relations intended are obvious. Our impressions of rather free sign order might have been the result of the latter kind of situation.

Experiments on Sign Order

We decided to explore further the question of grammatical competence. We reasoned that if the grammar of ISL contained any rules of sign ordering, these rules would be observed by signers where the situation could not hint at meaning, thus requiring them to draw on all the grammatical resources at their disposal to get their message across. To construct such a situation we utilized a method based on that of Fraser, Bellugi,and Brown's (1963) investigation of child language, subsequently also employed by Cooper (1967) with deaf subjects. We carried out a series of experiments in which the signer was requested to describe to a deaf partner one of two or more drawings, which differed among themselves only on one aspect corresponding to a grammatical contrast—or rather, what in spoken language would correspond to a grammatical contrast (Schlesinger, 1971). An example of a pair of such drawings would be, e.g., (a) a black dog biting a white dog; (b) a white dog biting a black dog. The contrast involved in this pair is, of course, that between underlying subject and direct object.

In designing the stimulus pictures the possibility had to be kept in mind of the signer attempting to **enact** the situation instead of signing it sequentially—which, of course, would enable him to circumvent the use of grammatical means involving sign order that might be available in ISL. This may be illustrated by considering the statement that the ball is in front of the tree. ISL has a sign for each of the three terms involved: *ball, in front of,* and *tree.* The signer might make the sign for *ball* with one hand, that for *tree* with the other, and place his hands in the appropriate position relative to one another. In this way he would both avoid a communicative failure in the experimental task involving these concepts and defeat our purpose in the experiment. The use of these and similar means in American Sign Language has been described by Friedman (1976). A judicious use of situations to be described was therefore called for, which would prevent the signer's taking this way out.

In our main experiment we used a set of six drawings each involving (equal-sized) cartoontype characters depicting a monkey, a bear, and a man presented in a relationship which would, in spoken language, be expressed by subject, direct object, and indirect object. The six drawings depicted the six possibilities of A handing B to C, where A, B, and C are each either the man, the bear, or the monkey.

In analyzing the signers' messages we found that they did not consistently signal the difference between subject, direct and indirect object by sign order. There was a strong tendency to express the underlying subject first in the utterance, but beyond this there was considerable freedom of sign order even within the same sender. This lack of consistency in the signing sequence was probably why receivers of the messages found it quite difficult, on the whole, to understand what picture was intended by the sender. In everyday situations where such fine discriminations as those demanded by the experimental condition are very rarely called for, communication is naturally much more successful, and one (already mentioned) typical way of achieving this is the building of redundancy into the message. This was also sometimes attempted by our experimental subjects.

Another observation was made regarding signers' mastery of Hebrew. In Hebrew two word orders are permissible in simple active declarative sentences: subject–verb–direct object–indirect object,and subject–verb–indirect object–direct object; in both cases the indirect object is obligatorily marked by a prefix. The tendency of the signers in our experiment to use the sequence A–B–C (where A hands B to C) increased with their mastery of Hebrew, which points to the possibility that a process of importing something of Hebrew word order is in operation. This phenomenon of bilingual interference is of course of great interest, but the main problem which concerned us in this experiment was whether what might be termed "primitive" SL—by which we mean simply SL prior to spoken language influence, i.e., the language used by uninstructed and isolated groups of deaf people—does have any ordering structure comparable to that of spoken language.

It should not be assumed that we found nothing that can be regarded as rules of syntax in our experiment. Two such rules were adhered to very steadfastly by all the signers:

1.   The sign referring to the action did not come first in the utterance.
2.   The sign for the attribute followed that which it modified.

Rule 2, incidentally, holds for Hebrew word order too. One might assume that rules such as these would be less important for successful communication than rules for distinguishing, e.g., between subject and object. ISL, interestingly enough, appears to lack the latter. This finding was subsequently replicated in a more carefully controlled experiment where the interchanges between signers were filmed. The resulting sequences were carefully analyzed for the presence of subtle cues (such as pausing, emphases, etc.) which might help in signaling grammatical distinctions. No such cues were found.

We were also concerned by the possibility that the generally low rate of success in communication might have resulted from difficulty in distinguishing between six very similar pictures. To check on this, in the second experiment we varied the number of drawings in the set presented to each signer, using two, three, four, or six drawings. Allowing for the effect of guessing, we found no influence on performance with up to four drawings, while there was a possible drop with six drawings. But even for two to four drawings the mean success in getting the message across was no more than 68%!

Theoretical Implications

As argued elsewhere (Schlesinger, 1971), the finding that ISL lacks grammatical means to signal the "subject of" and "object of" relations has important theoretical consequences. If there is no fixed way of expressing these relations in the surface structure, then there is no reason to assign these relations to the base structure of this language. Such a conclusion was certain to prove uncongenial to those committed to the postulate of universal base structures. This is why we took care to replicate the experiment, trying to rule out possible artifacts.

Nevertheless, believers in universal base structures have lines of defense to fall back on. One of these is to deny SL the status of a language. If the criterion is the use to which SL is put, this argument is easily refuted by any observer of deaf signers who, as mentioned above, use SL as an independent means of communication for their daily purposes. If, on the other hand, eligibility to languagehood is to be determined by linguistic criteria, such as the presence of a syntax of the kind familiar from spoken languages, the argument becomes largely circular: Only those languages which conform to the universal base are considered to be languages, and hence the base is universal for all languages. This circularity is merely disguised by the claim that the universality hypothesis pertains only to spoken languages. Wasow (1973), however, has argued that there are some independent reasons for thus limiting the hypothesis, but discussion of his claims would be beyond the scope of the present chapter. For further discussion of these problems see Crystal and Craig (this volume).

Another line of defense is to plead a special case for ISL, on the grounds that it is an immature language (cf. Stokoe, 1972, p. 127, who points this out in his discussion of our experiment, although not in order to defend the universality hypothesis). Bonvillian, Charrow, and Nelson (1973) have suggested that perhaps because of the diversity of the Israeli deaf population (many of them are relatively newly arrived in the country), a "single" homogenous sign language has not yet been established. ISL, however, has been used for decades now, and already serves the needs of many second-generation signers. If lack of bilingual interference is to be a criterion for according a language full status, where is one to stop? Eventually, ISL will probably drift toward a sign order paralleling Hebrew word order, but this is itself an interference phenomenon. There is little evidence for the claim that the language will develop sign order rules of its own.

Our experiment has since been replicated with American Sign Language by Bode (1974), who obtained a very high proportion of correctly understood messages. Bode's American signers used a sign order paralleling English word order to differentiate between semantic roles. It would be premature, however, to conclude that these conflicting results were due to the different sign languages used (an explanation which would be in line with Bonvillian *et al.*'s argument). Bode's subjects were undergraduate students and thus well conversant with English, and with such subjects bilingual interference is to be expected. It will be remembered that our Hebrew-speaking subjects were also influenced by Hebrew word order.

Bode's own explanation of the discrepancy in experimental results refers to the subject populations used. The poor comprehension scores in our experiment, she argues, may have been due to the different degrees of mastery of Hebrew of our subjects. If the communicants differ in the degree to which their signing is influenced by the Hebrew vernacular, they are employing what are in effect different dialects. There may be some truth in this (cf. Schlesinger, 1971, p. 114). But it should be clear that our conclusions are not invalidated thereby, because we also found that those of our subjects who had a poor knowledge of Hebrew did not use **any** sign order consistently, which indicates the absence of a sign order rule in "primitive" SL. The fact that comprehension was far from perfect even when the sender and receiver used consistently the same sign order is further evidence that ISL lacks such a sign order rule.

The question, of course, remains why ISL (and, presumably, other "primitive" sign languages as well, though experimental data are still lacking) differs from spoken languages in having no fixed order of elements. One reasonable explanation has been advanced by Tervoort (1961), who also comments on the lack of fixed sign order. He refers to the iconic nature of signs and the fact that the signing sequence is replete with pantomime. The signer, argues Tervoort, reenacts the situation he wants to describe and may be therefore less dependent on the usual grammatical devices to get his meanings across.

Another possibility is that the differences may have something to do with the way the brain processes information in the visual and auditory modes. Wales (1971) has pointed out that there are indications for the existence of special auditory rehearsal mechanisms in short-term memory, and has speculated that the absence of parallel mechanisms for the visual modality may have led to limiting SL to "simple 'propositionalised' forms of communication where there is not the same need for structural constraints, such as ordering, to operate [p. 78]."

It is also pertinent to note in this connection that early stages of spoken languages are believed by Jespersen (1922) to have been devoid of a fixed word order (pp. 256, 372).

Although neither inflections nor relative position of signs distinguish communicatively important relations, like agent, action, and goal, the Israeli Sign Language functions well. The reason, as will have become apparent in the foregoing, is that the context serves to disambiguate the utterance. Out-of-context comic-strip-like situations of the sort depicted in our experiment do not happen in everyday life, and the breakdown of communication observed in our experiments seems to be restricted mainly to this highly artificial situation.

Analysis of a Signed Corpus

In addition to the experiments, we analyzed a corpus of spontaneous signing by deaf Israeli signers. It was felt that experiments would not suffice to provide a full answer to the problem of relative position in sign language. In the first place, there was always the possibility that the findings are restricted to the experimental situation. It should also be borne in mind that in our experiment only a single action term was employed, viz., *give* (or alternatively, the pictures could be described by *receive*). Moreover, it might be the case that a fixed sign order may hold for other relations than those tapped by the experiment. We therefore decided to find out how signers behave in more natural situations. For this purpose we analyzed a filmed corpus collected at the Jerusalem deaf club in semiformal situations, mostly addressing friends at club meetings.

In the following the results of the analysis are presented. We also include some findings reported in the literature for other sign languages. The peculiarities of SL entailed some awkwardness in reporting. The absence of parts of speech, commented on earlier, precluded the use of terms like "noun," "verb," or "verb phrase." Since our experiments led us to expect less structure than is usual in spoken language, there could be no justification for us to try to superimpose any elaborate syntactic framework on a language which might rather be described more simply in terms of a few concepts. We therefore preferred to state the regularities observed for ISL in general terms, such as "agent," "action," "modifier," and "goal," which refer to the function of the sign in the utterance as understood from the context.

AGENT AND ACTION

Our findings showed that the sign expressing the agent almost always came before that expressing the action,[3] for example:

---

[3]To avoid cumbersome statements such as: the sign expressing the action, etc., in the following we shall allow ourselves the rather imprecise formulation: The action follows the agent.

deaf come

policeman hit

This order would seem to be common to many sign languages; Leont'yev (1969), for instance, has remarked upon it for contemporary Russian sign language, and Hilde Schlesinger (this volume) has given some examples from the acquisition of American Sign Language. McCall (1965), writing about American users of sign, found the agent either at the beginning, or both at the beginning and at the end of a construction, for example, *me fall off me* (p. 40). One of the early sign language investigators of the German SL, cited in Tylor (1881), found, however, the contrary order (e.g., *knit I*) to hold more generally.

EXPERIENCER AND STATE

Similarly, we found that the experiencer almost always precedes the state, for example:

baby weigh

everyone happy

These two regularities, AGENT + ACTION and EXPERIENCER + STATE, can be reduced to the generalization that the topic of the utterance precedes the comment. (The topic–comment distinction is thought to be very early and basic one; see, for instance, Bruner [1975] and Hewes [this volume].)

Wundt (1904), treating sign languages of both the deaf and the North American Plains Indians, finds that as a general psychological principle the "subject" precedes the "predicate." Kroeber (1958) also proposed this order for Indian Sign Language. Hirsch (1961), writing about German Sign Language, found only one sign-order rule: that the psychological subject takes first place—the view taken by earlier authors such as Tylor (1881), who opted for the existence of a "natural order," which was "the same among the mutes of different countries, and wholly independent of the syntax which may happen to belong to the language of their speaking friends."

ATTRIBUTION

In expressions corresponding to adjective–noun constructions in spoken language the attribute almost invariably comes last, for example:

elections new

clock round

This order was also found consistently in our experiments. In the filmed corpus, however, there were a very few instances where the reverse order was observed, for example:

new chairman

(In this example, the signer—who was rated very high on knowledge of spoken languages, especially German—may have been following German word order.)

Instances of the attribute following the modified word (which is also the order holding for Hebrew) were very numerous throughout our corpus. This same order is found characteristic by many writers at different periods and referring to different sign languages, including Tylor (1881) for German Sign Language, Geylman (1964) and Leont'yev (1969) for Russian Sign Language, and West (1960) and Mallery (1879) for American Indian Sign Language (although the latter's informant found, in general, a wide variety of sign orders to be acceptable, and this order was common but not obligatory).

We note that the Gardners' chimp Washoe spontaneously signed *flower red,* in spite of the fact that her human companions used the opposite order (Gardner, personal communication). It is observed, in passing, that in a paired-associate learning experiment, Lambert and Paivio (1956) found that it was easier for subjects to learn the order noun + adjective than the converse order (with the latter resulting in fewer errors, however).

Like Tylor, Wundt (1904) saw the predominating noun + adjective order as exemplifying an underlying psychological principle: The object which the noun refers to can be conceived of as standing by itself, whereas the attributing expression cannot. Therefore the former has to be expressed first. A similar explanation is given by Kroeber (1958) for American Indian Sign Language. He observes that it helps to know what it is that is being communicated about. This establishes the context (say, a horse), and one may next sign that it is black. If *black* were signed first, the following sign might be expected to refer to any one of an indefinitely large class of black objects, or the information might even be about darkness or night. The fact that this alleged tendency does not apply to spoken languages, many of which have the adjective + noun order, is commented on briefly by Bühler (1934, p. 334). He observes that the explanation holds only for a language which forms a picture of what is described and hence does not hold for spoken language.[4] Kroeber (1958)

---

[4]Note, however, that this explanation predicts too much, since it would seem to apply also to quantifiers, which (in ISL) do **not** follow the term quantified, as will be seen.

suggests that in spoken language the rate of speaking is more rapid, and associated units are therefore more easily kept in mind; hence it is less important to adhere to the noun + adjective order.

An apparent exception, cited by Wundt, is the case where two nouns stand in some sort of attributive relationship to each other, and here the attribute rather than the attributed-to takes first place—e.g., "the tower of the church" is signed *church tower*. However, it seems that this may be regarded as a case of a compound sign. We found that for compound signs in the Israeli Sign Language the sequence of components is not fixed, and sometimes the determining component precedes the other component. For American Indian Sign Language (which is used by a large number of different tribes each speaking widely differing languages), Kroeber states that on the whole the determining element follows the one which is qualified except when two nounlike elements are compounded, in which case the determining element usually comes first. Kroeber suspects that the word order of spoken Indian languages may have influenced the order of elements in compound signs. For a monastic sign language, Hutt (1968) reports that the modifying element follows the one modified.

In her analysis of American Sign Language order, McCall (1965) does not find any fixed order for attribution; according to her optional trans-formational rules they may either precede or follow the term qualified. (We suspect that her subjects' knowledge of English may have been a factor influencing order preferences, as indeed we feel is the case with users of Israeli Sign Language.) According to McCall, where two attrib-utes modify a noun this may be placed between them, for example:

have many thing different

In this case, however, one attribute is a quantifier; as will be seen in the following, in ISL these typically precede what is quantified.

For many languages, there is a preferred adjective order. For instance, in English one says "a little old man" rather than "an old little man" (except in special cases). A small informal study on order between signs for attributes in Israeli Sign Language suggested that there is no fixed preference, and signers indifferently signed, for example, *flower red big* and *flower big red*.

QUANTIFIERS

In our corpus we found that quantifiers such as *all, much, enough*, and cardinal numbers always preceded the signs modified, for example:

two car

much money

On the other hand, ordinal numbers always followed the concepts modified:

time first (the first time)

The sign order in the above cases parallels that typical for Hebrew word order. ISL, however, also characteristically repeats the quantifier signs, which sometimes occur both before and after the sign for the quantified concept:

all number all

five=month five[5]

Kroeber (1958), discussing order of American Indian signs, reports that while the "qualifying adjective probably follows its noun, numerals and restrictive adjectives perhaps precede [p. 10]."

In her analysis of ASL, McCall postulated certain obligatory time transformations which resulted in a sign order different from that of English, resembling our above finding on the repetition of quantifier signs. For example:

soon week three (in three weeks' time)

year three year (in three years' time)

MODIFIERS OF ACTIONS AND STATES

We found a strong tendency for modifiers to follow actions, for example:

tell brief (briefly)

write=down correct (write down accurately)

This order is similarly reported by Leont'yev (1969) for Russian Sign Language, and Wundt (1904) too found that the adverb followed the verb. The psychological explanation he and others put forth in connection with attribution (see above) would seem to hold here as well.

Among the signers from whom we obtained our corpus there are two who deserve special consideration here in connection with location modifiers. One, who was altogether lacking in knowledge of any verbal language, used the order X + LOCATION very rarely and LOCATION + X very frequently (although for one particular expression both orders in

----

[5]Here and elsewhere, where in the translation of our sign examples into English glosses a single sign requires two words, these are joined a double hyphen (=). In the present example, the number *five* has been incorporated into the sign for *month* in the first of the signs.

fact occurred: *Tel Aviv discussions* and *discussions Tel Aviv*). The other
signer, who rated very high in knowledge of both German and Hebrew,
used both orders rather inconsistently, tending to prefer LOCATION +
X.

The temporal modifiers in our corpus were unlike other modifiers: They
tended to be signed prior to—but not necessarily adjacent with—the
related action or state (the order TIME + X occurred in about two thirds
of the cases), for example:

later talk

In McCall's American Sign Language corpus, temporal modifiers did
not have a fixed position relative to the action term—that is, she reports
each of the following to be permissible:

(We) meet my home Saturday

Saturday (we) meet my home

GOAL AND ACTION

The order ACTION + GOAL was used frequently by all our signers,
for example:

examine contract

give candy

my wife my spouse give=birth already daughter

But many signers also used the opposite order, GOAL + ACTION, quite
often, although with less frequency.

We also found instances of other constructions, such as GOAL +
AGENT + ACTION:

proposal Center reject refuse (the Center rejected the
proposal)

Two different goals could also be signed one before and the other after
the action

I work day lose money (I lost both a working day and
money)

For American Sign Language Friedman (1976) reports the following
orders: AGENT + ACTION + GOAL, AGENT + GOAL + ACTION,
GOAL + AGENT + ACTION, and GOAL + ACTION. The prevalence
of AGENT + ACTION + GOAL and ACTION + GOAL constructions
in ISL does not agree with that in the German SL, according to descrip-

tions by several German teachers of the deaf (Wundt, 1904). They report that the subject usually comes first in the sentence, as it does in many spoken languages, but that the object precedes the verb, for example, *the teacher the boy praises*. The same sequence of signs has also been observed by Leont'yev (1969) for contemporary Russian Sign Language, and, like Wundt, Leont'yev seems to believe this reflects a cognitive predisposition or "inner programming." For the American Indian Sign Language Mallery (1879) likewise reports the order: subject + attribute + object + verb.

Tervoort (1961) has suggested that various factors may influence ordering of signs, such as the chronological order of events or of perception, emotional importance, and also, the order prevailing in the spoken language environment. This may possibly explain those relatively few cases in our corpus in which, contrary to the prevalent order, GOAL preceded AGENT. One of the universals of (spoken) languages, according to Greenberg (1963, p. 76), is that the subject precedes the object, unless a special effect is desired. Wundt has likewise observed that the usual sign sequence might be changed on special occasions—for example, when there is a strong wish to obtain water, the order signed will be *water drink I*.

A comparison is in order here of our findings based on the filmed corpus and those of our experiments (see above). In our first experiment we had found the order GOAL + ACTION in about two-thirds of the cases. In our second experiment, however, we usually found ACTION before GOAL (as in the filmed corpus). This may have had something to do with the subject population: That of our first experiment included a considerable number of older subjects, whereas in the second experiment, the subjects' ages were, on the whole, somewhat lower, and it is possible that among the younger group the influence of Hebrew word order (typically AGENT + ACTION + GOAL) had made itself more felt in their signing. Here, however, the fact must be borne in mind that the only actions in question were "give" and, occasionally, "receive." The sample in our films included subjects with no knowledge of Hebrew at all as well as those with a fairly good knowledge.

OTHER COMPLEMENTS OF THE ACTION

No regularities could be found with other complements, i.e., those which in spoken language would be expressed by the indirect object. We found both ACTION + COMPLEMENT:

request UNO (request from UNO . . .)

later look=for municipality new site (the municipality
looked for a new site)

and COMPLEMENT + ACTION:

I B . . . talk I for club (I talked with B . . . about the
club)

I council wait (I waited for the council)

COMPLEX STRUCTURES

In ISL, what in spoken language would be a subordinate object clause
invariably follows the action sign. We found many instances of what
might be translated as subordinate object clauses without any sign marking them off. In these cases the subordinate follows the main clause.
Many examples were found for what might be regarded as object clauses
after the signs *understand, know, say, think, demand, ask, see, agree,
decide, be=glad=that,* for example:

B . . . say find substitute candidate (B . . . said he
would find a substitute candidate)

Haifa demand build basket=ball (the Haifa [center for the
deaf] request the setting up of a basketball pitch)

Think perhaps boy perhaps girl

I see take war give candy give cigarette (I saw soldiers
giving and taking candy and cigarettes)

I agree all branch build house (I agree that all the branches
of the club should build a center together)

I think why everyone strong oppose (I wondered why
everyone strongly opposed it)

The many cases of quotations in our corpus were invariably introduced
by a sign such as *X said* (*asked, told*):

R . . . say write=down everything (R . . . said
everything should be written down)

It is of interest in this connection that the main clause–subordinate
clause order is also preferred by hearing people in constructing sentences
(Jarvella, 1972).

One exception to the above occurs with some conditional statements,
where a special sign for *if* is used. When this occurs it is usually at the

beginning of a statement. But the idea of conditionality is sometimes implied with the help of facial expression and posture rather than being expressed by the use of any specific sign, for example in:

> *I lose I club here never* (If I lose [the elections] I shall never come to the club again)

Finally, there are some sequences which seem to resist attempts at formulation, partly because of the many repetitions of signs and sign phrases (see the following section), and partly owing to the prevalence of idiosyncratic, scrambled orderings, such as:[6]

> *I weigh=up perhaps know H . . . what say* (I don't know how to decide what H . . . is worth).

McCall found that complex sentences in American SL could be formed in various ways, such as:

1. The juxtaposition of two strings without the use of a conjunction sign, for example, *John say house near town*
2. The American sign conjunctions *and, because, or, why* (Here it should be noted that there is no Israeli equivalent for *and.*)
3. The sign *if.* In such cases sign order appears to parallel English word order.

(It should be kept in mind that these signers know English and there may have been some influence of spoken language.)

For German sign sentences, Tylor (1881, p. 251) reports that the cause is signed after the effect, and is not introduced by any sign such as *because,* for example:

> *died, drank, drank, drank* (died of drinking)

The main clause–subordinate clause order observed for ISL suggested the following question: Would this order also be adhered to in sentences with *after* clauses, where it would lead to a clause order which reverses the temporal order of events? Consider the English sentence "I went home after it started raining." Here the event referred to in the main clause—which is also the first clause of the sentence—follows the event referred to in the subordinate clause. Such reversals have been found to be difficult for children (Clark, 1973). Would signers, like children, prefer

---

[6]In translating the examples it was often a difficult matter to get across all the implications. It must be confessed that we felt a little uneasy about translating concise messages like: *say health work everything municipality* as "He said that matters concerning health and work and so on were to be dealt with by the municipality."

the opposite order in this case ("after it started raining, I went home"), putting the subordinate clause first?

There were no examples in our corpus to answer this question. We turned therefore to our informant, asking him how he would sign such a "rain—go home" sequence. He gave neither of the above two formulations but suggested instead:

Suddenly it rained; at once I went home.

This shows that: (*a*) The natural order of events tends indeed to be preserved in the signing sequence; (*b*) informants do not always give the kind of answers one is looking for.

NEGATION

There were surprisingly few instances of negation in the corpus analyzed. On the whole, signs such as *not* were found to precede what was negated, for example:

not get=excited

I Arab not Jew

but there were also examples of the sign indicating negation following the sign for what was negated:

jealousy not everyone peace (there will be no jealousy . . .)

In some cases the negating sign was repeated, occurring both before and after what was negated:

not rush=me not (don't rush me)

or, using two different negation signs:

they not see nothing

In fact the only clearly consistent finding was that negative signs always occur adjacent to what is negated.

In McCall's analysis of American SL, negation seems to follow the same pattern as in English. The negating sign would usually be placed before the predicate, and where "main" and "auxiliary" verbs occurred, negation would come between them. (She cites the example *me past not here,* where *past* acts as an auxiliary indicating past tense.)

For some sign languages it has been observed that negations consistently follow what is negated. West (1960) notes this as one of the only instances of firm ordering to occur in American Indian Sign Language. Geylman (1964) found this to be the case for Russian Sign Language, as did Witte (quoted in Kainz, 1960) for early German Sign Language. It is of interest in this connection that some writers report *no* following rather than preceding the negated element in early child language and point out the parallel with SL (Jespersen, 1922, p. 136; Sully, 1924, pp. 173–1974).

INTERROGATIVES

As was the case with negation, we found only a few instances of questions in our corpus. Question signs like *why?* and *what?* tended to come at the beginning of statements, for example:

why you no look=at=me?

The sign *who?* occurred both in first and last place:

who house? (whose house is it?)

much good who? (who acts well?)

McCall's (1965) findings on ASL, here as elsewhere, seem to parallel English word order: The signs *which?* and *who?* occur at the beginning of a string, while "where a modal and intransitive verb occur in juxtaposition, order may be reversed to form questions [p. 45]." She also found this occurring with noun phrases and intransitive verbs. The signs *what?* and *where?* appeared in different ordering patterns.

Question signs, like negating signs, are reported to occur typically at the end of statements, but West (1960) found them obligatorily placed at the beginning for Indian Sign Language. Writing about German Sign Language, Witte (quoted in Kainz, 1960) says that the question word comes at the end of the utterance (as in child language, he claims).

Are There Sign Order Rules?

It is time now to take stock. The above analysis of a filmed corpus has shown that for several semantic relations there is a tendency to assign certain relative positions to the signs expressing them. These are only statistical tendencies however. With the possible exception of attribution, none of the observed regularities is adhered to without exception.

It might be argued that not too much store should be laid by spontaneously generated utterances which are prone to irregularities (errors, false starts, etc.) due to various "performance" factors. A different picture would perhaps have emerged from judgments of native speakers as to what is grammatical in their language. But acceptability judgments typically do not render two dichotomous sets of grammatical versus ungrammatical sentences; there is little agreement between judges about a vast

set of utterances which lie between the clearly grammatical and un-
equivocally ungrammatical (see, for example, Greenbaum, in press). Let
us therefore rest content for the time being with our free speech samples,
and the elicitation technique used in our experiments, and ask ourselves
what the results imply concerning the nature of Sign Language grammar.
Can the observed regularities be regarded as rules of the grammar of Sign
Language which the native speaker has incorporated as part of his linguistic competence? There seem to be two possibilities here:

1. The predominant sign order in ISL reflects the operation of a
   syntactic rule. The existence of such rules does not preclude occasional variations—even in inflectionless languages the normal word
   order is sometimes deviated from when emphasis or other special
   effects are desired.
2. There are no syntactic rules of relative position in ISL. The
   predominance of certain sign orders may be explained by the tendency to put whatever is salient first in the utterance, or other such
   psychological factors as suggested by Wundt and other writers.

The data available seem to favor the latter alternative. If 1 were correct,
one should expect that when pressed hard to convey an otherwise ambiguous message, signers would fall back on their grammatical resources
and adhere to the internalized relative position rule. Our experiments
show that this is not the case.

On the other hand, some corroboration for 2 comes from the findings of
other sign languages where usually very similar sign orders seem to
predominate. The fact that various independent sign languages have similar surface structures—which is patently not the case for spoken
languages—may indicate that the same psychological factors are at work
leading to preference of one order over another. Similar factors also
operate in spoken language and may explain the preference of one surface
form over the other, where both are synonymous or near-synonymous.
Thus, it has been found that English passive sentences are resorted to
when the goal term is focused on (Anisfeld & Klenbort 1973); otherwise,
the active voice is preferred.

Further support for the saliency hypothesis comes from a study by
Susan Goldin-Meadow (1975) of the signing of 2–4-year-old deaf children
who had no experience of a conventional sign language. Goldin-Meadow
analyzed their spontaneously created gesture language in terms of
"roles," i.e., "relational concepts such as patients, acts, recipients,
agents . . . [p. 131]." The children did not always sign all roles
explicitly, and there were certain preferred roles. These preferences were
related to the sign order adhered to by the children in the following way.

The role which was "more likely to be produced . . . occupies the initial position of the two-gesture phrase, and the less likely role occupies the second position." Now, the role more likely to be produced is presumably the one which tends to be more salient for the child. These findings also parallel the evidence for a natural word order in speaking children (Schlesinger, 1976).

Even when this argument is accepted, the status of the X + ATTRIBUTE regularity, which, as we have seen, has no exceptions, remains doubtful. Should this be regarded as just another manifestation of psychological principles, or is this a rule of relative position imposed by SL grammar? There is something strange about the idea of a grammar which has a single rule of a certain type. But on the other hand, if we disregard the binding character of this rule and assign it to the realm of "mere" psychology, what would entitle us to regard even a language which has many such rules as being governed by a grammar, as long as a psychological explanation can be found?

These reflections seem to indicate that 1 and 2 above are perhaps not really true alternatives. The early origins of grammar are anything but well documented, but it stands to reason that a grammar is built, at least in part, on the foundation of the natural tendencies of speakers, which gradually crystallize into hard-and-fast rules. If this is so, then ISL might be regarded as a language in the early stage of this process—a language on the way toward forming a grammar containing rules of relative position. Be that as it may, the question of whether ISL has a syntax with sign order rules turns out to be a rather complicated one, which cannot be answered by a simple, unequivocal yes or no.

Adjacency

While the signing sequence in ISL does not adhere steadfastly to rules of relative position, there is another principle which, as far as we know, is observed invariably: The more closely related the denotata of two signs, the stronger is the tendency to place the signs close to each other. This principle of adjacency results in much weaker claims than rules of relative position. It may be illustrated by referring to the following diagram, adapted from Wundt (1904), which sums up his findings on sign order:

object

subject   adjective   verb   adverb

This "tree" structure (presumably familiar to readers from contemporary linguistic writings) represents a hierarchical constituent structure. The constituents are ordered: Subject comes before adjective, object before verb, etc.

But, as we have seen, in ISL the order of the various branches is fixed only for subject and adjective (X + ATTRIBUTE). The object may occasionally come after the verb and adverb, and verb and adverb are still more frequently interchanged. This suggests that instead of a tree we may imagine the above diagram to represent a mobile: Each of the vertical branches (except that of subject–adjective) may turn around its axis with greater or lesser facility. The hierarchical structure is preserved, however: The terms subject, adjective, object, etc., are still firmly fixed to their branches. This means that not all permutations are possible. For example, object, verb, and adverb may appear in the sign sequence in the following permutations:

object —verb   —adverb

object —adverb—verb

verb   —adverb—object

adverb—verb   —object

The two remaining permutations are impermissible:

adverb—object —verb

verb   —object —adverb

This is because, as shown by the mobile structure, the link between verb and adverb is stronger than that between these two and the object. Similarly, verb (and adverb) and object are more strongly linked together than object and subject. From this it may be predicted that the subject will not come between object and verb, and in fact our corpus has only very few examples of GOAL + AGENT + ACTION, and none of the order ACTION + AGENT + GOAL.

The principle of adjacency is also satisfied by the sign for negation, which, as noted above, is always adjacent to the sign for the negated term. The temporal modifier is often not adjacent to the action term, but temporal modifiers may perhaps best be viewed as modifiers of the utterance as a whole (cf. the sentential adverbs of English).

That adjacency of elements which (intuitively speaking) belong together may be of greater moment than any given sequence is also suggested by one of Tervoort's studies (1968). He tried out all possible different sequences of the signs in the statement *You me downtown movie fun* (you and I go downtown to have fun at a movie) on deaf subjects fluent in signing, to see if changes in the order of signs would lead to consistently different interpretations of the sentence. He found that so long as the grouping consisted of the signs *you* and *me*, in either sequence, and the signs *movie, downtown*, and *fun*, in any order, no matter which of the two groups came first, the same approximate meaning was attributed to the statement; but inserting one or more elements from one of the above groups into the other led to ambiguity. (The question, however, remains, whether all the sequences which were comprehensible to signers were also equally acceptable.)

In sum, the adjacency principle, which is a weaker rule than any position rule, may turn out to capture most regularities of the signing sequence. Is this rule therefore to be viewed as part of Sign Language grammar? Not necessarily, because the arguments advanced above in respect to the statistical regularities of sign order apply here as well. The adjacency principle seems to apply to other sign languages as well, and presumably stems from the ''natural'' tendency to mention together what belongs together. Spoken languages too follow this principle to a large extent, but here the tendency is occasionally overridden by the grammar, which introduces discontinuous constituents. Apparently, inflections, function words, and other grammatical devices ensure the comprehensibility of utterances with discontinuous constituents, in contrast with the signed utterances that violated the adjacency principle in Tervoort's experiment.

THE GRAMMATICAL ARMORY OF SIGN LANGUAGE

The preceding section has shown that relative position of signs plays only a subsidiary role in expressing those notions which are usually expressed by a grammar. To express such notions, Sign Language has various other means at its disposal, and in the present section this grammatical armory (the term is Kroeber's, 1958) will be presented. The devices employed in SL fall under two main headings:

1. **The use of special signs.** As in several uninflected languages (notably Chinese), SL employs signs as functors to express certain grammatical relations and concepts. These special signs are often transparent, but not invariably so (their original iconicity perhaps wore off through frequent use). Occasionally—as in the case of signs expressing temporal notions—they represent a transfer of meaning to spatial concepts.

2. **The modulation of signs.** There are various ways of modifying the manner in which a sign is executed—by changing the direction of the movement, or by the addition of suprasegmental features analogous to the paralinguistic features of spoken language (see earlier section entitled "The Problem of Sign Language Grammar").

One of the more important of these devices is the **reduplication** of the sign. As shown in the following sections, reduplication may serve to indicate plurality, aspect, degree, or emphasis. In this connection the following distinction should be kept in mind. The use of reduplication as a grammatical device differs from the reduplication of a movement in signing a single lexical item. Thus the sign for *tailor* is performed by a movement repeated twice or more (imitating the action of plying a needle). Such signs, which are constituted of a repeated performance of a movement—generally with only minimal performance changes within the movement—will be considered incorrectly performed when made without such reduplication. In some cases there is a difference in meaning between the reduplicated and a nonreduplicated version of the sign. Thus the sign for *luck* when reduplicated means "loan."

Analysis of reduplication and its grammatical functions is further complicated by the tendency of signers to be repetitive (see earlier section "The Problem of Sign Language Grammar").

In the following it will be shown how SL expresses such various notions as plurality, comparison, and what takes the place of tense, prepositions, conjunctions, etc., in spoken languages. The data are mainly from our informant on ISL (our corpus was not large enough for some of these phenomena to surface). They are supplemented by several quotations in the literature pertaining to other sign languages.

Sentence Boundaries

Stokoe, Casterline, and Croneberg (1965, pp. 274–275) have described the way the end of a sign utterance is indicated in American Sign Language. It is our impression that their description fits ISL as well. These writers state that at the end of an utterance the signing hand comes to rest on the other hand, or close to some part of the body, or on some object such as a piece of furniture. If the utterance expresses a question, at its end the hands do not drop to rest as usual, but remain suspended in position, or reach out toward the person to whom the question is addressed.

In American Indian Sign Language (West, 1960) both a "paragraph final juncture'' (hands held down, folded, or crossed), and a "phrase final juncture" are described.

Number

Some signs in ISL can be rendered in the plural by reduplication, a finding also reported for American Sign Language by McCall (1965) and Fischer (1973). The reduplicated versions are not, however, "superimposed" one upon the other at the same point in space, but are executed side by side, as though a number of separate and distinct images of the same object are conjured up. Interestingly, reduplication is used to indicate the plural in at least one spoken language (Sapir, 1921, p. 60). Another way of indicating plurality is by adding the sign *all* (cf. Taylor, 1975, on Indian Sign Language), or *many* (ISL).

Temporal Concepts

Signs denoting actions and processes are not inflected for tense. Temporal notions and relations are usually rendered, by a transfer of meaning, into spatio-directional expressions. A fixed point of reference—the present time, or some other point previously established in the context of discussion—is associated with the signer's body, or one of his hands, while the other hand points, turns, or moves from this starting point in a direction analogous with the meaning intended. Movements made outward and ahead of the signer are related to "future" or "forward," while movement back toward the signer's body or over his shoulder indicate "past" or "behind." This was found for ISL and has also been reported for other sign languages (Goodridge, 1960, p. 2; Hirsch, 1961, pp. 169–170; Stokoe *et al.*, 1965, pp. 282–283; Tylor, 1881, p. 178). It is of interest to note in this connection that these spatial analogies seem natural to hearing persons (cf. Werner & Kaplan, 1963, pp. 234–235). Kainz (1960) cites experiments carried out by Witte in 1930, in which hearing persons were asked to express temporal concepts such as "today," "yesterday," "tomorrow." They used gestures very similar to those used by the deaf. In fact, the use of spatial metaphors for temporal terms is very widespread among the languages of the world (cf. Seiler, 1970).

The way temporal concepts are signed is not quite as "obvious" as would at first glance seem to be the case, however. Consider the ISL signs *before* and *after*. In both cases initially one flat hand is held horizontally, thumb parallel to the chest; the other hand is held above this "platform," palm facing the chest. To sign *before*, the moving hand is lowered toward the signer, so that it enters the space between the signer's body and the "platform" serving as reference point. To sign *after* the moving hand is lowered to the other side, so that the "platform" lies between it and the signer. It would seem as though a temporal sequence of events is perceived as a kind of procession from first to last, facing the signer, first in line being nearest to him. *Until* is expressed in ISL by moving one hand in an arc from a position where the index finger touches the other shoulder to a position where it touches the hand or forearm of the other hand. If the signer wishes to express a longer duration of time he may stretch out the arm serving as background so that the distance between point of origin and point of termination of the movement is increased to the maximum.

Here and *now* are expressed by the same sign in ISL, pointing at the ground beside the signer.

The past, present, and future for action signs are usually expressed by using the specific signs translated by the English words "past," "once," "now," "future," etc. ISL has specific signs for *day, week, morning, Sabbath*, etc., and these may be used to set the temporal context. Sometimes direction and handshape can combine to form a sort of blend such as *last=week*, or *last=year*. Once the temporal context has been established it is usually unnecessary in subsequent utterances to indicate time again, unless there is a change or a doubt about it.

The translations from our ISL corpus presented in this chapter are usually in the present time, but actually the signs referring to actions were largely neutral as to tense, the time of the event referred to being understood from the context.

In Indian Sign Language, too, tense "can be indicated where necessary by independent signs" like *now, soon*, etc. (Kroeber, 1958).

In American Sign Language, as in ISL, time can be indicated by space in relation to the signer's body, by special signs (*before, after, then, last month, next week*, etc.), or by combining these two (e.g., *month* with backward or forward movement). *Month, day*, etc., without further specification refer to the present. Still another way of representing time is by body position: Past time is indicated by the signer leaning slightly backward or inclining his head backward (Friedman, 1975).

An artificial attempt to translate temporal into spatial concepts was reported by Hutt (1968), writing about monastic sign languages. Movements in a backward direction indicated the past as in Sign Language of the deaf, but she mentions an up–down movement sometimes used to refer to the future. (Repetition of a descending movement denoting *tomorrow* rendered this *the day after tomorrow*.) Handshape differences denoted fine distinctions between French tenses. A manner of translating and differentiating among the French past simple, perfect, and pluperfect was devised for the deaf by de l'Epée (Wright, 1969), involving a "flicking of the hand" a different number of times for each of the three tenses.

Tylor (1881) believed, apparently, that the signer's facial expression "made it clear whether an event was anticipated or being recalled."

Aspect

Signers can indicate that a process or action is ongoing, recurrent, or habitual. In our corpus we found:

Here club always quarrel quarrel

Once once Arab bomb bomb shoot Israel airplane

Reduplication of the action sign here indicates a characteristic of the action. A similar way of indicating the recurrence of an activity is to reduplicate the sign indicating the time it took place. Thus, *two=year two-year* means "every two years" and *night night* means "every night." It should be pointed out that such reduplication is also frequent in the Hebrew vernacular ("day day" means 'daily', "year year" means 'yearly', etc.).

For American Sign Language Susan Fischer (1973) has explored the regularities governing the use of reduplication to indicate recurrence. She points out that whereas in those spoken languages which use reduplication the word is usually repeated once, the reduplicated sign appears generally three or more times. She also distinguishes among various kinds of reduplication (fast and slow, horizontal, rocking and regular) and shows how these are used to express the continuative, iterative, habitual, and other aspects.

Comparison and Degree

ISL has several signs which are used similarly to the ways "more" or "less" are used in English. These signs may be juxtaposed with other signs to express comparison. One of the two signs we found for *more* is made by holding the flat hand horizontal, palm down, and raising it upright by a wrist movement so that the palm faces the interlocutor. The height at which this sign is performed may express the extent of the difference intended. (An approximately converse performance of this sign is glossed as *less*. The other sign is made by two hands in contact; cf. Cohen *et al.*, 1977, sign 9.13). The two signs were used apparently interchangeably by our informant, the choice of sign perhaps stemming from whether the preceding sign involved one or both hands, or other reasons of physical convenience of performance.

We found one specific sign for *better,* but no sign for "worse." The *better* sign was sometimes used to qualify or form a comparison, for example, *this good better that* (implying that the first mentioned object, etc., is superior in some respect to the second).

Apart from the use of specific signs juxtaposed with the terms to be qualified, comparison can sometimes be iconically expressed by juxtaposing two performances of the referents to be compared, where these differ on some dimension such as relative size, height, velocity, etc., so that the intended comparison is self-evident. For instance, a certain shape is shown, followed by a larger or smaller version of the same overall shape. Thus the signs for *child* and *adult*, or *tall* and *short*, differ only in the height presented.

Smallness or largeness is indicated by holding the hands near or far from one another, presenting an extra small space between the fingers, or extending the arms wide apart. Moreover, each signer seems to have his own standard size for a sign, and any conspicuous deviation from this may serve to indicate size or degree.

In the Indian Sign Language "more" and "less" are signed by adding the signs *big* or *little*. The superlative, and also the concept "very," are indicated by the sign for *strong* (Mallery, 1879). In ISL there is no sign for "most" and we found no way in which this concept, or other superlatives, are concisely expressed. The sign *very* (made by shaking from side to side a flat hand, fingertips pointing upward, near the cheek) is used to qualify modifiers (such as *healthy, heavy*) as well as *love*.

Paraphasing, typically used to express superlatives, is illustrated by the way one of our informants signed "richest": *rich very very better everyone.*

Another way in which ISL expresses degree is by the repetition of signs: *very very, cheap cheap, rich rich, small small.* (Whereas only the first of these examples is common to English, all the other forms exist in the Hebrew vernacular too.) "A bad cold" can be rendered in ISL by *cold cold.* "He loves her very much" can be translated into ISL by *he her love love.*

A closely allied use of reduplication is in signing "a lot of" something. For example, to sign *money* one rubs the side of the index finger against the ball of the thumb (as in the popular gesture). Normally this sign would be made by just two such rubbing movements, but to indicate a lot of money the rubbings would be much more numerous.

ISL has signs expressing *excellent, special* (in the sense of specially good), *expert, fancy* (in appearance), etc., which may all on occasion be used to qualify other referents, providing another means of expressing degree.

In American Sign Language the difference between *more* and *most* is one of emphasis (size of movement), according to Falberg (1963, p. 95). The sign *most* usually precedes the modifier to which it pertains. However, where the smoothness of the movement requires this, *most* comes after the adjective; thus, "best" is signed by *better* + *most*. McCall (1965) gives some examples of how "John is older than I" may be rendered in American Sign Language:

John more old me

John old me

John more old

For "John is as old as I am" she reports the utterance:

John same old me

While ISL has several specifically intensifying signs (*very, much,* etc.), these signs themselves, as well as the signs for the referents qualified, can be performed with wide variation in their physical extent, speed, etc. Referents can often be qualified without using additional intensifier signs by such variations in performance as:

1. Amplifying the dimensions of a movement, lengthening its path, widening its diameter, etc.
2. Speeding up or slowing down the usual tempo
3. Adding an intake or expulsion of breath to the total performance
4. Adding vocalizations
5. Adding head or body movements which would not otherwise be included
6. Modifying the accompanying facial expression.

More than one of the above features may co-occur. This happens especially in the case of facial expressions, which are an almost constant accompaniment to signing.

For illustrative purposes we present in Table 3.1 the way a small selection of ISL signs are qualified.

Possession

There is a single sign in ISL indicating possession, translatable as "of." It is made by a fist, with the index finger and thumb forming a circle, their tips touching. This handshape, which is common to many other ISL signs (see Cohen *et al.*, 1977), comes between possessor and entity possessed in signing such constructions as "the car of the man."

TABLE 3.1

Examples of Intensification of ISL Signs[a]

| Sign | Intensifying features | | | |
	Amplification	Speed	Breath	Facial expression
fat	+	+	+	+
light, clear	+	+	+	+
hard	+	+	+	+
like, love	+	+	−	+
happy	+	+	−	+
beautiful	+	+	−	+
very	+	−	+	+
fed up with	+	−	+	+
wide	+	−	+	+
mean	+	−	vocalization	+ plus head movement
raining	+	−	−	+
dark	+	−	−	+
hate	+	−	−	+
sick	−	−	−	+
dirty	−	−	−	+
hurts	−	−	−	+
crowded	−	−	−	+
small[b]	−	−	vocalization	+

[a] + stands for presence, and − for absence of a given feature.

[b] The sign *small* is modified first by decreasing the space between the fingers. To sign "very small" the eyes may be narrowed; "very, very small" may be made by additionally adding a vocalization based on the Hebrew word for "small."

The *of* sign may appear in blends in personal pronouns of ISL, as shown in the section on pronouns below.

Kroeber (1958, p. 11) also mentions a single sign for possession in the Indian Sign Language.

Pronouns

Pronouns in ISL are pointing signs. Pointing at self or speech partner means *I (me)* and *you*, respectively; repeatedly swinging the index finger between interlocutor and self means "both of us," and swinging the hand round in an arc inscribing a horizontal circle between self and a group of speech partners means "all of us." Imaginary locations in space to the right and left of the main speech partner are used to indicate the third person. (We have found that the signer does not simply point at these locations to refer to absent persons, but may incline his whole body to appear to be speaking from the appropriate location when directly quoting one of these absentees.)

These pointing signs are performed with a clenched hand and extended index finger. Possessional pronouns differ from them only in the hand-shape: As in the sign for possession (see above), the tips of the index finger and thumb touch and pointing or tapping the chest is done from their point of contact.

Pointing may be incorporated into signs describing actions so as to indicate both the actor and the "endpoint" of the action. This is the device of directionality, mentioned in the earlier section entitled "The Problem of Sign Language Grammar." Thus pronouns *I, me, you, he, him,* etc., are expressed by a modulation of the action sign in *I ask you, you ask me, you ask him,* etc. Kroeber (1958, p. 11) also reports a "centrifugal–centripetal" inversion to express the distinction between, for example, "give" and "give me."

The pronouns of American Sign Language, as described in Stokoe (1972, pp. 59–61, 70–72), and Friedman (1975), those of the German Sign Language (Tylor, 1881, p. 168; Stoevesand, 1970), and the British Sign Language (Goodridge, 1960) are similarly pointing signs.

Omission of "I"

Some observers have been struck by the infrequent use of the sign for *I, me*, even comparing this phenomenon with the same omission on the part of infants acquiring speech (cf. McNeill, 1970, p. 30) and citing it as a demonstration of a kind of "egocentrism" of the deaf. However, such conclusions fail to take into account the pronounced tendency of Sign Language to incorporate pronouns into action signs, etc. In fact all signs beginning at the signer's body potentially incorporate first person, unless additional context is given to counteract this.

Negation

ISL has three general ways of negating utterances, all similar to gestures of negation used by hearing people in Israel accompanying or replacing speech. One sign is made by wagging from side to side the clenched hand, with index finger extended and pointing upward. When this is done with considerable intensity it means "forbidden." A second sign involves a headshake accompanied by a slightly frowning facial expression. The third form of negation is a slight shrugging of the shoulders with the above facial expression. The second and third forms can be performed simultaneously with other signs. A simultaneous headshake has also been found to function as negation in child language (see Bloom, 1970, p. 153).

A kind of cancellation sign, a variant of the first sign above for *no*, is made by drawing a large X in the air, and may be used by a signer when he feels he has expressed himself wrongly and wants to start his message again from the beginning.

The position of *no* signs in ISL and other sign languages has been discussed in the section entitled "Relative Position of Signs."

No signs appear as simultaneous components in several ISL signs, such as:

1. *impossible:* A downward movement of a clenched hand with two fingers spread out is the sign for *possible*. Changing the direction of this movement and simultaneously signing a *no* sign results in the sign *impossible*.
2. *disagree:* Signed like *agree* (two extended fingers touch the palm of the other hand), accompanied by a headshake.
3. *not yet:* This also involves a headshake; however, the second component of the sign, performed by the hands, does not mean "yet."

We note in passing that there are several intrinsically negative signs which do not include any of the above versions of *no, not*—for instance, *never* (resembling an Arab popular gesture), and *don't=want*,[7] which involves a movement evoking a rapid expulsion, rejection, or wafting away of something from the mouth or body. *None* or *nothing* can be signed by drawing two zeros in the air or by spreading the empty hands, palms up.

Interrogatives

Facial mimicry and posture always form a crucial part in questioning in ISL:

1. **yes–no questions:** These can be made by accompanying statements with a questioning expression, without the use of any specific question sign (rather as this may occur in spoken languages by using a distinctive rising vocal intonation). This questioning ex-

---

[7]*Don't=want*, signed thus, bears no resemblance to *want*.

pression seems to fulfill the function of an inflection. Performed simultaneously with certain signs it alters their meaning: Thus, *add=up, arithmetic* can be rendered "how much does something cost?" and *someone* becomes "who?" (In the latter case the signer may turn his head as well, as though seeking out the possible candidate.)

2. **Wh-questions:** These are made by the use of various specific question signs, all of which also include the questioning expression as an essential component.

One widely used, fairly general question sign involving rotating of hands accompanied by an appropriate facial expression may be simply translated "question" or "?". It serves for *what? how? when? where?* and *why?* with fine performance distinctions between each. Thus our informant adds a minute shrug of the shoulders to imply *why?* and turns his head very slightly from side to side, as though looking around for the right place to sign *where?* By comparison, interrogative signs of American Sign Language differ much more from each other (see the corresponding entries in Stokoe *et al.*, 1965).

The "question" sign of ISL can also be a simultaneously performed component in a compound sign: *Where?* can also be performed by adding it to *there*, and *why?* by adding it to *because*.

Another specific question sign is that for *where=from?* (where do [you] come from?). This is made by a kind of beckoning with two fingers, drawing the hand from a slight distance toward the body, and could be seen as a blend of *come (from)* with a questioning expression.

When a question is posed involving choice between two possible alternatives, the signer will often indicate each of these in a separate spatial location. For instance, in signing *coffee? tea?* (which would you prefer, coffee or tea?), the signer may make the sign for each on different sides of his body.

The place of questioning signs in the sign sequence has been discussed in the section entitled "Relative Position of Signs."

Prepositions

ISL has a number of specific signs approximately equivalent to certain English prepositions signifying spatial relationships, for example, *in-=front=of, behind, between, opposite, in, on, under, over, into, around.* All these signs are iconic, made by both hands held in a neutral or flat handshape, one hand serving as a background or reference point while the other describes the appropriate relationship to it (under, in front, etc.).

Sometimes the preposition need not be signed at all, since the way the action is portrayed in signing conveys the intended spatial relationship. For instance, to sign *climb down* the movements used for *climb up* will be reversed. Similarly, the spatial relations may often be "read off" from the way the signs for the various referents are placed relative to each other, thus making signing of prepositions unnecessary.

For American Sign Language, similar devices have been reported by Friedman (1975).

We did not find special signs for "from" or "to." These can usually be expressed by modifying sign movements so that where they begin, the direction taken, and terminal points can portray the direction or sense intended.

With or *together* is rendered by bringing two hands into proximity, keeping them on the same level.

The sign *there* is used to indicate places, especially towns and countries, and to distinguish these from nationalities, languages, etc. Thus, *England there*, *England speak*, and *England born* mean "England," "English" (the language), and "English" (the nationality).

A noniconic sign *for* (for the purpose of) is frequently used, and may have been imported, possibly based on finger spelling.

For prepositions pertaining to temporal relations see the discussion of "temporal concepts."

Conjunctions

ISL has the signs *because, for, therefore, but, perhaps, if, or, even if,* some of which are iconic and some of which bear some metaphoric resemblance to the concepts they denote.

There is no sign equivalent to "and." The signs which are to be conjoined are simply juxtaposed (sometimes with pauses between them), for example:

> *no money buy shoes sock*

> *He I friend old*

> *house clean* (pause) *elegant* (pause) *flowers around*

Occasionally, *more* is used instead of a conjunction:

> *go=trip who? first Danny more Ruth more Rina*

Alternatively, one may sign:

> *go=trip who? first Danny second Ruth third Rina*

American Sign Language has a sign for *and*, but conjoined expressions like the English "father and mother" or "eat and run" are rendered by simple juxtaposition (Stokoe, 1972, p. 66). In other respects the inventory of function words in American Sign Language seems to be largely similar to the ISL inventory (see Stokoe, 1972, pp. 63–73; cf. also Stokoe *et al.*, 1965, p. 287). Hirsch (1963, p. 170) describes the signs for *and*, *or*, and *but* in German Sign Language, by way of example, and Stoevesand (1970), who also lists signs for *therefore* and *with*, gives two additional ways to sign *and*, one of which constitutes drawing a plus sign. In British Sign Language, *and* and *but* differ only in direction of movement—left-to-right, or right-to-left (Goodridge, 1960, p. 12).

Gender

The term **gender** is used here only for convenience as a caption, for there is no gender in ISL in the grammatical sense. Sex distinctions can be made where necessary by juxtaposing the sign for *man, male* or *woman, female* with the sign it is required to modify. Thus, "grandmother" is signed by *grandparent* + *woman*, similarly, "daughter," "aunt," etc. (Our—male—informant tended to mark *girl, sister*, etc., in this way, while signing *boy, grandmother, uncle, brother*, etc., unmarked. It is not clear how consistent other signers are in using the sex marker.)

The only pair of signs in ISL which are both noncompounded and intrinsically masculine or feminine are *mother* and *father*, both opaque signs today.

In formal usage of American Sign Language, the sign for *male person* is the first element of the compounds *man, boy, father, grandfather, husband, son*, etc., and there is a similarly used sign for *female person* (Stokoe *et al.*, 1965, pp. 124–125, 172–173).

ACKNOWLEDGMENTS

We are indebted to Israel Sella, who acted as our informant, and to Mordechai Rimor (Mordecha), who helped with the experiments reported here, as well as to the many other people who participated in our project.

REFERENCES

Anisfeld, M., & Klenbort, I. 1973. On the function of structural paraphrases: The view from the passive voice. *Psychological Bulletin, 79*, 117–126.
Bloom, L. 1970. *Language development: Form and function in emerging grammars.* Cambridge, Massachusetts: MIT Press.

Bloomfield, L. 1935. *Language*. London: Allen and Unwin.

Bode, L. 1974. Communication of agent, object, and indirect object in spoken and signed languages. *Perceptual and Motor Skills, 39,* 1151–1158.

Bonvillian, J. D., Charrow, V. R., & Nelson, K. 1973. Psycholinguistic and educational implications of deafness. *Human Development, 16,* 321–345.

Bruner, J. 1975. The ontogenesis of speech acts. *Journal of Child Language, 2,* 1–19.

Bühler, K. 1934. *Sprachtheorie: Die Darstellungsfunktion der Sprache*. Jena: Fischer.

Chomsky, N. 1957. *Syntactic structures*. The Hague: Mouton.

Clark, E. 1973. How children describe time and order. In C. A. Ferguson & D. I. Slobin (Eds.), *Studies of child language development*. New York: Holt. Pp. 585–606.

Cohen, E., Namir, L., & Schlesinger, I. M. 1977. *A new dictionary of sign language*. The Hague: Mouton.

Cooper, R. L. 1967. The ability of deaf and hearing children to apply morphological rules. *Journal of Speech and Hearing Research, 10,* 77–82.

Dewey, J. 1971. The Psychology of infant language. In A. Bar-Adon & V. F. Leopold (Eds.), *Child language: A book of readings*. Englewood Cliffs, New Jersey: Prentice-Hall. Pp. 34–36.

Falberg, R. M. 1963. *The language of silence*. Wichita, Kansas: Wichita Social Services for the Deaf.

Fischer, S. 1973. Two processes of reduplication in the American Sign Language. *Foundations of Language, 9,* 469–480.

Fraser, C., Bellugi, U., & Brown, R. 1963. Control of grammar in imitation, comprehension and production. *Journal of Verbal Learning and Verbal Behavior, 2,* 121–135.

Friedman, L. A. 1975. Space, time and person reference in American Sign Language. *Language, 51,* 940–961.

Friedman, L. A. 1976. The manifestation of subject, object, and topic in the American sign language. In C. N. Li (Ed.), *Subject and Topic*, New York: Academic Press.

Fusfeld, I. S. 1958. How the deaf communicate: Manual language. *American Annals of the Deaf, 103,* 264–282.

Geylman, I. 1964. The hand alphabet and speech gestures of deaf-mutes. In E. Smith (Ed.), *Workshop on interpreting for the deaf*. Muncie, Indiana: Ball State Teachers College.

Goldin-Meadow, S. J. 1975. The representation of semantic relations in manual language created by children of hearing parents: A language you can't dismiss out of hand. Tech. Rep. XXVI. Philadelphia: Univ. of Pennsylvania.

Goodridge, F. 1960. *The language of the silent world*. Carlisle: British Deaf and Dumb Association.

Greenbaum, S. In press. Current usage and the experimenter.

Greenberg, J. H. 1963. Some universals of grammar with particular reference to the order of meaningful elements. In J. H. Greenberg (Ed.), *Universals of language*. (2nd ed.) Cambridge, Massachusetts: M.I.T. Press. Pp. 73–114.

Hirsch, A. P. 1961. Zur Genese der Taubstummengebärde. *Neue Blätter der Taubstummenkunde, 15,* 240–252.

Hirsch, A. P. 1963. Einführungsplan in die Volksgebärde. *Neue Blätter der Taubstummenkunde, 17,* 16–174.

Hutt, C. 1968. Etude d'un corpus: Dictionnaire du langage gestuel chez les Trappistes. *Langages, 10,* 107–118.

Jarvella, R. 1972. Starting with psychological verbs. Paper presented at the Midwestern Psychological Association, Cleveland, May.

Jespersen, O. 1922. *Language: Its nature, development and origin*. New York: Holt.

Kainz, F. 1960. *Psychologie der Sprache*. Vol. 2. Stuttgart: Enke.

Kroeber, A. L. 1958. Sign language inquiry. *International Journal of American Linguistics*, *24*, 1–19.

Lambert, W. E., & Paivio, A. 1956. The influence of noun–adjective order on learning. *Canadian Journal of Psychology*, *10*, 9–12.

Leont'yev, A. A. 1969. Inner speech and the process of grammatical generation of utterance. *Soviet Psychology*, *7*, 11–16.

Mallery, G. 1879–1880. Sign language among the North American Indians, compared with that among other peoples and deafmutes. First annual report of the Bureau of Ethnology to the . . . Smithsonian Institution . . . 1879–1880.

McCall, E. A. 1965. A generative grammar of Sign. Master's thesis, Dept. of Speech, Pathology & Audiology, Graduate College of Univ. of Iowa.

McNeill, D. 1970. *The acquisition of language: The study of developmental psycholinguistics*. New York: Harper.

Neumann, H. 1968. *Sprachliche Einschläge in sogenannten sprachfreien Tests*. Kettwig: Verlag Hörgeschädigter Kinder.

Paget, R. A. 1944. The origin of language. *Science*, *99*, 14–15.

Raffler-Engel, W. von. 1970. The function of repetition in child language as a part of an integrated theory of developmental linguistics. *Bolletino di Psicologia Applicata*, *97–99*, 27–32.

Sapir, E. 1921. *Language: An introduction to the study of speech*. New York: Harcourt.

Sapir, E., & Swadesh, M. 1946. American Indian grammatical categories. *Word, 2*, 103–112.

Schlesinger, I. M. 1971. The grammar of sign language and the problem of language universals. In J. Morton (Ed.), *Biological and social factors in psycholinguistics*. London: Logos Press. Pp. 98–121.

Schlesinger, I. M. 1976. Is there a natural word order? In W. von Raffler-Engel & Y. Lebrun (Eds.), *Baby talk and infant speech*. Amsterdam: Swets and Zeitlinger.

Seiler, H. 1970. Semantic information in grammar. The problem of syntactical relations. *Semiotica, 2*, 321–334.

Sella, I. 1969. *Some impressions of an Israeli signer abroad*. Working Paper No. *10*. Jerusalem, Hebrew Univ.

Shunary, J. 1969. Social background of the Israeli Sign Language. Working Paper No. *9*. Jerusalem, Hebrew Univ.

Stoevesand, B. 1970. *Tausend Taubstummengebärden*. Berlin.

Stokoe, W. C., Jr. 1972. *Semiotics and human sign languages*. The Hague: Mouton.

Stokoe, W. C., Jr., Casterline, D. C., & Croneberg, C. G. 1965. *A dictionary of American Sign Language on linguistic principles*. Washington, D. C.: Gallaudet College Press.

Sully, J. 1924. *Studies in childhood*. London: Longmans Green.

Taylor, A. R. 1975. Nonverbal communication systems in native North America. *Semiotica*, *13*, 329–374.

Tervoort, B. T. 1961. Esoteric symbolism in the communication behavior of young deaf children. *American Annals for the Deaf, 106*, 436–480.

Tervoort, B. T. 1968. You me downtown fun. *Lingua, 21*, 455–465.

Tervoort, B. T., & Verberk, A.J.A. 1967. Analysis of communicative structure patterns in deaf children. Final report Project Nr. RD-467-64-65, Vocational Administration, Department of Health, Education and Welfare, Washington, D. C.

Tylor, E. B. 1881. The gesture language. *American Annals for the Deaf, 23*, 162–178, 251–260.

Wales, R. 1971. Comparing and contrasting. In J. Morton (Ed.), *Biological and social factors in Psycholinguistics*. London: Logos Press. Pp. 61–81.

Wasow, T. 1973. The innateness hypothesis and grammatical relations. *Synthese, 26*, 38–56.

Werner, H., & Kaplan, B. 1963. *Symbol formation: An organismic-developmental approach to language and the expression of thought.* New York: Wiley.

West, La Mont, Jr. 1960. *The sign language: An analysis.* Vols. I and II. Ann Arbor, Michigan: University Microfilms.

Wright, D. 1969. *Deafness: A personal account.* Allen Lane.

Wundt, W. 1904. *Die Sprache.* Leipzig: Engelmann.

4

Contrived Sign Language

DAVID CRYSTAL
ELMA CRAIG

PROBLEMS OF DEFINITION

Questions of definition face the student of human signing behavior from the very beginning, but on the whole they have been given little systematic discussion. In the present paper, for example, we immediately encounter two widely used terms, **contrived** and **language**, yet we have been unable to discover any adequate discussion of the implication of either in the context of deafness. But it is surely particularly important to operate with an explicit and well-explored concept of language, so that on the one hand we do not subsume too much manual activity under the heading of **sign language**, whether contrived or not, and on the other hand do not exclude too much either. Without theoretical and methodological clarification, it would seem impossible to develop any typology, or even to discuss points consistently.

It is generally taken for granted that the meaning of the term "sign language" is sufficiently evident for it to form part of the postulates of any discussion. This partly reflects a reaction against traditional pejorative attitudes to signing as an essentially "inferior" or "debased" form of communication: it was only natural—though equally unsupported—to assert that signing was "just as much" a language as speech. But it presumably also reflects the state of the art: Until a reasonably detailed classification of manual communicative systems is developed, it is not surprising that similarities should be noticed at the expense of differences;

and there are evidently enough broad similarities between speech/writing and signing to motivate the extension of the term "language" from the former to the latter. However, when we come to classify signing behaviors, as required for the present paper, then these postulates need more formal support. Classification presupposes criteria of differentiation, and questions of definition are no longer able to be avoided. Are all possible signing behaviors "languages"? Are some? How should we decide, when faced with a range of phenomena to be accounted for that includes popular gesture, musical conducting, secret society signing, the American Sign Language, and the Paget Gorman Sign System? If they are all grouped together under the same heading, at what point does the application of the term "language" cease to be literal (in the sense of "spoken language") and become metaphorical (as in "the language of music")? They are presumably not all language in the same sense, but what does "language in the same sense" mean? (Cf. Bellugi & Klima, 1974, p. 6.) Some answer must be given to these questions in order to justify the selection of material made later in this paper. And there is little agreement in the literature on signing, even when the discussion is restricted to deaf signing systems. On the one hand, there are Anthony, Vetter, Fant, and others, claiming that "sign language is as much a real language as any other [Vetter, 1969, p. 233]"; on the other hand, we have such statements as that of Cohen, Namir, and Schlesinger (1977, p. 3): "Sign language differs in many respects from spoken language to a far greater extent than do spoken languages from one another"; and in between, we find such statements as Stokoe's (1972a, p. 90): "The sight, shape, and sense systems of sign language seem to be just similar enough, yet enough different, to cause maximum difficulty, maximum negative interference for the [deaf] person learning English as a second language."

There are many possible positions that can be taken up as regards the linguistic status of signing behavior, ranging from the use of unrealistically narrow formal criteria to very general consideration of functional equivalence. The former position is nowadays usually avoided, with the advent of more sophisticated typologies of language, but may be illustrated by such arguments as those which deny any linguistic status to signing on the grounds that it omits such grammatical features as inflections and function words, and operates with indistinct parts of speech. General linguistics has clearly shown how far from being universal such features of language are, and the point is probably no longer controversial. At the other extreme, we are faced with the broadly functionalist positions of such writers as Stokoe, who argues (e.g., 1960, p. 14) that "a symbol system by means of which persons carry on all the activities of their ordinary lives is, and ought to be treated as, a language." Here one might ask how essential is the emphasis of "all"? To what extent would it be arbitrary to exclude signing behaviors which have a restricted function, as in the case of racing bookmakers' tic-tac signs? Also, does this definition allow for varying degrees of signing success in "carrying on the activity of one's ordinary life"? In a more recent paper (1974), Stokoe is rightly cautious about definition. He points to the nineteenth-century belief that signing is "a single semiotic system . . . pancultural . . . a species-specific human attribute . . . universally intelligible [p. 354]," agrees that there are similarities between the various systems, but adds that only a complete and systematic comparison can succeed in showing whether they are in fact all congruent. He then argues that non-language-based signs (such as the gestures of musical conducting) are not properly language: "Some have a very limited lexicon of signs, others a narrowly circumscribed range of denotata, and most a simple and direct sign-to-signified relation which is not much like that of language. . . . Semiotic systems which have a broad or unlimited semantic range are more fittingly classed as sign languages [p. 355]." On these grounds, he follows Voegelin in denying language status to American Indian signing, in that "its use was confined to situations of fairly limited and predictable contexts [p. 355]."

This emphasis, though welcome, does not take us very far. We want to know whether these are the only criteria for language status, or whether there might be others as relevant. Also, we would like to see how the various deaf signing systems would fare when measured against the same criteria. Stokoe (1974) suggests that there are differences, but it is only at the very end of his paper that he raises the question which so far everyone seems to have begged: "How much of a language can a sign language of the natively acquired class be?" Unfortunately, there is little discussion provided, and what there is raises further questions of principle. To begin with, he proceeds to paraphrase this question as: "Does American Sign Language have duality of patterning? [1974, p. 367]." His answer is yes, and this is amplified as follows:

ASL grammar has the same general form as other grammars. There is in this language a small closed set of distinctive features, meaningless in themselves which nevertheless combine in ways peculiar to this language to form morphemes, i.e. signs which denote meaning as do the morphemes of other languages. But this language also has ways of combining these morphemes into meaningful "signs" so numerous and with so many meanings that the familiar symbol "S" represents them as well as it does the large, open, nondenumberable set of sentences in any language. Its users, like the native speakers of other languages, also reject or do not generate or produce combinations of the morphemes of the language in any but grammatical ways [p. 367].

Now there are important empirical questions here: In particular, one wants evidence for the assertion that native speakers reject certain strings as ungrammatical (see below), and that there is qualitative as well as quantitative comparability between the set of "sentences" generable in signing and speech. But for the moment, let us raise the basic question of the legitimacy of Stokoe's paraphrase: Duality of patterning is an essential feature of language design, but on what grounds may we take it to be the only salient criterion? What other criteria could there be?

One answer would be to look at the framework within which the notion of duality of patterning was originally developed. Duality is in fact well down the list of design features for language developed by Charles Hockett and others (see Hockett, 1958; Hockett & Altmann, 1968; Thorpe, 1972), and we propose to examine the remainder of this list in detail below, to see what relevance to our topic the other criteria may be said to have. But before doing so, it may be as well to anticipate an objection to this approach, arising out of Schlesinger's discussion of the relationship between signing and linguistic theory (1971, p. 99). He argues: "I see no reason to accord sign language . . . a special status as far as the problem of universality of language is concerned. We are dealing here not with finger spelling . . . but with an independent language. . . ." He continues: "To show why sign language is to be regarded as a language **in every respect**, a short description of its **uses** will be given here. . . ." These are our emphases, and they are intended to draw attention to two stages in his formulation which we consider to be weak. At the very least, we expect clarification of the phrase "in every respect," and propose to initiate some discussion on this point below. But whatever our arguments, it is unlikely that a description of language **use** by itself would be an adequate justification. Arguments to do with the formal structure of language must also be provided, and their weight properly evaluated. It is our contention that this evaluation—focused as it is on the range of application of the term "language"—must come from linguistics, and our own criteria, presented in due course, stem from a consideration of general linguistic factors (cf. also the orientation of Bellugi & Klima, 1974). Schlesinger seems to doubt the force of this orientation (1971): "To claim that sign language has no relevance to the problem of universality because it lacks a certain characteristic of syntax, or simply because it is 'primitive' . . . is to indulge in a circular argument, according to which those languages which fail to fit into a given scheme of universals of language are simply pronounced to be 'out of the game' [p. 100]." We certainly support his criticism of those unthinking attitudes which seemed to wish to exclude signing from serious intellectual inquiry, but this reasoning cannot be applied to the study of signing as a whole, in the context of linguistic science. For what else is there with which to judge the linguisticness of a phenomenon, other than a particular linguistic theory—which will presumably include "a scheme of universals of language"? Without such a datum, it is difficult to see how the dangers of overestimating or underestimating the structural or functional capacity of signing behavior can be avoided, and a coherent typology of such behaviors developed.

In this paper, then, we propose to approach the study of signing specifically from the viewpoint of the characteristics of speech. Our aim is to answer the question "How similar are the various signing behaviors to speech?" There are of course alternative ways of investigating signing, which do not put the question in quite such a linguistic way. We have done so because we see in speech the traditional focus for the application of the term "language," and because the study of the structure and function of speech has provided more detailed analytical models, capable of being used for comparative studies, than in the case of any other communicative behavior.

DESIGN FEATURES FOR LANGUAGE

In the absence of any clear or formalized semiotic theory to justify a definition of language within a taxonomy of communicative behaviors, we must start with those attempts at comparative study which postulate an arbitrary set of language properties, or design features, and then apply this grid to the classification of other signaling systems. Such approaches raise interesting questions at an appropriately general level. It should therefore be helpful to take up the suggestion made above that the inventory proposed by Hockett and others—which has generally been applied only to the study of animal communication—could be used as an evaluative framework for signing. Briefly, the 16 features of the revised list make the following claims about human speech (quotations here and below are all from Hockett & Altmann, 1968, pp. 63–64).

1. It uses a **vocal–auditory** channel.
2. There is **broadcast transmission** and **directional reception**.
3. There is **rapid fading**.
4. There is **interchangeability** (i.e., "Adult members of any speech community are interchangeably transmitters and receivers of linguistic signals").
5. There is **complete feedback** (i.e., "The speaker hears everything relevant to what he says").

6. There is **specialization** (i.e., "The direct-energetic consequences of linguistic signals are biologically unimportant").

7. There is **semanticity**, "associative ties between signal elements and features in the world."

8. **Arbitrariness** requires that "the relation between a meaningful element in a language and its denotation is independent of any physical or geometrical resemblance between the two."

9. There is **discreteness**, a lack of continuity between the elements of the signal.

10. There is **displacement** (i.e., "We can talk about things that are remote in time, space, or both from the site of the communicative transaction").[1]

11. There is **openness** (i.e., "New linguistic messages are coined freely and easily, and, in context, are usually understood").

12. **Tradition** requires that "the conventions . . . are passed down by teaching and learning, not through the germ plasm").

13. **Duality of patterning** (i.e., "Every language has a patterning in terms of arbitrary but stable meaningless signal-elements and also a patterning in terms of minimum meaningful arrangements of those elements").

14. There is **prevarication** (i.e., "We can say things that are false or meaningless").

15. There is **reflexiveness** (i.e., "In a language, we can communicate about the very system in which we are communicating").

16. There is **learnability** (i.e., "A speaker of a language can learn another language").

Not all of these properties are at this level of analysis methodologically relevant for the study of signing, of course. Property 1 is ruled out by definition, and there are restrictions on the extent of broadcast transmission and directional reception, as well as on the nature of the feedback, which are also due to the different kinds of channel being used. But some of the other differences are less trivial. The most noticeable difference between signing and speech is in respect of property 8, **arbitrariness**. The potential iconicity of signing, while varying in its extent and degree of stylization from behavior to behavior, is a point of major difference whose effect on the communicative status of the phenomenon as a whole it is difficult to assess. On the one hand, the physical resemblance of many signs to their referents must make meaning more transparent and univer-

---

[1]Note that this is a different sense from that used in the literature on signing (e.g., by Cohen, Namir, & Schlesinger, 1977), where it refers to the lack of congruence between a signing limb and the object or action it represents, e.g., signing *walk* with the fingers.

sal, thereby facilitating intelligibility and interlanguage communication. On the other hand, physical and perceptual limitations must considerably restrict the range of an iconic vocabulary, and hinder the use of various processes found to be important in the analysis of speech—for example, the process of extension and restriction of sense in metaphorical expression, and the like. Tervoort, for instance, has pointed to the rarity of spontaneous metaphorical uses of sign (1961, p. 106).

Property 10, **displacement**, is also much involved in any comparison. It would seem that many signs are dependent on the immediate context for a correct interpretation, i.e., part of the formal identity of the sign resides in the accompanying situation, and the more use that a signing behavior makes of this, the more differences from speech one must conclude there to be. Under this heading, for example, we would include what Cohen *et al.* (1977) call **covariance**—those iconic signs which vary in form depending on the nature of the accompanying object, event, etc. (for example, the sign for *carry* depends on exactly what it is that is being carried). Other examples would be the use of pointing to a specific referent for pronominal deixis, or the dependence of certain sign senses on facial expressions—for example, the contrast between positive and negative using head movement, or the use of a distinctive facial configuration as an obligatory part of a sign (e.g., *lemon* or *odor* in Israeli Sign Language).[2] Further illustrations can be found in Stokoe's commentary (1973a, pp. 14–45). The overall impression we have of signing systems for the deaf is that they are context-dependent to a degree that is unlikely in speech, and that the notion of displacement does not readily apply. The argument applies a fortiori to most of the other systems of signing referred to below, e.g., in aircraft marshaling and radio production. (We shall comment separately on the distinct notion of situational redundancy.)

[2]Whether facial expression is part of the sign or part of the context is a methodological question which most writers leave unclear. We have noted the use of the term **sign** as a formal manual notion, e.g., by Stokoe (1972a, p. 110): "A signer's hand may be performing the sign 'like' while his face and head are signalling negation." On the other hand, it is also used with reference to the semantic identity of a formal configuration which includes face, hands, etc., as in some of the examples cited below. A similar problem has been identified in prosodic studies: "Scholars have been anxious to restrict the formal definition of intonation to pitch movement alone . . .: but when the question of intonational meanings is raised, then criteria other than pitch are readily referred to as being part of the basis of a semantic effect [Crystal, 1969, p. 195]." Presumably the dilemma facing the intonation analyst faces the analyst of signing too. As Crystal goes on to say: "This is a theoretically undesirable situation, and one must make up one's mind which way to follow: either one adopts a relatively narrow definition of the phenomenon, and simplifies the formal description of intonation at the expense of the semantic, or one allows intonation a wider definition, with resultant increasing complexity in the formal stage, but an ultimately less involved semantic statement [pp. 195–196]."

Other differences between speech and signing in terms of the Hockett and Altmann list seem less significant. There would seem to be a greater use of continuous scales of signing, compared with the essential discreteness of speech (Bergman [1972, p. 21] refers to the former as an "analog language," in fact); and reflexiveness is less easy to demonstrate. But apart from these, Hockett's properties would seem to be present in a large number of human signing behaviors, and his approach accordingly makes few useful discriminations in this area. Are there, then, other differences which the limitations of this particular list of design features force us to miss? Two factors in particular seem relevant. The first of these, **dimensionality**, may be briefly mentioned; the second will be given more extensive discussion below. Dimensionality refers to the availability of two limbs, facial expression, bodily posture, etc., to allow for simultaneity of transmission of partially or wholly different messages (see the emphasis on this point in, for example, Bellugi & Fischer, 1972, p. 175). It has to be distinguished from the use of prosodic and paralinguistic features of speech, which to a limited extent have their own equivalent signing (cf. Covington, 1973). There is no possibility of simultaneous segmental or verbal use in the speech medium, and consequently the central linguistic notion of paradigmatic choice, which underlies the definition of a linguistic **system** through its implication of mutual exclusiveness of items (see below), would seem to require much modification before being applicable to signing.

ISOMORPHISM BETWEEN SPEECH AND SIGNING

The second question left unasked by the Hockett list is the extent to which there is a general correspondence between the structure of language and that of signing behavior. Presumably the more we can establish isomorphism between the two, the more plausible the ascription of the term "language" to signing will seem to be. As an initial orientation, we can take the generally used account of linguistic structure that recognises three levels, or components: phonology, grammar, and lexicon. According to Stokoe (1973b), signing displays three comparable levels: "Sign is a natural language like hundreds of others on the face of the earth. It has its own symbolic, syntactic, and semantic system [pp. 14–15]." But how comparable, quantitatively and qualitatively, are these systems to those recognized in speech? If we take the lexical level, which is where most of the discussion has centered, it is clear that there is a certain correspondence between sign (however defined) and lexical item, or lexeme, but that the differences between, say, English and the most sophisticated signing behaviors must not be underestimated. The purely quantitative dimension cannot be simply dismissed—contrasting the three-quarters of a million items of contemporary English with the 6000 items of Seeing Essential English, the 2500 items of the Paget Gorman Sign System, or the 3000 morphemes of the American Sign Language, for example. It is not purely a pragmatic question of the number of signs increasing to comparable levels of productivity in the course of time. There is considerable doubt as to whether visual acuity can cope with any increase of such an order—of whether, for example, the signing behavior would not come to contain an intolerable amount of visual formal ambiguity, owing to limitations on the number of visually discriminable items. As Bergman says (1972, p. 22), "Owing to physiological limitations it is doubtful whether the total number of signs in ASL will ever exceed five thousand."[3] These are interesting, but generally uninvestigated questions. Moreover, there is the point that as vocabulary increases, it must surely become increasingly difficult to retain an unambiguously iconic relationship between referent and sign, or for visual memory to be able to cope with the number of arbitrary sign distinctions such as would make the signing behavior comparable to that of speech. (Similar points have been made in discussion of the merits and demerits of alphabetic systems, e.g., the learnability of phonemic as opposed to logographic writing.)

At the phonological level, apart from the writing-based codes such as finger spelling, there is no isomorphism between segmental phonology and signing behaviors, and only partial equivalence in the nonsegmental area. The absence of any equivalent for segmental phonology has of course always been recognized as a difficulty—for example, in relation to the signing of proper names, where finger spelling is regularly resorted to. Cohen *et al.* (1977) conclude: "In this respect the barrier between sign and spoken languages is much greater than that between any two spoken languages." Recent work has added a great deal to our knowledge of the nature of duality in signing (e.g., Battison, Markowicz, & Woodward,

---

[3]We do not see how this can be reconciled with the view that "a correctly trained signer can express himself in ASL with the utmost precision, whatever the nuances of meaning may be [Bergman, 1972, p. 22]." If this were so, it is difficult to see why there should be so much finger spelling (as indicated by Tweney & Hoemann, 1973, p. 78; Vetter, 1969, p. 238, and below). Similar claims are frequently made, e.g., Stokoe (1972a): "Because American Sign Language is the medium of communication used by a community of people . . ., anything expressible in another language can be expressed in it [p. 63]." These claims are premature, and hide massive methodological problems. Stokoe makes some progress in establishing equivalence between some of the most frequent words of written English and ASL, but it is not in the area of the most frequently occurring (largely unproductive, grammatical classes of) words that the problems of semantic precision, nuance, and the like mainly lie.

1975), but the distinctiveness of the units postulated at the "phonological" level is still in need of clarification, e.g., the level of abstractness at which the units operate (cf. Battison *et al.*, 1975 p. 293), and criteria which can place the proposed **emic** signing system into correspondence with that of speech now need to be evolved.

But it is under the heading of grammar that the comparative question is raised in its most crucial form, and here the evidence is unclear. Under this heading, we subsume both morphological and syntactic variation. To what extent do signing behaviors operate with any morphological or syntactic constraints? In view of the centrality of these notions for linguistic theory, establishing their role in any signing behavior is evidently fundamental, and the literature contains many generally phrased impressions of the situation. The absence of inflections and function words is frequently referred to, as we have already mentioned; Cohen *et al.* (1977, p. 23) talk about the "telegraphic style of sign language"; and the flexibility of sign order has also often been pointed out. But before we can investigate this question in detail, some terminological clarification seems necessary. It is widely accepted that signing is concept based. Sign language is an "idea language" (Madsen, 1972, p. 2) is a typical statement. Writers then conclude that the ordered properties evident in signing are essentially cognitive; for example, Vetter (1969, p. 235) talks about the "logical or natural" order of signs, Stokoe (1973a, p. 11) of the "larger to smaller units of reckoning" in the expression of time relationships as an utterance proceeds. Confusion enters in when one proceeds to talk about these essentially cognitive strategies using linguistic terminology, as to a great extent this begs the question. This is most readily illustrated with reference to the notion of the "syntax" of signs. An early example is in Mallery (1881):

> The reader will understand without explanation that there is in the gesture speech no organized sentence such as is integrated in the languages of civilization, and that he must not look for articles or particles or passive voice or case or grammatic gender, or even what appears in those languages as a substantive or a verb, as a subject or a predicate, or as qualifiers or inflexions. The sign radicals, without being specifically any of our parts of speech, may be all of them in turn. There is, however, *a grouping and sequence of the ideographic pictures*, an arrangement of signs in connected succession, *which may be classed under the scholastic head of syntax* [pp. 359–360]. (italics ours)

That this is a nonlinguistic conception of syntax is made clear a little later, where, in comparing Indian signing to that of the deaf, he asserts that they are similar "in figuring first the principal idea and adding the accessories successively in the order of importance, the ideographic expressions being in the ideologic order [p. 363]." Talking about sign syntax in this way, however, is highly misleading, and it is unfortunate that the metaphor has become so widespread. On the one hand, it is difficult to see what might constitute an agreed counterexample to the hypothesis that signing is "rule-governed" in a syntactic sense, as presumably any signed sequence might be said to reflect some particular process of conceptual ordering on the part of the user—this latter, however, being inaccessible to observation. On the other hand, it implies that the rules of the signing behavior are as conventional, well formed, and discrete as those of spoken syntax, and this is at best debatable, as will be discussed below.

How far are there syntactic constraints in signing comparable to those operative in speech? Our general impression is that there is little in common. Stokoe, working on American Sign Language, is the main investigator who has faced up to the importance of syntax (e.g., 1972a, p. 13) and attempted to investigate this question systematically, but even he comes up with very little, and most of his rules are capable of analysis in cognitive terms—for example, it is claimed that time adverbs are initial in an utterance, that conditional clauses precede result clauses, and that there are restrictions on subject–verb collocability. More detailed instances, in conventional syntactic terms, are: "Either/or" questions end in *which*; second person questions often end with the second person pronoun; verbs have mood, phase, and aspect variation, but not tense (see Stokoe 1973a, pp. 8–9; 1974, p. 95). Sentence boundaries are formally marked (Covington, 1973). In Israeli Sign Language, Schlesinger (1971) concludes that adjectives follow nouns, and that verbs do not occur initially, but he allows (p. 113) that cognitive saliency may have been a determinant of order in his experiment. Reduplication seems an important general process for expressing syntactic relations (Bornstein, 1973, p. 455), but it has been little studied. We are thus left with a number of isolated examples of types of potential syntactic significance, but no sense of a coherent, autonomous, formal system.[4] And even with the examples cited above, there is tentativeness over generalization. As a writer in *Signs for the Times* (11, 1972) said: "Some signers use some of the rules some of the time." For the most part, discussion of a "syntax" for signing is carried on in negative terms—there are **no** equivalents to such and such a feature in English (etc.) syntax.

A linguistic metalanguage is also used in the more detailed analyses of

---

[4]Autonomy refers back to the question of displacement, and is discussed below. There are a number of rules whose status is debatable because it is unclear how productive they are in displaced situations, for example, according to Stokoe (1972b, p. 87), agent/patient is distinguished by head–eye movement: "The signer's eyes, often with appropriate movement of the whole head, move *from* the agent *to* the patient."

signs. Stokoe, for example, suggests that within the structure of a sign, one component may be used in a "subordinate" way to "modify" another—for example, (1973a, p. 20), he points to the use of the eyes and face to modify the concept of *driving*, thus adding "adverbial" force, as in *driving sleepily, driving eagerly*. He emphasizes that there is considerable potential for communication here: "If close replicas of various English syntactic structures are not to be found, there is still no cause to find ASL syntax restricted; for the analogic representation in space, time and motion, over and above the separability and cooperative capability of hands and face, makes a continuum of subordination possible [1973a, p. 20]." A little earlier in the same paper (pp. 15–16), as part of his analytic commentary on a signing text, Stokoe illustrates the conceptual complexity which can be derived. He describes the use of the *light* sign used in the story to convey the visual experience of the night driver. In addition to the basic hand configurations, other positional and dynamic variables are used to produce an effect glossed in translation as "lights–tiny–glow–growing–bigger–and–bigger–glare–in–eyes." Stokoe concludes (p. 16) that "it is possible . . . to suggest that some of sign syntax must be manifested within the sign," and he draws a parallel with polysynthetic languages and the notion of the "syntax of the word."

But is this a legitimate parallel? We are of the opinion that there is no "syntax" in such signs, in the usual sense of this term; they are rather **configurations** of features (cf. Bellugi & Fischer, 1972, p. 176), interrelated primarily by the observer's awareness of cognitive probabilities—for example, a screwing up of the eyes may mean "glare" in the context of a story about night driving, but in a story about problem solving it might be glossed as "difficulty." Moreover, while kinesic and other effects are undoubtedly more important for the signer than the speaker, it is an open question whether the use of these effects in the two media is anything more than a difference of degree. The complexity and subtlety of these effects in conversation between hearing people has only recently begun to be appreciated, but it is obvious that semantic nuances of the type illustrated by the above example could equally well be carried kinesically in the context of speech. In which case, possibilities of terminological confusion abound, for if one includes kinesic variables under the heading of syntax for signing, one would in all consistency have to do likewise for speech, and one would end up with two senses of syntax for the latter. The most important argument, however, is that there is little evidence in signing of the formal sequential constraints of sign upon sign comparable to the constraints of word order in speech. What would this evidence consist of? One of the clearest supports for the view that signing is a language would come from the demonstration of unacceptable sequences.

As Gleitman, Gleitman, & Shipley (1972) say: "The one task that provides the main data base for modern grammatical theories [is] . . . whether a sentence is or is not well-formed [p. 138]." Woodward (1973), for example, asserts that "people can and do make mistakes in ASL [p. 82]," but there is no illustration (cf. also Fischer, 1973, p. 11). We have found no discussion of what would count as a mistake, but two papers (Schlesinger, 1971, and Tweney & Hoemann, 1973) have investigated experimentally aspects of signing acceptability and these do shed some light on the linguisticness of signing.

In Schlesinger's experiment, two signers tried to communicate message sequences involving subject, direct object, and indirect object; it was found that the subjects did "very poorly . . . their degree of comprehension was quite low [pp. 114–115]." He comments: "The reason is that there is apparently no rule which all users of ISL employ consistently to distinguish between the subject, the direct object and the indirect object [1971, p. 115]." He goes on: "A rule can be said to belong to the competence of users of a language only if they are able to use it consistently either in encoding or decoding. In our experiment such consistency was crucial for success in the task imposed on the subject, but no consistency was found [p. 115]." In the light of this, his conclusion reads surprisingly: "All this does not imply that the 'original' ISL has no syntax. There seem to be at least two rules adhered to steadfastly by all signers: one, concerning the sequence of the noun and its modifying adjective, the second specifying where the verb may *not* appear in the declarative sentence [p. 115]." It perhaps does not need emphasizing that the distance between a communicative system which has two, or three, or ten rules and the syntactic rules of speech is very great. Schlesinger, however, is more concerned to discuss why it is that ISL can do without the fundamental relations (subject of, etc.), when "experience shows that ISL is an adequate vehicle for everyday give and take of the deaf [p. 115]." He does not go into the question of adequacy (to deal, for example, with degrees of achievement, or what counts as "give and take"), but argues that his informants did not do well in this experiment because it posed them with problems they were not used to. Normally these grammatical rules are unnecessary in signing, "because the situation is usually such that the meaning is unambiguous," whereas "in our experiment the unusual lack of situational redundancy may have made it too hard for some of our subjects to supply enough linguistic context [p. 116]." But the implications of this reasoning for the notion of "sign language" are serious. In discussing the relevance of his experiment to the question of universals as viewed by a transformational approach, Schlesinger refers to the fundamental distinction between cognitive structures and linguistic structures. What his experiment shows, it seems to us, is the reliance of ISL users on certain common cognitive (or possibly semantic) structures or strategies. We have seen that there is little evidence for any formal syntactic linguistic patterning. To talk about "language," then, when what is being referred to is cognitive organization, seems to us a confusion of levels. This experiment, in other words, can offer little direct support to the view that signing contains a syntax in a linguistic sense.

The second experiment was carried out by Tweney and Hoemann (1973) using back translation. Written English sentences were translated by a deaf adult into ASL, the resultant signs videotaped, and played back to a second adult deaf person who translated it back into English. The two versions were then compared. The basic results show considerable preservation of meaning, within the restrictions of the experiment (no further context was supplied, the participants were not allowed to ask further questions, etc.)—about 27% resulted in no change, and a further 63% produced semantic equivalence. They conclude (1973, p. 67): "While the frequency of structural changes in back translation supports the view that ASL is a separate language differing in important ways from English, there was no evidence that ASL is an inferior language" (though for some reason they see as exceptional to this statement "the frequent loss of plural markers"). They feel that the misconceptions about the nature of ASL as a language system have been due to the lack of appropriate tools for its study. They criticize the use of literal glosses for signing sequences (as in Tervoort, 1968): "Literal glosses of ASL tend to obscure the subtlety and sophistication of distinctions that ASL is capable of making, just as literal translations of any language lend themselves to ethnocentric judgments that the other language sounds crude and inferior compared with the native speaker's [p. 69]." These distinctions are such events as facial expression, body posture, and spatial localization: "Presumably a formal grammar of ASL would need to incorporate these features of manual communication in its treatment. The difficulty facing a formal grammar of ASL is not that ASL is 'ungrammatical,' but that it is grammatical in a different sense than spoken language [p. 69]." Earlier (p. 62), they suggest that it may be these features that might resolve Schlesinger's paradox, referred to above.

We certainly support the emphasis of this research, and look forward to its extension to other cases. But it leaves the question of linguistic status very much open. One criticism was made by Stokoe, in a comment on the paper in the same number of *Sign Language Studies* (2, 1973), who doubted the generalizability of the experiment's results, on the grounds that the investigators examined only one variety of sign language (what Stokoe calls the "high" diglossic variety: See 1969; 1972a, p. 125 ff.), and that this was the kind which was most English influenced. The implication of this criticism, of course, is that if they had used the "low" variety, less influenced by English, and continued to use back translation as a method, there would have been less equivalence between the translations, and the difference between ASL and spoken language would have been much greater. For Stokoe, this reflects on the inadequacy of back translation as an analytic method. For ourselves, we have noted the use of back translation successfully as a regular part of foreign language teaching procedures, and feel that if it is unable to be used in relation to "low" variety ASL, this is in effect a recognition of the distance away from spoken language that ASL is.

A second point concerns the role of kinesic and proxemic features. Tweney and Hoemann are right to emphasize the need to study these factors, but it would be premature to assume that the answer to their questions will necessarily be found in this area. There is the point already made, that these features co-occur with speech too, and that therefore the grammar in this respect may not turn out to be so different as Tweney and Hoemann anticipate. But in addition, it should be emphasized that there are only so many discriminable kinesic/proxemic possibilities, and many of these are semantically nonspecific. It is therefore debatable how productive a "grammar" of these phenomena could be, or whether it could in principle provide the degree of precision to make signing comparable to speech. The basic problem is that we are dealing here with behavioral continua, not discrete segments, and with patterns that do not display any duality of structure. These basic differences between the "verbal" properties of speech and the "nonverbal" aspects of behavior have for too long been played down. It is in fact only recently that some of the distortions and simplifications of extending the notion of phoneme (originally devised to handle variability in sound segments) to the area of nonsegmental phonology (thus talking about pitch, stress, and juncture "phonemes") have come to be widely discussed, though the basic criticisms have been around since the 1940s (see Bazell, 1954, p. 133; Bolinger, 1949, 1951; Crystal, 1969, 1974). Haas (1957, p. 159) has criticized the "segmental principle," as he put it—that all things reduce to unit-segments—as being a major prejudice in the linguistic field. And the criticism that discrete techniques are dubiously applicable to gradient phenomena presumably applies all the more to those other areas of human behavior that Pike (1967) used the notion of "-eme" to help describe. It is too early to say, but there are grounds for thinking that a formal grammar of kinesic effect cannot be written—or at least, there are grounds for doubting whether these features can carry the weight of interpretation that Tweney and Hoemann suggest they have. We accept that they have some relevance to syntax, but do not feel (*pace* Stokoe, 1960, p. 63) that they are "the key to syntactical structure." Rather we feel that (as in the case of Schlesinger) it is the factors of situation and presupposition that explain most semantic equivalence—and these are not linguistic factors. And we await the presentation of evidence which will show that kinesic features are being used differently in connection with signing than in connection with speech.

CLASSIFICATORY CRITERIA FOR SIGNING BEHAVIOR

Our argument so far may be summarized as follows. In order to investigate those behaviors generally referred to as "sign language," it was necessary to develop classificatory criteria. It seemed likely that the term "language" would provide a useful starting point for inquiry, and that some usable criteria would emerge from a consideration of communicative design features (such as Hockett's) and from the literature on signing in the deaf. We have however found that Hockett's features are not wholly applicable and are in need of extension when used with reference to types of human signing (presumably because of its original zoosemiotic orientation), and subsequently that the literature on signing is inexplicit and inconclusive regarding its use of the term "language." We have not found the criteria we were looking for, and consequently we have found it necessary to suggest our own. We have therefore selected 12 characteristics of language, which we feel are at or near the center of any definition of that phenomenon, and which seem to be sufficiently specific to permit a meaningful classification of a wide range of human signing behaviors.

A. **Productivity**. An infinite number of meaningful units (cf. "sentences") can be generated.

B. **Finiteness**. The rules governing the construction of these units are finite and learnable.

C. **Range**. The vocabulary is capable of indefinite extension.

D. **Reciprocity**. The majority of the units are conventionally understood by the whole of some community (cf. "speech community"), there being some formally definable standard of shared usage.

E. **Acceptability**. Some units will be considered unintelligible by all members of the community, and some will be considered intelligible but unacceptable in terms of their formal structure.

F. **Constituency**. Some units can be analyzed into a string of minimal meaningfully contrastive formal units (cf. "morphemes").

G. **Hierarchy**. There will be at least one level of formal organization between the level of the largest formally definable unit of meaningful sequence (cf. A) and that of the minimal meaningful unit (cf. F).

H. **Idiom**. The meaning of larger units is not necessarily analyzable as the sum of the meanings of the smaller units out of which it is constructed.

I. **Duality**. Each minimal meaningful unit is identifiable with reference to a set of minimal distinctive but meaningless elements (cf. "phonemes," "distinctive features").

J. **Systemicness**. The minimal meaningful units are organized into systems. A system has finite membership, and the units are mutually exclusive and mutually defining (cf. Quirk *et al.*, 1972, p. 46; Halliday, 1961).[5]

K. **Autonomy**. If a set of minimal units constitute a system, there will be theoretical interdependence between the units, such that every unit is capable of being defined in terms of some other unit; there is no essential dependence on events or phenomena outside the system (cf. Hockett's "displacement").

L. **Disambiguation**. There are ambiguous formal sequences, some of which are capable of having the ambiguity resolved through the use of transformational processes.

Using these 12 criteria, some of the salient differences and similarities between the various forms of signing behavior that have all on occasion been referred to as "languages" can be established. These behaviors include:

1. Various kinds of symbolic dancing or pantomimic activity, e.g., classical or Thai (see Coomaraswamy & Duggirala, 1917; Mawer, 1932; Zung, 1937)

2. Religious or quasi-religious ritual signing, such as the Masonic, Hung (see Knight, 1818; Ward & Stirling, 1925)

3. Monastic signing, e.g., of the Cistercians, the Benedictines (see Barakat, 1969; Herrgot, 1726; Hutt, 1968; Rijnberk, 1953)

[5]"Mutual exclusiveness" requires that at a given place in a sequence, only one unit from a given system may be used; "mutual definition" requires that it is possible (and usually more economical) to state the meaning of an item in terms of the other members of the system than in terms derived from outside that system. Standard examples of grammatical systems would be the personal pronouns, determiners, and auxiliary verbs. Bellugi and Klima (1974) in their work argue for the importance of the notion of systemicness "based on recurring shared elements or aspects of signs [p. 36]," emphasizing the importance of such evidence as slips of the hand.

4. Signs used in sports or entertainment, e.g., between acrobats, cricketers, in musical conducting.
5. Signs for conversation on restricted areas in certain speech communities, e.g., Indian, Aborigine, Neapolitan (see Mallery, 1881; Rosa, 1929; Roth, 1897; Seton, 1918; Tomkins, 1926)
6. Signs used in various professions: gambling casinos (to indicate the state of play, or problems that might affect the participants in a game), theaters and cinemas (signaling the number and location of seats), sales and auctions (signaling type and amount of selling or buying), aviation marshaling (signaling direction and position of aircraft, state of the engines), radio and television direction (signaling amount of time available, instructions about loudness levels, etc., information about faults and corrections; see Carlile, 1947), diving (signaling depth, direction, time, and kinds of personal difficulties; see Becker, n.d.), truck driving (signaling difficulties, courtesy, information about the state of the road), crane driving (signaling direction of movement), the fire service (signaling directions concerning the supply of water, pressures, and use of equipment), bookmaking (signaling the number of a horse or race, and its price), and those tasks where environmental noise makes auditory communication difficult (e.g., in cotton mills).

A general discussion of these areas may be found in Critchley (1939) and West (1960); some further information is given in Stokoe (1974) and Brun (1969). With very little empirical work having been done, it is accepted that any classification is arbitrary to some extent, and that generalizations about the defining characteristics of any signing behavior are tentative in the extreme. Nonetheless, we have attempted to analyze a sample of these behaviors using the 12 linguistic criteria above, and hope that despite the proliferation of question marks (which reflect our lack of knowledge) some interesting tendencies will emerge (see Table 4.1).

The genesis of this table may be seen by illustrating from radio and television signing. The signs used by a radio/TV director to people on the air may be characterized as follows:

A. They have a certain, limited productivity (signs can be used recursively for specifying the amount of time or variation in loudness required).
B. They are finite.
C. The vocabulary is extremely limited; certain semantic fields only are used.
D. The director's signals will be understood by the person on the air,

TABLE 4.1.

Classificatory Matrix for Signing Behaviors

	A	B	C	D	E	F	G	H	I	J	K	L
Cricket signs	−	+	−	+	+	−	−	−	−	?−	−	−
Aviation marshaling } Truck/crane driving }	?+	+	−	+	+	?−	−	−	?−	?+	−	−
Orchestral conducting	+	+	−	?+	+	?−	?−	−	?−	?+	?	?
Radio/TV signaling	?+	+	?−	+	+	?−	?−	−	?	+	?	?
Divers' signs	+	+	−	+	+	+	?	+	?−	+	?	−
Indian signs	?+	+	?−	+	+	+	?	+	?−	+	−	?−
Symbolic dancing	+	+	−	+	+	+	?+	−	?−	+	?	?−
Tic-tac signing	+	+	−	+	+	+	+	−	−	+	+	−
American Sign Language	+	?+	?−	?	?+	+	?	+	?+	?+	−	?
Paget Gorman Sign System, etc.	+	+	?−	+	+	+	+	+	+	+	+	+
Speech	+	+	+	+	+	+	+	+	+	+	+	+

159

and he may (hence the question mark) use signals from the same set in return.

E. There are many contradictory signals (e.g., "speak up" versus "speak quietly"), and these would not be used in direct sequence.

F,G. It is unlikely, but unclear from our sample, whether there is any constituent structure.

H. No instances of idioms were found.

I. It is possible that some of the signals can be analyzed in terms of duality, but on the whole this was not so.

J. There are clear formal systems, related to the various semantic fields (e.g., time qualification, loudness level, fault specification, movement direction), each containing a finite, mutually exclusive set of elements.

K. Many of the signs are dependent on physical characteristics of the ongoing situation.

L. There is no evidence of disambiguation using the signs; writing is often used when further clarification is needed.

Comparing the various signing behaviors with each other, it is possible to detect a gradual increase in complexity in respect of their formal characterization, and we tentatively propose categories as follows:

1. Behaviors (e.g., cricket, aviation marshaling, truck and crane driving) which satisfy the criteria of finiteness, acceptability, and reciprocity, but containing little or no systemic organization of elements (i.e., the signs are more like an inventory than a system).

2. Behavior (such as orchestral conducting) where, in addition to being finite, acceptable, and reciprocal, there is evidence of more complex systemicness in operation and a wider semantic range.

3. Behaviors (such as the case of radio/TV direction) where in addition to the above some productivity must be recognized (though of a very limited kind), and where there is more structuring of the semantic fields involved (possibly suggesting the existence of some duality and constituency).

4. Behaviors (such as Indian signs) which in addition to the above have more productivity and range, and more formal structure (constituency, duality, and idiom).

5. Behaviors (such as some systems of symbolic dance) where, in addition to the above, there is a measure of autonomy. A clear example of this is tic-tac signing (Brun, 1969).

6. Artificial signing systems for the deaf, such as Signing Essential English or the Paget Gorman Sign System (see below), are clearly linguistic in respect of these criteria, though there is the doubtful

question of the extent of their lexical range, referred to above. ASL, it will be seen, falls in between these systems and the others, though nearer to the former. The question marks in the line for ASL primarily identify areas for empirical research, but it is worth pointing to two areas in particular, D and E (Reciprocity and Acceptibility). **All** other signing behaviors are positive in respect of these criteria: it would therefore seem crucial for ASL's status to determine the facts here (cf. the discussion of the experimental reports above).

The point of introducing a matrix of this kind is that it helps to identify the salient contrasts between signing behaviors: As we move down the table, we encounter more conceptual organization and more formal structure in the behaviors. In other words, more can be said—there are more things to be said, and more means for unambiguously specifying them. It is premature to draw any firm conclusions, when so little empirical work has been done (on even the "high" varieties of ASL), but we do feel confident in stating that the assumption that signing behaviors in general are capable of description in linguistic terms is wrong, and that it would be preferable to talk instead in some more neutral way. We ourselves prefer to use the term **system** until such time as one can demonstrate a reasonable isomorphism between a signing behavior and the structure and function of spoken language. Perhaps in the end the choice of term is unimportant; but what cannot be shrugged aside is the fact that signing behaviors display different kinds and degrees of structural isomorphism with spoken language,[6] and this must be taken into account in the premises of any discussion.

CONTRIVED SIGNING SYSTEMS

We now feel in a position to make some typological remarks about those systems which are at the "most linguistic" end of the signing continuum—positive in respect of all or nearly all of the above criteria. These systems, the signs of which are in a one-for-one correspondence with the words or morphemes of spoken English, have not developed naturally, though most of them have incorporated as raw material some of the data of natural signing. They may therefore fairly be called **contrived**.

1. *Seeing Essential English* (1971), edited by D. A. Anthony, with a number of contributors, provides written descriptions, based on

---

[6]It is also likely that similar reasoning will be applicable to claims made about functional parallels; it is debatable, for example, whether the range of sociolinguistic functions for a signing system for the deaf is equivalent to that of speech.

one-handed finger spelling, of approximately 6000 signs. It is published by the Educational Services Division, Anaheim Union High School District, P.O. Box 3520, Anaheim, California 92803.

2. *Signing Exact English* (1972), edited by G. Gustason, D. Pfetzing, and E. Zawolkow, provides line drawings and written descriptions of approximately 1400 signs. It is published by Modern Signs Press, National Association of the Deaf, 814 Thayer, Silver Spring, Maryland 20910.

3. *Linguistics of Visual English* (1971), edited by D. J. Wampler, and published by Early Childhood Education Department, Aurally Handicapped Program, Santa Rosa City Schools, Santa Rosa, California 95402. (We have been able to see only a small part of this material, while preparing this paper).

4. *Signed English* (1969). *Signs for Instructional Purposes*, edited by B. Kannapell, L. B. Hamilton, and H. Bornstein, and in a number of subsequent writings, provides a series of children's books of drawings. It is published by Gallaudet College Press, Washington, D.C. 20002.

5. *Paget Gorman Sign System* (1964, revised 1970), formally known as "A Systematic Sign Language" (see Paget, 1951), edited by G. Paget and P. Gorman, provides 2500 signs. At present, this material is restricted to those who can attend a course of instruction (as is the case with item 3 above). Information is obtainable from the Association for Experiment in Deaf Education, Royal National Institute for the Deaf, 105 Gower Street, London WC1. (A discussion and analysis of this system is to be found in Craig, 1973.)

6. *Improved Techniques of Communication* (1970), edited by H. W. Hoemann, with a number of other contributors, is a training manual which provides line drawings and written descriptions of approximately 270 signs (assuming knowledge of ASL).

The aims of these systems are broadly similar. In *Seeing Essential English*, for example, the aims are said to be "the presentation of English as a visual, visible medium to complement speech . . . to introduce English to manual communication, to effect a marriage between the two, to meet a social as well as an educational need, and to give shape and form to English language processes . . . not only to give but to get from the deaf ease of communication and speed of comprehension in correct colloquial English [p. ix]."

The eight aims of the *Paget Gorman Sign System* read as follows:

1. To provide correct patterns of English to enable the deaf child to learn language at an age which is more commensurate with the natural optimum age for language

learning in normally hearing children. 2. To increase the deaf child's comprehension by giving clearer patterns of correct language than those which are available to him by speechreading alone. 3. To enable the deaf child to build up an understanding of correct language in conjunction with speech and speechreading; to provide a sound foundation for the future use of speech and speechreading to be used by themselves where possible, or for correct fingerspelling to be used where this form of communication is considered to be the most appropriate for the individual concerned. 4. To encourage in the deaf child a desire to communicate verbally. 5. To accelerate the learning of all school subjects by providing clear unambiguous patterns of correct language. 6. To encourage the deaf child to express English which would be considered acceptable for his age and environment. 7. To increase the probability of the deaf child's reaching a reading level which would enable him to read with facility. 8. To offer a method of remedial teaching for those deaf children, or other language disordered children, whose language has not been adequately developed by other methods of teaching [pp. 18–19].

These in turn relate readily to the list of aims of *Signed English*, as given by Bornstein (in *Signed English: A Manual Supplement to Speech Intended to Further Language Development*): that it be usable at home as well as school; that it be attractive and pleasurable for child and adult; that it be informal and nonacademic in character (no grammar or metalanguage imposed upon the adult); that each aid be self-contained (usable without recourse to other materials or system logic); that it be supportive of pleasant experiences with books; that it provide the child with access to our common cultural heritage; and that it meet the immediate practical needs of the home.

All these systems are designed to supplement and not replace speech; and all are in the process of development, with additional signs being regularly added. All the systems have as a main aim some degree of isomorphism with English discussed in general terms earlier in this paper. They may therefore be classified in terms of which particular areas of English they choose to make their primary focus, and the extent to which they have developed a signing system which replicates these areas of English in all or most formal respects. In this way we recognize the following taxonomy of possibilities:

1. All the above are systems where the aim is to follow the language's syntax as closely as possible, and autonomously (i.e., there is no dependence on some other code or medium). They may thus be distinguished from signing behaviors where there is no such aim (as in many of the naturalistic, concept-based types) and those systems where the language's syntax exercises a varying influence on the signing (as with some varieties of ASL).
2. The syntactic systems may now be subclassified in terms of whether they aim to represent morphological structure in addition to syntax.

All the above have a morphological level, which is used in varying degrees. They are therefore distinct from the general use of Siglish (Fant, 1972, p. iii), which follows word order without morphological variation. *Linguistics of Visual English (LVE)* and *Seeing Essential English (SEE₁)* analyze morphological processes most fully; *Signed English (SE)* has so far introduced little at this level, and is not concerned with an internally consistent level of representation. *Signing Exact English (SEE₂)* and the *Paget Gorman Sign System (PGSS)* fall between these extremes, in respect of the amount of morphological structure explicitly represented.

3. In addition, we have to recognize a further distinction which crosscuts the above to some extent, namely, the fact that the *PGSS* gives formal representation to a notion of "Basic Sign," whereas the other systems do not. "Whenever possible, words with a common theme are grouped together, and each group has its own 'Basic Sign'; each word in that group makes use of the Basic Sign for that group, together with an identifying gesture [p. 21]." Thirty-seven Basic Signs are recognized, and the authors claim that their use enables greater ease of learning of those words which the signs represent. It should be noted, however, that in this respect the system is going **beyond** the formal properties of spoken English, and in its degree of contrivedness would be opposed by, for example, the authors of *SE*, whose concern is to follow English order with as little additional systematization as possible.

These distinctions may be summarized as shown in Figure 4.1. The focus of interest, then, would seem to be at the center of this figure: To what extent are the systems outlined there simply notational variants of each other? A comparison of selected areas of syntactic operation would show that there are many differences among the systems, a number of which involve matters of linguistic principle and raise major educational issues. A clear example is to be found in the treatment of the various primary and modal auxiliary verbs ("have," "be," "do," "can," "may," etc.). Despite broad similarities of approach to the analysis of this area of the grammar, there are numerous differences in the morphological and syntactic analysis of these verbs. For example, whereas all systems have markers indicating past tense and past participle, *SEE₁*, *SEE₂* and *PGSS* incorporate these in the signs for *was, were*, and *been*, while *SE* and *Improved Techniques of Communication (ITC)* use *be + n* to describe "been." The American systems other than *SE* sign "has" and "does" as *have + s* and *do + s* respectively, giving no clue to the phonological

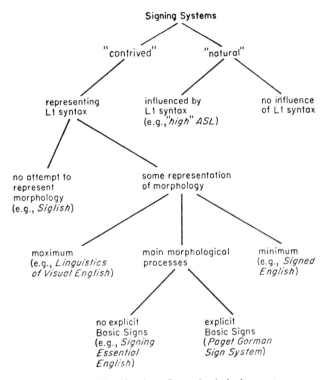

Figure 4.1. Classification of contrived signing systems.

change in the words—a point of some importance when considering the extent to which these systems can be used along with speech in the teaching situation. The *PGSS* has no official sign for the third person singular -*s*, and so there is no recognized sign for "has" or "does." None of the systems appear to differentiate among the uses of "do," with the possible exception of *ITC*. Some of the systems (*SEE*$_1$, *SEE*$_2$, *PGSS*) use the sign for the lexical item *have* (in the sense "possess") as the auxiliary verb. *SEE*$_1$ and *SEE*$_2$ treat the "paired modals" as Verb + Past Participle ("can/could," etc.); *SE* treats "can/could," "will/would" and "shall/should" in terms of Verb + Past Tense; *ITC* describes only "will/would," with "would" being treated as *will* + *d*; "should" is treated as a separate lexical item. *PGSS* treats all the modal auxiliaries discretely, and the link between the pairs is not obvious. *SE, SEE*$_1$ and SEE$_2$ all recognize the need for abbreviations '*m*, '*s*, '*ve*, '*ll* and *n't*. *SE* treats "don't" and "can't" as separate signs since the authors believe that young children regard these as holophrases before understanding their components. The lack of the "-n't" abbreviation in *PGSS* and *ITC* prevents the use of interrogative phrases (e.g., "can't you?"), since the full word "not" is not used in such constructions.

Other areas of grammar and lexicon bring to light similar differences, e.g., over the marking of irregular morphological forms for number, person, tense, and comparison (*SE* and *ITC* mark irregular past tense and plural, for instance, but the other systems do not). *SEE*₁ makes use of a large number of signs for affixes, whereas *PGSS* has no regular system for affix representation (though Craig, 1973, makes numerous suggestions for modification in this respect). It is also possible to be critical of many of the decisions made in the analysis of individual words. *SEE*₁, for example, has been criticized for overemphasizing criteria of formal identity (such as spelling) and not paying enough attention to meaning. Analyses of "any" as *an* + *y*, or "also" as *all* + *so*, or (to give an example from a different area of the lexicon) *mot*- being given as the common stem prefix for a set of items including *motor, motife*, and *motivate* raise fundamental questions of morphological method. All these cases raise questions of linguistic analysis, many of which do not have a single solution.

Bornstein (1973) outlines a number of other salient differences among the various systems, and it is evident from his examples and those just cited that any comparison of contrived signing systems will be a complex matter, raising questions of educational, psychological, and linguistic principle. For instance, we have not in this paper discussed the relative merits of the actual signs used by the various systems, in terms of their iconicity, clarity, fluency, or learnability, as little seems to have been done relating these notions experimentally to questions of linguistic analysis. But in the long run it is clear that many decisions in the linguistic domain are going to be affected by extralinguistic considerations of clumsiness, speed of delivery, and so on. We therefore look forward to systematic comparisons of contrived signing systems from this point of view, once their form has become more stable and their material more widely disseminated. In much the same way as no one morphological theory seems universally suitable for the description of all languages (see Matthews, 1974), so it is likely that the various systems which have been devised for English will find themselves with different and complementary futures if and when their principles are taken as models for use with languages other than English. But for such developments to be realistic, a much more thorough analysis and comparison of the linguistic principles of the available systems needs to take place. It is as part of a prolegomenon to a comparative study of this kind that we hope this paper will make a contribution.

REFERENCES

Barakat, R. A. 1969. Gesture systems. *Keystone Folklore Quarterly*, Fall issue, 105–121.

Battison, R., Markowicz, H., & Woodward, J. 1975. A good rule of thumb: Variable phonology in American Sign Language. In R. Fasold and R. Shuy (eds.), *Analyzing variation in language*. Washington, D.C.: Georgetown University Press. Pp. 291–302.

Bazell, C. E. 1954. Choice of criteria in structural linguistics. *Word, 10*, 126–135.

Becker, V. A. n.d. *Underwater sign language*. U.S. Divers Corps, Catalog No. 1919.

Bellugi, U., & Fischer, S. 1972. A comparison of sign language and spoken language. *Cognition, 1*, 173–200.

Bellugi, U., & Klima, E. S. 1974. Aspects of sign language and its structure. In *Proceedings of the NICHD Conference on "The Role of Speech in Language."*

Bergman, E. 1972. Autonomous and unique features of American Sign Language. *American Annals of the Deaf, 117*, 20–24.

Bolinger, D. L. 1949. Intonation and analysis. *Word, 5*, 248–254.

Bolinger, D. L. 1951. Intonation—levels v. configurations. *Word, 7*, 199–210.

Bornstein, H. 1973. A description of some current sign systems designed to represent English. *American Annals of the Deaf, 118*, 454–463.

Brun, T. 1969. *The international dictionary of sign language*. London: Wolfe.

Carlile, J. S. 1947. *Production and direction of radio programs*. New York: Prentice-Hall.

Cohen, E., Namir, L., & Schlesinger, I.M. 1977. *A new dictionary of sign language*. The Hague: Mouton.

Coomaraswamy, A., & Duggirala, G. 1917. *The mirror of gesture*. Cambridge: Cambridge Univ. Press.

Covington, V. C. 1973. Juncture in American Sign Language. *Sign Language Studies, 2*, 29–38.

Craig, E. 1973. *The Paget Gorman Sign System: A report of the research project 1970–1973*. (University of Reading: Dept. of Linguistic Science).

Critchley, M. 1939. *The language of gesture*. London: Arnold.

Crystal, D. 1969. *Prosodic systems and intonation in English*. London: Cambridge Univ. Press.

Crystal, D. 1974. Paralanguage. In T. A. Sebeok (Ed.), *Current trends in linguistics XII*. The Hague: Mouton.

Fant, L. J. 1972. *Ameslan: An introduction to American Sign Language*. Washington, D.C.: National Association of the Deaf.

Fischer, S. D. 1973. Two processes of reduplication in the American Sign Language. *Foundations of Language, 9*, 469–480.

Gleitman, L. R., Gleitman, H., & Shipley, E. F. 1972. The emergence of the child as grammarian. *Cognition, 1*, 137–164.

Haas, W. 1957. The identification and description of phonetic elements. *Transactions of the Philological Society*, 118–159.

Halliday, M. A. K. 1961. Categories of the theory of grammar. *Word, 17*, 241–292.

Herrgot, Abbé. 1726. *Vetus disciplina monastica*. Paris: Osmont.

Hockett, C. F. 1958. *Course in modern linguistics*. New York: Macmillan.

Hockett, C. F., & Altmann, S. A. 1968. A note on design features. In T. A. Sebeok (Ed.), *Animal communication*. Bloomington: Indiana Univ. Press. Pp. 61–72.

Hutt, C. 1968. Etude d'un corpus: Dictionnaire du langage gesturel chez les Trappistes. *Langage, 10*, 107–118.

Knight, R. P. 1818. *An inquiry into the Symbolical language of ancient art and mythology*. London: privately printed.

Madsen, W. 1972. *Conversational sign language*. Washington, D.C.: Gallaudet.

Mallery, G. 1881. Sign language among North American Indians compared with that among other peoples and deaf-mutes. *Smithsonian Institute Bureau of Ethnology*, 263–552.

Matthews, P. H. 1974. *Morphology*. London: Cambridge Univ. Press.

Mawer, I. 1932. *The art of mime*. London: Methuen.

Paget, R. 1951. *The new sign language*. London: Kegan Paul.

Pike, K. L. 1967. *Language in relation to a unified theory of the structure of human behavior*. The Hague: Mouton.

Quirk, R., Greenbaum, S., Leech, G., & Svartvik, J. 1972. *A grammar of contemporary English*. London: Longman.

Rijnberk, G. van 1953. *Le langage par signes chez les Moines*. Amsterdam: North Holland.

Rosa, L. A. 1929. *Espressione e mimica*. Milan: Hoepli.

Roth, W. E. 1897. *Ethnological studies among the North-West-Central Queensland Aborigines*. Brisbane: Government Printer.

Schlesinger, I. M. 1971. The grammar of sign language and the problems of language universals. In J. Morton (Ed.), *Biological and social factors in psycholinguistics*. London: Logos Press. Pp. 98–121.

Seton, E. E. T. 1918. *Sign talk*. London: Curtis Brown.

Stokoe, W. C. 1960. *Sign language structure. Studies in Linguistics* Occasional Paper, *8*. Washington, D.C.: Gallaudet College Press.

Stokoe, W. C. 1969. Sign language diglossia. *SIL, 21*, 27–41.

Stokoe, W. C. 1972a. *Semiotics and human sign languages*. The Hague: Mouton.

Stokoe, W. C. 1972b. A classroom experiment in two languages. In T. J. O'Rourke (Ed.), Psycholinguistics and total communication. *American Annals of the Deaf*, 85–91.

Stokoe, W. C. 1973a. Sign syntax and human language capacity. Forum Lecture in the 1973 Linguistics Institute, Ann Arbor.

Stokoe, W. C. 1973b. Linguistics, sign language, and total communication. Mimeo.

Stokoe, W. C. 1974. Classification and description of sign languages. In T. A. Sebeok (Ed.), *Current trends in linguistics XII*. The Hague: Mouton.

Tervoort, B. 1961. Esoteric symbolism in the communication behavior of young deaf children. *American Annals of the Deaf, 106*, 436–480.

Tervoort, B. 1968. You me downtown movie fun. *Lingua, 21*, 455–465.

Thorpe, W. H. 1972. The comparison of vocal communication in animals and man. In R. A. Hinde (Ed.), *Non-verbal communication*. London: Cambridge Univ. Press. Pp. 27–47.

Tomkins, W. 1926. *Universal Indian sign language of the Plains Indians of North America*. San Diego: for the author.

Tweney, R. D., & Hoemann, H. W. 1973. Back translation: A method for the analysis of manual languages. *Sign Language Studies, 2*, 51–72.

Vetter, H. J. 1969. *Language behavior and communication*. Itasca, Illinois: Peacock.

Ward, J. S. M., & Stirling, W. G. 1925. *The Hung Society*. London: Baskerville.

West, L. 1960. The sign language: An analysis. Unpublished Ph.D. dissertation, Univ. of Indiana.

Woodward, J. C. 1973. Language continuum: A different point of view. *Sign Language Studies, 2*, 81–83.

Zung, C. S. L. 1937. *Secrets of the Chinese drama*. London: Harrap.

5

Bilingual Interference

BERNARD T. TERVOORT

INTRODUCTION

Bilingual interference is taken to be the influence, unilateral or—usually—mutual, of one language upon another. To cause it, two different languages must be in close contact. Within one and the same language there can be no such interference. In that case, diglossia or the mutual interaction of different social codes, like high and low, can occur.

In order to cause interference, the co-occurrence of the languages involved has to be such that their speakers meet regularly with each other, such as inhabitants of national borderline areas, immigrants and other types of ethnic minority groups within a majority, or groups living together without majority or minority status, but coming from different linguistic environments.

A complete study of bilingual interference implies not only a linguistic analysis of the languages involved, in order to understand fully the extent and character of the borrowing and the resulting blended forms, but also a sociological analysis of their speakers' historical and geographical background, their social situation, their value codes, and so on. Quite often it is not so much the smaller or greater complexity of the differences between the contrasting languages as the smaller or greater willingness to integrate and to compromise that decides the specific issues of bilingual interference. What is finally accepted into usage can be either the way it is said and expressed in one of the two languages—often but not necessarily the dominant one—or it can come out as a new creation, showing the influence of both. Such choices can lead to slow changes in both languages, even in the subsequent usage in the monolingual setting. They can also result in the establishment of a new communication system functioning in between the two languages for the situations of mutual interchange, implying the coexistence in continuing separation of two adjacent subcultures. In a successful integration, however, the newly created blend of the two languages can gain significance to the point that the originally contributing languages start disappearing in that area.

So there are different possibilities, all with their varied implications for a linguist's analysis of the system of interfering, disappearing, and dominant features. A sociologist will turn to different aspects, such as the social interference and the co-occurrence of stable versus changing relations of the groups of people involved. For a complete evaluation, the two will need each other. All this is common knowledge, and it will suffice here to present a simple and accepted frame of reference, pointing out that this part is written by a linguist, not a sociologist, and is, therefore, incomplete.

To give only a bare minimum in supplementary references, I refer the reader to Diebold's (1961) article in *Language,* which still reads as a good outline of the subject, and to Weinreich (1953) and Haugen (1964), who dealt with bilingualism in a fundamental way. The notion of "diglossia" is, of course, to be found in Ferguson's (1959) article of that name in *Word.*

The Uniqueness of the Bilingualism Dealt with Here

Among all people of different tongues living together one way or another, the deaf living among the hearing are in a unique situation. On the one hand, most of them take a highly integrated part in society in many different ways. They hold positions no different from the hearing; they live together with hearing friends, relatives, and, often, members of their own family; they do their shopping, in some countries take part in traffic, read newspapers and magazines, go to movies, watch television, and so on. On the other hand, their handicap sets them apart, communicationwise, in a far more vital and penetrating way than any other group of handicapped, or, for that matter, any other linguistic minority.

It is this difference, between their means of communication among themselves and the means of communication of all other people, that makes their type of bilingualism so unique, and the interference so different. Where all other types of bilingual situations are of the same kind insofar as they all imply the interference of one spoken language with another, in the present case we are dealing with the coexistence of a basically acoustic system with a basically visual system, namely, the communicative code that the deaf use for communication among themselves. As will be dealt with extensively elsewhere in this chapter, two systems of this kind are based upon a totally different set of fundamental principles that stand irreducibly apart, such as: absolute linearity of acoustic versus relative simultaneity of visual forms; a high degree of possible detachment from the speaking partner versus a mandatory person-to-person and face-to-face contact with the deaf partner; arbitrariness as a characteristic feature of words versus iconic motivation as overt or covert concomitant feature of signs; the fact that saying words needs less time than making signs (Bellugi & Fischer, 1972); and so on. As some of these matters are dealt with more fully in other chapters, it seems enough to state here that such basically different features all follow from the fundamentally different perceptual functioning of the listening ear and the seeing eye, and that all details of bilingual interference to be set forth in the sequel will be consequences of a set of such basic principles.

Bilingual situations between deaf and hearing people are different from those to be found between groups of hearing people in some other ways too. The latter can be located geographically; their ethnic, social, political, economic, etc., implications are dependent on different local factors; and the interwovenness of the two languages is based upon the coexistence of two independently occurring linguistic systems. The deaf live all over the world among hearing people of different tongues. It is taken for granted here that almost nowhere do the deaf live together in such close-knit and independent groups as do some other minorities, and that they never have in early childhood an adult, fully developed linguistic system available. This latter statement can be demonstrated most easily by pointing to the fact that from earliest childhood on the deaf child is reared and taught in the language of his parents, his school, and his country. Yet, in those childhood years also lie the roots of the bilingualism that characterizes the communication of every deaf person to a greater or lesser degree. It is my intention, therefore, to go into these years of schooling more deeply, and to make the analysis of this initial interference the focus of my contribution.

It is possible to obtain similar information in a different way. Bellugi and Fischer (1972) used hearing children of signing deaf parents, after checking whether these subjects were well versed in the signing of their parents as well as in English. I shall come back to their study on different occasions.

As far as I know, the deaf child all over the world is educated in the language of the country in which he or she happens to live. Of all the almost 120 schools for the deaf I have visited or worked at during almost 25 years now, this was always the basic philosophy. The final goals could and did differ to a great extent, particularly so where it was believed the accent had to rest upon an oral (speech and speech reading) or on a simultaneous or total (signing and finger spelling in combination with speech and lip reading) communicative competence. The means were different accordingly, e.g., in the ways speech, writing, and spelling plus signing were given greater or lesser predominance compared to each other. But I have never encountered the philosophy that English, Dutch, German, French (and so on) were to be considered foreign tongues for young deaf children born in these countries, and that one of these languages therefore ought to be taught only after a sign language, as a completely different language, has first been acquired the natural way as a mother tongue.

Historically speaking, this has not always been the case. De l'Epée and Sicard in late eighteenth- and beginning nineteenth-century Paris, for example, held the different philosophy that this indeed was the best thing to do; but even they did not teach deaf children at the early age at which primary language acquisition takes place, and even they tried to arrive at a written competence in French for their pupils, not as a foreign language but as the highest level of the signing system they had designed. Anyhow, theirs was a philosophy that since has been abandoned—and, in my opinion, rightly so.

Matters have not become simpler since, however. For there can be no doubt, I believe, that:

1. Such an approach, in which a pure and independent sign language were developed and taught, is entirely possible.
2. Such a sign language would be an easy and natural code for deaf children to acquire and to handle.
3. It would differ more fundamentally from any of the surrounding languages than any set of acoustic codes known.
4. It would, moreover, also differ considerably from the system created by de l'Epée or the systems that are still in existence nowadays and that go back to the French-inspired code.
5. Such a sign language would set deaf children raised and taught in its system completely apart from their social environment.

Whether a deaf child raised in such a sign language—which, as an independent and fully grown linguistic system does not occur in a monolingual setting—would be better able to learn English, Dutch, etc., as a second language afterwards than all the deaf children who struggle with it under the prevailing conditions, is a matter of speculation. The extent of the existing struggle, and all the problems originating from the interference of existing visual codes that have developed in dependence on the surrounding languages, make me, at least, not so optimistic about the outcome of such an experiment. So far, not only do all schools for the deaf teach the language of the parents and of the country, but even deaf parents who do not use speech in communication will sometimes (or often) finger-spell, and when they do, they use words. Furthermore, if they sign, they often sign an adapted version of the acoustic language, at least as far as syntactic ordering and some of its morphology are concerned.

Although I do not intend to get involved in educational issues or in the controversy about what would be best for the deaf communicationwise, their specific bilingual situation and the status of sign languages as part thereof can still not be fully evaluated without a sketch of how a deaf person is introduced into life and language contact with fellow human beings during his or her school years. A deaf child, after all, spends an average of 15 years at school, in a far greater dependency on his teacher for all his communicative capacity, than any other child, handicapped or not. The school is mostly responsible for his further orientation toward or against the prevailing linguistic system of the society to which he is supposed to belong.

All this might be true, or might be challenged by those who believe otherwise, but the fact remains that, in the meantime, deaf children keep coming together in the classroom, on the playground, in the dormitory, and so on, and that they keep communicating among themselves, more or less beyond the control of their educators. It is this initial and fast-growing private communication of deaf children that has been intriguing me for the past 25 years, and it is from this angle that I shall look at bilingual interference here.

Anyone who has ever visited a school for the deaf and observed its pupils, especially the younger ones, more than very superficially must have noticed the striking difference in their behavior in situations in which so called "good" language, to be used on behalf of a hearing partner, is requested from them, and their behavior in circumstances in which they are left free to communicate as they please among themselves. In the first instance, their behavior is awkward, inhibited, and hesitant; it reminds one of a foreigner, unfamiliar with the language, who tries to utter something which he has to put together by thinking hard and using the little he knows. In the latter case, however, the deaf children's behavior is that of partners at ease who focus upon the subject matter at hand, to be dealt with in a communicative code the use of which is a matter of course. It is only partially the requirement of speech and speech reading that prompts the first type of behavior. Let them try writing down what they want to say and cannot, or else succeed only with great difficulty in doing, and the result will come out the same. Neither is the use of their hands, for the benefit of those hearing partners who do know signs or finger spelling, of any great help in producing an acceptable grammatical utterance in the language of the hearing environment. Any young deaf child, enrolled in an educational system that adheres to the simultaneous—or total—approach, who signs a "good" English sentence (using the right order of elements, with a verb and a subject, and the like) is complimented on such a performance. So, producing English with one's fingers and hands is not a matter of course in that type of school either. Certainly, a pupil there might have some advantage over the orally taught deaf child insofar as he can forgo speech (not in a truly simultaneous or total system, though, which includes speech too, by definition), but for the rest he has to try equally hard to achieve as much; his problems with English (etc.) grammar are no different, and he shows the same type of change in behavior when he is left free to turn to his comrades and to communicate as he pleases.

So, obviously, deaf children must be bilingual to a certain extent: They have two different codes, one for outside and one for inside use, the former the difficult foreign language of their teacher, their parents, their hearing mates, the grocer, the bus driver, the princess in the fairy-tale book, and everybody else, and the latter the easy and familiar one that nobody knows except for a few mates living under the same conditions. During school years this latter code can slowly merge with the former in such a way that it leaves only a few traces in a monolingual usage throughout of the language taught. This type of deaf youngster is, or has become, monolingual; he knows English (etc.) and nothing else. Again, whether or not his mode of communication leaves out speech in some instances does not make too much of a difference, although it means the absence of some of the structural features at the word level, and the occurrence instead of other, manual features of a visual nature. In principle, however, what he then uses is as much English (or Dutch, etc.) as it is sign language. Stokoe (1972, p. 159) was facing this problem when he proposed to use the terms "high" and "low" for the two versions of the American Sign Language, and where he states that the former version amounts to English. There are, obviously, many inalienable visual features present, in the high variety too, which could never be termed English, and which belong in the other code—but still it is English to a great extent: Let those who sign "grammatically" write down literally what they were signing, and it will turn out to be English. Or do as I did—film them and decode the filming in script: It turns out to be English again. In these cases, there is hardly any bilingualism left. But the same manual features are also present in the more genuine occurrences of bilingual interference in the so-called low variant, and there they have to be dealt with as such—as characteristics of the private and visual code.

The opposite occurs if the mastering of the school's and the society's language remains to a great extent unsuccessful. If English does not become the language in which the deaf child can think (if I may say it that simply), can read and write, can express himself and can understand others, little or no integration of his private communication system into the language taught takes place. In this case, it can make quite a difference whether the educational situation is oral or simultaneous. The former enforces speech and lip reading while discouraging the use of manual communicative support; in case of failure the pupil ends up with almost no structured language at all. His private code could not develop through coaching and channeling of manual expression toward the difficult code. Because it was suppressed all the time, it remained in a nascent state and stayed poor in terms of structure and vocabulary.

Still, such deaf children, while growing up, keep communicating one way or another with their family, friends, and former classmates. Many of the characteristics of their privately used code reveal features of true visual structuring and functioning, and—according to my observations— often more so than the interchange of adult deaf, who live and communicate much more under the influence of the acoustic code. The simultaneous system, on the contrary, not only accepts signs as part of a whole that includes speaking and finger spelling as well, but it also coaches and integrates these children into an existing, fully accepted, and adult system, usually termed sign language. In fact, this latter system relates to the language of the society at large in so many ways that it hardly can be discovered any longer as a language of its own. I have argued elsewhere (Tervoort, 1973a) why, on the one hand, the so-called sign languages that are in existence everywhere are not independent linguistic systems like English, Dutch, and so on, but rather English or Dutch as far as some important syntactic and semantic aspects are concerned. I have voiced my strong conviction, on the other hand, that independent visual communication systems not undergoing such permanent interference at all levels from surrounding acoustic codes—i.e., from the existing natural languages based upon speech—are, obviously, feasible. In all instances known to me, the communication of the deaf shows features of both: the influence of the basically acoustic outlook of the country's language as taught in every school for the deaf, as well as the influence of the basically visual outlook of the deaf person's codes as developed in relation to others with the same handicap.

So far, analyses of sign codes, trying to demonstrate the existence of these codes as languages, have met with the handicap that all occurrences were dependent on prevailing acoustic codes. Basic differences at the level of semantic and semiotic functioning between manual and verbal signifiers can easily be, and have been, demonstrated in quite satisfactory linguistic analyses (e.g., by Stokoe, 1960, 1965; see for the analysis of one detail Fischer, 1973). The difference between the functioning and the structure of word and sign is quite obvious. Syntactic analyses meet with greater handicaps and have been less successful in analyzing the existing differences (cf. Stokoe, 1972, with Tervoort, 1973a; see also Schlesinger, 1971).

In this context I should like to discuss one study at some length. In an analysis of some features of American Sign Language (ASL), Susan Fischer (Bellugi & Fischer, 1972, pp. 185–198) touches upon the relations between English and ASL on several occasions. The informants studied were bilingual in the sense that they were versed in both English and ASL. Many of Fischer's observations concur with earlier ones on my part; the fact that our frames of references are not identical does not lessen the value of her analysis—or of mine, I hope. The Bellugi and Fischer article's main theme is that it takes more time to produce signs than words, but that, in terms of propositions ("something that can be considered equivalent to a simple underlying sentence [p. 184]"), the same information can be carried across in the same time. Or, to quote them directly: "The rate of articulation for words is nearly double the rate for signs for each of our four subjects [p. 180]." "The rate of articulation for speaking is considerably higher than the rate of articulation for signing, even when both languages are produced at the same time [p. 183]." And, finally, "the mean number of seconds per proposition we have found in signing alone, speaking alone, and signing and speaking simultaneously, are not consistently different from one another . . . [p. 185]." In passing, the authors mention bilingual co-occurrence, or—as they put it—"the effect of producing two languages at the same time." "We notice in some instances that the two languages influence one another and that one finds 'errors' in one language that are related to the other [p. 182]." Subsequently, they give only two, rather trivial, examples (the use of the word "cook" because that was what the sign meant, and a spoken "then" simultaneously with a signed *than*).

Departing from the central theme of the Bellugi and Fischer presentation, Fischer, in an appendix, then puts the question: Given the fact that signing is more time consuming and yet comes up with the same amount of information, timewise, if one looks at the propositions, "What are the mechanisms by which sign compensates for this limitation—what are the unique properties of sign on which the language capitalizes [p. 185]?" She then lists the following features: (*a*) doing without (the "get-rid-of-it syndrome"); (*b*) incorporation; (*c*) body movements and facial expressions. I shall come back to all of these in the following sections.

Of the answers she has found so far, Fischer says that they are "by no means complete." She has outlined some basic features of one sign language, but has not dealt with bilingual interference as such. I therefore propose to demonstrate the bilingual interference between the two languages a deaf person is exposed to mainly from the information from an 8-year project dealing with just this specific topic (Tervoort, 1967a, 1975). In order to avoid interim explanations, a short summary of that project as a whole is presented in the following paragraphs.

In 1950 I filmed two 12-year-old deaf subjects with a telescopic camera for 45 minutes, while they were engaged in a conversation in their own code, using speech and signs. Subsequent analysis confirmed in great detail the hypothesis on bilingualism *sui generis*, as described above (Tervoort, 1953). Two questions were left unanswered, though:

1. What is the situation, in terms of bilingualism, before and after that age?
2. How much of what has been found is typical for any deaf child?

To find some of the answers, a longitudinal project was designed in 1958 carried out between 1959 and 1965, and accounted for in a report between 1965 and 1967. Each year 24 deaf subjects in the United States, taught with the simultaneous method, and 24 in Holland and Belgium, taught orally, were filmed in conversation. Their age range was 7 to 12 in the first, and 12 to 17 in the last year.

The results showed an overall dominance of the private code, termed **esoteric**, during the earlier years, making way with growing age for the difficult code of English or Dutch, termed **exoteric**. The level of significance of this growth was .001. There was little exoteric use at ages 7 and 8, although the influence of the means of instruction on the private communication was already quite noticeable. Beyond the ages of 13 and 14 most subjects used the language taught fairly well for mutual interchange, with the exception of a small minority who had not mastered it. Growing exoteric grammaticality of the utterance appeared to bear no overall significant relation to the modes of execution, words versus signs. Under both conditions, the competence in the language taught grew. The modes that were preferred in a highly significant way were signs-plus-words or signs-only; at the above level of significance the words-only mode was rejected. This will be elaborated in the following section.

WORD AND SIGN

Introductory Remarks

For a generic term to indicate the use of a word, a sign, or both at the same time, I propose to use the generic term **signifier**, using the term **sign** to mean a manually executed sign only in the present context. Names and transcription devices for the signifiers as they occur in the bilingual setting are:

(1)	**spoken-only**	*(just)* *(spoken)* *(words)*
(2)	**spelled-only**	WORDS WRITTEN IN THE AIR
(3)	**spoken and spelled**	*WITH MOUTH AND FINGERS*
(4)	**spoken and signed**	*with mouth and hands*
(5)	**signed-only**	just manual signs

Stokoe (1960; Stokoe *et al.*, 1965) has developed a complete notation system for signs. Another such system is to be found in West (1960). The reasons I opt for translations into words, or glosses, are that Stokoe's or West's systems are difficult to read, and that my subjects gave words for every sign I asked the meaning of, so there was some kind of identification already (see the next section, "Identification of Word and Sign," and Tervoort, 1967a, where I discuss this notation system at length.). Still I agree with Fischer's (1972) conclusion, when she writes:

> We have mentioned the notation for writing sign down, developed by Stokoe in his *Sign Language Structure*. It notes for any given sign the hand configuration involved, the point of articulation, the direction of movement, and to a certain extent, the manner of this movement. For us, our glosses serve the same purpose—we have developed a consistent code such that there is a one-to-one correspondence between our gloss and an entry in Stokoe's notation—and are a convenient mnemonic. The problem is that hands, movements, and location—and indeed the signs made up from these—are not the only parameters involved in the language, as we shall show below. It is partly for this reason that the gloss is inadequate [p. 187].

As will be shown, I interpret the inadequacy of the gloss a little differently from Fischer, though.

To return to the form of signifiers occurring in my study, although there appeared to be some difference between schools and individuals, in general it can be stated that the category which occurred the least and showed the poorest development over the years was (1) **spoken-only**; (5) **signed-only**, on the contrary, occurred most frequently from the earliest ages on. The conclusion that, therefore, signs are the true vehicles for most subjects's private, esoteric, interchange, is warranted. That words stay foreign to such a system per se is not correct, however. On the contrary, they can and do influence it to a very great extent. This is best demonstrated by the prevalence of category (4) **spoken and signed**, the frequency of occurrence of which lies only slightly below that of category (5). Finally, there was no overall significant difference to be found in the frequency of occurrence of (3) **spoken and spelled** versus (2) **spelled-only**; in any case, only words are used in both. From the frequent simultaneous occurrence of spoken words with spelled signs it becomes clear that words penetrate and are incorporated somehow into the esoteric system. Even if this were restricted to the school years and to only some of the students—the continuing use of words and the number of deaf individuals using them later on being subject to various social conditions—the conclusion would still have to be that, apparently, two signifiers of completely different origin can and do co-occur and thereafter blend into a new complex one. The means of execution of the manual sign and of the spoken word in such a simultaneous, complex signifier is obviously less interesting than the semantic implications in the present context. I therefore only list in passing some such features of interference in the execution, for example: the rhythmic patterning of the polysyllabic word being transferred to the sign; the reduplication of the sign being carried over to the word, which, as a consequence, is repeated; morphological markers which are characteristic for words, like plural -s or past tense -ed, being added to the sign in finger spelling, and so on. The following sections will forgo these external aspects and will enter into the semantic ones more deeply.

A most extensive elaboration of the morphological features of the sign signifier is to be found in the notation systems mentioned (Stokoe's and West's). There is little use for these precise analyses here since there is no interference between the sign signifier and its verbal counterpart in terms of the physiological aspects of the signifiers other than the phenomena just mentioned.

Finally, it should be noted that there are various degrees of incorporation of the word into the sign. There are words that do not have a sign counterpart but are always spelled—if not also spoken. And there are signs which in fact do not get a spoken counterpart. Moreover, there are all kinds of possible variations stemming from individual attitudes, family habits, and educational practices which—all taken together—can have as their result at the one extreme the deaf person who never opens his mouth, at least not to try to utter words, and at the other extreme deaf people who speak during all communication. I once filmed some deaf children over whose mouths I had tied a towel with the instruction to try to communicate. They were not able to do so with their hands only, although they had been signing simultaneously with speech just a couple of minutes before (Tervoort, 1953, vol. 2). The spoken Dutch was mandatorily incorporated as an integral part of these children's communication system despite the fact that that system was absolutely different from Dutch.

Identification of Word and Sign

The conclusion from the foregoing can be that the relation between sign and word is close enough to warrant the term identification. The following arguments for such an identification can be given:

1. The regular simultaneous occurrence
2. The recognition of the sign through the counterpart word
3. The recognition of the word by means of the sign
4. The alternating occurrence of either the sign-only or the sign + word signifier.

I would like to elaborate a little on these four arguments.

1. I shall come back to the fact that more than one sign can occur at once; here, the interesting feature is the simultaneity of two signifiers coming from two different systems. This simultaneity is different and more complete than, e.g., the one that occurs when someone is reading aloud, or giving simultaneous translation; just because it is more complete, it leads to a strong identification.
2. In all traditional sign dictionaries signs are named and paraphrased with words—to which sometimes drawings and photographs are added, but only to display proper execution, not to code the sign in print. Transcription codes, rejecting the word in print as the equivalent of the sign made (like West, 1960, and Stokoe *et al.*, 1965) remain difficult to decode into signs again and prevent quick reading. Even after the decoding has been performed, it leaves one only with the correct execution, not with the meaning, unless—again—the word is added, or the reader knows the system throughout. Furthermore, these transcriptions remain utterly foreign to the native users of signs. When asked to write down a sign made, every deaf person will write down a word, the appropriate word. This word to him is not a translation but the sign itself, as written down.
3. This is the argument the other way around. Any deaf person, when asked to sign a word—either spoken, spelled, written down, or in print—will do so, provided of course that such a sign exists and he knows it. He will, moreover, always make the same sign for the same word.
4. This alternating occurrence indicates that the same concept is pro-

duced by the partners of a conversation who use sometimes the word, sometimes the sign, and sometimes the simultaneous combination of the two. This characteristic was found to occur in all schools and at all ages among a majority of the subjects. The occurrence of any one of the modes of execution was random, the choice between them was free, and the meaning did not change in any way under any of the conditions.

This strong identification is somewhat similar to the one between the spoken and the written word; it also has some characteristics of the close relation between two different words with the same meaning in two different languages. On the other hand, however, the equivalent word-sign also has other aspects. There appear to be limitations to the identification just elaborated. These limitations do not necessarily make the identification less strong, just more specifically conditioned. The very nature of the word as feature of the acoustic system versus that of the sign as characteristic phenomenon of the visual one brings about these limitations. In the following section, I shall argue first that signs can not be distinguished into the classes of an acoustic system per se, but that they tend to borrow parts of the word classification, on the basis of the co-occurrence and the identification. The section thereafter will try to demonstrate that signs function like words linguistically, insofar as they are based upon agreement on arbitrary features, but that signs continue to differ from words because of their concomitant iconicity. We shall now turn to this feature.

Category Forming

Any linguistic theory divides the words of a language into a number of grammatical categories on the basis of a range of both structural and semantic features which correlate with each other to some extent. It is one of my points of criticism against some of the distinctions made in equating signs with verbs, nouns, etc., that this principle is neglected, and that such distinctions are made according to semantic content only.

A fairly recent distinction is the one between those categories that are regarded as grammatically basic and the ones that are not, for example, as discussed by Schlesinger (1971). I shall return to these later but for the time being want to revert to a traditional, if less good, distinction which I have used before, and which Fischer also uses for the same purpose (Bellugi & Fischer, 1972, p. 186). This very simple division is between content words and function words and looks acceptable as a start, sufficing to make a point. Some words name "reality" or aspects thereof—using this term as an abbreviation instead of a lengthy account—which are easy to delimit in a more direct and less grammatically involved way than do others. The latter refer to more complex and relational aspects in "reality," and they do so via all kinds of grammatical rules in a sometimes very indirect way. Formally, these two groups are distinct from each other in that classes of so-called content words are countless and infinitely extendable, whereas all classes of so-called function words contain a limited and unchanging number of words only.

This distinction remains an oversimplification, since:

1. Content words are subject to grammatical rules, no less than function words.
2. Function words have meaning, no less than content words.
3. Within the category of content words there is quite some difference in the directness of the relation between word and "reality," with concrete nouns at the one end and many adverbs at the other.
4. There is not much difference in the grammatical complexity of functioning of some adverbs on the one hand and pronouns and prepositions on the other.
5. It remains to be seen whether the distinction primarily based upon lexical versus grammatical functioning covers adequately the one based upon limited versus unlimited number.

Yet, as inadequate as it might be, the content word–function word distinction makes some sense. Apparently, the more direct lexical content versus the more grammatical functioning of words, in combination with the observation that some word classes are finite and unchangeable and others are not, has kept it in use in applied research of a different kind. (Compare direct translation of content words versus differences in grammatical rules implied by some function words in foreign language learning.)

The applicability of the distinction here seems obvious. Signs show some characteristics of content words and none of function words. They name "reality" for which the acoustic languages most often use the word classes nouns, verbs, adjectives in English, but they never mark them for plural, tense and the like. They also name some of the aspects of "reality" covered by adverbs, pronouns, and prepositions but, again, never display the functioning of exoteric grammatical rules that mark these categories, say in English or Dutch. The mere lexical functioning, if we may call it that, shows, however, no formal and semantic classification over these categories, or any other for that matter. This does not mean that signs could not be categorized on visual principles, and in fact they are. It just means that it is quite evident that classification of visual signs into formally marked and rule-governed categories is not by necessity similar to that of acoustic languages. On the contrary, and to all appearances so far, it is not as all-pervasive as it is there. I hope to argue later that this is a logical outcome of the visual system.

It is, furthermore, quite evident that only the regular simultaneous co-occurrence of a given sign with one and the same word over the years and as used by everyone gives the sign its borrowed classification as verb, noun, adjective, etc. Even so, in the bilingual occurrences too many signs remain homonymous, and their classification depends completely on the translation. This translation of the signed data from the films was always given to me by the subjects themselves; from it this ambiguity in terms of relation with one specific word class became quite evident. So, there are no good reasons to speak about such categories if a signifier is not marked and ordered like words, morphologically and syntactically, and if it can have verbal, nominal, adnominal, adverbial, etc., meaning, depending on the situation in which it occurs, signifying activity, quality, entity, relation, etc., respectively. That these conceptual distinctions in "reality" are no sufficient ground on which to base linguistic distinction is a trivial remark. But in this case it is even not necessarily so that in a sequence of signs a sign specifically signifies **either** activity or entity, etc.; this often remains unspecified, and is largely a matter of interpretation for the purpose of translation into a language where such a choice has to be made. It is therefore not trivial any longer in this context to point out that even indicating an entity or an activity exclusively does not make the first signifier a noun and the second one a verb in any language, as long as no grammatical rules that differentiate them have been discovered. The numbers of so-called nouns occurring as "verbs" is very large, and many "nouns" occur as "adjectives" as well. Including an "adjective–adverb" classification makes little sense, as this distinction is obviously even more foreign to signing than the others mentioned. A few examples may clarify the point. The same sign may signify:

Activity	Entity	Quality	Relation
(to) *dance*	(the) *dance*	*exultant*	
(to) *sleep*	(the) *sleep*	*sleepy*	
(to) *hope*	(the) *hope*	*hopeful*	
(to) *bathe*	(the) *bath*		
(to) *swing*	(the) *swing*		
(to) *snoop,nibble*	(the) *candy*	*sweet*	
(to) *blossom,bloom*	(the) *blossom*	*pink*	
(to) *pile up*	(the) *top*	*high*	*up*
(to) *move back*	(the) *past*	*former, last*	*ago*
	(the) *fun*	*funny*	
	(the) *mistake*	*wrong*	
	(the) *friend*	*friendly*	*together*

In all these instances, representing many others, the same sign was used; homonymy was not solved by grammatical means but by correct interpretation of situational and contextual information. It could also remain unsolved when such a decision was unnecessary. It is quite obvious that there are indeed also a great number of signs that indicate entities exclusively. These signs are too easily labeled with the term "noun." Signs like those for *daddy, vase, nose*, and many thousands more seem to raise no difficulty. Even there, though, it remains very much in doubt whether there exists any classification other than the one based upon implicit recognition of semantic features like *animate + personal + male + family + parent* for "daddy." Yet, no safeguard for any real linguistic categories is present, as long as such a set of features is not bundled into a signifier which is grammatically classified as noun. Verb, noun, etc., are technical terms; even a person's name can be turned into a verb: "Don't you Johnny me," "There he goes—Nixoning again."

That is why I have some problems with Fischer's 1973 article on reduplication of verbs. She classifies verbs in ASL in terms of the semantic features "stative" and "non-stative," indicating the signs she is dealing with through words that name English verbs. That, of course, is all right. But she does not define "verb-in-ASL" in any other way than, for example, stating: "A durative verb . . . denotes an action which can last some amount of time, e.g., *sleep, watch T.V., talk, rest*, etc. A nondurative . . . verb . . . denotes an action of rather little duration, e.g., *kill, win, leave, find*, etc. [p. 472]." This is quite evident for English where these are indeed verbs, as we know beforehand, and where "verb-in-English" is to be found in any grammar. But here it means presupposing that there are verbs in ASL, which has yet to be proven. What one would like to know is whether the rules of grammar Fischer finds—and which I do not intend to challenge at this point—are syntactic proof that we are indeed dealing with a verbal class, distinct from, say, a nominal one—that is, a class with specific privileges of occurrence that would, for example, distinguish "sleep long" from "long sleep," "win big" from "big win," or "again" in reduplication from "repeat" or "repetition."

Schlesinger (1971) has met with the same problem too; he puts it this way: "Although it is doubtful whether one may refer to word classes in ISL [i.e., Israeli Sign Language] it will be convenient to use the customary terms *noun* and *verb* [his italics] for signs denoting things and actions respectively [p. 119, fn. 3]." I share Schlesinger's doubts wholeheartedly, but I feel that his convenient use of the customary terms is unacceptable either here or in his article, where important linguistic conclusions follow which, in part, are based on this weak premise. I submit the more conservative hypothesis that word classes, as well as syntactic functions like subject, direct object, indirect object, modifier, and the like—about which Schlesinger is writing and to which I shall return in a later section entitled "Bilingual Interference in Utterances"—are characteristic for languages based upon speech, but that signs do not function that way, certainly not a priori, by necessity or on their own. The presumption is on the contrary that such typically verbal functioning is brought about by spoken language influence and thus could be better left aside in a sign analysis.

Fischer's (1973) statements about signs are all acceptable to me, as long as she does not claim to be writing about verbs. If signs are found to show real word class features, the first question should obviously be whether this has to be ascribed to their co-occurrence and therefore identification with words. Unless and until there is definite proof to the contrary, one should avoid such conclusions.

Signs and words in their relation to each other are no exception to the situation of words of one language in their relation to those of another one in a bilingual setting. Some are easily translated and sometimes blend into one new word; some are not. A transcription or a circumlocution then is the best that can be expected. As stated before, content words generally create fewer problems; it is the group of function words that proves to be difficult. In the same way, it is not so much the lexical but the grammatical functioning of words which sets languages apart and puzzles foreign visitors, translators, and all those functioning in a bilingual setting. Now, after having made my introductory point with the all too simple distinction between content and function words, I shall leave that distinction behind and try to improve on it, as follows.

Expressing concepts and referring to "reality" can be accomplished with manual signifiers as easily as with spoken words. This equally adequate capacity of functioning lexically answers the questions of how many signs for words there are, and vice versa, and why some words do not have a counterpart in signs. Signs have no word grammar; if many words are idiosyncratic grammatical tools with some sort of subtle grammatical meaning attached (like, for example, the conjunction "that" or the article "the" in English), they are typical not only for that language versus another language, but they are also typical as features of that language as an acoustic system (with linear ordering, for example) together with all other languages which display analogous features, versus any visual communication system. Insofar as signs can and do express activities, entities, etc., lexically, they can be and are identified with words which have the same function. This does not by any means show or prove, however, that there must therefore be anything grammatically nominal, verbal, etc., about the sign. Signs do not express exoteric conjunctions, articles, the prepositional aspect under grammatical rules of a preposition, or the adverbial aspects under different grammatical rules of an adverb. They can and do express what is conveyed by the lexical part of such words, if the words are not purely grammatical and have some "reality"-naming function left. The use of different articles, for example, for a new topic ("a cat") versus one that is known already ("the cat"), or for different gender in Dutch, are purely grammatical and utterly foreign to signing; if there is something in "reality" here, signs express that in another way. This does not mean that such a difficult part of the spoken language can not be learned and translated into the visual system, and expressed by a sign–signifier made up for that specific purpose. Signs for such words, however, like for the conjunction "that" or the article "the" remain borrowings from a foreign language. The fact that these words are finger-spelled does not incorporate them into the visual system, of course. Finger-spelling an internally structured word like "un-mis-ta-ka-bly" does not make its structure more transparent to the deaf person, unless he has enough knowledge of English. This might sound like stating the obvious; another seemingly trivial remark that might not be superfluous either is, that all this says nothing about signs being poorer or less capable of expressing concepts. It just happens to be the case that the conjunction, the article, etc., are atypical for a visualization of "reality" as much as "unmistakably" is a buildup that is absolutely tied in with an acoustic way of signifying a structured linear whole. I shall come back to some of this when dealing with similar features in syntax. First, the characteristic functioning of the sign-part in the word + sign signifier has to be analyzed further by considering its origin. This will be done now.

The Ontogenesis of the Word + Sign Signifier

The ontogenesis of the complex signifier can be such that first the sign was known and the word was learned thereafter until, finally, the two merged, or vice versa. It is not difficult to see that first there is the whole range of environmental distinctions the very young child has learned to develop by agreeing with his mother and—eventually—other people, upon signifiers that can be used to handle that environment more efficiently than by just operating upon it. I leave aside here both the setting in which the mother—and others—hand over to the child in his first years of life an existing sign system, and the opposite setting in which manual communication is suppressed fully in favor of the exclusive use of the visual–oral communicative channel—both the deaf mother of a deaf child who knows a sign language and the hearing mother of a deaf child who can effectively prevent all signing are exceptions. For a more complete description of the ontogenesis of the sign at such earliest stages, see Tervoort (1961).

Signs originating in such a process between young deaf children, for example, in preschool and kindergarten, are mostly imitative, "iconic" in origin, but there are others which are deictic, emotive, response-eliciting, affirming or denying, and so on. With the exception of all these, the majority of the signs initially and originally are iconic lexical signifiers *in statu nascenti*. One of the prerequisites of signs for their development toward a linguistic level—by which I mean the level at which it can be safely assumed that language is being used as far as the feature under scrutiny is concerned, and that there is not any longer just imitative behavior, role playing, and the like—is that each single sign can be isolated from a communicative cycle of signifying behavior. As long as such a cycle consists of acting or reenacting, that part of it certainly is not linguistic. This also goes for the sign that is still functioning exclusively at the imitative level. Since both clusters of role playing and purely imitative signs occurred regularly in my data among the younger subjects, and since they obviously mark phases of development, I have termed them sublinguistic, in order to indicate that they are not absolute and isolated phenomena, but ephemeral tokens of growth. A lot of signing begins by playing parts or imitating concrete "reality," by visualizing striking parts thereof. Such signs are based upon true and careful imitation and subsequent associative recognition by the partner. The imitation is not exhaustive; that would be very inefficient. Both the choice of the detail or details to be imitated and of the subjective execution are free. Under these come the dialectal varieties and the different names in the different sign languages. For "dog," for example, I have observed: (*a*) the slapping of one's knee; (*b*) the biting of one's hand; (*c*) the snapping of one's thumb and middle finger; and (*d*) the outlining of the animal's muzzle with a hand in the C position of the finger alphabet coming forward from the face of the speaker. The American sign for my country, Holland, is in origin the depicting of the long Gouda clay pipe, but I have met with the variant depicting the Volendam girl's cap with both hands at the sides of the head.

At the primary and primitive level of origin, the recognition-by-association is strictly situation-bound. As a means to distinguish between such purely ad hoc imitations and true linguistic signifiers, I executed the signs which I suspected were still functioning at a sublinguistic level without context while asking the subjects the meaning of such signs. If there was a uniform and immediate recognition, I concluded that the sign could evidently be isolated, and that—in all probability—it was more than a situation-bound imitation. But if there was nonrecognition or no uniform agreement, the sign was considered to be still in need of contextual information and to function still at a stage of development toward the status of a linguistic sign.

I use the term "development" on purpose. The life span of such ad hoc imitations was short. They either disappeared or they were picked up by partners; in the latter case they developed very fast toward the linguistic level. Sometimes the acting or role playing as a communicative means was such that no single signifiers could be isolated as minimal free units. I was able to achieve some insight into these primary stages of development owing to the fact that data of young deaf subjects were collected. Information from preschool children would have given much more information; however, the youngest age at which deaf subjects can assist in the translation of their signifying behavior is seven—at least in my experience.

Once the recognition of a sign is established as a convention, it is no longer associated with "reality" but identified with it. The sign then functions as a word does in this respect. Careful imitation to evoke correct associative recognition is no longer necessary, since now there is an agreement upon the meaning of the sign between the partners who use it. From then on the iconicity recedes to the level of concomitant feature. For the purpose of quick and efficient use of the sign, it is executed in a streamlined, shortened way that accentuates some features and leaves out others or treats them as optional. Such a sign follows linguistic realization rules in which onomatopoeic functioning no longer plays a role. Once all this is established, the sign, like the word, is identified with that "reality" it names and vice versa. It is normal to ask: "What is this?" "What do you think that is?" not "What do you call that?"—just as it is normal to get the answer: "Oh, well, I think that is some sort of a bottle," and not "Oh, that is called a bottle." Only if there is a context explicitly dealing with name giving, as in second language learning or being in a foreign country, will conversational partners turn consciously to the naming aspect of a word as distinct from the "reality" it names. In all other instances, signs as well as words function as conventional, arbitrary forms when, at least, the signs have reached the adult stage of development. Yet there remain differences, also at that level, between signs and words. To restate the obvious, words are acoustic and signs are visual. Signs can be traced back to their iconic past in many instances, words can not as they do not have such a past. Some specific types of interference in the semantic functioning of the word + sign signifier will be dealt with in the next section.

The Differences in Arbitrariness of Word and Sign

There remain some differences between the semantic functioning of words and signs, even if the latter name as words do in the sense described above. These differences have something to do with the fact that the original iconicity remains a concomitant feature, implying that somehow it keeps playing a role in the communicative process. One of the ways this comes to the surface can be best demonstrated by giving a few examples.

To pick was performed by a group of subjects as follows: The right fist, thumb on top, makes a quick turn while moving toward the body. In fast conversation this sign can be made at chest level, no matter what is picked. It can also be made in a more depicting way, however, especially in a colorful, emphasizing, emotional, narrative situation. Then, strawberries, flowers, blueberries, cherries, and apples are picked successively a little higher. There can be accompanying pantomimic behavior of different sorts; often, the eyes show a flash of a searching look in the appropriate direction; the movements of the head—as if searching for the fruits—are accordingly different. In one instance, while conversing about picking strawberries, a subject making the picking sign stooped a little, while her partner, who was sitting on a chair, moved her legs aside to make room for her hand getting down, while she in turn was signing the picking of strawberries. The signing of picking blueberries was accompanied by an imitation with the left hand of the pushing aside of the shrubbery. While signing the picking of an apple, a deaf boy held his head supine for a short while. At another occasion, the picking sign for a pear was accompanied by a hardly noticeable lift of the body because the feet indicated that the picking had been done on tiptoe. None of these additional features, pertaining to the performance, to the execution-in-fact, to the ambiance of accessory picking circumstances, was obligatory for the linguistic realization of the signifier. It seems hard to find other than psychological determinants of such behavior. Most of the time alternating sets of such optional features were present. The important aspect I want to bring forward, though, is that **no optional feature or set of features could ever be used in conflict with the real activity and its circumstances.** Picking strawberries with the neutral and quick execution of the sign but with a searching look at the sky, or picking apples with the same neutral sign but with a searching look at the ground were simply not accepted or caused amusement or misunderstanding. By the same token, the height at which the picking sign is made predicts the kind of flowers that still have to be introduced into the conversation. If one makes the sign fairly high, for example in a general context about a garden, the expectancy is that the flowers going to be picked in the story will be lilacs, roses, or some others from bushes; they could not be tulips or pansies.

Tall, long, high—as well as some other measure-indicating adjectives—

are usually signed by the subject with one or two hands (depending on whether the measurement is longitudinal or vertical) which, at the same time execute the constant conventional, arbitrary features together with changeable modalities adapting to each situation at one's free choice. *Tall* or *high* can be a quick going up of the hand, palm down, and *long* an extending of both hands, palms facing each other, no matter whether the height of Daddy or the Empire State Building is the topic of conversation, or again the length of the skipping rope or of Main Street is at stake. Daddy's height can, obviously, be indicated much more precisely if Sonny stands up and makes the sign reaching about that much above his head; for the extreme height of the Empire State Building he could add the optional features of reaching as high as he can and looking up; there are more behavioral variations to stress the point. The proud indication, by one of the youngest subjects, of the size of a big fish her daddy had caught was performed in such a precise exaggeration that it had to be talked down by her partner several inches.

Province, country: a group of Dutch subjects indicated the position of a province or a country (in Holland or in Europe, respectively) on the map by making a circular movement of the right hand, fingers spread, at the more or less appropriate location on an imaginary map in the air. The sign was not a pure imitation ad hoc but had a core of conventional features according to the recognition test: If made without context and in a neutral way, it evoked the response, "What country?" An additional interesting feature of specific word–sign bilingualism was that the sign by itself meant something like "country-in-general" or "any-province," not specifying the country or province; this was done by the simultaneously spoken word. So the sign-only was ambiguous, as long as the country or province had to be introduced into the conversation as new; the word-only was hard to read from the lips, but in combination, the two worked in perfect cooperation, the sign narrowing down the possibilities of misunderstanding considerably by introducing the generic indication of "somewhere on a map," and the word specifying the sign. Furthermore, the same optional features in the performance of the sign were possible, for example, in relation to the area and the shape of the country named. I found, by the way, at that same school more of these typical combinations of a word + sign where the sign-part had the function of signaling a generic category and the word pinpointed the individual, for example, *person-in-general* + "spoken name," *place-where-one-lives* + "name-of-town," *some-river* + "name-of-the-river."

Returning to the features we found in *country* and *province*, and also in *to pick, tall, long*, and *high*, I think the point is not that the same can be found in the actual performance of some signs for *dance, laugh, sleep, cough, ugly, game, cold, shake hands*, and numerous other signs, but that visual and acoustic signifiers function both similarly and differently. They function similarly in that they both operate removed from "reality" in an arbitrary agreement which frees them for abstract use at different levels. But they function differently in that signs are embedded in ad hoc behavior that is inseparably interwoven with the arbitrary features, and therefore condition the latter. Before elaborating upon the consequences of all this in terms of bilingual interference between word and sign, some more introductory remarks have to be made. Concomitant iconicity comes to the surface in still other, but similar ways. Again, a few examples can replace much explanation.

To like among some subjects was a sign made by crossing the arms across the chest, originally indicating the embracing of a person. A foreign visitor gave each pupil of a class a candy bar, whereupon some of them told each other that they liked the fellow, using this sign. I was working in that classroom and had seen it all. I got an idea and asked: "Would you actually embrace the fellow if he were still here?" They were pleasantly shocked at the idea and explained patiently to me that they just found the man kind and sympathetic. Obviously, the connotation "embrace" had not entered their minds until I brought it up. One would conclude that the sign was an arbitrary one, and that its iconicity was something of the past. But about half an hour or so later, I was offered part of one of the candy bars; I turned it down, saying and signing "*No, thank you, I don't like milk chocolate*," using—on purpose, of course—the same sign for *like*. I was then laughed at for using it, because "you can't hold a piece of candy that way." The proper sign to use in their system would have been to rub my stomach. We then decided to settle the matter in terms of what linguists call semantic features, which looked easy enough until we tried. We first tried one sign for people and, possibly, things that can also be embraced, and the other sign for things that one can put into one's stomach—more or less, and without too great a risk—but it turned out to be so complicated that we gave it up for the time being. A beautiful tree, a mailbox, a new car, all kinds of toys, even very small ones, could be "liked" with the first sign; the second one was not limited to edibles or drinkables which tasted good, but was used for different sorts of sensations, depending also on the mimicry, and whether the heart or the stomach was rubbed.

House among most subjects, American and Dutch alike, was signed by indicating a slanting roof with fingertips touching, then going apart and down. I have never noticed any difficulty with houses that did not have slanted roofs; the same sign was also used for these in both countries. In America the twice-repeated sign was used for "downtown," indicating the complete abstraction of the implication "slanted roof." I have tried on several occasions to confuse my pupils and my subjects in the project, asking them if they were sure that the house they were talking about had indeed a roof that was slanted. Sometimes they said that they did not know, or only realized that such was indeed the case when I asked them, but they always explained to me that it did not matter. That was also their answer when the house in question did not have such a roof. On occasion they just shrugged their shoulders, saying something like "I guess so," to get rid of me. But when I insisted sometimes that a flat or rectangular roof ought not to be outlined with the sign they used, they showed puzzlement, or disagreed. The sign meant "house," period. Like the little girl in another experiment on child language, whom I asked why she called her doll a "doll" (hoping she would come up with a self-invented name); her answer was: "Because it is a doll, you nut!" Of course, both the young lady and the deaf children were absolutely right. Evidently, the slanting was not part of the denoting features of the linguistic signifier. But a problem arose when a whole class of Dutch deaf children kept understanding the "House of Orange" as the well-known and beautiful white palace of Queen Juliana, not wanting at first to accept the meaning "The family of the Oranges all the way back to William the Silent." They protested in chorus that such a thing could never be signed with the slanted-roof sign because you could not live under it. They made the sign higher up above their heads, in their arguing about it, to indicate that a house meant something over your head.

To take among one group was a grasping hand moving toward the body while closing the fingers. When a boy told me that he had gotten his driver's license and was going on a ride during the coming weekend, he signed: *I take my girl friend*. I then asked whether he planned to grab his girl like that, whereupon he laughed, slightly mad at me, tapped his forehead and pointed at me, meaning, of course: "You stupid." But 5 minutes later, when I stopped the conversation with the signed and spoken utterance *"You better take that shower now,"* he did not understand the taking of the shower that way. He protested against my signing, arguing that he could not envisage handling a shower in such a way.

Place to one of the younger Dutch subjects meant her seat in the classroom, dining room, chapel, etc. The sign had been motivated in its origin, as was evident from its shape: hands with palms down making conjuring "sit down" motions. Place-in-line caused no problems, although the sitting implication was nonadaptable, neither did the place of her bed in the dormitory. But "Amsterdam is such a nice place" could not be signed that way.

There are numerous other examples of all these features, but the points have been made, I hope, and more eloquently by the examples the children gave me than by me. From these examples it becomes clear that the semantic features of the word-part and the sign-part are not always identical, although they are used together and even simultaneously in the word + sign signifier.

Now, shifts of meaning as a consequence of different combinations of semantic features are, of course, a well-known phenomenon in bilingualism. It is quite evident that many words can hardly, or only in part, or in a certain context, be translated into words of another language. "Bank," for example, means "bank" in both English and Dutch insofar as a trading place for money and checks (or something of that kind) is concerned; it means, moreover, "bench" in Dutch and not in English, and the "bank" of a river in English but not in Dutch.

However, in the word + sign signifier bilingual interference there is more to it than just a partial, more or less accidental or historic difference in some semantic features, like in sets of words from two different languages. As is shown by the examples, concomitant iconicity starts interfering when some semantic word features disagree with what the sign originally depicted. It thus is not any arbitrary agreement that happens to differ between two languages which blocks the usage, but the fact that **suddenly the native user of the sign realizes that the sign can not be envisaged to handle "reality" like that.** The limits of what a sign can—and implicitly does—signify can be discovered by methodologically challenging its original motivation. It then becomes clear that the semantic load of a sign always reflects its original iconicity.

For an even better understanding of the semantic functioning of the word + sign signifier, one has to consider the basically different relations to "reality" of the sign-part and of the word-part. Words represent acoustically a "reality" which is both spatial and acoustic; signs represent spatially only a purely spatial world. One should not forget that the deaf lack a whole dimension. No spatial and acoustic environment can be represented by sound giving only in a signifying communicative system based upon sound imitation; such a system would obviously be utterly inadequate. "Reality" seldom is acoustic; even where it is, sound is one of the characteristics of the source of sound only, never the source itself.

Furthermore, the sound-giving apparatus would be inadequate for the imitative task. As a consequence, words—essentially—make abstraction from sound and sight in the way they sound; using an acoustic signifier implies no indication whatsoever of the sound or shape of the specific "reality" referred to.

An exclusively spatial environment, however, can be represented quite well by its shapes' outlines, movements, and the like. Visual signifying utilizes reshaping, depicting with one's communicating body as one of the most obvious, easy, and convincing ways of representing (that is, making **present** in a signifier) "reality." Iconicity as concomitant feature means having at one's disposal an enormous evocative power of the signifiers as they not only refer to reality in some sort of detached way, but at the same time have it in them to (re)create the presence of such "reality."

Fischer's observations concerning ASL (Bellugi & Fischer, 1972) are similar to the ones described above, but her analysis does not take iconicity into account as I have done. She refers to a feature "incorporation," of which she lists the following types: (a) "incorporation of number," for example, *park-a-car* with one hand, *two-cars-parked-side-by-side* with two hands; (b) "incorporation of manner," for example, "In one story, a person *said*, 'and there was a *terrific* explosion.' In the signed version, the sign for 'EXPLODE' incorporated the manner adverbial and indicated that it was indeed a 'terrific' explosion."; (c) "incorporation of size and shape," for example, "The sign RUN incorporates legs, but the sign BITE incorporates something like mouth [pp. 191, 192]." At the end of this section, Fischer writes:

> It is beginning to look as though the incorporation of size and shape involves some sort of feature system, since we need a method of cross-classification in order to attain maximum generality. Thus, EAT-ICE-CREAM-WITH-SPOON employs the same hand-shape for the signing hand as the sign for removing something with a spoon, while SCREW-ON-TOP-OF-JAR has the same base hand as the sign for removing something from a jar [p. 192].

One would like to know, what "system" Fischer is writing about here. It looks to me more like adding ad hoc rules to many signs that are evidently partly imitating and therefore rather obeying psycholinguistic or psychological than linguistic rules. I take it that Fischer means something of the kind when she states:

> While many signs which incorporate the size and/or shape of various elements are optional, and seem to be used somewhat to add color to a signed utterance, there are some verbs for which this type of incorporation is obligatory. Thus, the verb CLOSE *requires* the signer to specify *what* is being closed [pp. 192–193].

This is like the sign for picking something, which I gave before; the difference is that I also found a "neutralized" version. If one thing is certain, it is that more research will be necessary to find more answers.

Briefly summarizing this section, it can be stated that true bilingualism of some kind is present wherever a compound word + sign signifier is used, because and insofar as an acoustic and a visual counterpart meet, blend, and are identified with each other. The data from my 6-year project clearly bear out the conclusion that such a signifier occurs very frequently and becomes one of the modes of easy usage among all deaf living amidst hearing people. Although there are limitations to the degree of identification, one of its obvious results is that the grammatical exoteric word category is borrowed by the sign. Simultaneous occurrence might be preceded by the occurrence of either word-only or sign-only usages; in the course of the first years of life of a deaf child, visual communication will rely mostly on signs that are to a large extent imitations in origin. Iconicity thereafter remains a concomitant feature that is a powerful asset to the creativity and liveliness of the conversation. In the analysis of the semantic functioning of the word + sign signifier the bilingual interference is, to a large extent, due to this iconicity as a truly functioning feature.

BILINGUAL INTERFERENCE IN UTTERANCES

Introductory Remarks

So far we have dealt with some aspects of the bilingual interference at the level of the signifier in and by itself. In the process of communication of deaf persons, both among themselves and when facing hearing people, bilingual features are apparent all the time. Again, it has to be emphasized that we are dealing with a unique sort of bilingualism because of the fundamental difference between acoustic and visual communication. There is no interference here between two known natural languages based upon speech. Here we are always dealing on the one hand with one such language—English or Dutch, for example—for which fairly complete and sophisticated grammatical analyses are available, and on the other hand a system whose very status as a language might still be controversial among some linguists. As I have argued extensively elsewhere (Tervoort, 1973a), I am not among those who doubt this, insofar as I am willing to accept at face value a system of communication which, obviously, functions adequately among its users, without worrying too much about what to call it before it has been thoroughly analyzed.

It seems better to me to accept any signing system between the deaf as

some sort of a language, while awaiting what future research will come up with. Maybe there will then appear to be reasons indeed to deny signing some of the fundamental features of language—with the qualification that we mean specifically speech-based language—without having to deny it the status of language altogether as a consequence. There might even appear to be some good new arguments for revising the old definitions of what a language fundamentally is and is not. One of the problems of analyzing a sign language is that it hardly occurs independently of the language(s) around it, nor is it ever on an equal level of development and sophistication in general, unless it has bilingual characteristics. It might be possible to find deaf persons who have had hardly any education at all, and therefore are to a far lesser extent bilingual—although they will always be functioning within a society of words and of speaking and writing people. But even then it would be as risky to neglect the factor of poorer intellectual development and cognition in conclusions concerning the features of their communication, as it will be difficult to keep the two apart. For how are you going to do it?

In this context, some of Schlesinger's experiments are worth mentioning again. Schlesinger (1971) was confronted with bilingual features of Israeli Sign Language (ISL) and Hebrew in these experiments; he found various degrees of interference between the two. The more competent his deaf subjects were in Hebrew, the more able they were to get across to their partners through signing the relation between subject, verb, indirect object, and direct object. Mostly, those who knew little Hebrew failed in this task. Their signing had some rules, such as that the adjective always follows the noun it modifies (as in *dog white* or *man big*), or that the verb never stands in first position; they lacked, however, the means to express the relations between subject, verb, and object.

Schlesinger concludes that this does not make the sign language under discussion less of a language, because ISL is adequate enough to express those and other relations in a nonlaboratory, everyday situation. According to Schlesinger, the implications for the theory of universals of language of these features not being present in this type of sign language are that hereby the hypothesis discussed in Bach (1968), "there are certain grammatical relations—such as 'subject of' and 'object of'—which appear in the universal base structure" is falsified [quoted by Schlesinger]. Schlesinger (1971) then states: "This particular version is extremely vulnerable because it claims that whatever appears in the universal base appears in the base structure of *every* language [p. 116, italics his]."

I doubt whether this is the complete picture, or whether this reasoning will finally solve the problem, In what sense is a sign language a language?

What Bach and many others are writing about are natural languages **based upon speech acts, speech production, and speech perception**; a visual communication system obviously can lack some of the basic features of an acoustic one and still be termed a **language sui generis**. I therefore understand Schlesinger much better when he writes:

> Elsewhere (Schlesinger, 1968) it has been shown that adults, using spoken language, may decode an utterance by means of semantic cues without analyzing its syntactic structure. The present study seems to indicate that this substitution of semantic for syntactic cues is far from being an isolated phenomenon. Instead *ISL* seems to resort regularly to semantic cues, both in encoding and decoding [1971, p. 116].

And I would like to add: The hypothesis does not seem too farfetched that all occurring sign languages, apart from being almost always interfered with by a dominating language spoken and written around them are specifically *sui generis* in that they are a mixture of some conventional agreements between partners (particularly as far as their signs and their vocabulary as listed in a special lexicon are concerned) and a whole range of communicative bodily behavioral features resulting from psychological influences rather than from linguistic conventions. Through these latter features roles are played, feelings expressed, parts are acted or reenacted, partners are elicited or rebuffed, others are mimicked, pointed at, and so on and so forth. Precisely because all these characteristics together are basic for a visual human communication system, their co-occurrence makes such a system fully capable of expressing semantic content. In my opinion, it is on these terms that signing can be truly a language.

Observing deaf people, or deaf children going full blast in animated interchange shows all this. Theirs is a total communication which is really person to person; they read each other's semantic intent from the face and the whole person of the partner. I see no difficulty in stating that this is not a language in the traditional and usual sense of the word. That is the direction in which, I think, Schlesinger's answer would go most successfully against Wasow (1973), who comes to the conclusion that if ISL can not express basic grammatical relations, it is not a language.

Obviously, to establish the exact nature of some feature of syntactic interference between two languages, one has to analyze first the origin of such an interference by tracing the occurrence of that feature in the two languages involved. Usually, and in the case of two spoken languages, one can rely upon existing extensive grammatical analysis of both. In the case of bilingual interference between a spoken language and signed communication, however, such extensive knowledge is available about the spoken language only, not about the signing. No complete grammars have been presented of any sign language yet; one of the reasons is that they are masked and dominated so much by the co-occurrence of the spoken language. Stokoe (1972) puts the problem as follows:

> If sign language were a uniform, homogeneous, and well ordered system throughout the ASL population (or as some assume throughout the total population that signs), then statistical and sampling procedures to secure subjects informants would be valid. But American Sign Language has no such uniformity, and the selection of informants for its study calls for as much care as is exercised in any linguistic research—indeed more care for ASL is nowhere found in isolation so that the linguist is forced to consider its relation, inside the informant, to the other language, American English, in the same community. Early in the research an ideal informant was thought of as an intelligent, adult, fully enculturated member of the ASL community who used little or no English. Such an informant was never found, of course. One mark of an intelligent adult signer is the competence he has in the language surrounding him. This is not to say he must be proficient in lipreading (intelligence and lipreading skills are often negatively correlated) nor skillful in producing audible and intelligible speech. It is instead to understand that he has competence in the semological and morphological systems of English which he uses, not through phonology, but through fingerspelling as well as through the conventional writing system of a literate technological culture. One must then settle for a bilingual informant [p. 122].

I have argued (Tervoort, 1973a) that this

> is hardly convincing to those who claim that such a dependent communication system can not be a true language. All there is to the signing of the deaf, they will argue, is that they convey messages in some visual VOCABULARY CODE (looking like some pictorial riddle to which only they have the key) but in a linguistic system based on the syntax of the hearing environment. Granted, they often fall short of the task of producing grammatical sentences, but there is no reason to confuse ungrammatical-ness with "using an exotic language" as if it existed on some remote island. Even SYSTEMATIC ungrammaticalness proves nothing more than the occurrence of typi-cal mistakes, the so called deafisms [p. 376].

In his last chapter, Stokoe (1972) tries to find the solution by calling the relation between ASL and English that of diglossia. I do not think this solves the problem, though:

> Ferguson's term DIGLOSSIA applies to the situation where "two or more varieties of the SAME language are used by some speakers under different conditions" (Ferguson, 1959, 325), which varieties he terms high (H) and low (L), giving a number of character-istics of the latter to demonstrate his point. In a note, he states that "no attempt is made in this paper to examine the analogous situation where two DISTINCT (related or unrelated) languages are used side by side throughout a speech community, each with a clearly defined role." (ibid.) The accent should be put on the words SAME and DISTINCT (which I therefore have emphasized) [Tervoort, 1973a, p. 377].

At the end of his book, Stokoe—who is one of the great promoters of

ASL as a language in its own right—comes to the conclusion that ASL's high variety is nothing else than English. The conclusion then seems unavoidable to me that the low variety of ASL is either English too, be it of a lower variety, or that it is non-English, and therefore a completely different language from ASL high.

The better answer, in my opinion, is that the use of grammatical English—especially as far as word order and the use of function words are concerned—increases inversely with the use of characteristic features of the visual code, and vice versa, of course. One should keep the two codes apart, methodologically speaking, without denying the evident fact that—in actual performance—they blend permanently. But that does not make sign language English, or vice versa. It is, of course, easy enough to discover features of English and of "something else" in the communication of American deaf; but a closer inspection will show that there are all kinds of degrees of co-occurrence of these features, and almost no occurrence of just one of the extremes. A deaf-born perfect speaker of the language is as rare as the adult signer who has undergone no influence whatsoever from the language spoken and written around him. This goes also for deaf persons of different nationalities, meeting each other. They all have been exposed to, as well as educated in, acoustic systems that—in most instances—were linguistically of one language family.

Theoretically speaking, I have had the opportunity of meeting signing that was as independent from any other language as possible, and studying it. While on an inspection tour in Dutch Guyana (Surinam) in 1970 to assess the extremely problematic multilingual situation in the schools of that country and its analphabetism, I came across a small group of illiterate, noneducated deaf-mute Indians living in one of the remote jungle villages. Unfortunately enough, I had no time or opportunity to give their communication more than passing attention. My strong conviction after watching them and communicating with them for some time was that upon scrutiny they might well have turned out to be native and monolingual signers of a purely visual communication system which had undergone no influence from the village dialect.

At any rate, if in all other cases there is always a blend of a language—say English—and of "something else," and if that "something else" is indeed a language different from English, then we are dealing with bilingualism, not with diglossia. However, if that "something else" is not a language but only a subsidiary, supporting, pantomimic—or what have you—system, we must speak of a high and a low variety, but in this case of the English, etc., language.

A more or less complete inventory of all the attempts at syntactic analyses of sign languages is beyond the scope of this chapter. Elsewhere

I have published my attempts at such an analysis (e.g., Tervoort, 1953, 1967, 1968a, 1975). A very elaborate analysis, of American Indian sign language in this case, with a very extensive survey of the literature is to be found in La Mont West (1960). The variety of theories concerning sign language grammar is sketched by him in a few words as follows:

> The observers thus fall in three main postures in respect to the evaluation of syntax in sign language:
> 1. Those who regard the grammar of sign language as chiefly confined to syntax and characterize the syntax as relatively firmly structured: Kroeber, Tomkins, Tylor, for example.
> 2. Those who search for the grammar of sign language on the syntactic level and note its actual great variability. These in turn fall into two categories:
>   a. Those who conclude that the sign language has little grammar of its own and must be supplemented by non-linguistic context to serve as a communication medium: Tervoort, for instance.
>   b. Those who search further and discover an elaborate grammatical structure tied to a spatial, rather than temporal framework: Mallery, West, for example.
> 3. Those who attribute sign syntax to derivation from spoken language [p. 93].

I cannot see that the theories sketched under (1) and (3) have yet been proven to be on firm ground; I am appreciative of being listed under (2). Since my analyses were confined to the private communication of deaf **children** who were in the process of learning Dutch or English, I am quite willing to accept that it is possible to "search further"; but then I would add with different informants. However, it seems also to me that, where bilingual interference between spoken language and signing is concerned, deaf **children** are the best informants, because:

1. They are less influenced by existing, sound-language-dependent adult systems of signing and therefore better capable of clearly demonstrating the origins of visual communication.
2. They are under the constant and growing influence of the classroom language, and therefore show the beginnings of the bilingual interference as well.

Apart from developmental characteristics, universal features were also found, supposedly characteristic for a visual communication system as such. As my 6-year project comprised groups of subjects coming from different American English- and Dutch-speaking communities, I had a fairly good opportunity to make a first attempt at separating universal features from peculiarities, applying only to one subject, a small group, or just one code, and to focus upon the former.[1] Following is a short inven-

---

[1]My 1967 publication was issued in a very limited number of copies as a report to the

tory of the most characteristic universal features which exerted a strong influence upon the bilingual utterance:

The ordering of signifiers in the utterance
Omissions
Additions
Substitutions
Inversions

Initial, final, and modal markers
Initial markers and final markers
Initial markers and conjunctions
Modal markers

The function of the focus.

Each of these universal characteristics will be taken up in the following sections. In order to demonstrate the specific functioning of the particular type of bilingual interference under discussion, it is necessary both to discuss the growing influence of the school language and to include the gist of the analysis carried out upon the esoteric, systematically visual component of the dialogues.

The Ordering of Signifiers in the Utterance

It was a fairly easy task first to divide all the 14,341 utterances collected into two main groups: those that were grammatical Dutch or English or reasonably close attempts, and those that were not. The respective over-all percentages were 35.5% versus 46.5% (not counting the ± 12% one-word sentences and the ± 7% pure imitative clauses). In general, exoteric (i.e., Dutch or English) grammaticality was judged on correct word order and the proper use of function words—"words" standing here for either signs-only, signs + words, or words-only.

In the reporting itself, it has been argued extensively why it seemed justified to count all three varieties of the same signifier in one category where syntactic analysis is concerned. In a few words, it amounts to this: If, e.g., *(people)*, *people*, and people; *(like)*, LIKE, and like; *(Kennedy)*, *Kennedy*, and Kennedy occurred randomly, I accepted a sentence like People like Kennedy (signed-only) as equivalent in grammaticality to

Office of Vocational Rehabilitation of the Department of Health, Education, and Welfare, Washington, D.C., and to the Netherlands' Organization for Pure Scientific Research. A revised and shortened version was published in 1975 by North Holland Elsevier (Amsterdam) under the title, *Developmental features of visual communication: A psycholinguistic analysis of deaf children's growth in communicative competence.*

(*People*) (*like*) (*Kennedy*) (spoken-only) or *People like Kennedy* (signed and spoken).[2] I disregarded, in other words, whether the one or the other type of execution of the signifier was used. And if the subjects were switching like this all the time, I expanded this to all signifiers.

At the start of our study a subdivision of all the grammatical sentences was made in 1958. The following types were found to occur (G = Grammatical, S = Simple, I = Inversion, C = Complex):[3]

GS

(1)   Your mother *came*.

(2)   Me and THE boyscouts work.

(3)   SHE sits in A WHEEL chair.

(4)   *We went to THE movies in town last Saturday.*

(5)   I made some cookies for HER.

(6)   *I help my mother very much.*

(7)   Who WAS your DATE yesterday?

(8)   *TODAY IS mother DAY.*

(9)   *I love to help braid* the girlS HAIR.

(10)   *My grandmother will die today or soon.*

(11)   *Yesterday afternoon you got A BOX from your mother.*

(12)   After a while my sister won crown.

GI

(13)   Have you?

(14)   Do you?

---

[2]For a key to the transcription devices used here and in the sample sentences that follow, see p. 178.

Exoteric morphological marking—say of a plural, a past tense, or a third person singular present tense—although it is possible through added or superimposed finger spelling, did not occur very often. There was a highly significant overall increase in the use of the exoteric grammatical sentence with increasing age. The use of function words remained relatively low; of course, they are highly uncharacteristic for a visual communication system to begin with. They shall be dealt with only insofar as they are of direct relevance for our topic, under "conjunctions" and "modal markers" below. The issue to be discussed now is the ordering of signifiers.

[3]A reference number before a sample sentence indicates that it actually occurred in the data.

(15)   Where is your boyfriend?

(16)   WHEN *WILL HE RETIRE OF our SCHOOL?*

(17)   What KIND OF CAR DO you like best?

(18)   WHAT says your boy?

(19)   AREN'T you pretty enough?

(20)   Had you A nice time AT the PROM last week?

(21)   WILL you GO to the 500 races this year?

(22)   DO you like to get it on AUG. 31?

(23)   IS he going to BE superintendent?

GC

(24)   *I hope you will GO and SEE.*

(25)   I told Shirley I saw LIZ TAYLOR.

(26)   *IF you finish school will you go to college?*

(27)   *WHY WERE NOT you here IF you are sorry that you ARE
        not?*

(28)   *DID you GO* and DID you *LIKE IT?*

(29)   I want the movies to know what you always say.

(30)   *We saw* VOLCANOS ERUPT.

The samples given account for the subdivisions as well. For a complete
account of the subdivision, as well as for all the samples in Dutch, one has
to consult the original publication. In this chapter, no Dutch examples or
translations thereof will be given, unless stated otherwise. If not mentioned expressly, the Dutch examples show similar features. Samples (1)
through (30) serve to substantiate the statement that (nearly) complete
and diversified exoteric grammaticality can be arrived at within all the
expressive possibilities, and that this exoteric usage is the one extreme at
which bilingual interference comes to an end. I would not term this ASL
high variety; this is English, not sign language, although signs are used.
   This is not the complete picture, though. In the nearly 5000 utterances
that were termed grammatical English or Dutch, over 5000 small "mistakes" occurred, making most of them "nearly" grammatical only—in
other words, not more than performance attempts at such grammaticality.

At first sight this might seem quite an unusual way of using the term "grammatical," to put it mildly, but one should not forget that we are dealing with unusual data too. The fact that a clear-cut division could be made between exoteric-grammatical and esoteric-definitely-not-grammatical if weighed against English or Dutch grammar—in other words, the fact that all these 5000 sentences were evidently intended to be English or Dutch and the rest clearly were not—warranted the division. The important point is that each of the small deviations found in these sentences was a clue for the interfering influence of the visual system. The four generic categories found appeared to be exhaustive. We shall deal with each of them briefly, again referring to the original publications for further information.

The categories were: (1) Omissions; (2) Additions; (3) Substitutions; and (4) Inversions.

OMISSIONS

Both the English and the Dutch subjects rarely left out nouns or other types of content words. On a few occasions a main verb was left out, but only if it could easily be reconstructed from the context. For example:

(31)   Last summer my FAMILY together to OHIO.   [went]

(32)   I HER STEP sister.   [like]

(33)   Our TEAM almost basketball in tournament.   [won]

(34)   My father HA HA!   [laughed]

All subjects, however, often omitted the different types of function words, including the copula and auxiliary verbs. The omission which occurred the most was the subject personal pronoun, followed by the object personal pronoun. Some samples are:

(35)   Yes will GO to the SLUMBER PARTY next Friday night.   [I]

(36)   Told about Chicago.   [I]

(37)   *NO next year will play basketball.*   [I]

(38)   know my FAVORITE MARTIAN man IS my father.   [You]

(39)   I like TAG but I DO not know.   [it]

(40)   *DO you miss?*   [him]

(41)   *I like YES.*   [her]

(42)   *Well I bought for fun.*   [it]

As will be argued in a later section entitled "The Function of the

Focus," in an esoteric utterance the noun-subjects as well as the pronouns "I"/"we," "you," "he"/"she"/"they" often function as the focus in a way that can be compared to the functioning of an NP-subject in an English or a Dutch sentence. The striking aspect of that esoteric functioning is, however, that it does not matter whether these signifiers are actually expressed within such an utterance or just given in the context. In either case, they keep exerting their focal influence. There seems to be no rule of grammar enforcing their actual use if this use is redundant. The omission of the object personal pronoun shows that, in these cases also, if the context supplies the information wanted, there is no rule prescribing its use. It will be explained in the discussion of "The Function of the Focus," why I do not speak in the latter case—or in the case of an omitted verb—of a focus. The reason the focus is not worked out here, is that it is a typical esoteric feature; and as long as we are dealing with omissions, we are taking the standpoint of exoteric analysis. Esoterically speaking, there are no omissions. There are only if one is looking at it from the outside, from the English. In that sense, all function words are left out frequently. As stated before, they are typical for an acoustic system and foreign to any visual code; they carry little immediate semantic information and are sound-grammar-specific. By the same token, all English and Dutch copulas and auxiliary verbs were subject to frequent omissions, as well as articles, prepositions and conjunctions. Here follow some items:

Copulative Verb

(43)   What yours?

(44)   Who older?

(45)   My favorite MARS.

(46)   Because I tired.

Auxiliary Verb

(47)   What you gave mother?

(48)   I not like snow because IT IS cold.

(49)   Because president Kennedy not let OSWALD live in US.

(50)   Yes today I think now who teach us how to speak.

Article

(51)   J., K., and I ARE on COMMITTEE.

(52)   Now sun is rising.

(53)   Dutch man come here.

(54)   *I like warm wind now.*

Preposition

(55)   *But MAY we will study MEXICO.*

(56)   I live ROYAL CENTER.

(57)   You go SANFORD.

(58)   I will go California in JUNE because my father will work in
        THE MARINE CORPS in SAN DIEGO.

Conjunction

(59)   I like shorter better long.

(60)   My father played card bridge won.

(61)   Yes *your brother mother father* love you.

(62)   Are you happy he comes?

Note: There are, of course, some similarities between features of child language development and characteristics of the communication of the deaf subjects under discussion, for example, the types of omission and the reasons for them. These similarities should not be overemphasized (as is sometimes done while arguing that deaf children's language is no different from that of their hearing mates but only somewhat retarded) for the following reasons:

1. There is a big age difference, given features always occurring at a much younger age among the hearing.
2. There remains a great difference in the frequency of occurrence of any specific feature.
3. There remains a great difference in the frequency of occurrence over the different subjects.
4. Apart from variables like age and frequency of occurrence, which are extrinsic to the features themselves, of course, there are a good number of features which are universally characteristic for the communication of deaf children that have no correspondence whatsoever in the primary language development of hearing children at any age level. These features are due to the fact that deaf children are in a bilingual situation, and hearing children are not, or not per se and as a rule.

ADDITIONS

Additions are the opposite of omissions; they seem to arise:

1. Because of overcategorization in the attempt to use the exoteric code
2. Because of the influence of the great freedom to insert a new sign in the chain of signs

The first case can be demonstrated quite well by giving some examples of superfluous use of some prepositions and the article. The counterparts in the same learning process are the omissions of same.

(63)   Yes I go home for on mother day.

(64)   *I wonder WHY OSWALD SHOT to HIM.*

(65)   *We learn A MEXICO next fall.*

(66)   *If I play there maybe I will make THE our TEAM win.*

The second case can be demonstrated by showing the superfluous addition of some adverbs. These are harder to pinpoint because inserting adverbs is more free in English and seldom superfluous or even ungrammatical. Consider:

(67)   Yes I think sometimes Miss G. always scold us to me good.

(68)   I AM SO glad that our CAMPUS IS more THE most beautiful CAMPUS in THE USA.

SUBSTITUTIONS

The substitutions that occurred in the data give a good impression of what is difficult to learn in the two languages involved and what, evidently, is foreign to the esoteric system. Another possible conclusion from the substitution data is that the subjects knew that they had to choose from a certain exoteric category but picked the "wrong" word (+ sign) from that category. It seems significant to me that no substitutions beyond the category occurred; all were from within the same exoteric grammatical category, at least in the grammatical and the grammatically acceptable sentences. Substitutions included several cases of "wrong" article, "wrong" preposition, "wrong" pronoun, and the like, for example:

(69)   NO I DID not have the good time because IT WAS A hard JOB.

(70)   Yes I like the NYC.   [New York City substituted for "town"]

(71)   *We leave to CAMP AT 8 o'clock to 3:30.*

(72)   SO I slept with NG'S home.

(73)   Sure me hurry but I can't.

(74)   You mean I AM fat AS HER.   [HER substituted for "she"]

In cases of finger spelling or unambiguous speech, even some types of morphological substitution could be traced down, such as "wrong" tense, "wrong" number, infinitive for participle, and the like:

(75)   After a while I GO to school.   [should be "went"]

(76)   *WHAT MERIT BADGE DO you get?*   [should be "did"]

(77)   Who ARE SHE?

(78)   *DO you have any more JOKE to tell me?*

(79)   *My class* paid *75 cents* for GO eat.

(80)   *I have enjoy fishing but I DID not catch any one.*

INVERSIONS

Inversions are the most important deviations since two or more signifiers are involved and since temporal ordering of signifiers is so central to the interpretation of sentences. Omissions, substitutions, and additions have, of course, a smaller, or sometimes no, effect on the order of signifiers. It has been argued by several authors that the absolute temporal and sequential ordering of any acoustic communication system has no equally absolute counterpart in visual systems; there, any sequence occurring in time is relativized by the possible simultaneous co-occurrence of two or more signifiers of different meaning. (See, for example, Bellugi & Fischer, 1972; Stokoe, 1970; Tervoort, 1958, 1967b, 1975; West, 1960.) This possibility of simultaneous occurrence can obviously influence the rigid temporal order of the words in spoken sentences in the following way. Any time two or more simultaneously occurring signs in the esoteric system have to be transmitted sequentially because of the presence of the word-part in the compound word + sign signifier, the choice of what has to come first requires knowledge of one or more rules of the English language; the wrong choice results in the use of an incorrect inversion in the exoteric system.

The possibility of simultaneous occurrence is, of course, not the only reason for deviant exoteric word order. It is quite evident that, in general, the esoteric communication is characterized by a great freedom of order. There seem to be only a few weak order rules at work. This freedom makes it possible in esoteric communication to arrange the sequence of signifiers according to the following nonlinguistic parameters (in the order of importance):

1. The chronological order of the events
2. The coordinating concatenation
3. The visual order of the situation referred to
4. The emotional expression of the self.

The final and least important influence upon the sequential ordering was the exoteric (*in casu* Dutch) word order (Tervoort, 1953, Vol. 1, p. 263). Some of the weak rules (as described in Tervoort, 1968a) are:

1. The stronger the semantic relation between signifiers, the closer they have to be to each other.
2. Any insert-signifier weakens the coherence between signifiers thus separated.
3. Semantically strong and topically central signifiers attract others to them.
4. Semantically weak and peripherally commenting signifiers must be disambiguated by others.

None of these rules is specific for a visual versus an acoustic code. Other rules are. They are the third reason for the interference in the word order of the exoteric system, after the possible simultaneity and the great freedom of the sequencing in the signing. One of the specific rules for the signing codes is the fixed position of some signs after others.

Schlesinger (1971) notes this postposition for the verb and for the adjective following the noun–subject and the modified noun, respectively. Apart from the fact that, again, I take issue with his easy way of accepting these signs as having by themselves the status of grammatical word class (which I prefer to derive from their co-occurrence with words with which they are thereby identified, as I have argued), I think his observation is interesting and his explanation quite correct, as follows:

A post-hoc explanation of this fact which suggests itself is that the sign denoting 'give', 'hand over' or 'receive' conveys no clearly visualisable picture when standing in isolation. The sign denoting the action becomes 'meaningful' only in connection with a sign standing for the agent, the object of the action or its recipient, and since its interpretation thus depends on the noun, the noun will be found to precede it in the sequence of signs [p. 106].

I have made the same observations, and I have termed such ordering of signs the logical one. The most surprising and elucidating samples I found were the "postpositions" of the preposition, as in: (I look) mirror into, (He is hiding) cupboard behind, (We all hid) table under, (The book lies) chest on, etc. (translations from the Dutch, 1953). My reasoning was similar to Schlesinger's, as follows. There has to be a mirror put into presence first, by means of the signing hands using the appropriate sign before one can look into it, or a table before one can sneak under it, or a desk before one can put the book upon it, or a cupboard before one can hide under it, etc. If relations like "in," "under," "on," "into" are expressed first, they cannot be specified and keep dangling in the air. This is true for the spatial relations more clearly, but temporal ones are not excepted. The logic of such "postpositions"—just like the modifiers that follow the noun—has obviously to do again with the latent iconicity as a constant concomitant characteristic of the visual communication as such. The relation to "reality" is expressed in an adaptation to that reality—the "up" of a cupboard being higher than the "up" of a chair—so the "reality" has to be signified first.

Schlesinger (1971) explains the rule he found in Israeli Sign Language that the sentence never starts with a verb with the same argument, based upon universal characteristics of sign languages. I have not found this to be universally so with the verbs in my data; there were more utterances of Dutch subjects that started with a verb than of the American ones. I think this has to be ascribed to the fact that we are dealing with a bilingual situation in which the subjects are learning to use more of the language of the environment, and that Dutch can have sentences beginning with a main verb (all questions, all imperatives, and some dependent clauses in complex sentences can begin with a verb), whereas in English only imperatives can, and those sentences that begin with an auxiliary. This would then explain why there are more utterances beginning with a verb in the Dutch than in the English data. The question, however, remains, why—against the rule of the English language and, supposedly, even against a universal rule of sign systems—the American subjects can and do use verbs sometimes in first position, where the English does not.

The first reason seems to be that, quite often, the utterance is of the esoteric type, with no focus present (see the section entitled "The Function of the Focus," below). Sometimes the utterance then can start with a verb:

(81)   Go visit Statue of Liberty.

(81a)[4]   I went to visit the Statue of Liberty.

[4]Sample sentences marked with an "a" are English paraphrases.

(82)   Know turtle know turtle my.

(82a)   You know my turtle.

(83)   Have home white polish.

(83a)   I have white polish at home.

(84)   Look fun silly.

(84a)   Daddy looked funny and silly.

But even with the actor present and expressed in the utterance, the verb can be the first signifier:

(85)   Can't I hard.

(85a)   I cannot do such a hard thing.

(86)   Grow grass there.

(86a)   There the grass is growing.

(87)   Came ate my aunt uncle came my home.

(87a)   My aunt and uncle came to eat at my home.

(88)   Come ANN and BUTCH tent fall again.

(88a)   Ann and Butch came and the tent fell again.

This does not occur too often, but frequently enough to challenge the claim about the existence of some universal rule prescribing the contrary. I think that the possibility of the verb's being in first position—apart from the contextual explanation—has to be explained from the fact that at least some verbs have a strong expressive power of their own and are not as dependent upon other concepts that would have to be put into presence by a signifier first in order to specify them, as, for example, prepositions, adjectives, possessive pronouns, or numerals.

The relation modifier–noun is similar to the relation between the two parts of a compound word in which the first word-part modifies the second. Compare:

(89a)   My mommy.

(90a)   Your baby.

(91a)   Twelve apples.

(92a)   Trackmeet.

(93a)   Firedrill.

(94a)   Classperiod.

In the first three examples, the words "my," "your," and "twelve" specify the following noun in a way comparable to the way the first parts of the compound words specify the second parts. We are dealing with a specific "mommy" and "baby" and a definite set of apples, just as we are dealing with a specified type of "meet," "drill," and "period." The deaf tend to follow the universal visual rule, and therefore we found:

(89)   Mommy my.

(90)   Baby your.

(91)   Apples twelve.

(92)   Meettrack.

(93)   Drillfire.

(94)   Periodclass.

These had the same meaning as the samples given first, under (89a) through (94a). This looks more amazing to us for the compound words, but it stands to reason. The rule that a firedrill has to be some sort of a drill and a drillfire must be some sort of a fire is self-evident to us, because such a rule goes for all English and Dutch compound words composed that way. Not so for the deaf child and his esoteric system, apparently. He has to pick up the rule in the bilingual setting the school provides (Tervoort, 1968a).

Initial, Final, and Modal Markers

INITIAL MARKERS AND FINAL MARKERS

When awake, a hearing person cannot turn off his ears, but he can avert his eyes. If a hearing person begins to speak, all he has to do to reach his hearing partner is to make sure his voice is loud enough. But if a person starts to sign to a deaf partner, he has to make sure this partner is looking in his direction. If this is not the case, he has to try to get his partner's attention by giving visual signals, which I have termed Initial Markers or IMs (1967, 1975). They were characteristic for all esoteric communication of my subjects throughout, regardless of the country or the language. Final Markers or FMs perform a somewhat similar function. In speech, intonation patterns are used, among other means, to mark the end of an utterance; any hearer can tell when the speaker comes to the end of his sentence and begins anew. In visual communication, the end can be marked by a split-second rest of the moving hands and the communicating body; apart from that, there are some specific signs to signal that there is an (intermediate) end. FMs are as typical and as characteristic for the subjects' private interchange as IMs. Both the beginning and the end of an esoteric sentence can be marked specifically by an attention-caller or a cut-off.

A very interesting and important aspect of IMs and FMs is that they both form a generic category in which different subcategories occur with slightly different functioning. I found the following types (in the English schools; the Dutch samples followed the same subcategorization). The translations—as always—are those of the subjects themselves:

IMs

1. Simply asking the partner to pay attention:
   you
   you listen
   listen

2. Indicating the self as beginning to communicate:
   I
   me
   mine
   my

3. Affirming the foregoing and/or appealing to the partner's knowledge:
   yes
   know
   I know
   think
   thought
   remember
   well
   oh
   wow
   you know
   imagine

4. Adverbial or conjunctionlike signal:
   after a while
   a while

while
that
before
then
last
touch

FMs

1. Simply marking the end:
finish
finished
enough
good
period

2. Confirming what has been said:
yes
wow
ugh
oh

3. Switching the initiative to the partner:
you
now you
your turn

4. Appealing to knowledge of self or partner:
know
remember
think
you know

5. Adverbial or conjunctionlike signal:
that
before
maybe
then

The overall percentage of all sentences having an IM- or FM-marking was 14.5%. This is quite high, if one takes into account: (*a*) that under the influence of the teaching of English and Dutch the use of IMs and FMs decreases with increasing age; (*b*) that—apart from the one-word sentences—short sentences do not need IMs and FMs as much as do longer ones; and (c) that all conversations were filmed between partners who were sitting and continuously facing each other, decreasing the need for IMs and FMs. It should be mentioned also that the use of FMs decreased in proportion to the increase in the use of exoteric syntactic structures; apparently, the latter can sometimes serve the purpose of marking off a sentence. This is especially so where the simplified model-sentences are used methodologically in the teaching; this effect was noticeable. The FMs then are partially replaced and their number decreases.

The relevancy for the topic of bilingual interference is not so much the fact that the IMs and FMs decrease with growing age, nor that they never disappear completely because there remains a need for them time and again. It is quite obvious why they keep occurring in the exoteric use of the subjects: Sometimes people do not look, and sometimes the end of a sentence is not self-evident. It is also not too interesting in itself that a visual communication can be started with a "please watch," "watch me now," "yes I know," "don't you know" variation; or that it can be finished with a "that's it," "yes," "now it's your turn," or "you know." What is interesting is that the beginning (much more than the end) can be marked by a signal that is semantically something more than just a start- or end-variety, that is at the same time also an adverbial or a conjunction-like signal. It is exactly the special way such a signal functions that can give more insight into the functioning of signifiers in the visual system in general, and specifically in growing syntax of some other markers that occur at the beginning of sentences and clauses in English or Dutch and are taken over.

Some of these conjunctionlike signals grow into English or Dutch conjunctions after some time, but sometimes something else, the other way around, also happens: The conjunction of the exoteric language gets incorporated in the visual system and starts functioning esoterically, as an initial marker, adding, at the same time, a given modality to the utterance. This will be worked out in the following section.

INITIAL MARKERS AND CONJUNCTIONS

Not all occurring IMs and conjunctions can be dealt with more extensively; we have selected only a few that show the mutual influence between English and signing more clearly. In principle, the two extremes are: an IM exclusively notifying the partner about a start with no further implication for either content or structure to follow, versus a conjunction introducing a causal, temporal, conditional, consecutive, etc., clause or (part of) a sentence. Conjunctions like *and* and *or* were used frequently but gave little reason to suspect the occurrence of interference phenomena; conjunctions like *although, since, so, while* occurred so seldom that nothing definite could be said about them. I shall subsequently deal with signifiers functioning somewhere in between the two extremes mentioned and occurring often enough among different subjects of different schools to warrant the conclusion that we are not dealing with the idiosyncracies of a few. Everything stated here can be substantiated with Dutch examples of similar items occurring in the same ways. The claim for universality of the feature is therefore again fairly strong.

The few IM-conjunctions chosen here are: *before, that, because,* and *but.*

BEFORE

Before is a good example of growth of an exoteric conjunction into an esoteric sign. It occurred 72 times, and only in two instances was the use exoteric and grammatical:

(95)   That HE want visit me before HE go away.

(96)   *One time in THE fall before my father got married my father was in the army.*

On no other occasion did *before* occur either as a conjunction, a preposition, or an adverb, so the following types did not occur at all:

    conjunction: I like to eat before we leave.

    preposition: Okay, would you like a drink before dinner?

    adverb: Yes I would, although I never had one before.

Before in esoteric usage occurred 70 times. It has to be divided into:

1. An adverbial-type item, occurring at any place in the utterance, with the meaning "some time ago," "in the past." It then determines either the preceding, the following, or both. As such, it occurred 25 times.
2. A conjunctionlike item, also meaning "some time ago," "in the past," always occurring in initial position, and thus functioning as an IM at the same time. As such, it occurred 45 times.

The meaning of *before,* namely, "some time ago," could easily decrease to a weakened "in the past," and so to a mere past tense signal. One has to keep in mind that there is no verb, in the sense of a specific category of signifiers expressing activity and grammatically marked as such. So, not until the identification begins to grow with the exoteric

English verb through the classroom teaching and through the use of the words and the compound word + sign signifiers can there be any certainty about verbs being present in the esoteric system, through borrowing. But even then a time marker using tense stays foreign to the sign system. Time is not marked in the private communication of the subjects through verb morphology, but differently, as by pinpointing the point in history, if that is relevant—as in "last Sunday," "Christmas vacation," "tomorrow afternoon"—or by weaker time signals indicating past or future which have no connection with the verb and which bear as much syntactic relation with the rest of a sentence as interjections. Their effect can be compared to that of sentences like:

That smile of hers—years ago—I shall never forget.

He keeps crying—this was in 1969—until I hug him.

When functioning as an IM, *before* frequently attenuates to merely a weak past tense marker. It can occur repeatedly if one storyteller keeps talking and talking. If then a whole context is in the past, *before* just signals the renewed start of a new bit of information, like the "And then . . . ," "and then . . . ," "and then . . ." chaining in a certain type of primitive storytelling.

There now follow some samples of *before:*

Adverbial

(97)   *Same before* dog small *before.*

(97a)   I had the same small dog before.

(98)   *Why* before dog?

(98a)   Why did you have that dog some time ago?

(99)   I remember before boy throw A BALL fly.

(99a)   I remember that some time ago a boy threw a ball that flew away.

(100)   *Me tired before tired.*

(100a)   Some time ago I was tired.

Conjunctional/IM

(101)   Before old glasses break.

(101a)   Then I broke my old glasses.

(102)   Before I was in ship SHIP.

(102a)   Then I was in a ship.

(103)   *(Before)* I *(have)* fish.

(103a)   Then I had some fish.

(104)   Before *I GO WHITE LAKE.*

(104a)   Some time ago I went to White Lake.

So, *before* departs from normal prepositional, adverbial, and even conjunctional usage and can and does grow into an esoteric connotation of the
past tense, more as an adverbial item in the included position, and more as
a conjunctional initial marker where it often diminishes into a very weak
tense marker. The subjects of both schools in the United States showed
these characteristics, not using *before* in any other, exoteric way.

THAT

That as a conjunction (not as a demonstrative pronoun) was used 136
times, 60 of which were exoteric occurrences of the conjunction between
sentences, as in:

(105) I CAN HARDLY believe that next fall we will BE
        SENIOR.

The esoteric items were those in which *that* was used as a pure IM (35
instances); in the other occurrences, an incomplete structure made it hard
to determine what exactly the function of *that* was (41 occurrences). I
shall deal with the latter first.

That is an English word to begin with, having at least two different
syntactic functions and meanings, namely conjunction and demonstrative
pronoun. Subsequently, *that* is incorporated into the private communication system of some of the subjects. In about half of the instances it
functions the English, exoteric way. But, especially among the younger
subjects, the esoteric types of *that* occur, as discussed here. I am not sure
about some of the 41 occurrences, because the "syntactic" information
sometimes is so scant that it is impossible to discern whether an originally
pronounlike or conjunctionlike *that* is intended. The "incompleteness"
of the "syntactic" information is, needless to say, purely a matter of the
person who studies the structure and tries to decode it with English
grammar in the back of his mind, wanting to decide whether the "that"
under scrutiny is more likely to be the one or the other. For the subjects,

there is, in all probability, nothing incomplete about their interchange. They certainly are using *that* in a curious way sometimes, however, and the first impression is that it often shows characteristics of both.

Initially, I was inclined to come to the conclusion that a conjunctionlike *that* is used if something of a verb can be identified in the rest of the utterance, and that the matter had to rest undecided between conjunction and demonstrative in all other instances. The more I kept studying the samples, the more I became convinced that *that* in included position, if it is not very evidently a demonstrativelike item, always functions more like some sort of a conjunction. Maybe some samples can clarify the matter:

(106)   You know that KE move new home KE.

(106a)   You know that K.E. moved to a new home.

(107)   *IS excited that IS spring will come* tomorrow *MARCH twenty one.*

(107a)   He is excited that tomorrow, March 21, spring will come.

(108)   When I was in car riding my half brother told me that *bee* above your head.

(108a)   When I was riding in the car my half brother told me that there was a bee above my head.

(109)   Know that ten cents.

(109a)   I know that it costs ten cents.

(110)   *Yes I think* that name tulip.

(110a)   Yes I think that it is named a tulip.

(111)   *You say that* FUR cute.

(111a)   You are saying that its fur is cute.

(112)   Know you true that newspaper read.

(112a)   I know that you really read that newspaper.

(113)   See that *tall.*

(113a)   I saw that it was tall.

There are two reasons why *that* must be a conjunction in all instances, also where it seems somewhat doubtful, as in (109) to (113): First, because usually (not always), if used as a demonstrative, its execution is different (a pointing finger, instead of a spelled Y which is put down in the palm of the left hand), and second, because the utterance, taken that way, makes better sense—the reference implied by *that* as a demonstrative hardly ever fits smoothly into the context. This reasoning is reinforced by an analysis of *that* as an IM, which is the main reason for dealing with *that* in the present context in the first place.

In English, both a conjunctional and a demonstrative *that* can, of course, begin a sentence:

That you like him is quite evident.

That is the man you seem to like best.

The esoteric IM *that* functions completely differently, though; it is hardly probable that it derives from either one. A better hypothesis is that it developed from the included *that* indicating nothing more than the beginning of a new clause or some other separate part of an utterance. If one leaves out the first parts of (106) to (113) and lets them start with the *that* they all have, the result, every time, is a perfectly acceptable utterance in the subjects' communication, just like others they are using. The following samples, used exclusively with *that* as IM's can prove as much:

(114)   That *scares scares scares* me bee.

(114a)   The bee scared me.

(115)   *That some boys pick girls.*

(115a)   Some boys pick girls.

(116)   That me visit my friend.

(116a)   I visited my friend.

(117)   That me nothing afraid.

(117a)   I am afraid of nothing.

(118)   That food poor.

(118a)   The food was poor.

(119)   That I came Holland, England, Sweden, Denmark, and
         Norway.

(119a)   I went to Holland, England, Sweden, Denmark, and
         Norway.

(120)   That last year last year that two turtles die.

(120a)   Last year the two turtles died.

(121)   That now you turn.

(121a)   Now it is your turn.

There is no preceding sentence, sentence part, or any other context, explaining such uses of *that* in a way that reduces it to something similar to the exoteric use. Some of the samples given are even the absolute beginning of a conversation by one of the partners. *That* then can only mean: "Watch me, I am starting (again)"; it is a pure IM, maybe with some emphasis deriving from the fact that the sign can easily be executed emphatically, and that the going down of the hand in Y position can, at the same time, be a wave to catch the attention.

So, the conclusion can be drawn that an exclusively English word has grown into an exclusively esoteric sign. No doubt, this was an ephemeral phenomenon: The esoteric use of *that* as demonstrated was far more typical for the subjects of one school than for the others; it was limited to some, and it was not found before the last year of the project. Still, it remains no less good an example of the extent of bilingual interference between the two codes.

BECAUSE

Because is used as a conjunction between sentences or clauses; it occurs, moreover, as an IM. The construction "because of"—as in "Because of sickness . . ."—never occurred in the data. The meaning of *because* is always causal; its use was exoteric in 47 instances and esoteric in only 11. The usual way in which *because* occurred—both exoterically and esoterically—was as an answer to a(n implicit) WHY-question. It is easy to see how it then can develop into an IM, used to start an utterance in which causality is involved, even without previous WHY. Grammatical English does not accept *because* as a conjunction introducing a clause without a verb; the subjects did. Some samples are:

(122)   I hate BEATLES because ugly HAIR.

(123)   Because my *father too busy my mother too busy too.*

(124)   Because same white.

(124a)   Because my dog is as white as snow.

(125)   Because today spring flower grow grow again.

BUT

But is used as a conjunction between sentences or clauses; like *because* it is also used as an IM. Its meaning is always adversative; its use was exoteric in 103, and esoteric in 79 instances. The usual occurrence of *but* was when an adversative turn in the conversation was to be taken in between two sentences or two clauses; both possibilities exist in English. *But* can develop into an adversative IM, the same way *because* can. Compare the following samples:

(126)   My father will establish swimming POOL near my home but IF my father have money.

(127)   I AM GLAD to come BE here and because BECAUSE I like ARIZONA CLIMATE and but my friends.

(128)   Once time almost drown in water but almost get OUT OF water.

(129)   Beat us but three boys FLU.

(129a)   They beat us, but three of our boys had the flu.

(130)   One girl fat but good guard.

(130a)   One girl is fat but she is a good guard.

(131)   But If rain will postpone to other day.

(131a)   But if it rains we will postpone it to the other day.

(132)   But he jealous of me.

(133)   But still alive.

But is used so often that it evidently has become part of the esoteric vocabulary. As such, it functions sometimes as it does in English, and sometimes deviantly, insofar as it can introduce any clause, or function as an absolute IM. The different usages show that incorporating a word like *but* can mean the esotericization of such a word in several degrees.

Of the conjunctions occurring as IMs, *before*, *that*, *because*, and *but*, the latter two have their exact counterparts *omdat* and *maar* in Dutch, showing the same partially deviating features and following the same esotericization (as do others that have not been dealt with here, like *when* and *if* with their Dutch equivalents). So, for all conjunctions/IMs it can be stated that they can function as they do in English and Dutch, introducing a dependent clause, as in:

If you meet him, you must thank him again.

However, they show a tendency to shorten their range, so to say, to the smaller clause or even the single signifier that follows immediately. What this means can be best demonstrated by examples like:

This road is slippery when wet.

This stuff does not mix if dry.

These seem to come close to the limit of what still is grammatically acceptable. Sometimes the structure becomes more acceptable with a participle, but apart from that it does not seem that it can be used unrestrictedly. Compare:

This door squeaks if closed.

No box is insured if opened.

Do not go if afraid.   [?]

These mushrooms are edible when yellow   [?]

Among the utterances of the subjects there are numerous examples of English and Dutch conjunctions used this way.

The possibilities for use of some members of a very typically exoteric word class—that of the conjunctions—have therefore been expanded and changed in the esoteric, visual communication system.

MODAL MARKERS

An analysis of the puzzling way some English or Dutch words are used in the esoteric system to indicate modality can, again, give more insight into the peculiar type of bilingual borrowing in both directions with which we are dealing. I would like to consider first the different ways of marking modality in an acoustic language and in a signing system.

One of the possible ways of denying a statement someone is making is by vigorously shaking one's head while the other is still talking. Even before we get an opportunity to interrupt him and to say "That is not true," we can already deny what he is saying using visual signifying behavior. We can, moreover, reinforce the shaking of the head by muttering "No, no, no." Apparently, that is what the shaking of the head means; these words could serve as some sort of a translation thereof. What we never do, though, is make a statement ourselves and, at the same time, deny it by simultaneously shaking our head. That, however, was what the subjects did repeatedly. It was one of the means they had to express negation. They would sign—and sometimes spell or speak—an utterance while shaking their heads indicating thereby the "no" or "not" of what they were communicating. They also did the opposite, that is, nod their heads to reinforce the truth or "yes" value of their communication. English, like Dutch, offers no possibility for such simultaneity. It has, moreover, different grammatical rules for "no" versus "not," "not" versus "yes," "yes" versus "true," "true" versus "truly," etc.

There are numerous other modalities in a signing system, however, that have to be expressed in a nonsimultaneous way, simply because they cannot be conveyed by movements of the head or by mimicry but must be conveyed by the hands; and as long as they are needed for making other signs also, the modal signs have "to wait their turn," so to speak. Take, for example, the alternatingly going up and down of "weighing" hands expressing doubt, or the shrugging of the shoulders (also preventing free use of the hands for something else) expressing ignorance, or the shaking of the fist expressing anger or threat. If such signs blend with one and the same word or clause—which is usually the case—such a word + sign signifier from then on can be identified as "maybe," "I don't know," and "I'm mad" or "mad," respectively. This is where bilingual interference starts.

"No," "not," "yes," "truly," "maybe," "I don't know," "I'm mad" are only a few of many variations; there are, of course, many more modalities that can all be expressed visually and can be translated into an other communication system, and—finally—start interfering with means used in such a system. As words or clauses, such translations represent different grammatical classes in English; the corresponding signs follow other rules than these words or clauses would, for example, as far as the limitation of the possibility of simultaneity is concerned in case the hands are needed for some other signs. The functioning of the *maybe* sign and the *I am mad* sign, for example, is not in any way different because the first is translated by an adverb and the second by a parenthetical sentence. In the visual system they can both be inserted anywhere in a chain of signs where the expression of their particular modality of doubt or anger is fitting. The diverse way they relate to surrounding—preceding, simultaneous, or following—signs can sometimes better be translated into English by changing "maybe" or "I am mad" into a noun-, adjective-, or verb-substitute, like "doubt," "dubious," "hesitance," and "threaten," "maddening," "anger," and so on. This demonstrates that signs have no grammatical word class characteristics and function differently in their relation to each other.

Changes in function start to occur only when a specific identification with a word and a generic, long-term exposure to the language of words introduce word-classification plus exoteric functioning into a sign. This happens continuously, whereby—over the years of symbiosis—words in their turn can begin to function in part as a sign, as we have demonstrated, for example, in the previous section for *before*. The sign taking over word-features and vice versa make the bilingual situation under discussion an ever-changing continuum.

In their combination with signs, some words have lost most of their possible English or Dutch functioning and turned into modal markers, sometimes with change of semantic features. They can be inserted as one-sign parentheses adding a certain modality to the utterance. In one of my publications (Tervoort, 1953), I have listed 10 pages of these (Vol. I, pp. 209–219), of which I select a few here. The translations are literal, word for word.

ZEGT ("SAYS")

Zegt ("says"), if used without subject—which cannot be derived from the context either—indicates that what is said rests upon an authority (saying so, but that is not expressed).

(134)   *Prinses verjaardag zegt.*
         "Princess birthday says."

(135)   *Morgen bezoek zegt.*
         "Tomorrow visit says."

(136)   *Snoep lekker zegt.*
         "Candy delicious says."

Sample (134) means: "Sure the princess has her birthday" (it was in the newspapers); (135): "They surely will visit me tomorrow" (it said so in the letter); and (136): "Candy is delicious; that's what everybody will confirm."

KAN ("CAN")

Kan ("can"), if used without identifiable subject, conveys that the content of the utterance is possible. Compare:

(137)   *Vader kan dansen dansen.*
         "Father can dance dance."

(138)   *Kan ziek.*
         "Can sick."

(139)   *Kan lang licht hoofdpijn.*
         "Can long light headache."

Sample (137) means: "Daddy said, 'It is possible for you to go dancing' ";
(138): "It is possible to get sick"; and (139): "It is possible to get a
headache if one sits under lights that burn long."

MOET ("MUST")

Moet ("must"), if used without identifiable subject, indicates the
necessity of what is stated, for example:

(140)   *Moet goed bidden.*

         "Must well pray."

(141)   *Ik hoop mee moet.*

         "I hope along must."

(142)   *Ik hoop later moest.*

         "I hope later must."

Sample (140) means: "It is necessary to pray well"; (141): "I hope I can
get along with them, that it cannot be avoided"; and (142): "I hope that
will be most necessarily so later on." The reason I add "most" is because
the Dutch *moest* is the past tense of *moet* (both "must" in English); but
this past tense *moest* is not used here to indicate the past but as a
superlative of *moet*. This became evident because every time *must* was
used the meaning was "most necessary" and the sign used indicated
superlative, being the same as the one for *meest* ("most"), *mooist* ("most
beautiful"), etc. (Tervoort 1953, p. 237 ss.)

The same type of parenthetic modal functioning was found more than
10 years later in another Dutch school, e.g., again with *zegt* ("says") in
the sense of "This is based upon an authority who says so." An American
example occurred in the interchange between two young subjects over
2 years. It was *touch,* meaning "What I am saying is not really true,"
"I am just kidding," "This is make believe." A similar sign/word is listed
in the 1953 series under *fop* ("kid").

Some samples of *touch* are the following:

(143)   Me touch make chair.

(144)   Me home how touch tree know you that me cut.

(145)   Touch know mistake cat play floor.

The meaning of these utterances is—(143): "I made a chair, but not
really"; (144): "You know I cut a tree at home, but I am just bragging";
(145): "You know the cat played on a diving board where it had gotten by
mistake, but it was just a make believe movie."

With these last examples, we have reached the lower limit of what still can be called samples of mutual influence between the two languages. In *zegt* ("says"), *kan* ("can"), *moet* ("must"), *fop* ("kid"), and the other Dutch examples, there still is a shade of meaning of the word left; in *touch* even that is lost.

The Function of the Focus

The bilingual interference under discussion means, among other things, that the English of the deaf deviates now and then because of their signing, and that their signing now and then shows the influence of the English. In this section, I would like to pay some more attention to the inner coherence of each utterance and the way it is interpreted, because I feel that a better understanding thereof might lead to a better understanding of some bilingual features, specifically the order of the signifiers and the rationale for their occurrence or omission. I think that there is one specific organizing principle which decides the interpretation of every utterance, more so in a semantic and psycholinguistic than in a syntactic and linguistic way.

Searching for a point of departure to start distinguishing and classifying all dominantly esoteric utterances, I came upon the notion of **focus** for the following reason. On the one hand, there is no structure that does not, here or there, escape known rules (with the exception of the ones mentioned under "Inversions," and perhaps some more nobody has found yet), while, on the other hand, there always, without exception, appears to be an indispensable reference point for the interpretation of every utterance. There is little misunderstanding between deaf partners using their own system; and I certainly do not accept the hypothesis that this is because of the evocative power of an exclusively imitating and mimicky behavior. Identifying such a reference point, or focus, and relating to it all elements of the utterance, is the key to understanding it, and the first operation in mentally processing the message.

As long as the reference point is not identified, an utterance remains uninterpretable, not because its lexical elements in the signifiers are not understood, but because their interdependency and interrelationship remain ambiguous. But the moment the reference point is recognized as such, the semantic relations between the signifiers fall into place and are instantaneously clear.

A few examples, at this moment, will help the argument. One utterance in signs-only goes as follows:

(146)   Statue upper lip?

The question mark represents the mimicry; the contextual information is that one of the 13-year-old boys is telling his friend about a trip to New York City and specifically to the Statue of Liberty. The friend then asks this question. It is impossible to interpret it, as long as one does not know what is stated by these three signifiers, which are unambiguous enough in themselves, in their relation to each other: What is predicated about what, what are the syntactic relations of the elements to each other, or—at least—what is the semantic interpretation of the whole?

The solution is that an unexpressed "you" is part of the context, in the case of the visit to the Statue of Liberty; so the "you" is part of that visit, is "in" the Statue, and therefore this same "you" is part of the semantic intent of the question:

(146)   (You) Statue upper lip?

This, instantaneously, makes clear that the question has to be understood as:

(146a)   Were you in the upper lip of the Statue?

Another example is:

(147)   Next fall GRADE five maybe see.

This was used by a 12-year-old boy, without much of a supporting context. The minimum available "context" obviously always is the talking and/or signing person. The hypothesis that the information given might fit the speaker himself is tried out successfully in this case:

(147)   Next fall (I) GRADE five maybe see.

The boy's own paraphrase in English for my benefit read:

(147a)   Next fall I will be in the fifth grade
          maybe, you see.

These two examples could give one the impression that the focus is never present in the utterance; on the contrary, it frequently is. But the number of times it has to be supplied is considerable. It was the instances in which it was not named within the boundaries of the utterance that gave me a first inkling of its functioning. Any time their shared context, actual situation, and general background ("context" for short in the following) made expressing the focus redundant, the subjects omitted or deleted it, while nonetheless handling it as reference point to an equal degree and without increased difficulty. The difficulties were mine alone, as I had to be assisted time and again in my correct interpretation of those utterances which missed such referent point. I just did not have the fluency of the native speakers in making the choices that were self-evident for them. It was hard to learn, because this fluency had more to do with contextual knowledge than with grammatical know-how.

The examples given can make clear how necessary retrieval of the focus is; it can only be done by scanning the "context" in actual performance. The written transcriptions of these utterances appeared to be uninterpretable, even for those who had handled them effortlessly before, as soon as the "context" was forgotten. Utterances that include the focus explicitly are more resistant and need less "context" to remain interpretable later on. I have tried out written transcriptions of the latter type compared to the same ones with the focus left out on purpose. Without reference point and without any "context," all written transcriptions of comprehensible utterances were turned into incomprehensible ones by the operation; all that was left was guesswork.

Some more examples in which the focus is mentioned are the following:

(148)   *Tired I tired I tired I I tired track now.*

(148a) I am tired of track now.

(149)   Real busy we lately grow up call with each other
        STEPsister.

(149a) We really call each other stepsisters lately while growing up.

(150)   Crazy you not coat.

(150a) You are crazy not to wear a coat.

(151)   Before you said you left there now you left DORM.

(151a) Some time ago you said that you now have left the
        intermediate dormitory.

(152)   Come down hill bad know man hear see.

(152a) The bad guy, you know, came riding down the hill, listened
        and looked around.

(153)   *My* sister *my* sister false decorate girl make false decorate
        false decorate.

(153a) My sister made false [wrong ?] decorations.

(154)   Grass grow pretty flower land my house.

(154a) Grass and pretty flowers grow on the land near my home.

(155)   Should win really PONTIAC 60.

(155a)   Pontiac 1960 really should win.

(156)   Rabbit rabbit true rabbit catch chicken.

(156a)   The rabbit did indeed catch a chicken.

(157)   Launch will airplane search found bring AS FLA.

(157a)   After launching, an airplane will search for him, and after
          having found him it will bring Alan Shepard to Florida.

Some other examples in which the focus has the same central function but
is left out and has to be retrieved from "context" are:

(158)   Have good time will will.

(158a)   I will have a good time.

(159)   Marry E. marry E. marry?

(159a)   Will you marry E.?

(160)   Sh! touch finish throw dirty popcorn finish touch.

(160a)   Hush! The man threw popcorn on the dirty floor, but not
          really.

(161)   *Give HIM money for ROCK launch good.*

(161a)   President Kennedy gave him (Alan Shepard) money for
          launching that rocket so well.

(162)   Yes grow.

(162a)   Yes they grow there [the grass and the flowers].

(163)   Not good swing around every day.

(163a)   My kite is not good, it swings around every day.

(164)   Yes A for give rabbit.

(164a)   Yes a pet store gives a rabbit for free.

While trying to identify the focus, where is one to look? The samples
suggest strongly that it is the subject of the sentence, if such terms be
permitted for a moment—or even the (pro)noun-subject of the sentence, if

such grammatical implications do not sound preposterous. Maybe we ought simply to say that it seems always to be the signifier that names an agent; if such an agent is missing, one must supply the unnamed agent that fits the action involved. This, however, is sometimes not the case. Compare:

(165)   Black my Lincoln black Lincoln black Lincoln.

(166)   Motor noisy motor well fair.

Both are comments upon cars by different subjects on different occasions. Their paraphrases in English read:

(165a)   Our Lincoln is black.

(166a)   The motor is noisy but, well, fair.

If *Lincoln* and *motor* are focus, that is the unmistakable reference point; the focus cannot be described generically as an agent that can be retrieved by searching who or what fits the action as its agent. The notion of focus would then also have to imply the reference point for a predicative adjective like *black*, *noisy*, and *fair*. This would bring the notion of focus a step closer to being like a grammatical subject. More proof is given by samples that show the retrieval of such a focus:

(167)   Large large brown little brown.

(168)   Bad not and nice.

which were paraphrased as:

(167a)   The shell was large and a little bit brown.

(168a)   My kid sister is not bad but nice.

These samples demonstrate that the same basic rule (relate everything to a reference point first, present or to be retrieved) works again in an identical way for predicative adjectives. So the focus seems to approach the notion of grammatical subject a little more. There are more problems, though.

All the subjects often reenacted or imitated in part what they were conveying; they also used to mimic the people they were talking about. Once in a while, they switched to the role of the person meant without, of course, quoting him—that would have been an exoteric means. In the Dutch data, the following statements occur in the course of a story in which respectively a daddy and a doctor played a role (given in literal sign-for-sign translation):

(169)   *Father can skate. (Vader kan schaatsen.)*

(170)   *Doctor can not. (Dokter kan niet.)*

meaning, respectively:

(169a)   Father said: "You can go skating."

(170a)   The doctor said: "You cannot go outside."

Some comparable utterances coming from American subjects were:

(171)   Please help mother help for me tomatoes for me.

(172)   While finish come mom open oh hurry late clean dirty over clean.

(173)   Man man work man work OK.

(174)   *Mr X man what R Ralph write.*

which read in the English paraphrase:

(171a)   "Please, help," Mom said, "help me with the tomatoes."

(172a)   While I was finishing, Mom came in, opening the door, and saying: "Oh hurry, you are late, clean yourself, you are dirty, clean yourself over again."

(173a)   The man who worked there said: "It's okay."

(174a)   Mr X, that man, asked me: "What did Ralph write?"

The complication we meet here is that, in role playing, the person mimicked and played is introduced as speaking while the signifier for "said," "spoke," "remarked", etc., is left out. Of course, this is an exoteric and extrinsic way of saying it: What actually is the case is that the deaf child switches roles—by just slightly altering his behavior or just his face—and thus reaches the "quoting" effect in a different way altogether. What the person portrayed, then, says or does is to be related, as to a whole, to him as focus-mentioned: *Father, Doctor, mother, mom, man, Mr X man*, etc. Thereafter, however, the focus within the quotation is the person addressed by the person mimicked, the former serving in turn as reference point for the elements within the quotation, without being mentioned. In (169) through (174), the person introduced as speaking at least was mentioned, but in some utterances even this reference point is left out and has to be derived from the context, as in:

(175)   Tell father but sorry patient tell father good character.

(176)   Disgust *what do scissors mad gone.*

to be paraphrased as:

(175a)   Mother said: "I'll tell father," but then I was sorry and patient, and she then said: "I'll tell him that you have a good character."

(176a)   Mother was disgusted: "What are you doing with those scissors, have you gone mad?"

These samples serve to demonstrate clearly that the consequence of what has been stated in the foregoing is that signing is dependent on the actual performance in such an intrinsic way that it can only partially be removed and abstracted from it, e.g., in writing (but in any other code in print also). The switch from ordinary conversation in which the subject "speaks for himself" to the role playing in which he speaks as the person quoted is performed by such altogether nonlinguistic means as looking and acting suddenly a little differently, like that person. Means like that are highly effective, even when applied in minimal doses; they do not need other, coded and abstracted cues, based upon arbitrary agreements. However, they are highly effective in actual performance only, from which they cannot be removed. See Fischer on this same issue under "Body attitude" (Bellugi & Fischer, 1972, pp. 195–196). I have argued this at length in my thesis (Tervoort, 1953).

Returning to the analysis of the functioning of the focus: The hypothesis that it refers to the actor, in a way the subject of an English sentence does, applies to the samples in which role playing occurs, and can therefore be maintained. There are still other types of utterances which need closer inspection, though, before the rule of the focus-reference is accepted as being universal. Compare:

(177)   Start spring start plow *maybe* plow plow.

(178)   Long time play to graduate finish.

(179)   Now after while afternoon play swing seesaw different play.

(180)   *Throw three store house throw.*

which read in paraphrase:

(177a)   In the spring they start to plow.

(178a)   One can play a long time (on the football team) until one graduates and has to finish.

(179a)   Now, after a while, we, all of us, can play on the swings, the seesaws, and different things.

(180a)   They will demolish that three-story house.

In all these samples, the focus cannot be derived immediately from the "context"; it comes from more general background information, shared implicitly between the partners, and it has the meaning of a more or less unidentified agent or group of agents acting out something that is generally accepted to be known or true. Sample (177) did not have "farmers" as topic or context; (180) was not embedded in a story about demolishers; (178) and (179) were stating what one or everybody could or would do. Such agents are expressed in English with words like "they," "people," "you," "one," etc. Similar words are used in Dutch, where this type of utterance occurred similarly.

In conclusion, the rule that a focus with noun-subject-like characteristics always serves as the basic reference point from which the utterance has to be interpreted appears to have universal value for all data. This is demonstrated by the fact that many utterances, not having such a reference point in the actual performance, remain uninterpretable as long as the focus is not retrieved from the context, including—as stated—shared actual situation and general background knowledge. It is demonstrated in a negative way insofar as other omissions—or rather non-occurrences—never served in the same way as the key to the understanding of the whole, functioning as the central point to which all other signifiers were oriented.

So the focus is always present, at least in the deep structure, and in the semantic intent. We found the same characteristic in an analysis of child language (cf. Tervoort, 1973b). If the claim of universality of this rule is valid, all utterances then must fall under its domain. This was checked and appeared to be the case: 99.4% of all utterances could be thus analyzed; only .6% of them remained uninterpretable and had to be left undecided. I would like to stress once more the point that this was found to be consistently the case over a period of 6 years among 48 subjects of different ages in four different schools in two different exoteric language settings. The claim of universality therefore looks fairly strong. The functioning of the focus shows an analogy between the acoustic and the visual communication systems in that both can relate signifiers expressing concepts like object, action, place, time, and so on, to a central point of reference, which is the agent and which governs the other signifiers in a way a grammatical subject does.

The means available in the acoustic codes are, of course, pretty well known, thoroughly analyzed, and defined again and again in grammars, as e.g., "subject," "object," "verb," "adverb," in terms of their functioning, their interrelationships, and everything else linguists could think of. Compared to all that, the means available in the visual codes have hardly been analyzed at all, giving a study of this type of bilingualism a terrific handicap to start with.

What can, even a priori, be stated about visual codes, though, is that those who keep creating and using them, by and large, have to deal with the same patterning in "reality" and with their concepts, evaluations, and feelings. That is the point of departure, structuring everybody's coding task to some extent. It is therefore not all too surprising to find, a posteriori, analogies dictated from such a point of departure. In other words, once the difference between the strongly rule-governed acoustic system and the strongly extralinguistically bound visual system is accepted, the functioning of the focus as a basic feature in the latter, similar to the function of the grammatical subject in the former, can be easily acknowledged.[5]

The dominating role of the focus which results from basic characteristics of the visual code cannot but play a great part in the bilingual setting in which the subjects were constantly switching from using their own esoteric code to attempts at using English. It did so in two ways. First of all, it facilitated the learning of the use of the grammatical subject of an English sentence, since esoteric focus and exoteric subject function so similarly as to become identified in many instances. Second, the fact that the focus was so often supplied by the "context" as self-evident in the actual performance led the subjects to leave out the grammatical subject in all those instances in which it looked redundant to them, information-wise. I shall give some attention to both extremes through a number of examples.

In utterances like:

(181)   My cousin big young *have* husband have and two child two
        one girl and one boy little.

(182)   Alligator many I see.

(183)   *My baby sister old two* BURN LEG BY *coffee.*

(184)   WHEN WILL *you* SHOW THE *fashion with* THE *dress?*

the focus points clearly are *My cousin, I, My baby sister,* and *you;* by the same token, they could be termed grammatical subjects of semigrammatical sentences, if these utterances can be accepted as English. In fact they are not, at least in my opinion. They are somewhere in between, melting the two codes into one composite.

In other utterances, such as:

[5] I have worked out the notion of focus more elaborately here because the analysis presented in this chapter deviates from the one I have given in the 1967 presentation (which is, as said, identical to the 1975 publication). The analogy between grammatical subject and focus, as worked out here, gives a better account, I feel, than the differentiation based upon beginning syntacticalization of different sentence types, as presented in 1967/1975.

(185)   I go become tan.

(186)   Have you dog picture hung?

(187)   If boy shoe broke I fix for boy.

(which, it will be noted, are all signed-only), the structure gets so fragmentary for English ears and eyes that one is inclined to term them esoteric, and to suppose that only seeing them would do them justice.

In still other utterances (which can also easily be signed-only, by the way), there is nothing esoteric left but the signs as different vocabulary items themselves; for the rest, they could and should be termed grammatical—if one cares, manual—English.

Compare:

(188)   WILL you GO to the 500 races this year?

(189)   But I will miss him if HE will not come here next year.

(190)   I am glad that JW and CS are here to watch us.

(191)   How long have you been going with your boy friend?

These exoteric examples, in which only a few spelled and no spoken words occur suggest that there is a gradual transition from esoteric focus point to exoteric grammatical subject. There are utterances at both extremes that can be quoted to demonstrate the difference; there are, however, also a great number of utterances in which there is no difference left: The grammatical subject is also truly the focus. And there are others in which it is, finally, hard to say what we have: a subjectlike focus or a grammatical subject that functions as a focus; there seems to be no difference left in such a proposition. But that, then, is at the end of a bilingual growth. On the other hand, and contrary to the school-inspired tendency in the direction toward English, there is the tendency to leave out the focus—or subject—under the influence of the practice in the other code (do away with the redundancy). As soon as it is evident from context, actual performance, and shared knowledge who or what is the subject of a sentence, such a subject can be left out, as if it were a focus in an esoteric utterance. We have met this already in the section dealing with omissions in general; in that context, utterances (35) through (38) can be cited again here. They show otherwise correct English sentences, missing the subject. There are numerous examples to be found, apart from these. Just a few might suffice here as further illustration:

(192)   Must learn more language, math, science.

(193) Will meet TRACK on MARCH 18 for SKYLINE
       CONFERENCE, OAK HILL, DREXEL,
       GLENALPINE and others.

(194) Next year will play basketball.

(195) Wait for hard wind to kite.

(196) HOPE you all will come here sometime in future.

CONCLUSIONS

A final section need not be another lengthy account, nor should it restate what has already been formulated at length. I would like to present it as a last, summarizing reflection on what we really have been doing. What did it mean that—in our search for the ins and outs of this sort of bilingual interference—we put signing next to speech? Have we not compared the incomparable? Did we extend the notion "language" too far, or at least stretch it dangerously thin? Or have we done injustice to signing? Signing and wording occur next to each other, even simultaneously. That was our starting point, and the origin of the questions about bilingualism in the first place.

Furthermore, it stands to reason that applying the grammar of English or Dutch to utterances in a sign system that appears to be a language *sui generis* leads nowhere. From all arguments I have brought forward here and elsewhere it is also evident that applying universal principles of analysis currently used for all natural languages based upon speech might be equally fruitless. Having to deal with bilingualism under the conditions set forward, it seems best, in the first instance, to see what is happening between two deaf persons who are communicating in a mainly or partially visual code embedded one way or another in a communicative environment of a different—i.e., acoustic—type, and worry at a later stage about the applicability or nonapplicability of acoustic versus more generally valid universals.

What soon becomes evident, if one is willing to look without bias, is that a visual system of communication apparently needs less of a strictly rule-governed grammar and therefore of syntactic coherence of its sentences. This has three main causes:

1. The absolute necessity of linear order of words is replaced by an ordering in which simultaneous superposition of signifiers is possible. This alone calls for rules of a type unheard of so far.
2. The latent iconicity makes signing always a potentially vivid por-

trayal of "reality," in which signifiers are embedded in a total bodily behavior that acts out "reality." It therefore has little or no need of the type of grammatical functions expressed through phenomena like morphological markers or so-called function words.

3. Each utterance is, finally, in fact and by necessity also embedded in the totality of the communicating person, who has to be watched continuously. No understanding is possible abstracted from mimicry and pantomimic behavior. The total amount of relevant nonlinguistic information to facilitate understanding is mandatorily present.

All this creates the possibility of mutual interchange in a way that depends greatly upon momentaneous interpretation of messages—as they remain to a great extent identical with their sender and therefore do not need some of the rules implied by a code that detaches message and sender from each other. This causes both more spontaneous creativity and more dependence on shared context, actual situation, and general background. It also appears to imply a great amount of freedom in ordering signifiers, the superfluity of classifying them as strictly as words in different grammatical categories, and the possibility of leaving out what is redundant for the ad hoc interpretation. This great syntactic freedom, this lack of grammatical classification, and this shortened way of expression are some of the main factors of influence from the esoteric language on the exoteric one in the bilingual setting.

If the person-to-person interaction is so much more an intrinsic part of signing, all this also has as its consequence that signing as a code embedded in such interaction cannot be transcribed, documented, and preserved as fully as can speech. What signing partners **do** is intrinsically different from what speaking partners **say,** for what partners **do** cannot be abstracted from them, whereas what they **say** can. Speech leaves a person, as any sound leaves its source, and can be distinguished from him. The bilingualism under discussion deals with two simultaneously occurring codes which influence each other in some very intrinsic ways but, on the other hand, are irreducible in others.

The reason this chapter has paid quite a bit of attention to the essence of signing is because its specific object, bilingualism, could not be encountered without sufficient insight into both languages involved. If this essence has been worked out more in terms of a psychological or psycholinguistic analysis of communicative behavior than in a linguistic way, formulating rules, this is due to the fact that signing is a mostly unknown language *sui generis*, essentially different from languages based on speech. Such a different language, in my opinion, has to be approached as a phenomenon of interpersonal human behavior first.

ACKNOWLEDGMENTS

I am greatly indebted to Catherine Snow, Ph.D., for editing this chapter.

REFERENCES

Bellugi, U., & Fischer, S. 1972. A comparison of sign language and spoken language. *Cognition, 1*, 173–200.

Diebold, A. R., Jr. 1961. Incipient bilingualism. *Language, 37*, 97–112.

Ferguson, C. A. 1959. Diglossia. *Word, 15*, 325–340.

Fischer, S. D. 1973. Two processes of reduplication in the American Sign Language. *Foundations of Language, 9*, 469–481.

Haugen, E. 1964. *Bilingualism in the Americas: A bibliography and research guide.* Montgomery, Alabama: Univ. of Alabama Press.

Schlesinger, I. M. 1967. *Problems of investigating the grammar of Sign Language.* VRA–ISR Project Paper 32–67. Washington, D.C.: Dept. of Health, Education and Welfare.

Schlesinger, I. M. 1971. The grammar of sign language and the problem of language universals. In John Morton (Ed.), *Biological and Social Factors in Psycholinguistics.* Cambridge, England: Logos Press. Pp. 98–121.

Stokoe, W. C. 1960. Sign language structure: An outline of the visual communication systems of the American deaf. Studies in Linguistics. Occasional Paper No. 8. Buffalo, New York: Univ. of Buffalo Press.

Stokoe, W. C., Casterline, D., & Croneberg, C. 1965. *A dictionary of American Sign Language on linguistic principles.* Washington, D.C.: Gallaudet College Press.

Stokoe, W. C. 1972. *Semiotics and human sign languages.* Approaches to Semiotics, 21. The Hague: Mouton.

Tervoort, B. T. 1953. *Structurele Analyse van Visueel Taalgebruik binnen een Groep Dove Kinderen.* Vol. 1, Vol. 2. Amsterdam: North Holland Publishing Company.

Tervoort, B. T. 1958. Acoustical and visual communications systems. *The Volta Review, 60*, 374–380.

Tervoort, B. T. 1961. Esoteric symbolism in the communication behavior of young deaf children. *American Annals of the Deaf, 106* (5), 436–480.

Tervoort, B. T. & Verberk, A. J. A. 1967a. *Analysis of communicative structure patterns in deaf children.* Vocational Rehabilitation Administration of the Dept. of Health, Education and Welfare, Washington D.C. Project No. RD-467-64-65. Nederlandse Organisatie voor Zuiver Wetenschappelijk Onderzoek Nr. 585-15. Groningen University Dept. of Psychology.

Tervoort, B. T. 1967b. Language development of deaf children. Some results of an 8-year project. *Het Gehoorgestoorde kind, 8*, 214–227.

Tervoort, B. T. 1968a. You me downtown movie fun? *Lingua, 21*, 455–465.

Tervoort, B. T. 1968b. Linguistics in language learning for deaf people. *International research seminar of the vocational rehabilitation of deaf persons.* Washington D.C.: Dept. of Health, Education and Welfare. Pp. 155–173.

Tervoort, B. T. 1973a. Could there be a human sign language? *Semiotica, IX*, 347–382.

Tervoort, B. T. 1973b. Van der Geest, T., Gerstel, R., Appel, R., & Tervoort, B. T. *The child's communicative competence.* Language Capacity in Three Groups of Children from Different Social Classes. The Hague: Mouton.

Tervoort, B. T. 1975. *Developmental features of visual communication.* A Psycholinguistic
    Analysis of Deaf Children's Growth in Communicative Capacity. The Hague: Mouton.
Wasow, T. 1973. The innateness hypothesis and grammatical relations. *Synthese, 26,* 38–57.
Weinreich, U. 1953. *Languages in contact. Findings and problems.* Publications of the
    Linguistic Circle of New York 1. New York.
West, L. M., Jr. 1960. *The sign language. An analysis.* Vol. 1, Vol. 2. Bloomington, Indiana:
    Indiana Univ. Press.

Part III

PSYCHOLOGICAL, SOCIOLOGICAL, AND EDUCATIONAL ASPECTS

6

Some Psycholinguistic
Aspects of Sign Language

RICHARD L. BLANTON
PENELOPE H. BROOKS

Sign language is a natural product of the drive to express. This drive and its expression appear in some of the higher animals, but only in man has led to the development
of a highly structured sign language. Both the drive to communicate and to imitate are
not only psychological functions but also are necessary results of communication between people. The drive to communicate results from feelings which accompany a mutual perception by two individuals. The feelings of the one person lead to impulsive
expression which triggers the same expression of affect in the other person, the
recognition of shared experience is the basic communication. The repetition of this
process slowly results in the development of a structure: the communication takes on
the form of voluntary directing and imitative signs. The various types of signs develop
to represent physical objects as well as mental concepts [Wundt, 1900, p. 218, pt. 1].

In this paper we will examine some of the perceptual and cognitive
features of language with special emphasis on sign language. We have
divided the paper into two sections. The first section is about the perceptual and cognitive determinants in language **production** and some of the
related empirical issues, and includes considerable material on early
work, notably by Wundt. The second section is about language **comprehension** and some theoretical and empirical accounts of the processes
involved. Since one of our goals was to elaborate some problems we think
are important to the study of sign languages (generic) and Sign (formal
languages of deaf communities), and since we are neither linguists nor

proficient in American Sign Language (ASL), our concerns are mainly psychological. Some of the relationships between input and output, knowledge of language and language behavior are considered, as well as our siftings of a large body of literature on the psychology of language and a small but growing body of literature on psycholinguistic aspects of sign language. Another goal of this chapter is to show how some past and current issues in cognitive psychology are relevant and necessary to the psycholinguistic study of sign languages—that is, we wanted to elaborate the principal features of a research domain which is as yet only vaguely outlined and not in any feature very detailed. We hope that some of the questions we raise will stimulate further research.

PERCEPTION AND THE PRODUCTION OF LANGUAGE

The basic decision in modern linguistics, says Dufrenne (1963), was taken by Saussure and consisted in distinguishing language from speech, making speech subordinate to language and thus establishing language as an object with structure which could be studied as such—an ideal system, as it were, separate from the specific examples given by occasions of use. This had the effect of elevating syntactics to a privileged status with respect to semantics; meaning was not in language, but attached to it by arbitrary assignment of words to experiences. The result has been a highly developed science of linguistics; formal and abstract systems lend themselves to structural and functional analysis. When one banishes from study the question of how signs come to mean what they mean, a host of difficult problems disappear; these are the psychological problems of perception, cognition, and the structures that subsume these complex processes. How is it that one person generates a message and another receives it? Questions of encoding and decoding, sensory information processing, storage and retrieval, the nature of language competence and its development, all become part of psychological study.

The phenomenological and introspective phases of the study of language are not new in psychology. They were well developed in metaphysics and the "mental sciences" before the first psychological laboratories were established. But the great problem for objective psychology has been to determine which of those questions derived from the armchair analysis of language can be answered or clarified by the collection of data under either natural or experimental conditions. The development of reliable methods of study has occupied psycholinguistics for some 75 years and can be said now to have hardly begun.

Language and Perception: The Studies of Wundt

The first psycholinguist was Wundt; he is also regarded by the two principal students of the history of the problem as the greatest as well (Blumenthal, 1970; Esper, 1935, 1968). In addition to his monumental work on spoken language (Wundt, 1900), he had a profound interest in sign languages and offered the first essay on the psycholinguistics of Sign, the source of the quotation at the head of this chapter. His interest in Sign was fundamental to his theory of language, and since the basic features of that theory have recently emerged in the "new look" in psycholinguistics (Blumenthal, 1970, p. 240 ff.), we should review it briefly here in order to understand his work on Sign.

Wundt's theory of **apperception** is fundamental to his theory of language. He defined **perception** as externally directed sensing and detecting. Internally directed scanning of the conscious field under the guidance of interest and affect and with the resources provided by memory and the structure of judgments and concepts was called **apperception**. Externally directed **perception** is passive, internally directed **apperception** is active. Associational processes are usually governed by externally directed features such as frequency, contiguity, or stimulus intensity, but the internal apperceptive processes usually override these features to permit, for example, the selection of a minor feature of the conscious field because of its affective relevance.

Memory was regarded by Wundt as a set of stored plans or processes for regenerating previous experiences rather than as stored traces of the experiences as such. The underlying affective level from which emotions, attitudes, and other aspects of apperceptive quality arise was three-dimensional, involving the feelings of pleasantness–unpleasantness, strain–relaxation, and activity–passivity. This "theory of emotion" was regarded by critics as elementalistic, though modern workers may see in it remarkable similarity to the "semantic differential" which Osgood (1953) isolated from the factor-analysis of scaled concepts. In fact, however, Wundt always insisted that the apperceptive process selects significant elements from the field entirely on the basis of their relevance as features of the *Gesamtvorstellung*, or whole impression.

Wundt saw apperception as expressive action, and expressive action as basic to language. Indeed, **overt** expressive actions are the fundamental forms of language. More complex language emerges from them in the following way: Expressive actions, especially in animals and children, arise from such affective processes as pleasure and fear which derive from simple sensory experiences. Associations between such expressive movements and other more complex feelings develop, but each experi-

ence has ideational elements, and the expressive movements come to
indicate these as well as the affective states. These ideational elements
then form the basis for gesture language. The indicating and imitating
gestures arouse in observers similar ideational elements, and these in turn
arouse affective states which correspond to, or in some cases, contrast
with, those of the signer. But, unlike affective processes, ideational elements are stored in memory in complex associational patterns. These
associations also have affective correlates which stimulate expressive
responses in the other person. In this way, **imitative** movements become
answering movements and a shared feeling is established. Communication
in itself is a highly gratifying process, and serves to motivate the development of the gestural system even further, taking it outside the
context of the present shared situation and allowing the development of
narrative and commentary. The primary function of language is not communication, however, it is the expression of ideas. Hence it naturally
follows, according to Wundt, that gesture language is not only more
primitive than spoken language, but more universal, since signs have a
closer and more natural relationship to their meaning than spoken words.
The etymology of signs is best understood by looking at their psychological meanings and their relationship to the general principles of expressive
movement.

This statement that sign language retains much of its original character,
a direct relationship between the sign and what it represents, is specifically contrasted by Wundt with speech. Natural signs are not arbitrary,
but motivated. Words, as Saussure pointed out, are arbitrary, which
makes for multiplicity in languages and difficulty in translation. Wundt's
theory about the transition from Sign to speech in the history of language
cannot be detailed here, although it contains features of interest. Our
principal concern at this point is to examine some aspects of the relationships between language and conscious experience as he describes
them—or to use the term in a more modern and looser sense, language
and perception.

As we have seen, Wundt saw language as grounded directly in perception, as part of the expressive activity of apperception. This process
involves several stages which ultimately provide us with a theory of
sentence formation. According to Wundt, the speaker begins with the
apperception of a general impression (the *Gesamtvorstellung*) which is
scanned by the apperceptive process for some feature from which to begin
the construction of a statement. Other aspects of the aggregate impression, including relational properties of its features, are then organized or
transformed in such a way as to generate a statement which more or less
corresponds to the original impression. Wundt emphasized that this cor-

respondence is often inexact; some impressions do not lend themselves easily to the organizational process. The application of grammatical rules to the process of sentence generation is also an apperceptive matter and serves to guide the process in the selection of subsequent members in the series. In this way, a speaker may find himself generating meanings which he did not intend, merely because grammatical relationships have this directional feature. In general, unless tradition forbids, words follow each other according to the degree of emphasis on the concepts; the strongest emphasis is on the concept that forms the main content of the statement. It is usually also first in the sentence, in some cases being the subject, in others the predicate. Wundt's statement here deserves quotation, since it bears on his view of the syntax of Sign:

> The psychological sense of this rule is easily understood; word positions do not first enter into consciousness as they are added to the sentence but rather are there from the beginning in the preceding *Gesamtvorstellung* as a slightly conscious psychological motive that stimulates attention. The order of perception is determined by the relative effects of the individual components of this motive. The speaker observes his cognitive structure of the moment in the same way that he observes a complex external object. He first perceives those features which make the strongest impression on his attention. Where word ordering is not restrained by arbitrary rules, the words emerge in accordance with the general psychological principle of the successive apperception of features of a whole according to the degree of their effect on cognition [1900, pp. 350–351].

Wundt wanted to distinguish his idea of **inner linguistic form** from the notion previously proposed by Humbolt, who had been interpreted to imply the existence of an ideal language structure in the mind of which the spoken language was an imperfect model. To Wundt, the inner linguistic structure is to be:

> understood as the psychological themes that bring about the external form as their result. Of all things that belong to the external side of language, only the phonetic aspect is relatively separated from these psychological motives or at least it is only indirectly related to them. Similarly, on the cognitive side this is true of the conceptual array and the related processes of the construction of meaning. Inasmuch as these are the shared cognitive structures encompassing the mental content of a speech community, they are the cognitive material that will be formed into language [1900, pp. 406–407, pt. 2].

They also provide the motivational or imitative feature of signs which accounts for the universality of natural signs, as Wundt noted. They may also account for the alleged poverty of sign languages, a matter to which we will return in discussion of Tervoort's studies of this problem.

WUNDT'S STUDY OF SIGN LANGUAGE

Wundt had studied a number of sign languages; he had examined sign languages of the deaf in German, English, and French. He had an especial interest in the sign languages of the American Plains Indians and of the Aborigines of Australia, since these could well be the production of a long evolutionary process. Special sign languages, such as those of the Calabrian peasants, were regarded as due to particular social needs, e.g., concealing communications from authorities. The sign language of the Trappist monks, a more recently developed system, was thought by Wundt to be very limited because of the repression of affective expression and the limitation of communication to bare necessities. In all cases, however, sign languages seemed to him to possess the same general features. There are two basic ways of expressing affectively loaded ideas through overt movement, according to Wundt: direction (or indication) and imitation. Hence there are two basic types of signs which are the original components of sign language. Imitative signs are further divided into copying, representing (*mitbezeichnen*), and symbolizing.

Directing signs are apparently the simplest and most primitive, appearing in the early communications of children. Newly formed sign languages should therefore show more directing signs retained principally for self and present persons, space, size, parts of the body, and their functions. **Copying signs** were observed by Wundt to include outlines of objects drawn with the finger and objects copied in continuous form with the hands. **Representative signs** are those in which an object is depicted by selecting some property or characteristic, e.g., the sign for man made by a gesture of lifting a hat. **Symbolic signs** were thought by Wundt to be unusual in natural sign languages, since the most important feature of gesture language is the absence of abstract concepts. He noted some instances, e.g., the sign for *truth* in both European and Dakota sign languages, made by moving the index finger forward from the lips, while *lie* was made by movement to the right or left, indicating straight and crooked speech. In Wundt's opinion, most such signs in modern languages for the deaf have been artificially constructed to permit the expression of concepts derived from spoken languages.

Wundt believed that natural sign language could be classified according to the three categories of **objects, properties**, and **conditions**, with the latter divided into the logical categories of **processes** and **actions**. Thus, classes of terms can be said to exist, but they are not in themselves distinguished as to form, although the way in which a sign is executed may suggest such a category. Auxiliary signs do exist, and others are especially introduced through finger spelling.

The syntax of Sign, according to Wundt, had two important features. First, natural sign language tends to follow the principle of strongest emphasis even more rigidly than spoken languages; and second, it follows the principle that a sign must be intelligible alone or through a sign preceding it. He notes, however, that formal training schools for the deaf have modified these principles in many respects to conform to the syntax of the spoken language. Wundt noted that this process was most fully developed in France, from which we might infer that he would regard American Sign Language as also highly modified in regard to English syntax.

Contemporary Studies of Sign

After Wundt's work, the study of sign language by psychologists was dormant for 60 years. Stokoe, in 1960, published a descriptive study of American Sign Language, to be followed by a linguistically structured dictionary in 1965 (Stokoe, Casterline, & Croneberg, 1965) and his general book on the subject in 1972. The impact of these contributions has been substantial and is reflected throughout this volume. It may be useful at this point to compare the early and recent classification studies since, so far as we can determine, they were performed independently.

While most of the signs in American Sign Language fit reasonably well the criterion of being arbitrary, a large number still have motivational features, retaining elements or cues linking them to their referents. Stokoe *et al.* (1965) distinguish six classes of these, five of them also discussed by Wundt:

1. Pantonymic: These are reenactment signs used mainly for verbs, and included by Wundt under the broad class of **Imitations**.
2. Imitative: Signs in which an essential feature of the action or object is used to represent the whole. Wundt used the word **Copying** to cover this category.
3. Metonymic: An unessential but distinctive feature of the object is used to represent it. These are Wundt's **Representative** signs.
4. Indicative: Pointing signs, which Wundt called **Directing**.
5. Initial Dez: The first letter of the word for the object is finger-spelled. Wundt did not report observing this, but he was not interested in "finger-writing," as he called it, feeling that it was a contaminant of the well-developed natural signs systems in which he was principally interested.
6. Name signs: These are specific to individuals or places, and may be

derived in any of the other ways listed, or may be arbitrary. Wundt mentions but does not discuss them.

Stokoe's work shows American Sign Language to be a rather highly developed system with many syntactical features which make it more readily translatable into English. In Wundt's studies, this sort of specialization of sign language was seen as characterizing work of the French schools; the English system was said to contain less of it. The German schools, he felt, were placing too much emphasis on finger spelling to the detriment of the useful system of natural signs which the middle-European deaf populations had developed over the centuries.

This negative attitude of Wundt toward attempts to force sign languages into the mold of the spoken language of the majority culture is interesting in view of the crusade against Sign by American workers with the deaf. The goal in the schools is, of course, the mastery of communication in English with the intent of maximal integration of the deaf into the general community. These goals have been criticized in recent years, especially by Furth, since they cannot be adequately met for substantial proportions of deaf children in the schools (Blanton, 1968; Furth, 1966). For Wundt, the great virtue of natural sign was in the vividness and empathic identification with the signer which it produced. This sense of immediacy was, he felt, an important advantage in the development of social cohesiveness. The relationships between language training difficulties in the schools and the mental health problems of the deaf reported by Schlesinger and Meadow (1971) and Stewart (1971) deserve study. This is not an appropriate place in which to discuss the matter of oral versus manual education, but the review by Alterman (1970) of the basic theses of each side of the argument supports the view that the suppression of Sign in the training schools has been primarily motivated by emotion rather than educational theory.

Of the standard psycholinguistic techniques, the word association method is one of the oldest and best established. Koplin, Odom, Blanton, and Nunnally (1967) found that the syntagmatic–paradigmatic shift in association frequency (increase in frequency of associations of the same form class as the stimulus, e.g., table–chair) comes some 2 years later in deaf than in hearing children when association is to written English words. Tweney and Hoemann (1973), however, report that when the associations are given by deaf in Sign-to-Sign stimuli, the shift occurs at a comparable age to that of hearing subjects. Schlesinger and Meadow (1971) find that stages in the acquisition of sign language closely parallel the stages in language acquisition by hearing children. Similar conclusions have come from the work of Tervoort (1967). Hilde Schlesinger's work is especially significant, since it covers the longitudinal development of language in four congenitally deaf children, thus enabling us to compare this development with that of hearing children as reported by Brown (1958), McNeill (1971), and others. Of significance for those concerned with the educational process is Schlesinger's finding that the amount of spoken English increased in the language development of her subjects as mastery of Sign increased. It is probable that the observations by earlier workers that free use of Sign tends to decrease use of English by children in residential schools is a social effect. Indeed Wilbur (1976) reviewed the educational situation regarding sign languages and found no evidence that teaching the deaf child to sign initially had a negative effect on subsequent mastery of English. It is primarily the problem of delay in acquisition of a communication system of any sort (which often occurs when hearing parents delay in the diagnosis of deafness in their child past critical stages of development) which is the more serious educational problem. Children of deaf parents who acquire early sign proficiency show better acquisition of English reading skill than children whose language acquisition has been delayed by diagnostic problems. There is some evidence that teaching deaf children a sign system approximating English structure is easier when they already have a basic sign system learned from their parents, and that such a sign English system is of some value in teaching reading, especially when combined with finger spelling. This supports our earlier conclusion that deaf children in the schools learn English as a second language, based on an existing sign system of some kind; the more comprehensive the better (Blanton, 1968).

THE PROBLEMS OF LINGUISTIC MOTIVATION
AND SYNTAX

If we disregard for the moment Wundt's theory of the origin of language in signing, he seems to have raised two major points about the psycholinguistics of Sign, the first being that of the absence of abstract terms in natural sign, and the second that of the relative absence of syntactical elements, i.e., function words and inflections. The first point should be examined first, and Wundt's discussion of the problem leads us directly to the work of Tervoort (1961). As we noted in an earlier discussion of this topic (Blanton, 1968), the observational data presented by Tervoort are used to justify the thesis that the imitational iconic, syncretic, or concrete meaning of a sign impedes its evolution to abstract usage. The perceptual feature causes it to adhere, as it were, to its original object, and it cannot be used in the process of generalization to instances which carry common features with the original object but not features included in the imitation. In other words, since signs are not so arbitrary as words, they are not so conceptually pliant as words. The abstraction process in language makes the sign a variable, denoting some features of the object and not others. If a feature of a new occurrence does not overlap with an iconic feature of the sign, it is not understood. But since an arbitrary sign has no features in common with its object, it can indicate any object agreed to by convention of assignment. This property even permits homonyms. Generalization from iconic signs would therefore depend upon the use of signs for "like" or "as" indicating similarity but nonidentity.

Bellugi and Klima attack the notion on the grounds indicated above, that signs do have abstract, separable elements which are not usually recognized as meaningful in isolation, although some of them may be hand configurations used in finger spelling. They also cite many instances (Klima & Bellugi, 1975) of wit, metaphor, and poetry in sign, outlining the aesthetic principles on which such "artistic" signing is judged by deaf observers. The relative poverty of ASL in abstract terms may, therefore, be due to the stage of its development on the one hand and reliance on finger spelling to use English abstract terms on the other. Other data seem to indicate that signs become less iconic with time. Film made at Gallaudet in 1913 shows deaf signers making many standard signs with more obviously iconic features than they now possess.

Tervoort's thesis, however, is an interesting one which seems to us to offer a number of directions for research. The questions raised for language development in the hearing child are as intriguing as those raised for sign language usage. We do not know the extent to which auditory–vocal signs are regarded by the child as formal or "proper names" attached to the original objects they designate. It is certainly the case, as Macnamara (1972) notes, that the distinction between proper names and variables—i.e., abstractions—emerges very early. What is required to generalize a term is to vary the contexts of its use. With natural or esoteric signs, this process may not occur very readily unless occasions are provided by adult users, just as they are provided by the parent of the hearing child in the generalization of the occasions of use of words. For those interested in the development of more general sign languages with greater resources of abstract terms, this observation may have many implications.[1]

Regarding the absence of syntax in natural sign languages, Wundt's observations are accompanied by the explicit comment that syntax makes possible the relationships between terms, and where these are given in imitation, no formal syntax is necessary. Indeed, in Wundt's view, syntax has primarily the function of structuring spoken language for interpretation, along with such features as rhythm and tonal emphasis.

[1]For other aspects of this issue, see Nelson (1973) on specific versus general nominals.

PERCEPTION AND LANGUAGE

Cassirer seems to have shared Wundt's perspective on the relationship between language and perception. Thus, in volume three of *The Philosophy of Symbolic Forms* (1957), Cassirer specifically denies that the word is arbitrary in its function as an expressive action:

> An expressive character is not a subjective appendage that is subsequently and, as it were, accidentally added to the objective content of sensation; on the contrary, it is part of the essential fact of perception. . . . Reality could never be deduced from the mere experience of things if it were not in some way already contained and manifested in a very particular way in expressive perception [p. 73].

Cassirer accurately perceived the limitations in Wundt's work, which treated language as a major subject for inquiry within social psychology, to which existing experimental methods could not be applied. Cassirer regards the study of language as fundamental to psychological method itself. For this reason, the work of such medical specialists as Jackson (1876), Head (1926), and Goldstein (1948) on the pathology of language assumes, in Cassirer's opinion, major importance for the question of the relation between the formation of language and the structure of the world of perception. After reviewing the literature on this topic, Cassirer (1957) concludes:

> The question of whether the new, i.e., pathological, form of perception comes first and that of language merely follows it—or whether conversely it is language that creates this form—need not trouble us. What is important for us is to recognize that a real separation is not possible, that the language of the sense and pure phonetic language develop hand in hand. . . . If perception did not embrace an originally symbolic element, it would offer no support and starting point for the symbolism of language. . . . Thus perception as such signifies, intends and "says" something—and language merely takes up this first significatory function to carry it in all directions, toward realization and completion. The word of language makes explicit the representative values and meanings that are embedded in perception itself [p. 232].

Osgood (1971) in a remarkable report on some empirical studies of describing, argues that prelinguistic perceptuo-motor behavior displays many of the characteristics of linguistic behavior, and that the perceptual signs and events must have meaning and structure, sharing a common representational system and set of rules with the linguistic signs and events. He believes that what is shared by both sign systems is not linguistic but cognitive in nature and that this nonlinguistic cognitive system is "where sentences come from" in sentence creating by speakers and "where sentences go to" in sentence understanding by listeners. Similarly, Deese (1969) argues that relational features of the perceptual systems give rise to cognitive categories that have languagelike features, including such features as **similarity** and **classification**. It is also clear that assumptions extrinsic to the speaking situation often comprise a complex array of presuppositions which underlie generation and interpretation of language, to which we will allude further below in discussing the work of Bransford, Barclay, and Franks (1972). Schlesinger (1971a) has offered the idea that a nonlinguistic "intentional" system underlies language performance. Paivio (1971) offers a theory of imagery as a substitute for theories of linguistic deep structure.

These citations of more recent literature indicate, it seems to us, that psychologists face an important challenge. Wundt was not able to advance beyond his observational analysis of these matters; they were excluded from his list of problems accessible to analysis by experiment. Oddly enough, Deese seems to share this viewpoint. It is true that most of the experiments in this area would be called "demonstrations" or "models" rather than measurement of adequately defined psychological dimensions. The function of such demonstrations is to point to domains of significant questions. The inventive scientist can subsequently begin the development of methods of more exact study and theory development. In his very clever work on the behavior of describing, Osgood (1971) seems to have made a substantial step in that direction. It seems to us that it has significant bearing on the study of sign languages of the deaf.

Wundt was concerned with making clear distinctions between natural signing and formal sign languages. Behavioral studies of signing in natural ways, without the use of formal sign languages, would probably illuminate the process of sentence generation with gesture languages. For example, describing tasks similar to those of Osgood (1971), which can be adequately carried out in natural gestures, might clarify such processes as the determination of determiners, the use of modifiers, and negation. Schlesinger (1971a) and Hoemann (1972) report sentence generation studies using Sign.

PHYSIOLOGICAL FACTORS IN THE PRODUCTION
OF SIGN LANGUAGE

There is at least one element common to the production of both manual and auditory–vocal languages—their expression is dependent on the organization and operation of motor systems. The gross motor component of sign languages makes them different systems. The first acquisition of signs by children of deaf parents has been studied by Wilbur and Jones (1974) and McIntire (1974). The first sign appears 2 to 3 months earlier than the first word of the hearing child of normal parents, i.e., at 9 to 10 months. For the hearing child of deaf parents, the first sign appears at 9 to

10 months, and the first word, depending on the availability of models, several months later. In such cases, spoken vocabulary complements sign vocabulary, with little overlap between the sets of terms. This indicates that the child is not simply translating from an already known term (Sign) to a synonym in another modality (speech).

With regard to vocabulary size, McIntire cited in Wilbur (1976) reports a 20 sign vocabulary and two-sign utterances at 10 months for deaf children of deaf parents at an age at which the learning child has the first word. The generally accepted average length of utterance for 18-month-old normally hearing children is two words. This may relate to the more rapid psychomotor development of hand musculature. But it also suggests that all children may develop cognitive and semantic skills farther in advance of their competence to produce spoken language than we had supposed. The much earlier ontogenesis of Sign would probably have been interpreted by Wundt as support for his theory of the primacy of sign language in the evolutionary development of man. It is a matter which must be studied more, since the number of children who have been carefully observed is still rather small. Of considerable interest in this regard is the work of Bates, Camioni, and Volterra (1975) who observed three normal infant girls for the emergence of preverbal communicative intentions expressed in gesture, pointing, the use of supports to pull objects nearer, object-to-object tool use, etc. These skills begin with primitive tool use at about 9 months and culminate with rather explicit "imperative" gestures and "declarative" pointing and exclaiming about 3 months later. They interpret these preverbal processes as protolanguage. The data obtained by McIntire on the children of deaf parents suggest, however, that this process may be refined and made considerably more exact and extensive with appropriate environmental demands.

The motoric aspects of the two language systems may also help determine the order of units in the language. The reader may recall that Wundt believed that words in a spoken language and signs in a gestural language conformed to the principle of strongest emphasis, i.e., the most important words or signs are emphasized. There seems to be little question that this principle is valid. Martin (1972) has elaborated it considerably, however, incorporating the concepts of rhythm, intonation, and syntax. He contends that there are properties peculiar to motor systems which affect the form in which ideas and elements are expressed. These properties include the size, speed, and inertia of the motoric components. Such characteristics have to be included in the temporal organization of the language system and are, therefore, highly structured in time. He believes this structure to be the essence of what is commonly known as "rhythm", and this rhythm of speech can be characterized in simple rules that specify the

relative placement of marked events (accented sounds) in time. The role of rhythmic factors in determining the order of language events is potentially enormous. That is, our syntax could be programmed in such a way that low information or redundant elements fall in unaccented periods. Thus, there may be intimate relationships between the mechanical properties of our speech apparatus and the time relations inherent in some syntactical rules. The most basic process would be temporal in nature with syntax being determined by rhythmical constraints instead of vice versa.

Indeed, Blesser (1969) concluded that syntax is almost entirely encoded in prosodic features. McNeill (1971) has speculated that temporal features, e.g., pauses, function to allow perceptual strategies to operate in production. The mechanical aspects of language production are important, then, in auditory–vocal languages. They are inherent in the production of manual language also. What function they serve with respect to a possible rhythmic structure of Sign is unknown. We can speculate that the ordering and pacing of information in time is an important aspect of the intricate synchrony between speaker and hearer—a mutual accommodation. The findings of Bellugi and Fischer (1972) that the rate of production of **ideas** by bilinguals is equal in Sign and spoken English would suggest that the speaker or signer has adapted to some temporal constraints on the listener's comprehension. The question of whether the rhythmic properties of auditory–vocal languages have a corollary in Sign and are organized so as to determine production rate and order, deserves consideration. We would hope that this perspective on the communication act will not be overlooked in future research on sign language.

PERCEPTION AND THE COMPREHENSION OF LANGUAGE

All of these accounts of the relationship between perceptual–cognitive events and language have for the most part been about the production of language and the mapping of the relationship between its production and perception. The creation of a language event is only half of the episode, however. Language output must also be perceived and comprehended by members of the community. Although the ability to understand language is just as important and just as complicated as the ability to produce it, fewer theoretical bases have been formulated to explain the comprehension aspect. Aside from his remarks on the universal comprehensibility of natural sign languages, Wundt did not deal with this problem.

In the following sections we will consider a few of the approaches to the problem of the receiver of language input, especially as they apply to the receiver of Sign. For the sake of organization we have divided this section into two parts, one on perception and one on comprehension. Some would argue that they are inseparable, and this probably is correct. Yet a given sentence or communication can be perceived and repeated by the receiver yet not understood in the sense of the receiver's being able to paraphrase it or act on it. Consider a sentence like "Write on the lemonade with the pacemaker." It is constructed with English words according to some gross constraints of English syntax, and according to our rather arbitrary distinction, is perceivable but not comprehensible.

The Problem of Speech Perception

The temporal features of motor-based language production systems seem to have correlates in the reception of communications. Liberman, Cooper, Shankweiler, and Studdert-Kennedy (1967) proposed that the perceptual identification of speech sounds is more a function of where and how the sound was made than the sound's absolute acoustic properties. To support their motor theory of speech perception, they report several studies that appear to demonstrate the discontinuous nature of phoneme perception. Similarly, Martin (1969), in proposing his theory of the rhythmic structure of speech, has shown that subjects can shadow a passage better if it conforms to good, natural rhythm patterns than if the passage is "offbeat." In a later study, Shields, McHugh, and Martin (1974) showed that accented sounds were identified with greater accuracy than unaccented sounds. Thus there is some evidence that speech production and speech perception are related for auditory–vocal languages. Martin (1972) has speculated that some elements in a sequence are more informative than others. Since a rhythm pattern entails predictability and enables listeners to anticipate, they can implement more efficient perceptual strategies such as attention focusing and cycling between input and processing.

It is an interesting question whether the auditory system has adapted either ontogenetically or phylogenetically to these special properties of auditory–vocal languages, or whether the language has adapted itself in its evolution to take advantage of special characteristics of the auditory system. The answer to this question is important in determining the relevant dimensions for comparing two diverse languages like Sign and an auditory–vocal language. If the vocal language has evolved to take advantage of the properties of the auditory system, then the changes or adaptations it has undergone are irrelevant in assessing the capability of a manual language. For example, some features of syntax in English may be no more than special rhythmic patterns that we overlay on our ideas in order to optimize the attentional operations of the auditory system.

Models developed for the study of memorial processes, format analyses, rhythmic features, and phrase marking, which are properties associated with the auditory system, may be quite inappropriate for studying visual–motor languages. Studies such as those of Smith and Smith (1962) and others indicate movement systems are hierarchically organized in postural, ballistic, and manipulative levels, and much work is needed to understand how these levels relate to each other in encoding and decoding. Thus the processes employed in visual–motor languages may be quite different in structure and logic from those involved in auditory–vocal languages—that is, perception and imitation of movement in free space undoubtedly involves processes structurally dissimilar in important ways to the ones used in perception and imitation of speech. Perhaps linguists interested in studying sign language would find it productive to examine models and grammars of visual perception, motor production, and choreography.

Neurophysiological Processes

The most salient property of sign languages is, of course, their representation in space and time and their consequent reliance on visual perception for decoding. One of the more intriguing aspects of this property is the implications it has for the theories of hemispheric differentiation and dominance.

The predominant view of hemispheric differentiation is that the two cerebral hemispheres not only innervate to a large degree contralateral halves of the body but also have different functions with respect to intellectual skills. Because of the numerous reports of aphasic disorders—e.g., impairment of language understanding, disturbances in naming, reading ability—that have been associated with left hemisphere damage, investigators have inferred function from dysfunction and planted language ability in the left hemisphere (in right-handed persons) or at least attributed a critical mediational function to the left hemisphere. Jackson (1876) proposed a special function for the right hemisphere. The right hemisphere, he concluded, was critical for visual recognition and visual memory. Studies by Weisenburg and McBride (1935), Hebb (1939), Brain (1941), Paterson and Zangwill (1944), Critchley (1953), and Carmon and Benton (1969) have found evidence that the right hemisphere in most people is specialized for coding and interpreting events that can be best characterized as spatiotemporal in nature. Deaf people who know Sign are unique in that their perception of their language is a product of both spatial and language abilities. It seems to us that a concentrated investigation of users of manual language on tasks designed to reflect different aspects of language and hemisphere functions would be a fruitful endeavor. We might be able to answer questions about the properties of Sign—e.g., grammatical properties, cognitive mapping, etc.—as well as answer questions about the definition of language, the necessity of a functional distinction between linguistic and spatial relations in the two hemispheres. One such psychophysical study was reported by McGuigan (1971), who was following research by Max (1937) and Novikova (1961). He took EMG recordings from the arms, lips, and legs of deaf and hearing subjects during thinking (problem solving). For the deaf subjects who were manual and oral, the increase in EMG was found in both lip and arm areas, suggesting to McGuigan that the arm and fingers act as part of a linguistic mechanism which in turn is a single functional speech analyzer system. He also found significant EEG changes in the left-hemisphere motor areas of deaf subjects during thinking, as well as greater EMG increases in the nonpreferred arm than the right arm. Although there were no recordings made from the right hemisphere, he concludes by speculating that deaf subjects may have unusual cerebral dominance or unusual location of speech regions in the right hemisphere.

The Understanding of Information Conveyed in Language

Roger Brown (1958) has captured the phenomenological character of comprehension with respect to reading:

> In reading, when I come upon an unfamiliar word or phrase I have a sensation of derailment. Some process that usually flows along smoothly has been interrupted. Some expected click of my mechanism has failed to occur. It has always seemed to be the principal task of psychology to discover the nature of this click. The meaningful linguistic form must set off some characteristic immediate effect in the person who understands. What is the substantial nature of this effect [p. 82]?

We will consider language comprehension from a semiconstructionist viewpoint, since this will enable us to incorporate alinguistic, experiential aspects of perception and cognition. A constructionist approach to language comprehension implies that the listener is actively processing the incoming information and that this active processing can be characterized as an enrichment process. The information is enriched with knowledge evolved from perceptual experience. The goal of this enrichment is the listener's ascertainment of the speaker's intent—that is, the listener must construct a cognitive match between his interpretation and what the speaker meant.

One of the foremost constructionist theorists is, of course, Piaget. His theoretical interests are not in language comprehension per se, but are addressed to how the child constructs and organizes the relational aspects of his experiences, or the act of comprehension. In this process, language plays a very secondary role. Piaget and Inhelder (1969) place verbal language in the general category of semiotic function, i.e., the representation of something by means of a signifier. Also in that category are mental images and symbolic gestures. Semiotic function does not appear until the end of the sensorimotor period because until then representation does not exist in the signifiers and they have not yet been differentiated from the signified. Semiotic function allows the person to think of objects and events that are not present; it detaches thought from action. Piaget and Inhelder (1969) note, with respect to the manual language of the deaf, that "this gestural language, if it were universal, would constitute an independent and original form of semiotic function [p. 84]."

Piaget distinguishes two aspects of intelligence—figurative and operative. The figurative aspect refers to a sort of representation or a particular, specific accommodation that is static and tied to the external features of the event. Operativity refers to cognitive actions or ways in which the figuratively represented events are structured via constructing, transforming, incorporating (definitions paraphrased from Furth, 1969, pp. 261–263). Language is neither necessary nor sufficient for the development of **operative** knowledge. Verbal communication is unlikely to transmit structures in any readymade way. If verbal transmissions about operations— e.g., mathematical operations, classificatory operations—are understood, it is because, in the child's knowledge, these structures are already elaborated. In other words, a child must already have the mature structures in order to understand linguistic communication about those structures. Sinclair (1971) provides considerable detail on what can be comprehended via language within Piaget's theory. To Piaget, then, language comprehension (and production) is a product of perceptual–cognitive operations.

Language may have its greatest influence at the level of formal or propositional operations, where a symbolic medium is regularly present as the figurative aspect of that functioning (Inhelder & Piaget, 1958) and where formal operations may be skill-specific. Furth and Youniss (1971) found that the ability to apply formal operations is, in part, dependent on the degree of figurative support inherent in the representation. They concluded that language is most closely related to formal operations rather than to concrete operations in that symbolically represented statements are the **object** of formal operative thinking, i.e., the ingredients to which certain operations are applied.

In one of his more recent reports, Furth (1971) reviewed the cognitive research with the deaf carried out between 1967 and 1969. He cites 39 studies in which the cognitive skills of the deaf children and adolescents were quite similar to those of hearing subjects. He concludes that verbal processes, in which the deaf are notably deficient, are not responsible for the emergence of cognitive skills or operations. Thus, linguistic learning and operative intelligence are viewed as independent.[2]

Another way of demonstrating the relationship between language comprehension and perceptual–cognitive processes is to show that nonlinguistic information (perceptual–cognitive) is necessary for comprehension to occur. Language comprehension in the constructionist framework needs a representational system, but it also becomes a product of a child's interaction with and transformation of reality. Comprehension may be viewed as another facet of the assimilatory process in which a child's experience, in the form of operations, is employed in the structuring of the information. Comprehension would be a successful incorporation or structuring of the input.[3] In this sense, comprehension applies to many more phenomena than just language.

The constructive and nonlinguistic aspects of reading were noted by Horn (1937):

> The author, moreover, does not really convey ideas to the reader; he merely stimulates him to construct them out of his own experience. If the concept is already in the

[2]Bornstein and Roy (1973) point out that Furth does not demonstrate conclusively language deficiency in the deaf. Their point is well taken. The readers of this volume should be asking about the proficiency of the deaf subjects in Sign. Furth asserts that the very small percentage of deaf children of deaf parents were the only ones that had any viable language before age 6. This statement needs statistical validation. Many deaf students have been receiving language input of some form before age 6. The assumption that deaf subjects can act as a natural deprivation group with respect to language is not valid; many of them may be deficient in **verbal** language, but until we know more about gestural language, no definitive statements about the deaf's **language** deficiency can be made.

[3]It is interesting to speculate about the temporal aspects of this process. Obviously, such assimilatory activities take time. In view of the constraints imposed by rhythmic structure, one might conclude that the function of this property is to pace information, to stretch it out in time so that the assimilating process can operate. Undoubtedly this involves the short-term memory competence and probably enhances the flexibility of the decoding process, enabling the listener to "replay" segments not adequately grasped initially. Bellugi and Fischer (1972) demonstrated that the rates of encoding in English and Sign were the same, but English is more "molecular" than Sign, containing more relevant units to be decoded. To equate the times, spoken language probably requires some chunking features, for which rhythm may be the principal means.

reader's mind, the task is relatively easy, but if, as is usually the case in school, it is new to the reader, its construction more nearly approaches problem-solving than simple association [p. 154].

Comprehension is not a rote process but is, as Horn suggests, very much like problem solving. Thorndike (1971) made this point clearly:

> Understanding a paragraph is like solving a problem in mathematics. It consists of selecting the right elements of the situation and putting them together in the right relations, and, also, with the right amount of weight or influence or force for each. The mind is assailed, as it were, by every word in the paragraph. It must select, repress, soften, emphasize, correlate, and organize, all under the influence of the right mental set or purpose or demand [p. 425].

Bransford and McCarrell (1974) believe that language comprehension occurs when the listener has sufficient nonlinguistic information to use the cues specified in the linguistic input to construct a meaning for that input. That is, comprehension is a function of the amount of information—properties and contexts—that the listener adds to the propositions specified in the linguistic input. They give several demonstrations that a prose passage or sentence like "the note was sour because the seam split [p. 55]," was better understood when subjects knew it was about a bagpipe than when other types of contextual information were given.

A sentence like "The man put the plane in the envelope" requires some degree of nonlinguistic information in order to understand: the size and shape characteristics of envelopes and of airplanes, and whether "man put" refers to "placement with his hand" or "placement by driving, pulling, pushing," etc. Part of the difficulty in understanding the sentence lies in a conflict between our knowledge of planes as large and bulky and our knowledge of envelopes as small flat containers and our knowledge of the spatial incompatability of the two. Bransford et al. (1972) in attacking interpretative linguistic approaches showed that recognition memory for sentences was actually memory for the semantic situations and relied on information not contained in the linguistic unit, e.g., spatial relations. Paris, Mahoney, and Buckhalt (1974) have shown similar kinds of effects with children. Thus if comprehension (and memory) demands the utilization of knowledge systems that are nonlinguistic in character, the nature of these systems and their mapping relationships to linguistic systems should be of fundamental interest to researchers interested in sign language and its adequacy in expressing ideas and communicating information. It would seem that much of the responsibility for expression and comprehension is in the heads of the participants, not in the communication media. The media can function optimally only if the communicators understand, and they can understand only if they can formulate the relations cued by the communication.

Studies of the Comprehension of Sign Language

One of the principal contributions to the linguistic study of sign languages has been Stokoe's identification of the principal dimensions involved in ASL, i.e., the location aspect (tab), the hand configuration (dez), and the movement of the hand or hands (sig). An exciting new contribution in this regard is the development of a comprehensive notation system at the Hebrew University in Jerusalem. The Eshkol–Wachman movement notation system is employed in a new dictionary by Cohen, Namir, and Schlesinger (1973). The system seems to parallel the phonetic alphabet for speech in having the properties of accuracy of designation and relative absence of meaning of the units. This offers the opportunity for a genuinely scientific analysis of sign languages, and for actual experiments in discriminability and/or meaning inference in sign languages, for example, the interpretation of fragmented sign sequences, Cloze procedure studies, and so on. For example, among the other features of ASL which distinguish it from spoken language is the permissibility of simultaneous signs. It would seem that interesting possibilities for encoding and decoding experiments would be provided by such features.

Wundt's observation that sign languages have substantial cross-cultural applicability impresses one as doubtful. It was generated in part, one feels, by his need to justify his theory of the original nature of language, and he does not offer actual data to support the assertion. One difficulty with testing this idea is, of course, that sign languages have been affected by formal educational systems and by spoken language penetration, so that none of them is very "natural," a point Wundt recognized. One of the few modern studies relevant to this issue was performed by Schlesinger (1971b). Schlesinger, in several studies of the sign systems in use in Israel, found that no grammatical rule was used by all deaf subjects, except that the verb never occurs at the beginning of the sentence and that the adjective always follows the noun. Relations such as "subject of" and "object of," much more crucial for accurate communication, were highly inconsistent. Indeed, the results of these studies suggest that communication between deaf of differing cultural backgrounds is very poor. Schlesinger's experimental method, involving the task of generating sign sequences to describe a standard stimulus, is a significant contribution to research in the field. While, in the work cited, it was used primarily to evaluate the accuracy of communication and to determine the grammatical rules employed by signs, it has merit also for studying the perception–language relationships for which Osgood's method was developed.

PERSPECTIVES AND CONCLUSIONS

Our historical review indicates that Wundt's work on the psychology of sign languages has had even less influence on research in modern psycholinguistics and deaf education than his general work on psycholinguistics has had on the modern developments in that field. Blumenthal (1970) has called attention to the startling modernity of Wundt's ideas, which indeed appear to fit very nicely into the new "mentalism" and the new look in the psychology of language.

This hiatus of 60 years is easy to account for. There are several factors, in addition to the notorious indifference of psychologists to their own history, which seem to us important.

The first of these, already alluded to, is that the educators of the deaf have given the development of sign language, and methods of instruction and research in it, a secondary position in the educational programs for the deaf, especially in the United States. The second reason for the hiatus is that experimental research methods in general psycholinguistics have a relatively short history, only about 20 years of development. It is understandable that research on sign languages would wait upon basic research in auditory–vocal processes.

A third factor, and a more basic one, was the growing dominance of behaviorism. The fundamental theory of Wundt in which language is grounded in perception was incompatible with behavioristic approaches. Esper (1968) traces the history of ideas in psycholinguistics from the work of Wundt to the present, and attributes the behaviorist standpoint to the influence of Geiger's *Der Ursprung der Sprache* (1878) on Max Meyer, who was the teacher of Esper's own mentor, A. P. Weiss, whose influence on Bloomfield is well known. Weiss transmitted to Bloomfield the objective naturalism of Meyer, combined in his own work with the experimental approaches of Watsonian behaviorism. The great failure of early behaviorism was its claim to be a valid theory of nature, rather than a theory of method to which modern criticism has reduced it. The first psycholinguist to recognize this weakness in behaviorism was de Laguna (1927).

Perspectives on directions for future research and study in Sign are not easy to attain. We really do not know what dimensions are important in the relationships between Sign and spoken language. For this reason, the transfer of research paradigms from general psycholinguistics to Sign is a doubtful strategy. Where an adequate analysis can be made, it is possible that some breakthrough work might be done. Fundamental studies of the perception–language relationship following an updated version of Wundt's theory of apperceptive-scanning in the language production process might produce a useful model for production studies. The development of a limited set of natural signs and a limited set of situations which they could effectively describe might enable us to use hearing subjects in studies of describing behavior similar to those of Osgood, discussed above. Comprehension studies like those of Bellugi and her associates (Bellugi & Fischer, 1972; Klima & Bellugi, 1975) offer useful approaches to problems in this area, where additional work, as indicated by the studies of Schlesinger (1971b) and Hoemann (1972), is badly needed.

How much syntax does Sign need? Many features of auditory–vocal language have the function of facilitating the encoding and decoding of serially ordered sense data. These syntactical features do not, for the most part, appear in Sign except to facilitate its translation into English. Schlesinger's observation that word-order variability is substantial among the Israeli deaf, and that confusion results from this, is a fascinating one, suggesting that more comparative studies in regard to this problem might be fruitful.

With regard to the problem of the motivational quality of signs, it seems to us that much useful work could be done. It is generally recognized that sound conveys many shades of meaning to speech, although psycholinguists have not done much useful experimental work on the subject. The comparative phenomenology of the senses has a most important role to play in cognition and communication. What aspects of communication and meaning are inaccessible to the congenitally blind, who cannot perceive gesture and facial expression? The eye provides us with most of our metaphors for understanding and cognition: "I see," means "I understand." The ear provides us with metaphors for social relations: "I hear," means "I obey." It is doubtful that these meanings would be accessible to any system for the accurate cross-sensory coding of information from a visual code or language to an auditory one, or vice versa. The absence of a writing system for Sign which encodes the temporal–spatial information has made the study of the problem very clumsy. Videotape offers some help in this regard, but it is hoped that further developments in Stokoe's notation system will also be useful. The new notation system of Conen *et al.* (1973) may prove to be a breakthrough for the design of experimental materials. The systematic production of nonsense signs, for example, would make it possible to study some interesting problems with more effective controls. The problems of generalizing from auditory–vocal phenomena, such as short-term memory span, to visual motor processes might be clarified thereby. In earlier work (Blanton, 1968), the problems of cross-sensory coding were discussed. We will not enter into the matter further here, but only want to point out that the area has not as yet been clearly conceptualized, and that much work remains to be done after that important step has been accomplished.

ACKNOWLEDGMENTS

Our thanks are expressed to Lula Drewes for assistance in translation.

REFERENCES

Alterman, A. 1970. Language and the education of children with early profound deafness. *American Annals of the Deaf, 115,* 514–521.

Bates, E., Camioni, L., & Volterra, V. 1975. The acquisition of performatives prior to speech. *Merrill Palmer Quarterly, 21,* 205–226.

Bellugi, U., & Fischer, S. 1972. A comparison of sign language and spoken language. *Cognition, 1,* 173–200.

Blanton, R. 1968. Language learning and performance in the deaf. In S. Rosenberg & J. Koplin (Eds.), *Developments in applied psycholinguistics research.* New York: MacMillan. Pp. 121–176.

Blesser, B. A. 1969. Perception of spectrally rotated speech. Unpublished Ph.D. dissertation, Massachusetts Institute of Technology, Department of Electrical Engineering.

Blumenthal, A. L. 1970. *Language and psychology.* New York: Wiley.

Bornstein, H., & Roy, H. 1973. Comment on, Linguistic deficiency and thinking: Research with deaf subjects 1964–1969. *Psychological Bulletin, 79,* 211–214.

Brain, W. R. 1941. Visual disorientation with special reference to lesions of the right cerebral hemisphere. *Brain, 64,* 244–272.

Bransford, J. D., Barclay, J. R., & Franks, J. J. 1972. Sentence memory: A constructive versus interpretive approach. *Cognitive Psychology, 3,* 193–209.

Bransford, J. D., & McCarrell, N. S. 1974. A sketch of a cognitive approach to comprehension: Some thoughts about understanding what it means to comprehend. In D. Palermo & W. Weimer (Eds.), *Cognition and the symbolic processes.* Baltimore: Erlbaum.

Brown, R. 1958. *Words and things.* New York: Free Press.

Carmon, A., & Benton, A. L. 1969. Tactile perception of direction and number in patients with unilateral cerebral disease. *Neurology, 19,* 525–532.

Cassirer, E. 1957. *The philosophy of symbolic forms: The phenomenology of knowledge.* New Haven, Connecticut: Yale Univ. Press.

Cohen, E., Namir, L., & Schlesinger, I. 1973. Some aspects of sign language. In *A new dictionary of sign language.* Part I. The Hague: Mouton.

Critchley, M. 1953. *The parietal lobes.* New York: Hafner.

Deese, J. 1969. Behavior and fact. *American Psychologist, 24,* 515–522.

Dufrenne, M. 1963. *Language and philosophy.* Bloomington, Indiana: Indiana Univ. Press.

Esper, E. A. 1935. Language. In C. Murchison (Ed.), *A handbook of social psychology*. Worcester, Massachusetts: Clark Univ. Press.

Esper, E. A. 1968. *Mentalism and objectivism in linguistics*. New York: American Elsevier.

Furth, H. 1966. *Thinking without language: Psychological implications of deafness*. New York: Free Press.

Furth, H. 1969. *Piaget and knowledge: Theoretical foundations*. Englewood Cliffs, New Jersey: Prentice-Hall.

Furth, H. 1971. Linguistic deficiency and thinking: Research with deaf subjects 1964–1969. *Psychological Bulletin, 74*, 1–34.

Furth, H., & Youniss, J. 1971. Formal operations and language: A comparison of deaf and hearing adolescents. *International Journal of Psychology, 6*, 49–64.

Goldstein, K. 1948. *Language and language disorders*. New York: Grune and Stratton.

Head, M. 1926. *Aphasia and kindred disorders of speech*. London: Cambridge Univ. Press.

Hebb, D. O. 1939. Intelligence in man after large removals of cerebral tissue: Defects following right temporal lobectomy. *Journal of General Psychology, 21*, 437–446.

Hoemann, H. 1972. The development of communication skills in deaf and hearing children. *Child Development, 43*, 990–1003.

Horn, E. V. 1937. *Methods of instruction in the social studies*. New York: Scribner.

Inhelder, B., & Piaget, J. 1958. *The growth of logical thinking: From childhood to adolescence*. New York: Basic Books.

Jackson, J. H. 1876. Case of large cerebral tumour without optic neuritis and with left hemiplegia and imperception. *Royal London Ophthalmic Hospital Reports, 8*, 434–444.

Klima, E., & Bellugi, U. 1975. Wit and poetry in American Sign Language. *Sign Language Studies, 7*, 203–224.

Koplin, J. H., Odom, P. B., Blanton, R. L., & Nunnally, J. C. 1967. Word association test performance of deaf subjects. *Journal of Speech and Hearing Research, 10*, 126–132.

Laguna, G. A. de. 1927. *Speech: Its function and development*. Bloomington, Indiana: Indiana Univ. Press.

Liberman, A. M., Cooper, F. S., Shankweiler, D. P., & Studdert-Kennedy, M. 1967. Perception of the speech code. *Psychological Review, 74*, 431–461.

Macnamara, J. 1972. Cognitive basis of language learning in infants. *Psychological Review, 79*, 1–13.

Martin, J. 1969. Temporal structure and the perception of speech: A preliminary report. Paper presented at the meeting of the Midwestern Psychological Association.

Martin, J. 1972. Rhythmic (hierarchical) versus serial structure in speech and other behavior. *Psychological Review, 79*, 487–509.

Max, L. W. 1937. Experimental study of the motor theory of consciousness: IV. Action-current responses in the deaf during awakening, kinaesthetic imagery and abstract thinking. *Journal of Comparative Psychology, 24*, 301–344.

McGuigan, F. J. 1971. Covert linguistic behavior in deaf subjects during thinking. *Journal of Comparative and Physiological Psychology, 75*, 417–420.

McIntire, M. L. 1974. A modified model for the description of language acquisition in a deaf child. Unpublished M.A. thesis, California State University at Northridge.

McNeill, D. 1971. Sentences as biological processes. Paper presented to the CNRS Conference on Psycholinguistics.

Nelson, K. 1973. Structure and strategy in learning to talk. *Monographs of the SRCD, 38*(1–2, Serial No. 149).

Novikova, L. A. 1961. Electrophysiological investigation of speech. In N. O'Connor (Ed.), *Recent Soviet psychology*. New York: Liveright.

Osgood, C. E. 1953. *Method and theory in experimental psychology.* New York: Oxford Univ. Press.

Osgood, C. E. 1971. Where do sentences come from? In D. Steinberg & L. Jakobovits (Eds.), *Semantics: An interdisciplinary reader in philosophy, linguistics, and psychology.* New York: Cambridge Univ. Press.

Paivio, A. 1971. *Imagery and verbal processes.* New York: Holt.

Paris, S. G., Mahoney, G. J., & Buckhalt, J. A. 1974. Facilitation of semantic integration in sentence memory of retarded children. *American Journal of Mental Deficiency, 78,* 714–720.

Paterson, A., & Zangwill, O. L. 1944. Disorders of visual space perception associated with lesions of the right cerebral hemisphere. *Brain, 67,* 331–358.

Piaget, J., & Inhelder, B. 1969. *The psychology of the child.* New York: Basic Books.

Schlesinger, H. S., & Meadow, K. 1971. Deafness and mental health. Final report, Social and Rehabilitation Service, Dept. of Health, Education and Welfare, Research and Demonstration Grant No. 14–P–5527019–03 (RD–2835–S).

Schlesinger, I. M. 1971a. The grammar of sign language and the problem of language universals. In J. Morton (Ed.), *Biological and social factors in psycholinguistics.* London: Logos Press.

Schlesinger, I. M. 1971b. Production of utterances and language acquisition. In D. I. Slobin (Ed.), *Ontogenesis of grammar: A theoretical symposium.* New York: Academic Press.

Shields, J. L., McHugh, A., & Martin, J. C. 1974. Reaction time to phoneme targets as a function of rhythmic cues in continuous speech. *Journal of Experimental Psychology, 102,* 250–255.

Sinclair, H. 1971. Sensorimotor action patterns as a condition for the acquisition of syntax. In R. Huxley & E. Ingram (Eds.), *Language acquisition: Models and methods.* New York: Academic Press.

Smith, K. U., & Smith, W. M. 1962. *Perception and motion: An analysis of space-structured behavior.* Philadelphia: Saunders.

Stewart, L. C. 1971. Problems of severely handicapped deaf, implications for educational programs. *American Annals of the Deaf, 116,* 362–368.

Stokoe, W. C., Jr. 1960. Sign language structure: An outline of the visual communication systems of the American deaf. *Studies in Linguistics,* Occasional Papers *8.* Buffalo, New York: Univ. of Buffalo Press.

Stokoe, W., Jr. 1972. *Semiotics and human sign languages.* New Jersey: Mouton (Humanities).

Stokoe, W., Jr., Casterline, D. C., & Croneberg, C. G. 1965. *A dictionary of American sign language on linguistic principles.* Washington, D.C.: Gallaudet College Press.

Tervoort, B. T. 1961. Esoteric symbolism in the communication behavior of young deaf children. *American Annals of the Deaf, 106,* 436–480.

Tervoort, B. 1967. Analysis of communicative structure patterns in deaf children. Final Report, Project No. RD–467–64–65, Vocational Rehabilitation Administration, U.S. Department of Health, Education, and Welfare. Gronigen, The Netherlands: University Press.

Thorndike, E. L. 1971. Reading as reasoning: A study of mistakes in paragraph reading. *Reading Research Quarterly, 6,* 425–434.

Tweney, R., & Hoemann, H. 1973. Sign associations in deaf children: Evidence for a paradigmatic shift. Paper presented at the annual meeting of the Midwestern Psychological Association, Chicago.

Weisenburg, T., & McBride, K. 1935. *Aphasia.* New York: Hafner.

Wilbur, R. B. 1976. The linguistics of manual languages and manual systems. In L. Lloyd (Ed.), *Communication assessment and intervention strategies*. Baltimore: Univ. Park Press.

Wilbur, R. B., & Jones, M. L. 1974. Some aspects of the bilingual/bimodal acquisition of Sign and English by three hearing children of deaf parents. In R. Fox & A. Bruck (Eds.), *Proceedings of the Tenth Regional Meeting, Chicago Linguistic Society*. Chicago: Chicago Linguistic Society.

Wundt, W. 1900. *Volkerpsychologie* (1), *Die Sprache*. Parts 1 and 2, Leipzig: Wilhelm Engelmann.

7

Sociolinguistic Aspects of the Use of Sign Language

AARON V. CICOUREL

In recent years the gestural sign language of the deaf has attracted the interest of researchers in anthropology, linguistics, psychology, and sociology. This interest stems from the fact that gestural sign language as used by persons born deaf to deaf parents (and hence native signing) constitutes a self-contained representational system whose development and use does not depend on auditory–oral inputs. Sign language studies have led to important questions about the origins of language, the use of sign language for cross-species communication with primates, the significance of language in a visual mode for a theory of language based on an auditory–vocal modality, and concern with the role of cognitive processes in sign language acquisition and use. The present chapter deals with sociolinguistic aspects of sign language use as derived from sociological field studies of the deaf.

The first section deals with issues in linguistic methodology as applied to sociolinguistic research on hearing subjects to orient the reader to salient problems. For example: What variations exist in a speech community? What constitutes an appropriate methodology and data base for sociolinguistic research? What is the significance of nonstandard versions of language? What is the relationship between the linguistic code used and the characteristics of the communicators, their language styles, and their use of code switching?

In the second section I discuss recent work on sociolinguistic aspects of sign language use. The issues of sign variation and styles include references to native signing, signing that remains faithful to oral language syntax, home signs, pidgin signs, the use of finger spelling, lip reading, and the creation of signs that correspond to oral language phonetic, phonemic, morphological, syntactic, and semantic levels of analysis.

A third section will present some recent data based on research in a deaf "community" in South London and three schools for the deaf. Variations in adult signing and speech are examined by recording the oral and manual representations of a written story transmitted on five separate occasions by the same deaf subject to other deaf subjects. Two of the schools for deaf children are in England, while the third is in California. The three schools place a different emphasis on the role of sign language, finger spelling, and lip reading in their education of deaf children. Recent work on the acquisition of deep and surface distinctions in hearing children was used to raise questions about the deaf child's acquisition of oral language rules and its relationship to sign language acquisition.

A fourth and final section examines the relationship between cognitive processes and representational systems. Recent research on visual informational processing, the role of internal representations, memory and dual coding is described briefly to indicate its relevance for understanding auditory–vocal and visual–kinesthetic communication. The concluding remarks discuss the issue of what is "language" and how we are to conceive of the interface between cognitive processes and representational systems.

LINGUISTIC METHODOLOGY AND
SOCIOLINGUISTIC RESEARCH

Research on sociolinguistics has been oriented toward field research with actual social groups (Gumperz, 1971; Labov, 1971). Earlier concerns by linguists with the notion of grammatical intuition have been described as exaggerated and the focus has been on the act of speaking (Labov, 1972). The researcher assumes, however, that the linguistic processes of today are the same as have operated to produce what is now considered historical data (Labov, 1972).

A serious methodological issue in all linguistic research is how to write a grammar of a speech community showing all of its internal variations, style shifting, change in progress, and still satisfy other researchers that we have matched the language used by natives when the linguist is not present to observe speech acts unobtrusively.

Sociolinguistic Theory and Research

One view of sociolinguistics deals with a macrolevel of analysis where, for the most part, the researcher is interested in aggregate data on the relationships between abstract social factors like social class and nationalist ideologies, and language dialects (Fishman, 1971). Hence there is a concern with the decay and assimilation of minority languages, the emergence of bilingualism, the institutional concern with standardizing languages, and how to plan for language development in emerging nations where a number of languages exist. At this level of analysis it is difficult to avoid political issues attached to all practical decisions involving the use of one or more languages for administrative, educational, and scientific–industrial development.

The study of sociolinguistic factors associated with sign language touches on macrolevel educational policy issues in the schooling of deaf children (Cicourel & Boese, 1972; Markowitz, 1972) and the problem of a minority language such as Sign. In this chapter, however, I will focus primarily on language use in face-to-face interaction.

A statement of how a linguist views the importance of language in actual use can be found in Labov (1971). The conditions discussed by Labov provide a useful framework for locating studies of the sign language of the deaf.

Labov is critical of linguistic research that fails to recognize that linguistic facts are embedded in social contexts, yet these contexts are not examined independently of the corpus used for analysis. Labov notes that the idea of a sociolinguistic approach to language is redundant and somewhat misleading because all language is a form of social behavior despite the fact that most theoretical linguists deal with language out of its social context (Labov, 1971, pp. 30–31). Modern linguists' decisions to address primarily the native speaker's intuition about language (Chomsky's "competence") without examining language in use as social behavior has led to a program of research that has barely touched the interface between actual speech performance in social contexts and the speaker–hearer's competence. The study of linguistic structure thus excludes the study of speech as social behavior because it is assumed that the portion of language behavior of interest to linguists is considered to be uniform and homogeneous (Labov, 1971). The idea put forth by linguists is that this uniformity and homogeneity of language behavior can be studied by accessing the intuitions of any native speaker of the language (Labov, 1971). Theoretical linguistic studies, notes Labov, idealize the dialectic and stylistic aspects of language in order to focus on what is assumed to be the speaker's intuitive knowledge of language.

Labov notes what he calls the Saussurian Paradox where the social aspect of language can be researched by studying one informant (the researcher as informant or native speaker–hearer), but where individual differences must be studied by research on language in use by many subjects in some social context.

Sociolinguistics deals with the study of language use by a few persons in one-to-one communication, and the verbal displays of one or many informants. Much of the work on sociolinguistics which follows the research of Labov has emphasized a survey research strategy wherein a large (by linguistic standards) sample of informants is examined to study variations and constraints in language use across social classes and regions.

The study of oral language communities has revealed alternate ways of claiming that the "same" thing has been said. Thus two lexical items may be different ("car" and "automobile") but are assumed to have the same referent (Labov, 1971). Phonological and syntactic options also exist, but as Labov notes, it is not easy deciding how to locate these variations in linguistic structure. He points out that the two clear options that exist place the variation outside of the linguistic system that is studied. One option sees the variation as belonging to different systems and hence the speaker exhibits "dialect mixture" or "code switching" in his use of alternations (Gumperz, 1971). The second option claims that the variants are to be viewed as exhibiting free variation within the same linguistic system (Labov, 1971). In the case of the first option, the speaker is assumed to possess a knowledge of two self-contained systems of co-occurring rules and to be able to move appropriately from one to another. In arguing for the existence of the second option of free variation, the researcher must show that the speaker remains within the same set of co-occurring rules (Labov, 1971). Labov notes that it is seldom possible to demonstrate either empirically. A key issue here is Labov's reference to the fact that selective variants within the same system are said to lie "below the level of linguistic structure" because both approaches locate the variation outside of the two systems that are studied. How do we account for this problem of explanation? Some kind of cognitive structure is implied but this structure is not incorporated explicitly into the linguistic model. I return to this issue in the section entitled "Cognitive Processes and Normatively Sanctioned Representational Systems."

The idea of converting meanings into linear forms of language use leads Labov to ask how stylistic meanings that cannot be explained by the notion of free variation based on code switching enter the linear translation process of sequential speech. He shows that linguistic distinctions (e.g., present and past tense) may not always be clear in the actual speech of some native speakers, and that the distinctions may not have any theoretical status in the rules attributed to competence or *langue*. Thus native speakers seem to exhibit normative patterns despite highly stratified variation in language use, but their intuitive judgments about syntax are not always uniform and do not fit the homogeneity implied in Saussure's notion of *langue* (Labov, 1971). Labov states that if we are to make use of a native speaker's statements about language, we need controls such as speech that is unreflecting or "natural."

Labov states that an initial concern of the linguist is to obtain large quantities of carefully recorded "natural" speech. He feels that the best data are obtained from tape-recorded interviews with one informant at a time. But such interviews should encourage the vernacular to emerge by diverting attention away from more formal speech. This means getting the informant to speak in such a way that he does not feel as if he is being interviewed at certain places over the course of the exchange. Certain topics or past experiences are seen as helpful here, as well as some standard probes common to most interviewing. He notes that a more systematic strategy would be to record the normal interaction of a group of peers. He assembled such a group to enable recording to occur on separate tracks after initial long-term participant observation of the group studied. Labov reviews a variety of methodological strategies for obtaining speakers' reactions to the speech of others where dialects and vernacular shifting are of interest. He notes that a dialect that is presumed to be superordinate will dominate when in contact with another assumed to be subordinate. Since language learning occurs at all times, an informant's grammatical rules can be influenced by the particular standard in operation during some period when the researcher elicits information from an informant.

Another sociolinguistic issue that can be applied to the study of sign language is raised by Labov (1971) in his research on black nonstandard English where he addresses the problem of the symmetry or asymmetry between production and perception. He notes, for example, that when speakers of black nonstandard English between the ages of 14 and 17 are given the sentence "I asked him if he did it," they provide an instant reply of "I axed him did he do it." Despite Labov's example, the reader should note that the difference between the two sentences could occur with high-school-educated adults who are white. We do not have comparable data for black and white adults with the same level of education. Labov concludes that the meaning of the sentence is understood clearly but its production is based on the use of black nonstandard rules and thus reveals asymmetry between perception and production. Labov (1971, p. 185) also notes that there are no intuitive judgments that the researcher can access that would reveal the member's competence "to accept, preserve, and interpret rules with variable constraints."

Labov thus acknowledges the role of cognition in language use, but he does not examine the consequences of his remarks for understanding intuitive judgments. He notes (1971, p. 185) that "native perception of our own and others' behavior is usually categorical" and hence does not reveal the capacity to use variable rules in some obvious way. But suggesting that we carefully study language in use to demonstrate the existence of this capacity to use variable rules presupposes a model of verbal information processing that extends beyond linguistic rules.

One way to identify cognitive processes in language use is to examine the differential perception of a socially defined setting where it is necessary for participants to recognize the interplay between dialect differences and standard forms of speech. The linguist assumes that dialects involve low-level rules that remain unstable in the presence of more standard forms of speech. But the social perception of complex cultural circumstances required here by the participants presumes cognitive processes the linguist does not include in his model. Labov's use of a survey research approach to sociolinguistics makes it difficult to study how cognitive processes influence language perception, comprehension, and speech production. The elicitation of survey-type data does not reveal how the interviewer and informants make tacit use of meanings based on the ethnographic history the members have of each other and a reliance on emergent features of the social exchange.

A basic assumption of micro-sociolinguistic research is that linguistic selection or the choice of lexical items, syntactic structures, and sound patterns, is an integral part of the organization of the everyday social exchanges of every hearing group or society. Hence the ways the members of a group or society seek to express insults or humor or doubt or a variety of emotional concerns and beliefs, presume that there are underlying rules of speech that are associated with the social meanings that can be attributed to surface or observable linguistic features (Ervin-Tripp, 1971). This view also assumes that the members of a group can easily recognize when there are deviations from norms about language use. Research on micro-sociolinguistics focuses on the linguistic code utilized and the relationship of this code to characteristics of the communicators and the everyday settings in which the exchanges occur (Fishman, 1967).

Considerable research on micro-sociolinguistics (Ervin-Tripp, 1971; Gumperz, 1971) tends to focus, for example, on a few areas of interpersonal exchanges: (1) rules of address in various groups or societies; (2) rules governing speaker selection and turn taking or general sequencing in discourse and in the opening and closing of conversations; (3) rules for recognizing the introduction or closing of topics; (4) the social selection of lexical items or pronouns or inflectional alternatives and their use for predicting later occurrences within the same utterance or conversation; (5) rules covering different language styles (polite or formal, colloquial, and slang) in different social strata; (6) rules for code switching among individuals as affected by the personnel they speak with, the situational constraints, the kind of speech act (greeting, identification of self, invitations, apologies, etc.), the specific types of assumed messages, and the presumed purpose of the interaction; and (7) rules dealing with various types of linguistic diversity involving types of social interaction within and across countries, regions, social classes, by frequency of communication, the forms of social relationships, and the identities of the speakers or hearers. Many of these areas overlap and the same data base may be useful for finding evidence to describe more than one area.

The above areas have been identified to give the reader a few impressions of the field of sociolinguistics. I have not tried to cover the entire range of research topics because their application to the study of the deaf community has been limited by difficult research conditions. Studies of hearing communities presuppose and rely on unexplicated notions of cultural or social organization, while seldom studying the basis for clustering groups into "social classes," or examining how members of a group decide what is an "invitation," or "apology" or "rejection" or "snub." Deviations or exceptions to "rules" governing address, the introduction or closing of topics, the use or mixing of one or more linguistic styles, are not studied from within a group on a day-to-day basis, but are often elicited from informants by the use of procedures that presuppose the conditions being studied. The idea of a "natural" conversation as a data base is an important view, but considerable work remains if we are to reveal how researchers obtained conversations, how different segments were selected for analysis, how corpora differ from one another, how it was decided that there might be differences between groups according to age, sex, and social relationships, and how a corpus is organized for analysis.

SOCIOLINGUISTICS AND GESTURAL SIGN LANGUAGE

The study of sociolinguistic features of gestural sign language usage among the deaf raises a number of issues that students of hearing subjects tend to ignore or take for granted. First of all, there is the problem of dealing with a language that can be self-contained, but which invariably is associated with a dominant oral tradition despite the fact that native sign systems in use by the deaf have more in common with each other than with a particular dominant oral system. The gestural and oral systems presumably share the same cultural settings. But here is where more difficulties emerge. It is difficult to evaluate the role that language plays in representing experiential knowledge of a culture. We cannot be precise about the differences between deaf and hearing subjects from the same group or society, despite claiming to have held "constant" such factors as age, sex, social class, ethnicity, and education.

When students of deaf sign language use bilingual informants, present minimal pairs of signs and ask what is the "same" or "different" in the hand configurations, movements, locations and orientations of signs, they are crossing modalities and must often rely on informants who are oriented to an oral conception of language. The sign language our informants produce is thus geared to an oral conception of social reality. When we study sociolinguistic aspects of oral language in our own culture as researchers, we assume that we share aspects of the "same" culture as our informants. The everyday world of the deaf seems to differ from the world of the hearing despite apparently sharing what appear to be the same norms of daily living in some ideal sense. The differences emerge over legal problems, educational issues, occupational activities, political conceptions, and daily social relationships. An understanding of the sociolinguistic aspects of deaf sign language use requires an examination of how the deaf shift back and forth between different representational or language systems when expressing their experiences.

One of the factors contributing to the intrusion of the hearing world on the deaf is the lack of a normatively sanctioned notational system for sign language. Hence when a linguist begins to study the sign language of the deaf, his or her presence creates an immediate authority about what is "correct" grammar. Attempting to elicit information from the deaf about variations in their use of native sign language can mean that a dominant oral tradition is being used as a standard with which to orient both the informant and researcher to the phenomena of interest. In the deaf community the deaf have always had to contend with hearing "friends" and teachers who have used oral language syntax as the basis for describing the "inadequacies" of sign language. A variety of signing and speaking forms emerges among signers of different educational backgrounds. Because of differential exposure to what can be called native sign language, the contextual variation of sign use across subjects with different educational backgrounds and different social relationships makes it difficult to write a grammar of native sign language and hold constant the intrusion of home signs, finger spelling or oral language words, pantomime, and signs adopted for use with oral language syntax.

Further complications arise when we recognize that the so-called deaf community is an ambiguous entity that is little understood in most countries. Depending on the size of a country's or state's or city's general population, we might find that the largest group of deaf subjects will be those born to hearing parents (Boese, 1971), but this designation does not mean a coherent group. Most of these deaf children will be exposed to an oral language tradition and yet never grasp this representational system as a native speaker–hearer is said to acquire oral language. On the other hand, deaf children born to hearing parents will seldom acquire proficiency in signs until they come into continuous contact with other deaf persons whose central means of communication is gestural sign. Those "home signs" (Stokoe, 1973; Woodward, 1971) created by hearing parents and deaf children may bear little or no identity to the signs developed by deaf children born to deaf parents whose central means of communication is gestural sign.

The notion of "native" sign language is not easy to define. In previous papers we have simply referred to the sign language used by deaf children and parents from deaf families (Cicourel & Boese, 1972). A more delimited description is provided by Woodward (1971) when he refers to signers born deaf to deaf parents, who have learned sign language before 6 years of age, and who use varieties of ASL that are not in correspondence with American English syntax. Other groups would be expected to use signs that closely correspond to American English equivalents; for example, deaf children born to hearing parents but not exposed to ASL until after 6 years of age, or children born hearing to hearing parents, who became deaf after acquiring some proficiency with oral language. The number of deaf children born to deaf parents whose first language is native sign is considered to be small. Studies of sign language (Stokoe, 1973; Woodward, 1971) have specified several varieties of American Sign Language (ASL) and how they combine with American English. Stokoe refers to High (H) and Low (L) versions of ASL and manually coded American English. The reference to "high" and "low" varieties of a language proposes a nonlinear, two-dimensional continuum. One dimension extends from signed English to ASL, while the other refers to constraints on code choice within English or ASL. At one end of the continuum would be "home signs" developed and used by two- or three-person groups not in contact with other groups using their own home signs (Stokoe, 1973). These groups are usually families with a deaf child and monolingual hearing–speaking family members. These signs, however, are not the "native" signs of deaf children and deaf parents. At the other end of the continuum would be signs derived from ASL but signed as grammatical American English. Stokoe notes that despite a reliance on grammatical American English these latter signs depend on facial and bodily activity that are part of a living nonoral cultural tradition. This high variety of ASL is used in large formal gatherings of deaf persons who have had considerable exposure to an oral language educational system.

Another code is called Pidgin Signed English (PSE) by Stokoe and Woodward and includes structures peculiar to ASL, English, and itself. There is a sign-for-word coding and finger spelling of American English that is represented visually, and thus PSE is closer to written than spoken English.

A third code of importance to this chapter is a signed version of American English that may employ finger spelling and is often called the SEE (Seeing Essential English) method. This code is used in some school settings and combines signs from ASL with strict adherence to American English morphological, syntactic, and semantic structures. The idea is to maintain a one-to-one relation between the morphemes of English and their sign equivalents. For a more refined discussion of high and low varieties of sign language the reader should consult the papers by Woodward (1971) and Stokoe (1973) and Ferguson's (1959) paper on diglossia.

Differences in the above codes provided by Woodward (1971) will be presented here for they will be applicable to later discussions of my research on sign language. High manual American English is illustrated by Woodward in (1):

(1)   *I* W-E-N-T *to the* S-T-O-R-E

A low version of ASL is illustrated by Woodward in (2) and shows a different grammatical structure from American English with little or no finger spelling.

(2)   *Touch finish California you question.*
                        (Have you been to California?)

The statement in (2) would be used in less formal situations and primarily by deaf signers. It should be construed as a rough English translation of a complex form of signing. Thus we have a diglossic situation (Ferguson, 1959) and a linguistic continuum in which different deaf persons will use different ends of the diglossic scale (Woodward, 1971).

Woodward notes that regional variations in sign language reveal more differences in the use of lexical items than in grammatical structure. Other sociolinguistic features of deaf sign language that parallel the so-called nonstandard English of black speech are noted by Woodward. For example, the deletion or hypercorrection of articles as in (3) and (4) below (Woodward, 1971):

(3)   *He is humorous sport.*

(4)   *I have a bread.*

Woodward states that several social variables, like social class or the educational level of the parents and the child, that appear to influence the speech of disadvantaged hearing children, also seem to influence the signing of deaf children. For example, in the case of deaf children, these social variables interact with whether the school attended was oral or manual to affect linguistic variations of Pidgin Signed English. The examples on deletion or hypercorrection of articles and (5) and (6) below illustrate the resemblance of deaf nonstandard American English to sociolinguistic variations in hearing subjects. Thus (5) and (6) are used in restricted (often classroom) situations:

(5)   *I finish been go to the store.* (I have gone to the store.)

(6)   *I have* (possession) *go.* (I have gone.)

In (5) and (6) we have American English syntactic word order along with a mixture of ASL. The reader needs to be warned about a difficult translation problem here. The English glosses presented in (1)–(5) should be read with caution because they tend to reify and underrepresent the amount of information conveyed by the signs but not depicted adequately by the English glosses. The glosses give a false impression of deaf sign language, perhaps giving some readers the idea that it is merely a pidgin language. Gestural sign language is not to be confused with pidgin versions of oral language.

The material from Woodward is useful because it shows that the deaf acquire combinations of sign and oral languages that are similar to hearing persons with different cultural and speech backgrounds. The contrast class, of course, is with hearing persons who are presumed to be from what has been loosely called a "middle-class" background and who presumably speak something called "standard" American English. Hence the sociolinguistic study of deaf sign language parallels the study of oral language because it can tell us something about the social aspects of communication among persons from presumedly the "same" country or nation-state, but where subcultural variations are assumed to be mirrored by speech variations.

The paper by Woodward suggests that variations in sign language exist that parallel sociolinguistic aspects of oral language according to regions, forms of social relationships established among participants, social class affiliation, educational level, and ethnic differences.

Research on the sociolinguistic aspects of sign language also differs from current work with hearing subjects because of the use of different modalities and the dominance of oral conceptions of language.

In my research I have followed the work by Stokoe and Woodward in a different research context. I began doing participant observation in a low-income club for the deaf in South London. After 7 months of observing the deaf in routine social settings at the club and in some of their homes, I devised procedures for obtaining more controlled information about the communicative competence of deaf children and adults. I became preoccupied with methodological issues that emerge when an idealized conception of oral linguistic structure is used to study a language in a different mode and where little is known about the latter's organization. A related preoccupation was with the cognitive processes that are necessary to produce displays in each language, and the fact that in both languages some reliance on other modalities is necessary even when using idealized representational systems of sound patterns and gestural signs. The concern with sociolinguistic aspects of sign and oral languages presupposes the study of the conversion of information from one or several modalities to another. This conversion may be likened to a mutual transfer of information between analogue and digital forms of representations. I will return to these issues in the section on "Cognitive Processes."

SOCIOLINGUISTIC IMPLICATIONS OF FIELD
STUDIES OF DEAF ADULTS AND DEAF CHILDREN

In this section I present a few findings from field studies of the deaf in England after spending 1 year doing participant observation with deaf groups in South London and making several visits to two schools for deaf children. I also include materials obtained a year later from a school for deaf children in California.

The sociolinguistic issues examined include the problem of what could be called different styles of sign and oral language usage that emerge as a routine part of two structured studies that were not intended to parallel sociolinguistic studies of hearing or deaf subjects, but which I hoped would reveal social aspects of deaf communicational strategies. The studies revealed features of code switching and the use of High and Low variations in sign language expression. In one study I had subjects sign a story to each other in the hope of eliciting simulated "natural" signing and was partially successful despite an initial reluctance on the part of a key informant to reveal spontaneous signing for the video camera. The kinds of signing that emerged revealed how the key informant was forced to alter his signing because of what he assumed to be the social and intellectual limitations of two other subjects to comprehend his initial use of signs and the details of the story.

The second study attempted to replicate work done with hearing children using sentences with adjectives that were difficult to understand. I wanted to reveal the problems of studying sociolinguistic aspects of sign language when it is not clear what "native" language structures the children possess. Hence I created a context where the child's teacher would have to reveal the social constraints of learning "language" in a classroom setting. The research context provided the conditions for observing different forms of oral and sign language usage.

The Holiday Story

One strategy that I used with adults to explore variations in the use of sign language was to create a story about a married couple discussing where to go on their holiday (Figure 7.1) (Cicourel, 1974). I assembled four signers who were considered proficient in "native" signing. Two of them were born hearing to hearing parents and the other two were born deaf but to hearing parents. The first and fourth signers (born hearing) became deaf at 7 years of age and had been exposed to sign language for over 55 years. The other two signers were born deaf and were exposed to sign language before the age of 6 because of attending deaf schools at an early age. All of the signers were from South London. A fifth person (Ce), hearing and exposed to sign language for about 14 years, acted as translator for the exercise. Each signer was asked to sign the holiday story to the next signer until the fourth signer told the story to the first signer. The

---

I have a story I want to tell you from the newspaper. A man was arrested in America last week because he threw his wife into a public fountain. The newspaper said the wife told her husband she was anxious to swim on their holiday. The husband then pushed his wife into a fountain they were walking past. The wife was not hurt but had the husband arrested. It seems they had been arguing all morning about where to take their holiday. Last year the husband had promised to take her to the seashore this year. But the man now said he wanted to go camping in the woods. They continued to argue while walking to a friend's house and were passing the fountain. The wife kept insisting that she wanted to go swimming on their holiday. Suddenly the wife was pushed into the fountain by the husband. The wife was not hurt but the husband spent the night in jail . . .

Figure 7.1 Adult sign language story.

exercise proved difficult because Le, the first signer, did not want to sign the story from memory but preferred to read it to the next signer. He was worried about projecting a negative image of signing that might be attributed to its "ungrammatical" status by contrast with oral language standards. A sixth person, Pe, hearing but born to deaf parents in South London, provided an independent translation of the videotapes. Pe's first language was gestural sign.

During the initial stages of the exercise, the first signer, Le, attempted to provide careful spoken oral language and gestural versions of the story to the second signer. He found it necessary to produce additional versions because the second signer had difficulty reading Le's lips and comprehending the H version of signing used. The second signer found it difficult to sign the story to the third signer. The first signer felt he should repeat the signing to the second signer and to the third signer because of their "nervousness" and apparent inability to follow the story. The videotape reveals changes in the iconic form of the signs as they are progressively rendered for an L or more native sign language recipient, rather than an H or signed version of grammatically correct spoken language, finger spelling, and the lip movements associated with oral language speech and syntax.

The five different versions of the story produced by Le were accompanied by his verbal shadowing of the written version of the story with subdued speech, making it possible for the translator to have access to the auditory rendition, lip movements, and finger spelling and gestural sign representations.

In the discussions of the videotapes that follow, I focus on the five interpretations rendered by the first signer (Le), the second language translator (Ce), and the translations of a native gestural signer (Pe), before and after the exercise.

I have assembled several levels of meaning. The different levels of meaning were derived from different scans of the video screen and my perception of the verbal reports. My knowledge of the original story prejudiced my attending to details on the video screen or available through Le's and Ce's oral translations. The translations seemed "obvious" during the initial viewings, only to be reinterpreted later on when I continually discovered discrepancies between the written text of the spoken version and the signs used. My attention to different parts of the video screen and to different elements of the spoken verbal reports sparked various interpretations of the story. The constraints of editing and integrating my analysis often mask the retrospective–prospective reasoning that produced my description.

In Figure 7.2 I call the reader's attention to the oral language structure

Oral Interpretation by First Signer	Oral Translation by Second Language Signer
I want to tell you a story from the newspaper. A man was arrested in America last week because he threw his wife into a fountain. The newspaper said the wife told her husband he was anxious to swim on holiday.	I want to tell you a story from the newspaper. A man was arrested in America last week because he threw his wife into a fountain. The newspaper said the wife told her husband he wanted to (pause) he was angry (pause) something about a holiday in America.
Written Literal Translation	Oral Translation by Native Signer
I want tell [say] you story newspaper, A-man w-a-s- arrest A-m-e-r-i-c-a America last week because you [he] throw wife [husband] in fountain water drink water throw. T-h-e newspaper say t-h-e- wife [husband] tell [say] yours [her]' husband [wife] you [he] w-a-s- anxious t-o swim when holiday.	I want to tell you a story from the newspaper (pause). A man was arrested (pause) in Amer. . . when he threw his wife into a fountain water he threw. The newspaper said that the wife told her husband that he was anxious to go swimming on holiday.

Figure 7.2. First three lines of first signer's initial version of story. (Brackets indicate alternate interpretation possible: dashes between letters indicate finger-spelled word).

that was evident in the first signer's verbal and signed renditions of the story. The translations by Ce and Pe were consistent with the first signer's changes of the original story. The use of signed English was fairly consistent and was displayed in an obvious manner.

In Figure 7.3 the second version of the signing by Le continued to use finger spelling and the oral language organization persisted but perhaps with less consistency vis-à-vis the original text of the story.

In the third oral version (Figure 7.4) the first signer again addressed the second signer but this time he began without looking at the script. He immediately altered the story by simplifying the first sentence; he left out the reference to being arrested in the second sentence, and added the information about how they were walking past the fountain. Le then looked at the script, added *her husband said* (not in the original script), paused, then provided an almost correct oral version of the script after substituting *wanted* for *was anxious* and deleting *their*. Ce's interpretations included a condensed version of the first sentence; she then added *arguing* in the second sentence, and acknowledged a mistake (*no*) in the third sentence. The literal sign interpretations revealed a premature refer-

Oral Interpretation by First Signer	Oral Translation by Second Language Signer
I have a story to tell you from the newspaper.	I have told a story from the newspaper.
A man was arrested in America last week because he threw his wife into fountain.	A man was arrested in America last week because he threw his wife into a fountain.
The husband said the wife was all (pause—signer shakes his head as if he were wrong and starts to sign and talk again.)	The husband told the wife (pause) mistake (pause).
The newspaper said the husband told her husband she was anxious to swim on holiday.	The newspaper said the wife told her husband she was anxious to swim when on holiday.
Written Literal Translation	**Oral Translation by Native Signer**
I want tell [say] story [implied] newspaper.	I've seen this from newspaper.
-A- man w-a-s arrest i-n- America last week because you [he] throw wife in water [water drink?] fountain.	A man was arrested in America last week because he threw his wife into a water fountain.
T-h-e husband say t-h-e wife tell h-e-r husband. (Subject stops and begins again.)	The husband said the wife told her no (pause) the newspaper (pause) the wife told her husband was anxious to swim when on holiday.
T-h-e newspaper t-h-e husband (spoken as husband) tell you [her] husband w-a-s anxious t-o swim when holiday.	

Figure 7.3. Second version of first three lines of story.

ence to *argue* in the first part of the third sentence, and also provided a less coherent oral English syntactic rendition of the third sentence (*The husband say newspaper say, the wife tell her husband she want to swim*). The interpretation by Pe, the native signer, also indicated a less coherent (*wanted been go*) oral English syntactic rendition of the third sentence.

The fourth oral version (Figure 7.5) of the first three lines by Le were altered, more telegraphic, and simplified. The oral English account included elements that occurred later in the story. The interpretation provided by Ce left out the reference to *newspaper* but was coherent and condensed. Ce's account reflected an informal use of spoken English. The literal sign version included a pantomimic depiction of someone reading a newspaper and a modified sign for *story*. This version strongly resembles native gestural sign language structure. The interpretation by Pe sup-

Oral Interpretation by First Signer	Oral Translation by Second Language Signer
I read a story from newspaper. A man pushed his wife into fountain they were walking past. (Pause to look at script.) Her husband said (pause) the newspaper said the wife told her husband she wanted to swim on holiday.	The story from the newspaper. A man pushed his wife into a fountain (pause) they were walking past and arguing (pause—now reading the script). The husband said, no, the newspaper said the wife told her husband she wanted to swim on holiday.
Written Literal Translation	Oral Translation by Native Signer
I tell you story from newspaper. -A- man wife push yours [his] wife in water [pool?] fountain fall. T-h-e-y walk past argue. (Subject stops. Can't seem to remember story and asks for script which he reads from as he continues signing.) T-h-e husband (spoken and basis for transcription) say newspaper say, t-h-e wife tell yours [her] husband you [she] want t-o swim holiday go swim.	I said story from newspaper. A man (pause) husband pushed his wife into fountain (pause) they walked past arguing. Husband said, newspaper said wife told her husband she's wanted been go swimming holiday.

Figure 7.4. Third version of first three lines of story.

ported this observation despite the fact that a reader could argue that an SVO (Subject–Verb–Object) structure is maintained for Ce and Pe's interpretations. Both Ce and Pe, however, were trying to preserve an oral English syntactic framework for a hearing audience. Le, the first signer, however, did not preserve oral English syntactic coherence in his oral and gestural sign renditions. I want to stress the importance of the constraints imposed by the use of written versions of oral and sign language glosses. These glosses make it difficult to represent the visual significance and internal consistency of native gestural sign language.

In the fifth version (Figure 7.6) of the first three lines (based on Le's recall of the story) there were a few modifications of earlier interpretations. Le's oral remarks were more coherent than in the fourth version, perhaps because he was not addressing the second and third signers with whom he experienced the considerable difficulty that led up to the native signing of the fourth version. Le paraphrased the story extensively by bringing in elements from later parts of the story. Ce's rendition was coherent but did not duplicate Le's remarks completely. This raises the

Oral Interpretation by First Signer	Oral Translation by Second Language Signer
The newspaper story. A man's wife walking argue, argue, argue about holiday. Wife want seaside because husband promised her last year. Wants to swim.	A man's wife walking along arguing about holidays. The wife wanted seaside because husband promised last year. Was interested in swimming.
Written Literal Translation	Oral Translation by Native Signer
I tell newspaper story (then two hands simulate holding newspaper) story. (Modified sign for story) Man wife walk go argue, argue -a-[bout?] holiday. Wife want you [her] sea[side] because husband promise sea [side]. Want swim. Husband change think [mind]. Want sea[side] don't [not].	Newspaper story (column it could be). Man walking along argue, wife want go to sea. Husband promise sea. Wife want swim.

Figure 7.5. Fourth version of first three lines of story.

question of whether she was reading Le's lips this time or remembering the story from previous occasions. The literal sign version retained a few elements of the native signing of the fourth version, like the modified (condensed?) sign for *about* and the telegraphic quality of the gestural signs. The significance of the fifth version can be found in the contrast between the oral gloss by Le and the literal interpretation of the signs. It is as if Le had finally managed to deal with the two activities on parallel tracks such that the qualities of both oral and sign language systems could be satisfied.

The different versions of the story as spoken and signed by Le reveal a consistency in the oral versions despite his condensing elements of the story, but the signed versions show a transformation of the signing from signed English to the use of native BSL (British Sign Language) with the elimination of finger spelling. Thus we can observe H and L versions of sign language use within this videotaped exercise that are consistent with the conclusions described above from Stokoe and Woodward. The interpretations by Pe, a native signer, provide still another perspective on the story and indicate some of the thinking employed by signers like Pe

Oral Interpretation by First Signer	Oral Translation by Second Language Signer
I'll tell you a story from the newspaper. A man pushed his wife into a fountain. The newspaper said they had been walking, arguing, all the time, about their holiday, but the wife said her husband promised to take her to the seaside because she was anxious to swim.	I will tell you a story from the newspaper. A man pushed his wife into a fountain. The newspaper said they were walking and arguing, walking and arguing for a long time about their holiday.
Written Literal Translation	Oral Translation by Native Signer
I tell you something from newspaper. -A- man push yours [his] wife in pool [drink] water. T-h-e newspaper say t-h-e-y walk, argue, walk, argue, long time, a[bout?] holiday.	Tell you story from newspaper. A man pushed his wife into fountain (pause) ring water. Newspaper said they walk argue long about holiday.

Figure 7.6. Fifth version of first three lines of story.

who have access to H and L versions of spoken English and sign language.

Methodological Issues

There were several methodological issues that emerged in my work with deaf children that I want to discuss before presenting more data. One problem deals with designing an experiment that would be compatible with field research conditions over which the researcher may have only minimal control. For example, how can we provide experimental controls and simultaneously face the difficulties of working with children who do not speak well and whose signing seems to depend on oral language syntactic knowledge, and who cannot hear but only read lips at a minimal level? I decided to use the child's teacher as an ''experimenter'' to insure the children had maximum exposure to someone whose lips they were accustomed to reading routinely. This procedure was designed to reduce errors that could arise because of an unfamiliarity with the sender of messages. Each child was expected to act out the same stimulus questions with two puppets who alternately were to take the role of object and agent in some sentences or either object or agent in other sentences. This description, however, does not resolve the issue of how we communicate the appropriate instructions to the deaf children acting as subjects. A prior problem consisted of convincing the teachers to use the same instructions: Show the child each puppet, ask the child to name the puppet, and then hope the child will understand the instruction "show me that" after being told the stimulus sentence each time. Some teachers would use the first two sentences (*The wolf bites the duck* and *The duck bites the wolf*) to elaborate the instructions. Other teachers actually showed the child how to interpret these sentences by moving first one and then the other puppet and perhaps pantomiming or mimicking a biting action.

If native deaf sign occurs in a diglossic context, then we have two types of rules organized around two or three (speech, visual and movement) channels of communication and we must hence presume a conversion of information between two representational systems.

In attempting to replicate Cromer's (1970) use of "crazy adjective" sentences with hearing children (see next section for details) to study English and American deaf children, I was aware of the fact that the sentences would probably be inappropriate for children whose command of English would not be based on native competence and performance. But it was this realization, based on prior experiences with American deaf children, which prompted me to replicate a modified version of Cromer's experiment. I felt that the kinds of language problems that deaf children would show in the two English schools from which subjects were obtained would underscore the difficulties of assuming the "naturalness" of oral language linguistic rules and of using an oral method of instruction with persons deprived of the acoustic modality necessary for the native acquisition of oral language. The American school in California presents another perspective because speaking and signing American English is a basic feature of the educational program.

The basic design of the study as conceived initially was to have the child's teacher read each of 16 sentences (Table 7.1) to the child with no other stimuli or gestural form accompanying the speaking. The child was to lip-read the teacher's spoken sentences. This was done by having the teacher read each sentence from a 3 × 5 card and asking the child to act out ("show me that") what was said.

I assumed that deaf children born to hearing parents and trained in the oral tradition would perform significantly better with the sentences as spoken to them than would deaf children born to deaf parents or who have hearing parents but have been exposed to native signing before 6 years of age and have been allowed to sign inside and outside of the classroom.

TABLE 7.1

Test Sentences Using Three Types of Adjectives:
S Type Where Deep and Surface Subject Coincide
O Type Where Deep Subject Is Someone *Other* Than Surface Subject
A Type Where the Deep and Surface Subjects Are Ambiguous[a]

	Correct answer to "Who does the biting?"	Adjective type
1. The wolf bites the wolf.	Wolf	
2. The duck bites the wolf.	Duck	
3. The wolf is **happy** to bite.	Wolf	S
4. The duck is **anxious** to bite.	Duck	S
5. The wolf is **tasty** to bite.	Duck	O
6. The duck is **easy** to bite.	Wolf	O
7. The wolf is **willing** to bite.	Wolf	S
8. The wolf is **hard** to bite.	Duck	O
9. The duck is **glad** to bite.	Duck	S
10. The duck is **fun** to bite.	Wolf	O
11. The wolf is **bad** to bite.	Either	A
12. The duck is **horrible** to bite.	Either	A
13. The wolf is **nice** to bite.	Either	A
14. The duck is **nasty** to bite.	Either	A
15. The wolf is bitten by the duck.	Duck	
16. The duck is bitten by the wolf.	Wolf	

[a] Adapted from Richard F. Cromer, "Children are nice to understand: Surface structure clues for the recovery of a deep structure." *British Journal of Psychology*, 1970,*61*, 397–408.

I planned a second round in which the sentences would be presented in L type gestural sign by a competent native signer. The deaf children born to deaf parents or to hearing parents but exposed to native sign before 6 years of age were expected to show significant improvement with the sentences signed by a competent native signer. The ideal conditions, however, were seldom realized. The difficulties of realizing the ideal conditions are instructive because they provide important information about our studies of sign language and the oral bias that dominates our theories and research.

For my research in England it was not possible to find a native gestural signer who could use only signs and not finger spelling. This was the beginning of a long series of compromises which I was either forced to make or felt I should make owing to the presence of informal pressure by the teachers and/or headmaster. In the case of School A I felt pressured to allow the teachers to use finger spelling and occasional signs during the first round, rather than insisting on their speaking the sentences and having the child rely on lip reading. The teachers told me they were accustomed to using whatever means were available to teach the child how to read, write, and speak. Many of the trials turned into occasional demonstrations by the teacher of how instruction proceeded in the classroom. In some cases I asked teachers to follow whatever procedures they deemed necessary to implement the task of having the children act out each sentence. This was done to observe if the procedures used in the exercise were similar to teaching routines I had observed independently in the classroom.

The English schools provided a nice contrast between two views of the use of the oral method as employed in the education of deaf children in England. In one school (A) the headmaster was open to the use of gestural signs, pantomime, lip reading, and finger spelling in the classroom. Some teachers were more proficient than others in their use of gestural signs, and a few felt they should be used minimally because the children must deal with a speaking–hearing world. My asking that only signs be used in the second round of the crazy adjective exercise met with approval by the headmaster and there was no apparent opposition by the faculty.

The extent to which the children at School A were dependent on the oral method was emphasized quite inadvertently. While videotaping a small part of the religious instruction to a few of our subjects, I asked my informant Pe to use only native signs if possible, to avoid finger spelling and not to use his lips. One of the students stopped him immediately to ask why he was not using his lips. The boy then signed that he and the others preferred that Pe use his lips while signing.

Children educated by a strict oral method of lip reading and reading and writing invariably learn to sign when thrown together at a school for the deaf unless very harsh methods are imposed by school officials. Historically, such methods might have meant having adults living in the same room with the children to prohibit any use of gestural signs, and the use of severe punishment when the children were found signing to each other. Deaf children left to their own devices will create a gestural sign representational system that may or may not interface with an oral representational system. The reader unfamiliar with the education of deaf children within an oral tradition may not realize that the deaf child may learn to lip-read, read, write, and even speak with enough success for a patient listener to understand. But when such deaf children are thrown together in a boarding school, this oral training is not much use for communicating amongst themselves. Some type of gestural representational system will surely emerge.

What remains unclear in circumstances such as in School A, a boarding school, is the kind of internal imagery the children develop, and how this internal representation interfaces with the external gestural signs and oral methods (Furth, 1966). I realized that because of difficulties stated above and the changes made during the exercise by the child's teacher, I might be forced to alter the research design on the spot to accommodate to the changing field conditions. The negotiated experimental conditions that emerged during the course of the trials at School A reflected the actual circumstances within which the children use oral and gestural sign representational systems, and made it difficult for me to pursue the hypothesis described earlier. It is not clear how we could describe the language socialization of our subjects in order to clarify their understanding of the signed and oral displays used. Nor can we be clear about the nature of the native intuition employed by these children when they make use of truncated fragments of oral and sign structures.

The situation at School B provided a contrast to the conditions at School A. The headmaster at School B was rather uneasy about the crazy adjective exercise because of my request to have a second round of trials using sign language. No signs were used at School B for instructional purposes, and all of the teachers sought to use oral methods with which to communicate with the children, especially those from deaf homes. There were four children from two deaf homes in the School B sample and they were all strong native signers. Two of them were in the preschool and kindergarten group. The teacher of this group would often use these children as informants. The four native signers provided the children from hearing homes with an important educational experience vis-à-vis learning gestural signs and cultural meanings that were not similar to the cultural experiences of hearing children of the same age and sex.

Most of the children at School B returned to hearing homes each night, but they used signs amongst themselves at school. The teachers, however, communicated the test sentences orally for the most part. The teachers used occasional facial expressions apparently to transmit information about lexical items felt to be difficult to understand, while the preschool–kindergarten teacher employed facial expressions and some signs in an effort to convey the adult meaning of the sentences. Two of the teachers provided adumbrated examples of their teaching methods. One teacher was requested to do this, while the other seemed to drift into the activity during the exercise. During the second round of sentences the gestural signer used finger spelling and gestural signs but sustained an oral English word order. This signer (Ce in the holiday story previously reported) used primarily H type signing and knew the children because of her social work with the deaf community.

The trials at School B differed from the others because I felt under pressure to hurry the exercise. The headmaster was not pleased by our use of signing during the second round of trials and would drop into the testing room periodically to inquire about how much time we expected to continue. His periodic presence seemed to lend encouragement to teachers who were anxious to show the benefits of the oral method. Both the headmaster and the teachers seemed dismayed by the sentences used because of the children's unfamiliarity with the crazy adjectives. They were concerned about the poor showing the children might make and were anxious to show what the children could do with the oral approach taught at the school.

My initial attempts to use "neutral" experimental conditions at Schools A and B quickly evoked concern on the part of the teachers and/or headmaster that the crazy adjective sentences were inappropriate for deaf children. Despite the use of subjects from two schools using the oral method of instruction, the children's performances on the crazy adjective sentences were ambiguous and very difficult to score. The problem is even more complicated, but I shall defer further discussion until later in the chapter.

The California school chosen is actually part of a hearing school but there are separate facilities for deaf children. The children are taught the oral method as well as signing of American English.

The teachers in School C used the simultaneous method of speaking and signing the verbal displays literally. A hearing person born to deaf parents employed a somewhat High version of ASL during the second trial, but only used those aspects of ASL that are congruent with signed English, while ignoring other features of ASL that are unique to this language.

The principal at School C was pleased with the format of the experiment and was not at all bothered by the use of ASL. He was successful in actively encouraging the hearing parents of deaf children to learn gestural signs, and all of his teachers are required to teach the children how to sign American English. The children were all from hearing homes, but it was not clear how much exposure the children have had to ASL signed by a native signer. Their performance with the crazy adjective sentences was also ambiguous and difficult to score. Hence it was not possible to assemble an unambiguous table of findings that would reveal differences in the children's ability to act out the crazy adjective sentences from an adult point of view by age, sex, and exposure to native signing. We lack important information on the children's language socialization.

Surface and Deep Structure in the Acquisition of Crazy Adjectives

Cromer (1970) addressed the problem of the acquisition of linguistic structures after 5 years of age. He used C. Chomsky's (1969) study of four complex syntactic structures. One structure, "John is easy to see," revealed how younger children mistook the surface subject "John" as being the deep subject of "see." That is, it was John who was doing the seeing. Chomsky used a blindfolded doll presented to the subject and asked, "Is this doll easy to see or hard to see?" This question was followed by the request, "Would you make her easy/hard to see?" The choice of "easy/hard" was to be decided by the child's response to the first question. Most 5-year-olds answered incorrectly that the doll was "hard to see." The percentage of correct answers increased with age until the children aged 9 all answered correctly that the doll was "easy to see." Questioning the subjects showed that younger children believed it was the doll that was doing the seeing in this sentence structure. Criticisms of this work noted that perhaps the child felt that if his own eyes are covered, others will not be able to see **him**. The general idea was that perhaps younger children believed it was necessary for one to see the eyes of others in order to believe it is "easy" to see them.

The interpretation of the sentence frame "John is _____ to see" depends on the particular adjective used in the empty space of this sentence, at least when nouns and verbs are held constant. In the case of the utterance "John is glad to see," the deep and surface structures coincide because "John" is doing the seeing. In the sentence "John is easy to see," the surface or superficial subject, "John," is not the deep subject. Someone other than "John" is doing the seeing. The work by Chomsky is derived from earlier research by Lees, Bolinger, and House-holder on how several types of adjectives influence the meaning of ambiguous sentences.

In Cromer's research three types of adjectives were considered:

I. S type—where surface and deep subjects coincide ("glad")
II. O type—where someone other than the surface subject is the actor ("easy" and "hard")
III. A type—where the sentence is ambiguous in structure, and the interpretation of actor or deep subject depends on the context ("nice," "bad," etc.)

Cromer wanted to know: (a) At what age do children acquire the ability to interpret correctly O type adjectives, i.e., to recover the correct deep structure and answer that "the other" is the real subject? (b) Does the acquisition of a new adjective and its classification as an S, O, or A type depend on a wide acquaintance with the new adjective (e.g., semantic properties, hearing it in several contexts), or can part of its properties be inferred from the limited experience of hearing it in one restrictive frame, i.e., a structure which allows only S type (or A type) adjectives or one which allows only O type (or A type) adjectives?

Cromer claims that Chomsky's original findings have been upheld in his own research. He found that children have less trouble interpreting sentences of the type "John is easy to see" after 6 years of age. But chronological age was not enough to understand what was happening. He used the Peabody Picture Vocabulary Test to differentiate children into three stages to show their differential acquisition of this particular structure. All children who failed to interpret the sentence "John is easy to see" by using one type of primitive rule (those who identified deep subject as being surface subject) were below mental age 5:0, while all children who behaved like adults in acting out the sentences were above the verbal mental age of 6:8. All other children were referred to as "intermediate."

The Use of Crazy Adjectives with Deaf Children

My analysis of the data I obtained from three schools deliberately avoids trying to code each sentence as if the sentence is to be treated as a stimulus for action on the part of the child and the child's movement as a response. To have done this might have created "objective" findings, but such a procedure would have ignored the ambiguity of the response setting (scoring the child's behavior), and how the teacher was motivated to produce various oral, facial, gestural, and tactile displays to generate some sort of communication with the child. A careful, literal transcription is necessary to reveal the auditory–oral aspects of the exchange, as well as my interpretations of nonoral activities. I treated each case as if it could potentially serve as the data base for my entire analysis. Thus despite possible age difference in how the deaf learn oral language syntax, **I want to argue that the crazy adjective sentences can perhaps be understood within the context of learning a foreign language, but where it is not clear that a comparable "native" language has been acquired by all of the children regardless of age.**

We cannot be clear about the attribution of native competence vis-à-vis oral English or a specified version of sign language. Hence we cannot be confident that our deaf subjects have acquired the native intuition we assume exists when studying the language acquisition of native speaker-hearers. Nor can we employ an unambiguous conception of mental age when such tests usually presuppose unspecified competence with oral language structures.

We are not clear as to how well the deaf children born to hearing parents in our sample know sign language in some High or Low sense, nor are we clear about how well the teachers know BSL and ASL even if we could control for the children's chronological and mental age. The teachers seemed to use some variant of signed English.

The various fragments of codes used in the exercise by different children and teachers complicate our study of the sociolinguistics of sign language use because we cannot assume native competence in oral language exists, nor can we clearly identify beforehand a "standard" native sign language system base line with which to study the variations that can be observed. No base lines have ever been identified for subjects, teachers, or experimenters. Hence the deaf situation is not easy to compare with conditions that exist for hearing subjects. We are faced with the intrusion of implicit oral language models of performance at every step. Hence we are forced to pretend that some base line exists, and this assumption immediately prejudices our analysis. But even our subjects are put into very constrained settings because what is "natural" for them as "language" consists of unclear mixtures of fragments of different codes often used as or derived from an oral language mode.

By using oral language "crazy adjective" sentences to study sociolinguistic aspects of gestural sign language use among the deaf, I deliberately create an ambiguous research design. The ambiguity stems from the use of bounded sentences employed in developmental psycholinguistic studies of hearing children (Chomsky, 1969; Cromer, 1970), where it is presumed that the acquisition of linguistic rules occurs in a series of stages and perhaps based on an innate capacity for acquiring "rules of grammar" derived from studies of adult performance.

I decided to use the same arrangement employed by Cromer because the children I studied had been in educational institutions for the deaf that stressed the necessity of teaching oral language syntax, phonology, and semantics. Hence differences in performance between hearing and deaf children could be attributed to their having differential access to language in different modalities despite the exposure by deaf children to oral means of communication in school. The differences could be due, notes Susan Fischer (personal communication), to an interference created by the structure of the crazy adjective sentences and the child's first language, e.g., some unspecifiable versions of BSL and ASL, some kind of pidgin system or home signs, or perhaps unknown aspects of the child's own internal processing system. Fischer also notes that we do not know how hearing adults would perform if presented with the crazy adjective sentences, and we seldom bother to use adults as a special control group in our studies of child language acquisition.

Table 7.2 reveals the ages and sex of the subjects used at the three schools and whether they were born deaf and have hearing or deaf parents. Six of the 34 subjects were born deaf to deaf parents. Hence most

TABLE 7.2

Description of Subjects for Crazy Adjectives Exercise by Age, Sex, and If Born Deaf, to Deaf or Hearing Parents[a]

	Male		Female	
Age	Hearing parents	Deaf parents	Hearing parents	Deaf parents
3	1			1
5			1	
6	1	2	2	
7	3	1	1	
8	2	1	2	
9	2		1	
10	2		2	1
11	3		1	
14			1	
16	1		1	
Total	15	4	12	2

[a] One female subject's age not reported. This child was born hearing to hearing parents and became deaf at 2 years of age.

of the sample has been exposed to an oral language environment. The use of crazy adjective sentences (e.g., "The wolf is tasty to bite") was designed to place some "strain" on the teacher of the deaf and the deaf child because I wanted to examine the prevalent idea among teachers of the deaf that the use of oral language is the "natural" way to teach "language" to the deaf.

I began my analysis by first reviewing parts of each of nine cases on one of the videotapes from School A. This tape depicted the student's teacher reading and/or using occasional elements of signed English to communicate the crazy adjective sentences the children were to act out with the two brightly colored foam rubber puppets of a "duck" and a "wolf" used by Cromer.

I reviewed several trials casually, stopping occasionally to write down some brief general comments about each case, to stimulate my recall of the original events. For example, in the first trial with the first case I wrote the following notes:

> The teacher (T) began by speaking to the child (aged 8) to describe how to use the two puppets. The child (S) was asked to identify each puppet. The teacher presented the first sentence (*The wolf bites the duck*). The child merely smiled "weakly" at the teacher and did not move either puppet toward the other. The same reaction occurred for the second sentence. The teacher did not use her hands but relied on her lip

movements. The child's left hand (holding the duck) moved slightly during each sentence, but the arm remained in the same position. The movement of the hand did not seem to be related to the content of each model sentence presented. The third and fourth sentences (*The wolf is happy to bite; The duck is anxious to bite*) were followed by long pauses, but there was no indication of movement that could be linked to the sentences, but the child's left hand continued to move slightly. The researcher (Res) interrupts here:

Res: Co, could you repeat "show me that," I don't know if she'll understand that.
T: Show me that (pause). Show me.
S: (The child makes some low sounds and moves her body slightly, but does not move one hand toward the other.)
T: The wolf is tasty to bite. (pause) Show me that.
S: (The child does not make any movements that seem related to an adult interpretation of the sentences.)

The teacher continued to present all 16 sentences with virtually the same response by the child as described above. During the actual videotaping of the initial cases it became obvious to me that I would probably not be able to follow Cromer's procedures as he described them. I encouraged some teachers to use whatever procedures they felt would be appropriate in the classroom when they encountered difficulties in communicating the test sentences. Because this first case seemed to yield no response on the part of the child, I decided to intervene in this and subsequent cases as follows:

I asked teacher to show the child what was expected from the child. Then I asked the teacher to go through the sentences again and do whatever necessary to communicate with the children. (Researcher goes over to the table and speaks with the teacher: "Why don't you just show her an example, and uh, and show moving her own hands, just to show *The duck bites the wolf*." The teacher proceeds to explain the exercise to the child.)

If I were to follow the format developed by Chomsky and Cromer, the analysis of each subject's performance in acting out the crazy adjective sentences should be fairly straightforward. I would simply code each stimulus sentence acting-out pair as "wolf," "duck," "wolf," "duck," "duck," etc., according to which puppet is supposed to be "biting" the other puppet. A table of "correct" responses could be assembled and I could compare my results with deaf children with the results obtained by Chomsky and Cromer on hearing children. Thus we could observe the child's proficiency with oral and signed English and obtain a measure of language acquisition among the deaf based on known performance among the hearing.

As I indicated earlier, coding the deaf subjects' performance proved difficult. As I began to code the first subject, it was immediately obvious that following the procedures set up by Cromer could simply imply that deaf children do not understand the sentences because of some of the lexical items used, or that they perhaps have not acquired "normal" oral language grammatical rules adequately, or that they could not read the teacher's lips, and so forth.

The strategy I developed for the analysis of the materials was to transcribe the first two subjects' performance at School A according to the teacher's oral activities, my description of the teacher's movements, and the child's responses. I followed the same procedure for the first two cases at School B and the California school before transcribing the remainder of the cases.

Table 7.3 reveals how the first teacher at School A altered her procedure in the second trial with the first child after my intervention. The teacher combined lip movements with pantomime to illustrate the sentences but she did not use conventional British gestural signs nor finger spelling. I intervened again here:

> Res: Okay, just go through it again and do anything that you think might work, okay?

In Table 7.4 the second round of the first five sentences are presented to give the reader some idea of how the teacher proceeded and how the child responded. In Tables 7.3 and 7.4 we are dealing with a data base that must combine a literal transcription of the teacher's oral remarks with her use of gestures or pantomime as seen by the researcher's description of these activities. In Table 7.4 the teacher employs various movements to supplement her oral remarks. In the presentation of each sentence she points to the puppets and proceeds to use pantomime (sentences 1, 3, 4, 5) and signs (sentences 2, 3) in an attempt to communicate the meaning of each sentence. The teacher continues to follow the same procedure for the remainder of the sentences. When the teacher points to each puppet while saying or repeating the sentence, she seems to be following the word order of the English sentence as if to indicate which puppet is the agent and which one is the object. But the teacher's comments and movements assume that she and the child share the same grammatical rule system governing the sentences and that the child is capable of detecting the ambiguity inherent in many of the sentences. The last two sentences involve passives. The teacher points to the puppets in the order in which each is to bite the other, thus eliminating the passive markers she used when she stated the sentence orally.

In the second case from School A we have a different teacher. The teacher sought to illustrate the relation between the objects in the sentence by using lip movements and different hand gestures. The teacher

TABLE 7.3

Second Explanation by First Teacher to First Subject of Initial Two Sentences

Teacher's remarks	Researcher's observations based on videotape
1. (a) The duck bites the wolf.	1. (a)
(b) Vi. this is the wolf, wolf.	(b) Pointing to the wolf.
(c) This is the duck, duck.	(c) Pointing to the duck while saying "duck" carefully and moving her lips in a somewhat exaggerated manner.
(d) I'm going to (pause) to bite, bite.	(d) Teacher puts her right index finger to her mouth as she simulates biting it.
2. (a) Now the wolf bites the duck.	2. (a) Teacher grasps the child's hand with the wolf on it with her left hand, and grasps the duck with her right hand and moves the wolf toward the duck to indicate a biting movement.
(b) The wolf bites the duck.	(b) Sentence said slowly as she releases her grip on the duck and points to the duck; by saying the sentence slowly the teacher provides time to grasp the puppets and simulate the biting movement.
(c) The wolf bites the duck.	(c) Holding each puppet on the child's hands but pointing with her right index finger to each puppet as she utters the sentence.
(d) Yes, show me. The wolf bites the duck.	(d) Pointing to the wolf and the duck as the terms are said. The child then has the wolf biting the duck.
(e) Yes? You show me.	(e)
(f) Bite! That's r-i-i-ight.	(f)
(g) Now, the duck bites the wolf.	(g) Teacher points to each puppet and places her hands on them while having the duck move toward the wolf.
(h) Bite!	(h) Teacher's right hand uses gestural sign for biting by having the right hand close slowly, and simultaneously making a sound like sucking in air.

placed the puppets on her hands and acted out the first sentence ("The wolf bites the duck") on three consecutive occasions. The teacher simulated the "biting" required of the puppets and showed the child the card with the sentence typed on it before having the child place the puppets on her hand. Table 7.5 presents the next three sentences.

The second teacher is more explicit in using signs to supplement her lip

TABLE 7.4

First Five Sentences Repeated by Teacher to the First Subject

	Teacher's remarks		Researcher's observations
1. (a)	The wolf bites the duck.	(a)	Teacher points to the wolf and then to the duck.
(b)	The wolf bites the duck.	(b)	Points again to each puppet and with right hand simulates biting by moving the mouth.
(c)	That's (the way?), good girl.	(c)	The child's reaction is not clear from the video screen despite the approving statement by the teacher.
2. (a)	Now (pause) the duck bites the wolf. Show me. Bite!	(a)	Gestural sign for *bite* made with right hand while pointing to the wolf. The child seems to have the duck biting the wolf.
3. (a	The wolf is happy to bite.	(a)	Teacher points to the wolf, smiles and makes gestural sign for *happy* and brings right hand up to the mouth area while signing *bite*.
(b)	(.?.) that's right.	(b)	
4. (a)	The duck is worried to bite.	(a)	Teacher uses sign for worrying by placing right hand on stomach area, sucking in air a little and pointing to the wolf, while pressing in the stomach a little while moving the hand on the stomach. Teacher's facial expression difficult to observe. No response by child.
5. (a)	Tasty to bite. The wolf is tasty. Show me.	(a)	Teacher points to the duck and sort of helps the child push the duck toward biting the wolf.
(b)	The duck (pause) nice.	(b)	Teacher moves right hand toward her stomach. It is not clear if the teacher is trying to say the child is doing "well" or that the wolf is "nice" to bite.

302

TABLE 7.5

Sentences 2–5 as Presented by Second Teacher to Second Subject

	Teacher's remarks			Researcher's observations
2.	(a)	Show me.	2. (a)	Teacher uses gestures for *show me*
	(b)	The duck bites the wolf.	(b)	
	(c)	The duck bites the wolf.	(c)	
	(d)	The duck (pause) which is the duck?	(d)	Child holds up the duck.
	(e)	Bites (pause) Bites (pause)	(e)	Child appears to have the wolf bite the duck.
	(f)	The wolf (pause)	(f)	Child has duck bite wolf.
	(g)	Bite.	(g)	Teacher makes gesture for *bite* with right hand.
	(h)	Bite him.	(h)	Child has duck bite the wolf.
	(i)	Yes, is that exactly, what you want?	(i)	Teacher speaking to researcher. (Researcher) "Yes, that's fine." Teacher shows the child the card to read and repeats the sentence, and the child has the duck bite the wolf.
	(j)	The duck bites the wolf. Show me.	(j)	Teacher then asks the child to sit up straight.
3.	(a)	The wolf is happy to bite.	3. (a)	
	(b)	The wolf is *happy* to bite	(b)	
	(c)	The wolf (pause)	(c)	Child holds up wolf.
	(d)	is *happy*, happy	(d)	Teacher moves right hand up to face grabbing the chin area, opening her mouth and simulating "happy laugh" and makes unclear sounds as she reads the card.
	(e)	is happy (pause) to bite	(e)	Child has wolf bite the duck.
	(f)	Look at it What's that word (pause) happy?	(f)	Teacher shows child the card and child makes unclear sounds as she reads the card.
4.	(a)	The duck (pause) is anxious to bite.	4. (a)	Teacher uses facial expression like frowning to signify *worry*, while moving her head, bringing her right hand up to around her eyes (forehead?) for the sign *think* while trying to interpret *anxious* to child. Teacher signs *think* while trying to give a "worried" look to her face. Thus "think-worried"="anxious."
	(b)	The duck (pause) is anxious, worried to bite (pause) to bite, (pause) to bite	(b)	Child seems to have the wolf biting the wolf.

(Continued)

TABLE 7.5 (Continued)

Teacher's remarks	Researcher's observations
(c) The duck (pause) is anxious to bite.	(c) Teacher pointing to duck here and she seems satisfied with the child's movements. The teacher speaks to researcher about needing a blackboard to show child what is meant by *anxious*.
(d) The duck (pause) is *anxious*.	(d) Teacher shows child the card.
(e) he wants to bite	(e) Teacher signs *think* and *want* and mumbles something to the child.

movements. My observations of this second case suggest that the teacher used part of her regular classroom procedure to communicate with the child. Hence rather than simply read each sentence, the teacher seemed to use the exercise to conduct a lesson so that the child could understand what was intended. This was accomplished by repeating the sentence, then repeating the lexical item the teacher felt appeared to be difficult for the child. The teacher used signs and pantomime, and finally showed the child the typed sentence on the card. Some of the presentation of the later sentences revealed more of the same type of "instructional" behavior by this teacher. But there were few occasions in which the child acted out the sentence according to adult conceptions of correctness. Sometimes the teacher produced an oral expression and a corresponding gestural sign. It seemed clear that the child could easily make such a correspondence in some cases, but it is difficult to say with what accuracy the child could comprehend the teacher's lip movements. This child seemed to have learned to recognize the puppets' names on the teacher's lips and an occasional term like "hard," but for most of the sentences it was difficult to say that there was obvious comprehension discernible.

Throughout the trials with the 34 children from the three schools for the deaf similar reactions were obtained from teachers and subjects. The teachers complained about the complexity of the sentences and some of them would interrupt the exercise to tell me that the children had not been taught the particular lexical items used, and that they had not been taught the grammatical constructions displayed in the sentences. The various teachers all used a variety of signed English sentences, pantomime, facial expressions, finger-spelled words, and various signs from BSL or ASL. The signing was clearly of the High variety, but because of the apparent difficulty in communicating the intentions of some of the sentences, the teachers would resort to other strategies in an effort to have the children do well with the exercise.

The basic issue that emerged over and over again was the unclear interface that exists between gestural signs, pantomime, pidgin-signed English, finger spelling, signed grammatical English, and the lip reading of spoken grammatical English. In virtually all of the trials the teacher would continually speak as if the deaf child possessed the communicative competence of a hearing child. Yet all of the teachers would recognize (as revealed by frequent remarks) that the children were often unable to understand the exercise. Twenty-eight of the 34 subjects were from hearing homes but their exposure to Low or native gestural signing is not clearly established. The difficulty of translating the sentences into native sign language was noted by my informants, and hence even the performance of the deaf children with deaf parents remains ambiguous and difficult to score. What is clear is that our sample, like most deaf children, is thoroughly embedded in an oral language educational system despite the use of gestural signs in Schools A and C. The signs used seemed to be subordinate to an oral language model.

Before I began the crazy adjective exercise in School A, I asked my informant, Pe, to help me devise English glosses for Low or native sign interpretations of the sentences. In Table 7.6 these glosses are presented to show how the native signer altered different lexical items ("worry" for "anxious") and the passive construction to create signs that would be intelligible to native signers. The native signer, Pe, also indicated some of the facial features that would be necessary to communicate the intentions of the sentences. The pointing gesture provides an order to the biting to resolve any ambiguity in the sentence, but the informant noted that the sentences are too artificial for deaf persons accustomed to native signing, and the lexical items presuppose complex meanings that are not commensurate with the way native signers would communicate their experiences. The sentences glossed in Table 7.6 presume unstated knowledge about how the deaf could make sense of the signs used. Several modalities or sources of information are necessary, but we cannot be sure that we have established equivalences between whatever conceptions the children have of the two systems, or how some kind of interface is achieved.

The conceptual distinction between High and Low versions of a language is an important beginning for an understanding of the sociolinguistic aspects of sign language. But we need more careful field studies that can link sign language use to the settings in which the exchanges occur, and then explore how what happens in the setting and the participants' assumptions about past relationships influence the signs used. It is difficult

TABLE 7.6

English Glosses by Native Signer of Gestural Signed Interpretations of Sentences with Three Types of Adjectives

1.	(Point)[a]	Wolf bite duck.
2.	(Point)	Duck bite wolf.
3.	(Point)	Wolf happy bite.
4.	(Point)	Duck "worry" bite bite (no sign for "anxious").
5.	(Point)	Wolf bite (point) taste good.
6.	(Point)	Duck easy bite (with expression of "ease" on face).
7.	(Point)	Wolf want (ing) (strong expression on face) bite.
8.	(Point)	Wolf hard bite (doubting expression and shaking head)
9.	(Point)	Duck glad bite.
10.		Bite duck fun (with laugh on face).
11.	(Point)	Wolf bite bad (expression of distaste and withdrawing action).
12.	(Point)	Duck bite horrible (expression of distaste and turning away).
13.	(Point)	Wolf bite nice (with expression of pleasure).
14.	(Point)	Duck bite nasty (expression of distaste).
15.	(Point)	Wolf bite through (or by) (thumb point) duck has.
16.	(Point)	Duck bite through (or by) (thumb point) wolf has.

[a]Point = *the* (in this context, using index finger of right hand or the thumb as indicated in sentences 15 and 16).

to apply our knowledge of sociolinguistic aspects of the hearing to the deaf when the former linguistic system is often attributed by fiat to the deaf subjects from whom we seek information about native signing in routine social settings.

COGNITIVE PROCESSES AND NORMATIVELY SANCTIONED REPRESENTATIONAL SYSTEMS

I would like to discuss sociolinguistic aspects of gestural sign in a broader context to emphasize the importance of cognitive processes in our understanding of sign language use in daily social activities. I wish to explore the role of internal representations in information processing descriptions of sign language, and then close this section by asking what we intend when we use the term "language" as if it were a self-contained system of rules.

Internal Representation of Visual Information

A number of recent studies (Clark & Chase, 1972; Cooper, n.d.; Cooper & Shepard, 1973a, 1973b; Horowitz, 1970; Paivio, 1971; Piaget & Inhelder, 1970; Richardson, 1969; Segal, 1971; Sheehan, 1972; Shepard & Metzler, 1971) have addressed the role of mental images in the performance of standard learning and memory tasks, and then asked about the nature or internal structure of whatever can be said to mediate the imagery. One prominent way to study the nature of internally generated representations is to examine the reaction time of subjects in matching tasks. The experiments seek to demonstrate the relationship of a visual stimulus to a corresponding internal representation. The visual stimulus in the case of some studies (Cooper & Shepard, 1973a, 1973b; Cooper, n.d.) had been rotated, or the subject is asked to rotate a suggested internal representation in preparation for a similarly rotated external visual stimulus. The studies suggest that the idea of internal representation is warranted and is used by subjects for cognitive processing when an appropriate external stimulus is not available (Cooper, n.d., p. 5). Researchers (Shepard & Metzler, 1971) have reported that subjects mentally rotate a representation of one element of a pair of objects into congruence with the second object and then check to see if there is a match or a mismatch in the shape of the perceived objects. Cooper and Shepard (1973a, 1973b) reported that subjects could evaluate a particular version of a tilted test character (letter or number) by mentally transforming an internal representation of the character to bring it into congruence with an upright normal version presumed to be part of the subject's long-term memory. Subjects were given variably timed advance information on the identity and orientation of a related test character that was about to appear. Cooper and Shepard note that when subjects were given enough time first to generate a mental image of one anticipated character, and could rotate it to the orientation that was expected, they could use the mental internal representation as a "sort of template" (1973b, p. 158) with which to compare the external test stimulus.

An interesting aspect of the Cooper–Shepard work has to do with the nonlinearity of the reaction times that were obtained with the alphanumeric stimulus when a simple rotated test character was used. The authors suggest that "familiarity" with the rotated or upright alphanumeric character may be the basis for the nonlinearity. They pursued this problem with the use of six random shapes but found the nonlinearity did not persist. In one experiment subjects first learned to discriminate standard from reflected forms of the objects used in the experiment before being asked to distinguish a presented form as a standard or reflected version. The reaction time was measured by how quickly subjects pushed one of two buttons and stated their choice orally. Further refinements included data on the process subjects are presumed to use to prepare for an upcoming, rotated test-stimulus. The general process seems to be one in which subjects mentally rotated an image of the standard version of the form that was about to be presented into the designated orientation by using an identity cue (Cooper, n.d., p. 52). This would enable subjects to perform a quick check to see if there was a match or mismatch between the image that had been transformed and the test form presented visually. In one case (pre-stimulus rotation) the subjects maintained an internal image of a visual object that had been transformed but which did not remain externally present, while in the other case (post-stimulus rotation) the subjects extracted the internal representation from an external visual stimulus that remained present throughout the rotational process that followed.

The evidence that human subjects carry out particular visual tasks by performing mental rotations on internal representations is suggestive for our understanding of the cognitive processes of nonoral communication. What is of interest here is the idea of human thinking that is not dependent on oral–symbolic activities but where we can expect the accomplishment of complex tasks that rely heavily on analog mental operations to plan the spatial organization of open and closed areas, solve difficult problems in some aspects of mathematics or engineering, and map nonoral experiential knowledge into a visual–kinesthetic external representational system. Hence what we mean by communicational structures would require a broader view of the relationship between cognition and the verbal skills that represent information with formally organized discrete units. The gestural sign language of the deaf provides one example of a self-contained external representational system which can be linked to internal representations and cognitive processes that do not require any reference to the rule systems of oral–symbolic skills to accomplish complex tasks of daily living. The deaf are capable of complex thought that uses an intricate manual–visual system of representation, but they also must convert information from this system into a digital oral–symbolic representational system or vice versa. Hearing subjects do this when receiving oral instructions to perform tasks in analog mental rotation experiments but they are not required to represent their thinking with a nonoral representational system.

A general problem of selective interference in studies of internal representations is described by Cooper (n.d.) as follows:

> Segal's experiments suggest that there are separate limited-capacity information-processing systems for each sensory modality. However, Brooks' output-conflict studies indicate that the important division between information-processing systems is at a high level—viz., between general spatial properties and verbal/articulatory properties. It may well be that modality-specific divisions are appropriate for sensory detection tasks like Segal's, while divisions between general, abstract systems are appropriate for the more cognitive classification tasks studies by Brooks [Chap. 1, p. 7].

Our research on the sociolinguistic aspects of gestural sign language may be clarified if we examine the significance of work on internal representation. Specifically, we would have to ask how an internal system is limited in its information-processing capacity because its generation of mental images (auditory–oral or visual–spatial) is disrupted by the nature of the external stimulus demands. When we have the possibility of two systems of external representation based on different modalities (perhaps only partially formed for children), then we cannot be satisfied with the use of an oral language linguistic model for studying sign language. We must ask if this interference is modality-specific, and if having two representational or language systems confounds information processing for deaf children or deaf adults who have not acquired a native competence in one of the systems. What remains unclear is how nonoral linguistic material (e.g., gestural signs) may be processed in a different way than oral linguistic material, and how perhaps nonlinguistic material can be processed in both oral and nonoral modes. Hence it is not clear if signs are to be considered "linguistic" in a strict oral sense or, as suggested in this paper, if these signs are to be viewed as a visual–symbolic system which we must also call a language.

CONCLUDING REMARKS

When we describe language origins and the structure of oral and nonoral systems of communication we often do so by ignoring the historical evolution of formal representational systems. It is difficult to compare the nature and complexity of language use under relentless daily conditions of harsh, primitive survival, with the extensive social organization of oral and nonoral communication in industrialized and technologically complex societies. The existence of elegant researcher-oriented rule systems for describing speech codes or levels of auditory abstraction (phonetic, phonological, syntactic, semantic, and conversational) can mask the ways in which speaker–hearers recognize and process auditory inputs during actual exchanges. If the complexity and form of human cognitive and social life are associated with the form and organization of oral and nonoral communication (Hewes, 1973), then we must refrain from first presuming and then imposing idealized rule systems on a communication system that has not achieved the same rule structures and metalanguage descriptions of itself (Cicourel, 1974). The study of the sign language of the deaf poses such a problem because the vocal–auditory channel is not needed for communication of complex ideas in a productive or generative manner.

The study of sign language use among the deaf born to deaf parents is central to a theory of language origins and the role of cognitive processes because this language lacks a formal prescriptive and proscriptive syntax and orthographic system. Hence the claim is made that the use of signs among native signers does not represent comparable classes of abstractions as those found among oral language users. I wish to stress the idea that the uses of sign language develop in ways that are comparable to the cultural and educational complexity of the everyday life in which they appear. Thus the limitations of gestural sign systems, if such limitations exist, are inherent in the cultural development of the deaf and not in the structure of sign languages.

Current theories of communication take for granted many aspects of how the representational system we call oral language can describe the past, present, and future settings they index. This representational system is assumed to be a standardized indicator of these settings. But these standardized auditory–oral displays presuppose unexplicated ideas about a memory system and normative conceptions of "normal" thinking and social activities. It is difficult to speculate about internal representations of experiences that may not be tied to a generative, normatively sanctioned external signaling system. Our description and analysis of communication among the deaf begins with the assumption that the organization of internal processes is structured by external representations similar to those of oral language.

The existence of gestural sign languages in all deaf groups (Boese, 1971) despite communicational exchanges that have different relationships to oral language (Cohen, Namir, & Schlesinger, 1977) suggests that a gestural sign system originally emerged in a context where "iconicity" was basic for depicting past, present, and future settings and social relationships among participants, and that this sign system initially led to different assumptions about the general knowledge of the world that each deaf person assumes of others and himself. In the case of oral languages, we do not have a clear basis for tracing the progressive emergence of more abstract symbolic forms from something we could say was comparable to the iconic forms of initial gestural sign systems, despite the knowledge we have about Chinese characters, and Egyptian and Sumerian hieroglyphics. Nancy Frishberg (1973) has noted that in the case of ASL and the French gestural sign system, these languages have evolved to the point where there is much less of the iconicity extant in initial versions of these systems.

The adults in the holiday story exercise exhibited behavior that confirms the idea of two generative oral and sign language systems that can be independent of each other despite their presumable reference to the same environment of objects. Variations in High and Low forms of sign were evident. The children from the three schools studied could be seen as exemplifying three variations of the oral method used by the majority of schools for the deaf. These educational variations provide a basis for understanding different styles of oral language used by the deaf in educational and social circumstances. The use of signs for educational purposes is rare in School B, inconsistent in School A, and rather systematic in School C. But all three schools assume that "language" means oral language phonology, syntax, and semantics. The role of native sign language remains somewhat ambiguous. We lack a clear normative model of native gestural signing that is relatively free of oral language conceptions of "language." Studies of the sociolinguistic aspects of gestural sign remain heavily dependent on our cultural experiences as hearing researchers when we design research problems and when we generate and interpret findings.

When we do studies of language acquisition and refer to the "language of the child," and insist on including deaf children, it is not clear how some sort of proficiency with the acting out of **spoken** sentences provides us with a specification of the hearing or deaf child's knowledge of "language."

Studies of information processing suggest that we examine carefully the interface between internal and external representational systems, and the different stages of cognitive processing that can exist in the construction of some level of abstraction identified by the researcher as auditory, phonetic, phonological, syntactic, semantic, conversational, finger spelling, pantomime, home signs, gestural signs, or "body language." We need to clarify how the internal organization of perceived or imagined experiences is represented by external systems of representation we call oral or gestural sign languages. The cultural basis of gestural sign language use requires that we examine the organization of experiential knowledge. The role of experiential knowledge is seldom addressed when the study of a gestural sign data base is dependent on oral language phonological or syntactic or conversational rules of analysis. I have stressed the idea of a visual–symbolic language system that is self-contained, and embedded in its own cultural milieu.

ACKNOWLEDGMENTS

The research discussed in this paper was done in London during 1970–1971 while the author held a National Science Foundation Senior Post-Doctoral Fellowship at the Sociological Research Unit of the University of London Institute of Education. Additional work was done at the Madison Elementary School in Santa Ana, California, with a small grant from the Faculty Research Committee, University of California, San Diego. The video recordings in

England were made possible through the generous assistance of the staff of the University of London Audio-Visual Center and its director, Michael Clarke; the Audio-Visual Center of Institute of Education and its director, Elizabeth Coppen; the Audio-Visual Center of Goldsmiths College and its director, Paul Barnes. In California, Marshall Shumsky helped me with the video recording. I am grateful to Percy Corfmat, Leonard Kent, Celia Shakeshaft, Ivor Scott-Oldfield, Monica Clare, T. Pursglove, Barbara Brandt, Roy K. Holcomb, and many others who wish to remain anonymous, for their help in making the study possible. I am grateful to Susan Fischer and I. M. Schlesinger for a number of helpful suggestions that have been incorporated into the paper.

REFERENCES

Boese, R. J. 1971. Native sign language and the problem of meaning. Unpublished Ph.D. dissertation, Univ. of California, Santa Barbara.

Chomsky, C. 1969. *The acquisition of syntax in children from 5 to 10*. Cambridge, Massachusetts: Massachusetts Institute of Technology Press.

Cicourel, A. V. 1974. Gestural sign language and the study of non-verbal communication. *Sign Language Studies, 4*, 35–76.

Cicourel, A. V., & Boese, R. J. 1972. The acquisition of manual sign language and generative semantics. *Semiotica, 7* (3), 225–256.

Clark, H. H., & Chase, W. G. 1972. On the process of comparing sentences against pictures. *Cognitive Psychology, 3*, 472–517.

Cohen, E., Namir, L., & Schlesinger, I. M. 1977. *A new dictionary of sign language*. Part I. The Hague: Mouton.

Cooper, L. A. n.d. Internal representation and transformation of random two-dimensional forms: A chronometric analysis. Unpublished manuscript.

Cooper, L. A., & Shepard, R. N. 1973a. Chronometric studies of the rotation of mental images. In W. G. Chase (Ed.), *Visual information processing*. New York: Academic Press.

Cooper, L. A., & Shepard, R. N. 1973b. The time required to prepare for a rotated stimulus. *Memory & Cognition, 1* (3), 246–250.

Cromer, R. F. 1970. Children are nice to understand: Surface structure clues for the recovery of a deep structure. *British Journal of Psychology, 61*, 397–408.

Ervin-Tripp, S. M. 1971. Sociolinguistics. *Advances in the sociology of languages, I*. The Hague: Mouton.

Ferguson, C. A. 1959. Diglossia. *Word, 15*, 225–340.

Fishman, J. A. 1967. Review of J. Hertzler: *A Sociology of Language*. *Language, 43*, 586–604.

Fishman, J. A. 1971. The sociology of language: An interdisciplinary social science approach to language in society. *Advances in the Sociology in Language, I*. The Hague: Mouton.

Frishberg, N. 1973. Arbitrariness and iconicity. Paper presented to the Linguistic Society of America, San Diego.

Furth, H. 1966. *Thinking without language*. London: Collier MacMillan.

Gumperz, J. J. 1971. *Language in social groups*. Stanford, California: Stanford Univ. Press.

Hewes, G. W. 1973. Primate communication and the gestural origin of language. *Current Anthropology, 14*, 5–24.

Horowitz, M. J. 1970. *Image formation and cognition*. New York: Appleton.

Labov, W. 1971. The study of language in its social context. In J. A. Fishman (Ed.), *Advances in the sociology of language, 1.* The Hague: Mouton.

Labov, W. 1972. Some principles of linguistic methodology. *Language in Society. 1* (1), 97–120.

Markowitz, H. 1972. Some sociolinguistic considerations of American Sign Language. *Sign Language Studies, 1*, 15–41.

Paivio, A. 1971. *Imagery and verbal processes.* New York: Holt.

Piaget, J., & Inhelder, B. 1970. *Mental imagery in the child.* New York: Basic Books.

Richardson, A. 1969. *Mental imagery.* New York: Springer.

Segal, S. J. (Ed.). 1971. *Imagery.* New York: Academic Press.

Sheehan, P. W. (Ed.). 1972. *The function and nature of imagery.* New York: Academic Press.

Shepard, R. N., & Metzler, J. 1971. Mental rotation of three-dimensional objects. *Science, 171*, 701–703.

Stokoe, W. C., Jr. 1973. Sign syntax and human language capacity. Summer Linguistic Institute, Linguistic Society of America, Ann Arbor, Michigan.

Woodward, J. C., Jr. 1971. Implications for sociolinguistic research among the deaf. Paper presented to the Linguistic Society of America, St. Louis.

8

Social–Psychological Aspects of the Use of Sign Language

LARS VON DER LIETH

> When I accept another person's language,
> I have accepted the person. . . . When I
> reject a language, I have rejected the
> person because the language is part of
> ourselves. . . . When I accept the sign
> language, I accept the deaf, and it is important
> to bear in mind that the deaf have a right to be
> deaf, we should not change them, we must
> teach them, help them, but we must allow
> them to be deaf, they have a right to be
> handicapped.
>
> —*Terje Basilier*

The quotation is from an interview in 1973 with the Norwegian deaf psychiatrist Terje Basilier on the official deaf program of Danish television. I fully share the respect with which Basilier refers to his deaf audience. It is a respect which not only concerns their sign language, but equally the culture which has often developed around their natural means of contact: the language of the hands.

With this in mind, it is my intention to give in the following pages an outline of the social–psychological importance of sign language for the individual deaf person and for deaf communities in different countries. This chapter will be based partly on my personal experience working with Danish deaf persons, partly on some important research projects within the following fields: **social psychology** (see, for example, Schlesinger &

Meadow, 1972; Switzer & Williams, 1967; Vernon & Mindel, 1971); **social psychiatry** (Harboe, 1967–1968; Rainer, Altshuler, & Kallmann, 1963; Schein, 1968); **sociolinguistics** (Lieth, 1967; Meadow, 1972; Stokoe, 1972); and **somato-psychology** (Goffman, 1963; Hviid, 1972; Meyerson, 1955).

As appears from the references, primarily American and European conditions have been described in the literature; therefore I shall attempt to describe the actual conditions of the deaf in the Western cultural sphere only, together with the existing traditions of special education and public assistance here.

BEING DIFFERENT

The fact that some people have a handicap, are different, has always caused their fellow citizens who are not handicapped, or who are capable of concealing their small defects, to feel, consciously or unconsciously, better or more normal than the handicapped (Goffman, 1963; Hviid, 1972). This feeling leads to an attitude of guardianship: There are those who receive assistance, and those who grant assistance. But this conception of the handicapped as patients in need of help makes us disregard the fact that groups of handicapped people—and other minorities—have a capacity for creating, among themselves, something of real value. Many handicapped persons lead rich lives because in their relations with other people, especially with their likes, they give and receive on an equal footing, whereas we tend to regard them as persons who only receive (Hviid, 1972).

A handicap can bind a group of persons together in a socio-psychological community, developing its own standards and habits which gradually come to constitute an entire cultural pattern; a subculture has arisen (Meadow, 1972; Schein, 1968; Stokoe, Casterline, & Croneberg, 1965; Vernon & Makowsky, 1969), which exists in harmony with—or in some cases in conflict with (Goffman, 1963; Vernon & Mindel, 1971, p. 104)—the general culture of the society in question. By culture we have in mind the aphoristic definition "culture is habits" (Frisch, 1961), i.e., that a culture is "the pattern of all those arrangements, material or behavioral, which have been adopted by a society as the traditional ways of solving the problems of its members [Krech, Crutchfield, & Ballachey, 1962, p. 380]."

In a way, this definition is in line with the same authors' definition of social psychology as "the science of the behavior of the individual in society [Krech *et al.*, 1962, p. 4]." In the following, "social-psychological aspects" and "cultural or subcultural aspects" will be considered as two sides of the same problem. For deaf persons especially, it is true, as pointed out by Meadow (1972), that those "who choose to consider themselves members of the cohesive sub-group can be said to form a linguistic community based on their knowledge and everyday use of American Sign Language [p. 19]," and she adds that this definition "is strengthened further with the knowledge that deaf persons are characterized by endogamous marital patterns [p. 20]."

A main social–psychological problem of the handicapped person is that he or she does not live in one society, but in at least two cultures (Meyerson, 1955), or rather in a marginal position where he does not belong entirely to either of the two cultures. The most striking feature in any description of deaf persons is the insoluble dilemma that they are forced to live in a hearing world where the major part of the cognitive communication takes place orally. A more difficult marginal position than that of the deaf person between the hearing world and the silent world in which he lives is hard to find.

In a description of the social–psychological aspects of the use of sign language, it is necessary to study both the situations where the sign language is shared by a group of people, and those where the sign language is understood by one of the parties only and where thus either the deaf person is isolated among the hearing, or the hearing person is isolated among the deaf.

SIGN LANGUAGE AND TOTAL COMMUNICATION

In an interpersonal communication situation, everything that a person says and does can be regarded as an element of this communication. The term total communication is used here to imply that the communication process consists of a wide spectrum of signals emitted from the bodies of the persons involved as well as from the total situation (Lieth, 1972–1973; O'Rourke, 1972).

Apparently, the concept of total communication was introduced by Margaret Mead (1964), but it has come to be applied especially to the sphere of deafness. The following quotation from David M. Denton, Maryland School of the Deaf (which now works on the basis of total communication), illustrates this usage:

> By Total Communication is meant the right of a deaf child to learn to use all forms of communication available to develop language competence at the earliest possible age. . . .
> Total Communication includes the full spectrum of language modes: child devised

gestures, formal sign language, speech, speechreading, fingerspelling, reading and writing [1972, p. 53].

Today, the expression Total Communication generally stands for "the simultaneous use of oral and manual language [Schlesinger & Meadow, 1972, p. 126]."

In some cases there are, in addition to a sign language, finger spelling and manual–phonetic systems, e.g., the mouth–hand system (Forchhammer, 1903; Holm, 1972), the result being what may be called a "combined deaf language [Remvig, 1971]." In these cases the different systems are so integrated that it is often impossible to distinguish readily between the use of signs, finger spelling, and the mouth–hand system (Lieth, 1969)—just as it is difficult to establish whether the speech reading functions as a redundancy for the manual system or vice versa—because the combined method is based on the structure of the spoken language and can best be understood as a dialect of the spoken language (Lieth, 1969).

In the American literature it has become customary to distinguish among at least three main types of sign language: Manual English, H-Ameslan and L-Ameslan (Meadow, 1972; Stokoe, 1972; Woodward, 1973a).

In the following, the term "Sign Language" will be used as representing a continuum of sign language varieties which can be distinguished scientifically, but which essentially constitute the means of communication of the deaf (Woodward, 1973b).

COMMUNICATION BETWEEN DEAF AND
HEARING PERSONS

The ordinary communication situation for adult deaf persons in our culture can be summed up as follows: The deaf person lives in a society in which the most important means of communication is the oral language of that society, both in its spoken and its written form. The individual deaf person masters the elements of this language to a greater or lesser degree so that he can (a) lip-read; (b) speak himself; (c) write; and (d) read. To this must be added that he masters the means of communication that is used by the deaf community of which he is a member; here there are also differences as to the linguistic levels of the individuals.

In a group of hearing persons the deaf person will soon get the worst of it when several persons speak at once. As was shown by Basilier (1973) and illustrated experimentally by Lieth (1972), even the hard-of-hearing function as **socially deaf** in groups with more than two hearing persons.

Only when one or several of the hearing persons of the group are fluent in sign language is there a chance for a deaf person to keep up with the conversation.

Only one society in which most of the hearing persons know the deaf sign language has been described. This is the village society in the island of Rennell in the Solomon Islands, where there is one deaf-mute person (Kuschel, 1973, 1974), now about 50 years old, who has, together with the hearing people of his village, invented his own apparently highly developed sign language. Kuschel observed that it is not usual for the people of the island to use many gestures in connection with spoken language.

SIGN LANGUAGE INTERPRETERS

Many of the hearing persons who work as interpreters come from families with deaf parents or parents working professionally as social workers, ministers, teachers of the deaf, etc. The technical standards and theoretical education of interpreters for the deaf vary from country to country. Only in a few countries is there actual training of interpreters, in which they receive both practical training in the means of communication of the deaf and an introduction to the linguistic, psychological, and ethical problems connected with interpretation (Quigley & Youngs, 1965).

The interpreter must vary his performance according to each individual situation. He must consider, for example, such factors as the linguistic abilities—oral and manual—of the deaf and hearing persons for whom he is interpreting; but first and foremost, the interpreter must adhere to his clients' preferences for systems of linguistic expression. On this point, Youngs (Quigley & Youngs, 1965) distinguishes between "translating" and "interpreting":

> When translating, the interpreter is recognizing that the deaf person is a highly literate individual who prefers to have his thoughts and those of hearing persons expressed verbatim. . . . For many deaf people, it is necessary to paraphrase, define, and explain a speaker's words in terms and concepts they can understand. This is interpreting [p. 1].

Many hearing persons associated with deaf persons—for instance, relatives, colleagues, shopkeepers, etc.—attend sign language classes in order to be able to communicate with the deaf without receiving any actual training in interpretation. Thus, in Denmark (where the deaf population numbers about 3000) about 600 hearing persons take sign language classes every year. Both deaf and hearing persons work as teachers. The Center for Total Communication was established in 1973 in order, among other things, to coordinate this education, which is uniform throughout the country. This is made possible through common textbooks, which have moreover been recorded on videotapes in order to unify the teachers' sign language.

In many countries there is an increasing interest in learning sufficient sign language to be able to communicate with deaf clients within one's profession. Several sign language dictionaries have been prepared for this purpose—one pamphlet is intended for airline stewardesses and contains those signs relevant for communication with deaf passengers (Bornstein & Hamilton, 1972).

FAMILY CONSTELLATIONS OF THE DEAF

The fact that relatives of deaf persons also take lessons in sign language should be seen against the background of the special situation in which the deaf as a minority group find themselves. Whereas most minority groups are common to parents and children, so that the children take over their parents' subculture, this is not the case for deaf children, only about 10% of whom have deaf parents (Stuckless & Birch, 1966). Stuckless and Birch find in their investigation that while more than 90% of the families in which both parents are deaf use sign language, only about 10% of the hearing parents state that they use sign language in communicating with their deaf children, and only 3% have used sign language since early childhood (Stuckless & Birch, 1966, p. 458). From these figures it can be concluded that four out of every five deaf children have not had the possibility of acquiring a systematic sign language during preschool age.

The figures quoted here from Stuckless and Birch (1966) are probably already obsolete. During the last decade there has been a new trend in the United States and in some European countries, among these the Scandinavian countries. "Early manual communication" (Meadow, 1968; Stuckless & Birch, 1966; Vernon & Koh, 1971) is becoming a slogan, and on the basis of total communication and combined methods such as "SEE" and "Signed English," pedagogical methods have been developed which are offered to parents of deaf children at an early stage (Denton, 1972; Howse & Fitch, 1972; Schlesinger & Meadow, 1972). Besides the ordinary sign language dictionaries (Bornstein & Hamilton, 1972), at the present time a series of children's books is being published which is illustrated in such a way that text, pictures, and Signed English form a unity enabling parents to tell the stories simultaneously by word and sign to their deaf children.

This increased interest in making it possible for parents to learn sign language, so that deaf children come to grow up in an environment of total communication, is connected with the fact that a number of investigations have shown that deaf children of deaf parents (i.e., children who are brought up in a sign language-using environment) do relatively better in school than deaf children of hearing parents (Stuckless & Birch, 1966; Vernon & Koh, 1971), although, as shown by Schlesinger and Meadow (1972), other factors—such as acceptance of the handicap, contact with more adult deaf persons, visual stimulation, and less cerebral damage (Vernon & Mindel, 1971)—are also important for the good results seen in deaf children of deaf parents.

Several surveys have shown that about 25% of the adult deaf never marry, and that 85–95% of those who do marry, marry deaf persons (Harboe, 1967–1968; Rainer et al., 1963; Schein, 1968). One investigation (Basilier, 1973) finds that 43% never marry and that 85% marry deaf partners: Basilier mentions that, unlike other investigators, he has investigated a population consisting of all living Norwegian deaf persons born between 1901 and 1910, including deaf persons in homes for the mentally deficient and in other institutions.

The high percentage of marriages between deaf persons may have many social causes, such as common schools, common clubs, etc., but it is incontestable that a common handicap and a common language play a major part in the choice of marriage partners. The security the deaf person must feel when, after having spent all day among hearing people without knowledge of sign language, he can retire to his home and here use his own form of communication, has been understood from an experiment where normal hearing was artificially reduced by means of a portable noise generator, which provided a hearing loss that within the speech frequency range was of approximately 55 dB (in free field) (Lieth, 1970, 1972):

> I spent the evening with my wife. Fortunately, she knows some sign language and masters the hand alphabet. We chatted for several hours, and I found that quite spontaneously I also began to use signs . . . it was in the nature of the whole situation, a pleasant, relaxed communication, and I did not have to exert myself. Now I understand better the deaf person's wish to be with other deaf persons: the rather hectic feeling I had all day left me then, and a wonderful peace took its place [Lieth, 1970].

As noted above, deaf children of deaf parents do relatively better than deaf children of hearing parents. But only 10% of the children who are born of deaf parents are deaf themselves (Basilier, 1973; Rainer et al., 1963; Remvig, 1971; Schein, 1968; Vernon & Mindel, 1971). Hearing children of deaf parents might be expected to encounter difficulties with regard both to the verbal–linguistic development and their personal development.

Apparently, the first-born hearing child is in an exceptional position; he will usually have sign language as his maternal language (Cicourel, 1973, Cicourel & Boese, 1972, Schlesinger & Meadow, 1972, Vernon & Mindel, 1971), but at the same time he will have to form a link to the hearing world. This duality of roles gives him a special position within the family, which may later cause him difficulties in adjusting himself to social situations where he has neither the responsibility nor the power he used to have in his home.

LINGUISTIC PROBLEMS IN CONNECTION WITH MENTAL ILLNESS

Perhaps the deaf person's dependence on sign language communication appears most distinctly in cases of mental illness. Here psychiatrists and psychologists agree that a very large percentage of deaf hospitalized as well as outpatients are unable to engage in oral communication but can only communicate via signs or total communication (Basilier, 1973; Denmark & Eldridge, 1969; Hansen, 1972; Levine, 1960; Rainer *et al.,* 1963; Remvig, 1971; Vernon, 1969).

When deaf patients were admitted to ordinary psychiatric wards, they were inflicted with an extra strain in the form of linguistic isolation (Hansen, 1929; Remvig, 1969). In order to prevent this isolation and to intensify the psychiatric treatment, hospitals in some countries have now established special wards for deaf patients where the whole staff has been trained in sign language (Altshuler & Rainer, 1970; Denmark & Warren, 1972; Hegerthorn, 1973; Remvig, 1973). The experience so far seems to indicate that the intensified treatment reduces both the period of hospitalization and the frequency of readmittance (Altshuler & Rainer, 1970; Remvig, personal communication).

THE DEAF AND THE CHRISTIAN CHURCH

The Christian church has always had a special relationship with the handicapped, and not least with the deaf. For a long time this relationship was a very negative one, St. Augustine and others having interpreted St. Paul's words—"So then faith cometh, and hearing by the word of God [Rom. 10:17]"—as meaning that deaf persons could not be confirmed because they could not receive the words of the Bible.

Later this attitude was replaced by a zeal to preach the Christian faith to the deaf—that is, to achieve communication with them. Thus the servants of the church contributed to the establishment of instruction for the deaf, notable names in this connection being the Venerable Bede, Pedro Ponce de Léon, Juan Pablo Bonet, Carl Michael de L'Epée (Hodgson, 1953; Werner, 1932). Through this instruction, the deaf obtained legal and religious rights, and foundations were laid for the first regular school for the deaf as established in 1765 by Abbé de L'Epée.

It is no coincidence that one-fifth of the authors of the sign language dictionaries in use today (Bornstein & Hamilton, 1972) are ministers and other servants of the Church. The Church has been of great importance to sign language, especially during the Victorian era (Vernon, 1972). While the teachers of the deaf suppressed sign language harder than ever in the schools, the ministers worked, not only through their preaching but also through sign language choirs, to develop and refine the language.

A number of countries have special ministers working for deaf parishes. In addition to their religious duties, they carry out extensive social work and often serve as interpreters (Kolb, 1971; Mermod, 1972).

ASSOCIATIONS AND CLUBS FOR THE DEAF

As Schein (1968) and Basilier (1973) have shown, deaf persons tend to migrate from sparsely populated areas to the large cities, where they have better possibilities for contact with other deaf persons. This migration, according to Basilier, should be seen as an indication of health because there are fewer psychic disorders among the migrating group than among those who remain in their own milieu isolated from other deaf people (Basilier, 1973).

Most deaf persons are attached to one or several deaf organizations. Schein (1968) found in his material that 68% are members of at least one deaf organization, half of these being members of more than two organizations. Harboe (1967–1968), in her survey of 138 deaf persons whose average age was 49 years, found that 14% are not members of any deaf organization, 65% are members of one or two organizations, and 21% are members of more than two organizations. Basilier (1973) found in his material on 120 deaf persons born from 1906 to 1910 that about 10% had no contact with deaf organizations, whereas 36% frequented the deaf organizations as often as once a week. The organizations mentioned in these surveys all have sign language as their primary means of communication. In some countries, however, there exist or have existed special organizations for deaf adults who do not want to use sign language.

According to Vernon and Mindel (1971), "The Oral Deaf Adult Section" in the United States numbers 150 members, whereas the largest deaf associations have more than 10,000 members each.

This impressive activity of the organizations should be seen as a consequence of this situation:

> Effectively isolated by this communication problem from sharing meaningfully with most of those with whom he rubs shoulders in the community, in the home, and on the job, the deaf person has sought and created special means to compensate.
>
> The chief characteristic of these means is that the communication barrier has been eliminated since all members use the sign language. The result is that deaf people move in and out of the larger culture according to their needs of the moment but always have available a complex of their own resources that enables them to live happy, reasonably balanced and profitable lives [Switzer & Williams, 1967, p. 253].

In addition to the social contacts, the deaf organizations fill a demand for information by arranging lectures, evening classes, study groups, conferences, etc.

Like Esperanto, sign language opens up prospects for international contacts. These may be more or less formal. Thus the World Federation of the Deaf arranges regular congresses for the deaf and for those who work with problems of deafness. Here, characteristically, sign language is used at different levels: During lectures and discussions several interpreters are usually at work, translating simultaneously into their own languages (soundlessly), and into sign language combined with finger spelling and/or phonetic systems; thus the educated deaf person with a good vocabulary can follow the lectures perfectly well. During intervals, however, hearing interpreters are not necessary; here everybody can communicate freely with their hands irrespective of differences in spoken language—but then the level of information is lower and more diffuse. From a linguistic point of view it may be argued whether this is sign language communication (Stokoe, 1972, p. 10 ff.), but from a psychological point of view it is de facto communication via sign language.

In the field of sports, the deaf also seem to prefer to organize their own clubs and arrange their own contests, nationally as well as internationally. Again, it is the combination of the hearing handicap and the common language which determines the segregation.

At an informal level, all deaf and hearing persons who master sign language know that when traveling one is welcomed cordially by deaf people everywhere; the language of the hands facilitates making contacts throughout the world (Lieth & Lieth, 1970). This is an observation of long standing, as can be seen from the preface of John Bulwer's *Chirologia* of 1644:

The Babe, whose harpe of speech is yet unstrung
speakes sense and reason in this infant-tongue
all tribes shall now each other understand
which (though not of one lip) are of one hand
Chirologie redeemes from Babels doome
and is the universall idiome.
—*Thomas Diconson*

BULLETINS AND PERIODICALS

In about the middle of the nineteenth century, deaf people in different countries began to organize. Soon a number of periodicals began to be published in which both deaf and hearing writers discussed the problems of the deaf. The oldest of these still being published is *The American Annals of the Deaf*, established in 1847, followed by *Blätter für Taubstummen*, established in 1853. Sign language is discussed in these periodicals among other subjects, but it was not until 1972 that a periodical specially devoted to sign language, *Sign Language Studies*, appeared.

In any attempt to understand the development of a deaf community, the study of bulletins for the deaf is an excellent source of information. Here deaf people's views of their own problems are described, often in the form of long, vehement discussions, especially between "oralists" and "manualists." From being mere inside sources of information, many bulletins have developed into mouthpieces of the deaf community to the authorities, parents' association, etc. One such bulletin—the Italian *La Settimana del Sordumuto*—appears weekly, some appear biweekly—for instance, the Norwegian *Døves Tidsskrift*—whereas most appear monthly.

Further literature on and by deaf people exists which can illustrate the social–psychological aspects of deafness and the ensuing dependence on visual forms of communication. Some examples will be given in the following section.

AUTOBIOGRAPHIES AND FICTION DEALING WITH THE DEAF

Unquestionably, the best-known description of the life of a deaf person is Helen Keller's *The Story of My Life*, which first appeared in 1903 and of which some sections have been filmed. Helen Keller, deaf and blind herself, describes in a fascinating way how she learned a language via the hand of her teacher, Miss Sullivan, in the following well-known passage:

> Some one was drawing water and my teacher placed my hand under the spout. As the cool stream gushed over one hand she spelled into the other the word *water*, first slowly, then rapidly. I stood still, my whole attention fixed upon the motions of her fingers. Suddenly I felt a misty consciousness as of something forgotten—a thrill of returning thought, and somehow the mystery of language was revealed to me. I knew then that "w-a-t-e-r" meant the wonderful cool something that was flowing over my hand. That living word awakened my soul, gave it light, hope, joy, set it free [Keller, 1958, p. 26].

Helen Keller was a figure of central importance for the hearing and seeing world's understanding of the problems caused by loss of vision and of hearing. At the same time she demonstrated, through her own example, that even such a serious multiple handicap can be overcome.

No complete survey exists of deafness as treated in fiction, and as is the case for the description of other handicaps, sentimentality often prevails in literature about deafness. One of the best books is Carson McCullers' novel, *The Heart is a Lonely Hunter* (1940), which has also been filmed. The best novel so far about the problems of the deaf is undoubtedly Joanne Greenberg's *In This Sign* (1970), with her deeply sympathetic insight into the world of the deaf. It is quite shocking for the nondeaf to follow the fight of deaf persons to communicate in their own way within an unsympathetic hearing world—which from their childhood, has filled the deaf with shame for their own language:

> They were always together after that, turning no attention to themselves, but sitting by the damp north wall that no one else would choose for an eating place. They sat close, hands hidden by one another's backs, and they talked, leaving only the last minute or two for the crazy eatwithoutchewing before the work bell broke them apart [Greenberg, 1970, p. 27].

A single play also deserves mention, not so much for its artistic merit as for its influence on attitudes toward deafness. Around the year 1800, Bouilly's play, *The Deaf-Mute* (with the original French title *L'Abbé de L'Epée*) was presented in several European capitals. The play was of importance in throwing light on the problems of the deaf and the necessity of establishing formal education for deaf children, thus preparing the way for schools for the deaf, and eventually forming the basis of deaf culture.

SIGN LANGUAGE DICTIONARIES

A survey of the sign language dictionaries that are used today throughout the world (Bornstein & Hamilton, 1972) shows that only 25 dictionaries are in use in 14 countries: Denmark, Sweden, Finland, the

U.S.S.R., the Ukraine, Bulgaria, Germany, England, Spain, Brazil, Poland, Haiti, Japan, and the United States. To these 25 should be added the 3 international dictionaries of the World Federation of the Deaf. The dictionaries comprise from 160 up to more than 3000 descriptions of signs.

My own investigations of older sign language dictionaries (Lieth, in press) show that great differences exist in the traditions for printed material concerning sign language in different countries. For example, the first sign language dictionary in the world appeared in France, edited by Sicard and partly based on the work of de l'Epée (Sicard, 1808). This dictionary, which primarily served as an ordinary dictionary for the deaf, was replaced around 1850 by no less than four books on sign language: three dictionaries proper (Brouland, 1855; Pélissier, 1856; Lambert, 1867) and a sign language ABC book for deaf children (Clamaron, 1873)—a unique work which constituted the first attempt to give instruction in total communication, each term being reproduced in writing, drawing, sign, and dactylology. Since the appearance of these books, however, no sign language dictionary has been published in France.

In Denmark, A. C. Nygaard, who was deaf and a teacher of the deaf, took the initiative in 1871 of publishing, together with deaf friends, the first Danish dictionary of sign language, containing the hand alphabet and 118 signs. In 1907 it was replaced by a description of 280 of the most common signs, edited by the first deaf minister in Denmark, Johs. Jørgensen. In 1926 another dictionary appeared (as the result of cooperation between deaf and hearing authors) with about 1500 descriptions of signs. Finally, in 1967 one of the world's largest sign language dictionaries to date was published with more than 3000 signs described in text and photographs (for the story of the Danish sign language dictionaries see Lieth, 1967).

This difference between France and Denmark is also apparent in the use by hearing persons of the deaf sign language. In France it appears to be difficult to find enough interpreters, and only a few teachers of the deaf master sign language (Blanc, personal communication). In Denmark, on the other hand, there are a few full-time interpreters; social workers, ministers, and many teachers act also as interpreters, and over 600 hearing persons receive sign language instruction every year.

The traditions and development of sign language in the different countries can be of great importance, for instance, if it is considered desirable to change the education of deaf children from the oral method to a method based on total communication (Denton, 1972). Whereas such a reorientation has already been started in Denmark, France—the native country of the manual method—still maintains a clearly oral educational orientation.

UTILIZATION OF FILMS, TV, AND VIDEOTAPE

With the development of motion pictures, the deaf have finally found a medium which provides full scope for their language. One obstacle is the expenditure involved in the production of films and videotape, and only in a few countries has it been financially possible to work continously with these media.

The Danish deaf are in the favorable situation of having their own film company, DØVEFILM, which, financed by the government, produces film and now also videotapes. The company has existed since 1963 and has produced about 100 educational and entertainment films for the adult deaf. Since 1973 the production has been altered to videotapes as the government has paid for 150 video recorders which are placed in the homes of deaf families and in organizations for the deaf. Once or twice a month specially recorded tapes are supplied; these are partly of an informative nature—about domestic and foreign political problems, etc.—and partly about activities within the organizations of the deaf.

Provision of video recorders is only experimental so far. It is estimated that about one-half of the Danish deaf have the opportunity to follow the programs, either in their own homes or with friends, or else in the deaf organizations. All Danish deaf have the opportunity to watch th monthly deaf program in the official Danish television (produced by *Danmarks Radio* in cooperation with the deaf). The films, videotapes, and television programs are based on the means of communication of the deaf, or on subtitles when hearing persons speak.

THEATER OF THE DEAF

In addition to scientific and social matters, the international deaf congresses also offer artistic activities. The most interesting feature of these is the theater and mime groups of the different countries. Dramatic arts have long been practiced by the deaf in a number of countries, covering a wide field from the classical white clown to the most sophisticated sign language theater.

In some countries dramatics form part of the program of the deaf schools; for instance, Gallaudet College in the United States has had, for several years, a female ensemble working with jazz ballet, rhythmics, drama, sign language chorus, etc. (Wisher, 1973). In Israel a choreographer has created a special drama form based exclusively on mime and gesticulation (Efrati & Scharir, 1973).

In England, the U.S.S.R., the United States, Germany, and the Scandinavian countries, ordinary plays have very often been performed by the deaf: The text is read aloud while the deaf actors either act the whole play in sign language and pantomime or illustrate the story in mime. Real pantomime and mime have been cultivated in, among other places, France, Poland, and Italy. In Sweden a special form of drama, *The Silent Theater*, has been developed, where body language is dominant and where the themes are often taken from the everyday life of the deaf.

As a rule, these theaters have amateur status, but the U.S.S.R., the United States, and Sweden have professional troupes giving performances for both hearing and deaf audiences. The Israeli ensemble is semi-professional. Through performances for hearing audiences the deaf theater has had a great public relations effect, giving these audiences an insight into the rich possibilities of visual communication and into the beauty of sign language.

CONCLUDING REMARKS

For the individual deaf person, sign language is of the greatest importance with regard to his development and his mental well-being throughout his life. Modern life depends on effective communication, from which the deaf are often excluded. With the aid of hearing interpreters and through the activities of their organizations, however, the deaf have been able to move with the times and to live as active, productive members of society, while at the same time they have been capable of strengthening and developing their own culture:

> L'homme élevé par l'usage des signes,
> à la dignité d'hommes
> —*Degerando*, 1800

ACKNOWLEDGMENTS

This chapter was supported by a grant from the Danish Research Council for the Humanities. Translated by Kirsten Jørgensen.

REFERENCES

Altshuler, K. Z., & Rainer, J. D. 1970. Observations on psychiatric services for the deaf. *Mental Hygiene, 54* (4), 535–539.

Basilier, T. 1973. *Hørselstap og egentlig døvhet i sosialpsykatrisk perspektiv*. Oslo: Universitetsforlaget.

Bornstein, H. & Hamilton, L. B. 1972. Recent national dictionaries of signs. *Sign Language Studies, 1* (1), 42–63.

Brouland, J. 1855. *Explication du tableau spécimen d'un dictionnaire des signes du langage mimique, mettant toute personne en état de l'apprendre seule*. Paris.

Bulwer, J. 1644. *Chirologia or the naturall language of the hand*. London.

Cicourel, A. V. 1973. *Cognitive sociology*. Harmondsworth: Penguin.

Cicourel, A. V., & Boese, R. 1972. The acquisition of manual sign language and generative semantics. *Semiotica, 3*, 225–256.

Clamaron, J. 1873. *Alphabet dactylologique orné de dessins variés présentant des exemples pour l'application de chacun des signes dactylologiques*. Paris.

Degerando, J. M. 1800. *Des signes et de l'art de penser considerés dans leurs rapports mutuels*. Paris: VIII–1800.

Denmark, J., & Eldridge, R. W. 1969. Psychiatric services for the deaf. *Lancet*, 259–262.

Denmark, J. C., & Warren, F. 1972. A psychiatric unit for the deaf. *British Journal of Psychiatry, 120* (557), 423–428.

Denton, D. M. 1972. A rationale for total communication. In T. J. O'Rourke (Ed.), *Psycholinguistics and total communication: The state of the art*. New York: American Annals of the Deaf.

Efrati, M., & Scharir, J. 1973. Paper given at the Fourth International Conference on Deafness, Tel Aviv.

Forchhammer, G. 1903. *Om nødvendigheden af sikre meddelelsesmidler i døvstummeundervisningen*. København: Frimodts Forlag.

Frisch, H. 1961. *Europas Kulturhistorie*. København: Politikens Forlag.

Goffman, E. 1963. *Stigma. Notes on the management of spoiled identity*. Englewood Cliffs, New Jersey: Prentice-Hall.

Greenberg, J. 1970. *In this sign*. London: Pan Books.

Hansen, B. 1972. En undersøgelse af hospitaliserede sindslidende døve. *Ugeskrift for læger, 134*, 45.

Hansen, V. C. 1929. *Beretning om Sindslidelse blandt Danmarks døvstumme*. København.

Harboe, A. 1967–68. De døves tilpasning til det normale samfund. *Sociologiske meddelelser, 12*, 85–104.

Hegerthorn, B. 1973. Paper given at the Fourth International Conference on Deafness, Tel Aviv.

Hodgson, K. W. 1953. *The deaf and their problems*. London: Watts.

Holm, A. 1972. The Danish mouth–hand system. *The Teacher of the Deaf, 70*, 486–490.

Howse, J. M. D., & Fitch, J. L. 1972. Effects of parent orientation in sign language on communication skills of preschool children. *American Annals of the Deaf, 117* (4), 459–462.

Hviid, J. 1972. *Frihed til at være handicappet*. København: Gyldendal.

Keller, H. 1958. *The story of my life*. London: Hodder & Stoughton.

Kolb, E. (Ed.) 1971. *Die Ausbildung der Taubstummenseelsorger*. Zürich.

Krech, D., Crutchfield, R. S. & Ballachey, E. L. 1962. *Individual in society. A textbook of social psychology*. New York: McGraw-Hill.

Kuschel, R. 1974. A lexicon of signs from a Polynesian outliner island. *Psykologisk Skriftserie, 8*.

Kuschel, R. 1973. The silent inventor: The creation of a sign language by the only deaf-mute on a Polynesian island. *Sign Language Studies, 3*, 1–27.

Lambert, L. 1867. *La clef du langage de la physionomie et du geste mise à la portée de tous*. Paris.

Levine, E. 1960. *The psychology of deafness*. New York: Columbia Univ. Press.

Lieth, L. von der. 1967. *Dansk døve-tegnsprog*. København: Akademisk Forlag.

Lieth, L. von der. 1969. Døves sprog; før og nu. *Døv i dag II*, 85–95.

Lieth, L. von der. 1970. En dag som socialt døv. *Hørelsen, 7*, 8–10.

Lieth, L. von der. 1972. Experimental social deafness. *Scandinavian Audiology, 2*, 81–87.

Lieth, L. von der. 1972–73. Le geste et la mimique dans la communication totale. *Bulletin de Psychologie, 304*, XXVI, 494–500.

Lieth, L. von der. Dictionaries of signs before 1950. In press.

Lieth, L. von der, & Lieth, M. von der. 1970. Pa rejse med tegnsproget *Tyst jul*.

Markowicz, H. 1972. Some sociolinguistic considerations of American Sign Language. *Sign Language Studies, 1*, 15–41.

McCullers, C. 1940. *The heart is a lonely hunter*. New York: Houghton Mifflin.

Mead, M. 1964. Vicissitudes of the study of the total communication process. In T. A. Sebeok (Ed.), *Approaches to semiotics*. The Hague: Mouton.

Meadow, K. P. 1968. Early manual communication in relation to the deaf children's intellectual, social, and communicative functioning. *American Annals of the Deaf, 113* (1), 29–41.

Meadow, K. P. 1972. Sociolinguistics, sign language, and the deaf sub-culture. In T. J. O'Rourke (Ed.), *Psycholinguistics and total communication: The state of the art*. New York: American Annals of the Deaf.

Mermod, D. (Ed.) 1972. *Entendre avec les yeux*. Genève: Labor & Fides.

Meyerson, L. 1955. Psychology of impaired hearing. In W. Cruickshank (Ed.), *Psychology of exceptional children and youth*. London: Staples Press

Moores, D. F. 1972. Communication—some unanswered questions and unquestioned answers. In J. T. O'Rourke (Ed.), *Psycholinguistics and total communication: The state of the art*. New York: American Annals of the Deaf.

O'Rourke, J. T. (Ed.) 1972. *Psycholinguistics and total communication: The state of the art*. New York: American Annals of the Deaf.

Pélissier, P. 1856. *L'enseignement primaire des sourds-muets mis à la portée de tout le monde, avec une iconographie des signes*. Paris.

Quigley, S. P., & Youngs, J. P. (Eds.). 1965. *Interpreting for deaf people*. Washington, D.C.: U.S. Department of Health, Education and Welfare.

Rainer, J. D., Altshuler, K. Z., & Kallmann, F. J. 1963. *Family and mental health problems in a deaf population*. New York: Dept. of Medical Genetics, New York State Psychiatric Institute.

Remvig, J. 1969. Three clinical studies of deaf-mutism and psychiatry. *Acta Psychiatrica Scandinavica*, Suppl. *210*.

Remvig, J. 1971. *Om surdo-mutitas og psykiatri*. København: Mentalhygiejnisk Forlag.

Remvig, J. 1973. Paper given at the Fourth International Conference on Deafness, Tel Aviv.

Schein, J. D. 1968. *The deaf community. Studies in the social psychology of deafness*. Washington, D.C.: Gallaudet College Press.

Schlesinger, H. S. 1972. Meaning and enjoyment: Language Acquisition of Deaf Children. In J. T. O'Rourke: *Psycholinguistics and Total Communication: The State of the Art*. New York: American Annals of the Deaf.

Schlesinger, H. S., & Meadow, K. P. 1972. *Sound and sign. Childhood deafness and mental health*. Berkeley, Calif.: Univ. of California Press.

Sicard, A. C. 1808. *Théorie des signes ou introduction à l'étude des langues où le sens des mots au lieu d'être défini, est mis en action*. Paris.

Stokoe, W. C. Jr. 1972. *Semiotics and human sign languages*. The Hague: Mouton.

Stokoe, W. C. Jr., Casterline, D. C., & Croneberg, C. G. 1965. *A dictionary of American sign language on linguistic principles*. Washington, D.C.: Gallaudet College Press.

Stuckless, E. R., & Birch, J. W. 1966. The influence of early manual communication on the linguistic development of deaf children. *American Annals of the Deaf, 111*, 452–460.

Switzer, M. E., & Williams, B. R. 1967. Life problems of deaf people. *Archives of Environmental Health, 15*, 249–256.

Vernon, M. 1969. Sociological and psychological factors associated with hearing loss. *Journal of Speech and Hearing Research, 12*, 541–563.

Vernon, M. 1972. Non-linguistic of sign language, human feelings and thought process. In T. J. O'Rourke (Ed.), *Psycholinguistics and total communication: The state of the art*. New York: American Annals of the Deaf.

Vernon, M., & Koh, S. D. 1971. Effects of oral preschool compared to early manual communication on education and communication in deaf children. *American Annals of the Deaf, 116*, 569–574.

Vernon, M. & Makowsky, B. 1969. Deafness and minority group dynamics. *The Deaf American, 21*, 3–6.

Vernon, M., & Mindel, E. 1971. Psychological and psychiatric aspects of profound hearing loss. In D. E. Rose (Ed.), *Audiological assessment*. Englewood Cliffs, New Jersey: Prentice-Hall.

Werner, H. 1932. *Geschichte des Taubstummenproblems bis ins 17. Jahrhundert*. Jena: Gustav Fischer.

Wisher, P. R. 1973. Paper given at the Fourth International Conference on Deafness, Tel Aviv.

Woodward, J. C. 1973a. Deaf Awareness. *Sign Language Studies, 3*, 57–59.

Woodward, J. C. 1973b. Language continuum: A different point of view. *Sign Language Studies, 2*, 81–83.

9

Sign Language in
the Education of the Deaf

HARRY BORNSTEIN

In the United States, at least, it is now possible to see manual communication involved in educating deaf people in ways which would have been almost unimaginable only a decade ago. The rapidity with which change has taken and is taking place suggests that this description of the educational scene will be dated rapidly.

In this chapter I shall regard the home and its relationship with the school as integral parts of the educational system. I do this because I believe that the principal weakness in the education of deaf children is that, with minor exceptions, the schools have assumed almost the full burden of teaching the deaf child language—a process which, of course, normally takes place in the home long before a child enters school. It really is a very open question as to how well schools can accomplish this task under the best of circumstances (Brown, 1973).

There are two principal reasons why an organized gesture system should be introduced into an educational setting: first, so that a person can **learn an accepted communication code**—a language—in order to be able to communicate better with other people; second, so that a person can **communicate** better with other persons who use that communication code. In both cases, the language could be Sign or a manual representation of the oral language of the country in which he lives, both of these, or some combination of both of these. Since I am most familiar with the American scene and the English language, I shall use the American Sign Language and English as my paradigm. When I discuss other settings and languages, I shall explicitly identify them.

In the current rush to employ manual methods in educational settings, the distinction between "communicating" and "learning a communication code" is often lost sight of. This is most unfortunate because the educational strategies which are optimum for each goal may be radically different. A sizable portion of this chapter will be devoted to the problem of optimum educational strategy.

THE VARIETIES OF LANGUAGE

To this point, I have used the term, the American Sign Language, as if it were a homogeneous language not made up of different language varieties and dialects. This, of course, is not the case. The American Sign Language coexists in the same culture with English and there are regional dialects in both languages. Recent sociolinguistic studies cited below on this coexistence reveal findings and hypotheses of the utmost importance for the education of deaf children. As these findings are fully described elsewhere in this volume, I shall deal with them skeletally as they appear to relate to education.

There have been a variety of ways of looking at the American Sign Language. The one I shall use begins with Stokoe. He used Ferguson's (1959) nine features of diglossia and was able to distinguish a high (H) and a low (L) Sign (Stokoe, 1970). Both Meadow and Moores (O'Rourke, 1972) have elaborated separately on these language varieties. Woodward (1973a) viewed these differences as occurring over a gradient. He hypothesized a continuum with Sign at one pole and Sign English at the other. These merge into language varieties between these poles called Pidgin Sign English. Obviously, the closer the variety of Pidgin is to a given pole, the more it will resemble that pole. There is a variety, or range, of dialects at each pole. A schematic of this continuum is given in Figure 9.1.

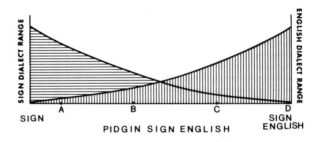

Figure 9.1.   A schematic of the linguistic varieties over the Sign to Sign English continuum.

This chapter will be organized around this characterization of Sign because I can usefully relate it to the dual purposes given above, i.e., to communicate and to learn a communication code. Here is a further description of the terms with implications that may not necessarily be consistent with those that Woodward would draw from his hypothesis:

Sign (the American Sign Language) is the language used by native speakers of Sign to communicate with one another. (Since this entire volume is concerned with definitions and descriptions of Sign, the obvious circularity of this definition need not concern us here.)

Pidgin Sign English is characterized by Woodward (1973a) as follows:

> It is generally agreed that pidgin languages are reduced in structure, contain a partial mixture of two (to several) languages, and contain structure common to none of the languages in the communication situation. Pidgins are used primarily in restricted social situations for communication purposes and are not generally used for socially integrative and personally expressive functions (Smith, 1972). . . . Generally along with this restricted function of language go negative attitudes towards the pidgin [pp. 39–40].

Exactly where on the Pidgin Sign English continuum a person can and does perform is dependent upon a variety of circumstances. The vast majority of hearing people learn manual communication late in life and only a very few of these ever become skilled in Sign. Most skilled hearing signers who can be regarded as bilingual are the children of deaf parents. Sometimes only the oldest child in such a family achieves this skill. Conversely, a very large proportion of deaf adults have difficulty with or are unsure of a variety of English structures and vocabulary (Bornstein & Roy, 1973; Furth, 1971a, 1973).

Another important consequence of viewing Pidgin Sign English as a continuum is that it is easy to deduce that individuals at different points of the continuum may have some difficulty in communicating with one another. I would suspect that such difficulties might be considerably greater than communication difficulties that might occur between users of different dialects of Sign or of English. There is abundant anecdotal evidence that suggests that this is the case, but I know of no formal study on the matter. The schematic in Figure 9.1 has been drawn to suggest that as a person's skill moves from a given pole, he would be less able to handle the dialectal variation characteristic of that pole.

The education of deaf children is conducted, for the most part, by hearing persons. It is directed quite properly at preparing children for life in a "hearing" world. It seeks to teach the child to read and write. It is not surprising therefore that in educational settings, the Pidgin Sign English variety is usually much closer to Sign English than to Sign.

Sign English is the other end of the continuum. Its basic purpose is to represent English manually. It employs signs in English syntax and the signs represent either words, or word parts, or morphemes, etc. It includes all the redundancies which are part of English but not of Sign, e.g., past tense markers for every verb in a message. It should be slower than Sign because of increased use of compounds (sign + marker sign). It can hardly be expected to be attractive to a native user of Sign.

Indeed, negative attitudes may be held by people toward performance in either direction as well as over different distances on this continuum. Thus in Figure 9.1, a person who performs at point A might dislike the language of all of those who perform at B, C, or D. But persons at point C might find many elements of D's performance especially objectionable as well. This is because Sign English is so clearly a contrived language. It is the imposition of one language channeled through a different modality onto another language. (Contrived Sign Languages will be described in full in another chapter. I shall, however, deal with them here in terms of their educational utility.)

In the United States at present there are those who advocate the use of Sign, variants of Pidgin Sign English, or Sign English for the education of the deaf. (Few would probably agree with this categorization, however.) My guess is that those I will label users and advocates of Pidgin Sign English would find that label rather objectionable. However, as I shall indicate later, I regard Pidgin Sign English as entirely appropriate for many educational settings.

A LITTLE BIT OF THE RECENT HISTORY OF THE EDUCATION OF THE DEAF

This review of recent research on manual communication in education will be highly selective for several reasons. First, two comprehensive reviews are already available (Bonvillian & Charrow, 1972; Moores, 1971), and almost every active investigator offers similar reviews as integral parts of his or her research reports (Meadow, 1968; Quigley & Frisina, 1961; Schlesinger & Meadow, 1972; Stevenson, 1964; Stuckless & Birch, 1966; Vernon & Koh, 1970). Second, there is a near unanimity in findings, which can be very simply stated: Those deaf students exposed to organized gesture systems achieve better than those exposed to unorganized gesture systems. The differences are small, however, and do not extend to speech intelligibility and speech reading. Where such are measured, better adjustment is also found for students exposed to organized gesture systems. Logically, the only thing surprising about these findings is that the differences are not very much greater and that they do not extend to speech intelligibility and speech reading. In this review, I shall attempt to explain why the obtained differences are not larger. Third, sophisticated linguistic treatment of Sign is so recent that most educational researchers have not had enough time to incorporate this into their strategy. Hence findings only a few years old are already dated and of limited value. Finally, the body of results summarized above and discussed below do not support established educational practices. It is time that this be accepted as fact without constant rehashing and that different issues be explored.

There are some clear methodological consequences of conceiving of these different language varieties as falling on a continuum. For example, if you wish to measure the effectiveness of communication it seems appropriate at least to describe the variety of language (*a*) used in the signal, (*b*) known by the person to whom the communication is addressed, and (*c*) used in the measurement technique designed to evaluate the effectiveness of the communication. There are already examples in the literature of the difficulty that may arise in the interpretation of the results of experiments that do not include this kind of information (Battison, 1973; Higgins, 1973; Stokoe, 1973; Tweney & Hoemann, 1973a, 1973b).

Turning now to the problem of trying to teach a child language in school settings, the language variety one chooses to work with should influence the instructional strategy followed. I shall describe strategies appropriate for each language variety after providing further detail about the circumstances under which these strategies might be used. Before this, let me describe briefly what has happened in the last decade to cause manual communication to warrant serious consideration as a technique in the education of the deaf in the United States and elsewhere.

In addition to being unable to hear, deaf children have been victimized (I can think of no term more accurate) by a bitter, wasteful controversy over pseudoalternatives for perhaps a hundred years. This is the so-called oral–manual controversy. There is not now a solely oral method of instruction nor has there ever been one in the past. And I know of no recent serious suggestion that educators use solely manual methods. Neither of these observations is original with this writer—far from it. So many observers have made similar comments in past years that it is pointless to try to document them. The reader can determine for himself that manual communication, e.g., gestures, pointing, pulling, pushing, touching, and "body language," are integral parts of communicating with deaf children merely by visiting any class or school for deaf children and watching the children and the teacher for an extended period of time.

There are two formal studies which illustrate the point quite objectively. Tervoort and Verbeck (1967) systematically observed that children ranging in age from 7 to 17 most commonly used signs in ingroup communication in spite of the "oral" instruction provided by their schools. The students in the study were educated at two schools in the United States, one in the Netherlands, and one in Belgium. (The results also show evidence of greater use of Pidgin Sign English as the American students grow older.) Additional and more pointed evidence can also be found in a current longitudinal study of hearing-impaired students in seven preschool programs which employ a representative range of communication methods, i.e., oral–aural, finger spelling, and total communication (Moores, McIntyre, & Weiss, 1972). Classroom observation revealed that gestures are used by both children and **teachers** to communicate with each other in all programs. When child communicated with child, gestures or signs were the most frequent communication mode in all programs. Clearly, only the most narrow view of education would regard child-to-child communication as an unimportant part of the learning process.

In fact, the choice of communication methods is between speech supplemented by an **untaught, unorganized** gesture system and speech supplemented by one of a variety of **taught, organized** gestures systems.[1] This way of stating the problem logically forces one to consider systematically which of the several gesture systems (organized or unorganized) would be most appropriate for which child and under what circumstances.

The gesture system which first seemed to some investigators to offer most promise is finger spelling or using the manual alphabet. Technically, the manual alphabet is not a Sign system. It really is a variant of English print. Nevertheless, any reasonable degree of skill requires one to function at a word rather than a letter level. To read at a comfortable rate of transmission one must be able to see words and sometimes brief phrases. When sending, there is usually no conscious awareness of the individual letters. For these and for historical reasons, I will consider it here a special case of Sign English. Further, I believe that the findings have important implications for Sign English and Pidgin Sign English.

There are several obvious advantages to using the manual alphabet. The complete English alphabet is transmitted and received by the communicator. This makes it possible to say anything that can be said in the graphemic version of English. It is a simple matter, requiring only a few hours, to learn how to form the letters with one's fingers. It takes a great

---

[1]There is a class of gesture systems which seeks to represent speech phonetically (Henegar & Cornett, 1971). Such systems are interesting and may be as useful as or more useful than those described in this chapter. However, they are not Sign languages as understood in this volume and will not be described in this chapter.

deal of practice, however, to attain proficiency in communicating by this means, with reading usually more difficult to learn than transmitting. There are some inherent characteristics of the finger spelling technique, however, which severely limit its usefulness.

Finger spelling is slow. A comfortable rate of finger spelling for very experienced adults is 300 letters (or 60 words) per minute (Bornstein, 1965). This estimate was obtained and replicated with 12 subjects on passages randomly selected from popular magazines. The standard deviation was 20 letters (or 4 words) per minute. Normal speech is about 150 words a minute and hence is about two and one-half times as fast. About the same ratio and similar absolute rates were found in a similar experiment performed in Russia by Martsinovskaia in 1960 (Solovjev, Shif, Rozanova, & Yashkova, 1971).[2] Hearing adults were slightly slower. They averaged 289 letters per minute, which is not surprising because 9 of the 32 Russian letters require movement of the whole hand as well as of the fingers. Only 2 of the 26 English letters, J and Z, require such movement. These extra movements, of course, take time, and this difference in the number of such letters could account for the difference in rate. The speed of the adults' oral reproduction was equivalent to 795 letters per minute. When they spelled and spoke simultaneously, the rate of oral speech dropped 300 letters per minute.

It is obvious therefore that finger spelling cannot parallel the normal speech system. It is simply too slow. This fact forces a speaker to speak very much more slowly than usual or to spell only a portion of what he says. The former choice results in speech which could be artificial and rather dull. It also severely limits the amount of language to which the child is exposed. The latter choice narrows down to spelling some, usually key, words. Because it is more comfortable to perform this way, I think it more likely to be followed by teachers. This latter alternative is also what has been objectively recorded in the study cited above (Moores, McIntyre, & Weiss, 1972). However, if we again refer to the Russian experiments on finger spelling, we find that the rate of speech and finger spelling of Russian deaf children is 270 and 281 letters per minute, respectively. They actually spelled slightly more rapidly than they spoke. I do not know if this reflects classroom practice.

There are still other difficulties. If language is to be expressed manually as early as possible in the life of a child, the average 18-month- or 2-year-old child simply does not have the perceptual and motor coordination to handle the manual alphabet at a rate remotely approximating speech.

[2]Withrow (1973) inferred from the phoneme–grapheme correspondence in Russian that the Russian manual alphabet would be more efficient, and hence the rate of Russian finger spelling would approach that of speech. As these results show, this is not the case.

Moreover, since finger spelling's closest counterpart is not speech but print, reading the manual alphabet may require him to read as he acquires language. Although there has recently been considerable question about the lateness at which reading is normally taught to hearing children in American schools, no one has contended that reading should precede language acquisition. Finally, it is extremely difficult, if not impossible, to parallel or approximate normal speech **rhythm** when you finger-spell.

There are several reports of the educational achievement of deaf children who have been exposed to finger spelling and speech (sometimes called the Rochester Method in the United States, and neo-oralism in Russia). While these yield favorable comparisons with "oral approaches," only one study is sufficiently rigorous to report here (Quigley, 1969). Sixteen matched pairs of preschool children taught in "controlled" residential settings were compared over a 4-year span. Initially, the children ranged in age from 3:5 to 4:5 years. For purposes of optimum language development this is a late start, perhaps 2 or even 3 years later than might be desired. Nevertheless, the results are still quite clear cut. "The data from the experimental study showed consistent and significant superiority of the experimental (finger spelling) groups on almost all of the measures used in the study. Not only did the experimental (finger spelling) subjects exceed the comparison group on reading and written language ability, they also exhibited superiority in the measures of speechreading ability [Quigley, 1969, p. 93]." Absolute differences between the groups, however, were rather small. About a fourth or a third of a grade level is the usual advantage.

From a Sign English point of view, there is one interesting aspect to the study. The film test used to measure ability to read finger spelling "required a reading level of at least third grade." This level exceeded the reading level of almost all the children in the study. The children obtained only a mean of 34% correct on the test, a level of performance below what their teachers believed they could do. The finding is consistent with the notion that the manual alphabet is a form of English print, and that reading it is dependent upon reading comprehension.

Quigley also reported on a 5-year survey of educational performance of older deaf children which compared three schools concentrating on finger spelling with three comparable schools using a variety of other communication techniques (including finger spelling). Formal classroom use of the manual alphabet began when these children were 9 years old in one experimental school and when they were approximately 12 in the other two experimental schools. At the beginning of the study the children averaged 13 years of age in both the experimental and comparison schools.

Although the results of this survey, in general, conform to that reported for the younger age group, there are some interpretation difficulties because the communication techniques used in the comparison school are not very precisely identified.

In any event, the data presented in Table 9.1 do offer a very revealing description of the English language performance of deaf adolescents. First, and probably most important, the reading scores of both groups are consistent with those reported in national survey data (Gentile & DiFrancesca, 1969). Both groups of students handle the English language badly. Although statistically significant, the one-half grade level difference in means is hardly of much practical importance. Moreover, the mean finger spelling tests scores in Table 9.1 show that many years of exposure still do not enable deaf students to decode a finger spelling film presentation at anything close to a perfect score. (This is the same test mentioned above.) As the standard deviations of these scores are quite large, a large proportion of these students clearly still have limited receptive capability. Again, reading comprehension could be the limiting condition.

In summary, I interpret the Quigley studies as indicating that finger spelling had a small positive effect when introduced at 4 years of age, clearly later than desired in life for a child. However, for reasons cited above, it is doubtful that it could be used very efficiently at much earlier ages. Accordingly, I doubt that finger spelling will substantially

TABLE 9.1

Finger Spelling and Stanford Achievement Reading Test Scores Taken from Survey Data[a]

| | | | Finger spelling schools | | | | Comparison schools | | |
| | | | Finger spelling | | Comb. read. mean grade level | | Finger spelling | | Comb. read. mean grade level |
Age	Year	N	Mean %	S.D. %		N	Mean %	S.D. %	
13	1	112	62	24	3.5	110	44	30	3.4
14	2	113	67	26	3.8	110	53	28	3.7
15	3	105	78	20	4.4	109	60	28	3.9
16	4	92	80	18	4.6	91	68	24	4.0
17	5	84	84	16	4.9	79	71	21	4.3

[a] From Quigley, 1969.

improve English language acquisition. As for the second purpose of using an organized gesture system, i.e., for communication purposes only, exclusive dependence on finger spelling again should yield very limited results. It will be decoded reliably only by those with English capabilities which match that inherent in the message. At the present time, this means a message complexity with which fourth- or fifth-grade hearing students can deal with reasonable facility.

As noted earlier, the 1960s and early 1970s saw a variety of studies which sought to evaluate the effects of manual communication on English language development, educational achievement, and/or emotional development of deaf children. The basic pattern followed in these studies was to compare the performance of children who had deaf parents with those who had hearing parents. The former were exposed to organized gesture systems in the home at a very early age, whereas the latter encountered only unorganized gesture systems. Before elaborating on these gesture systems and their possible effects on the basic comparison, I would first like to note again that the obtained differences favoring the manual communication group are usually modest in absolute terms. Moreover, academic achievement or English language performance on the part of the better groups is still very, very limited—far below that for hearing students at comparable ages. Why should this be? Schlesinger and Meadow (1972) offer at least one compelling explanation. When matched or comparison groups are formed, those children who have deaf parents come from a markedly lower socioeconomic strata than do those with hearing parents. The educational achievement of the deaf parents is also much lower. They read less themselves and they provide far fewer printed materials for their children. These facts in and of themselves could account for a sizable proportion of the variance from the mean hearing language performance and academic achievement.

If we examine the manual communication aspects of the situation more closely, it may be possible to account for still more if not most of the variance. In all probability, the gesture system learned in deaf parental homes is either Sign or a variant of Pidgin Sign English which lies close to Sign. Since very few deaf adults have been permitted to teach deaf children at the primary grades, much less in preschool, the principal language linkage between the "deaf home" and the class is the child's impaired sound system and a gesture system which is rarely consistent with the gesture system used in school. What the deaf child encountered was an unorganized gesture system in the classroom. **There was no linkage to the language he brought to the classroom** unless his speech was good enough to work with effectively. (Meadow, 1968, further notes the minimal help that deaf parents normally obtain for their children in the speech area.)

Verification of this poor linkage of manual communication and spoken language (including reading) can be found from an altogether different kind of investigation. Bolton reviewed nine factor analyses of correlational data on deaf students from primary grades through adolescence in Scandinavia, Great Britian, and the United States (Bolton, 1971b).[3] He reports that verbal skills are independent of nonverbal intelligence in all nine studies. In his own replicated studies of communication skills, he found four moderately related factors: (*a*) Nonverbal Intelligence; (*b*) Manual Communication; (*c*) Oral–Verbal Communication; and (*d*) Psychomotor Skill (Bolton, 1971a, 1972).

When a hearing child goes to school the teacher builds upon the language the child brings to the classroom. This clearly has not been the case with deaf children in the past, except for those who bring effective speech. There is evidence with a handful of children, however, that markedly improved language performance is a real possibility if classroom instruction is consistent with the language brought by the child (Schlesinger & Meadow, 1972, and Gallaudet Pre-School Program videotapes). The remainder of the chapter will be built around that premise.[4]

SOME CONSEQUENCES OF THE DEMOGRAPHY OF DEAFNESS

There are two central facts about the incidence of deafness which have the most pervasive consequences for the education of deaf people. These are:

1. The incidence of deafness in the general population is very low. Thus a very large country like the United States has only about 56,000 students enrolled in special programs for the hearing impaired (Reis, personal communication). A small country like Norway may have only several hundred (Basilier, personal communication).

---

[3]Hearing status of parents is rarely reported in these studies.

[4]Cicourel and Boese (1972) also stress the importance of linkage of gesture systems in home and class. However, they distinguish between a natural sign language and the American Sign Language. They consider the latter a second language. To my knowledge, it is a point of view **not** shared by other theorists. Because of this difference, the implications they draw for educating deaf children are congruent with rather than similar to those contained in this chapter.

2. Eighty-nine percent of deaf children have two hearing parents. Four percent have two deaf parents. Eight percent have one hearing parent, a third of whom may be hard of hearing (Rawlings, 1973).

These statistics suggest that the unit cost of materials developed for any age segment of deaf students must be very high. In fact, very little material has been prepared for deaf students on either a commercial or a nonprofit basis. Most are classroom made. Books on one or another variety of Sign are a seeming exception. But these books are really addressed to the hearing adult market which is, of course, considerably larger than any subgroup of deaf children. Such works are designed to introduce hearing adults to manual communication so that they can interact better with deaf people. These books have been published, in the main, by nonprofit organizations associated with the deaf, by church organizations, or by private printing. More often than not, the publishers are unable to pay for the services of professional writers, artists, photographers, linguists, scientists, and others involved.

If it is desired that manual communication be used with facility in the home by parents, siblings, and others, then the fact that the vast majority are hearing must be faced. It is these people who must (a) want to learn manual communication, and (b) be provided with the resources so that they can learn rapidly and easily. Which of the three language varieties discussed in this chapter is the most likely candidate for this situation? Since my own work on a preschool Sign English project clearly reflects my choice, let me state the considerations which influenced that choice.

For a variety of historical and social reasons, most Americans never become facile with a second language. Further, it is commonplace knowledge that the manual communication that most hearing adults learn is Pidgin Sign English. Although there are no statistics on the topic, it is generally believed that only a handful of individuals who are not born into deaf families, or who have not been deafened late in life themselves, learn Sign with much facility.[5] Apart from facility with a given language variety, what is the likelihood that hearing parents would think it appropriate to learn a manual language other than one that represents English? In all candor, it must be considered low since this is one of the arguments that has been traditionally and successfully leveled against the use of Sign. If parents do not think Sign appropriate, they simply will not achieve any reasonable level of skill with it. I know of no way around this difficulty.

[5]As noted in the following section, there really is very little material available which has been designed to teach Sign rather than Pidgin Sign English. Conceivably, improved relevant instructional materials could improve this situation somewhat.

Much of the remainder of this chapter will be devoted to an elaboration of these two points: ease of learning and appropriateness.

MANUAL COMMUNICATION INSTRUCTIONAL MATERIALS

A considerable amount of instructional material on manual communication has been prepared over the last decade, much of it in the last few years. Early in this period, the usual type of material consisted of a dictionary of signs which would serve as a course text or reference. In these books signs are most often drawn, sometimes photographed, and/or described in words. The number of signs varies from about 500 to 1000. Invariably, one or two English "equivalents" are associated with a sign. Exercise material, where supplied, is almost always in English syntax. Regardless of their titles, these are quite clearly Pidgin Sign English materials very close to the Sign English pole.[6]

The formats of the most recent works are much more varied, attractive, and ingenious. These consist of flashcards, playing cards, overlays, motion picture films, and videotapes. A general description of most items can be found in the Appendix of a text prepared by the Communication Skill Program of the National Association of the Deaf (O'Rourke, 1973). Some of these newer materials are designed to be self-instructional. Film courses are shown through use of 8-mm cartridge projectors. There are courses on finger spelling as well as Pidgin Sign English. A few courses run as long as several hours in segments of five minutes each. One videotape series offers as much as 13 hours of material in half-hour segments. Without doubt, such self-instructional materials are more expensive than texts. They also serve to develop some degree of skill, but it is also clear that none takes the learner very much beyond a beginner's level in receptive skill, if that far. Even that is a considerable accomplishment.

Only one work treats signs as Sign (Fant, 1972). Using a basic vocabulary of 465 signs, the text and associated films attempt to convey meaning within Sign syntax. There is a second text that treats Sign idioms and structures within a general English syntax (Madsen, 1972). The language complexity of the Pidgin Sign English work is considerably higher than that of the previous work. All of the works so far described work with vocabularies of fewer than 1000 signs.

[6]*A Dictionary of American Sign Languages on Linguistic Principles* is a conspicuous exception to the materials described in this section (Stokoe *et al.*, 1965). However, the dictionary is not often used for language learning purposes.

Sign English materials have also become available in the last few years (Anthony & Associates, 1971; Bornstein, Kannapell, Saulnier, Hamilton, & Roy, 1973–1974; Gustason, Pfetzing, & Zawolkow, 1972; Wampler, 1972). Since the object of these efforts is to represent "important" English words, the sign vocabulary included in these works is much larger than those cited above. They range in number from 2000 to about 6000. One system has built its instructional logic around the fact that a Sign, a printed word, and the shape of lips can all be represented together on paper and organized in stories, poems, and songs for preschool children and their parents. (Bornstein *et al.*, 1973–1974). The system is simultaneously being expanded and evaluated in class and home settings.

If recent materials are any indication, it seems very likely that instructional material will continue to increase in sophistication and provide an ever better means for parents and teachers to learn manual communication. There are certain areas in which I believe considerable development is both possible and desirable:

1. Instructional materials directed at teaching Sign or a Pidgin Sign English close to Sign should go beyond the core 500 to 800 signs currently found in such works.

2. A shift in general approach in presenting Sign and English "equivalents" might be helpful for hearing people. As noted above, one, occasionally two, English "equivalents" are generally offered to define a pictured sign. These signs are usually grouped in some functional manner. In essence, the English words are keyed to the sign. If this were reversed, if the pictured signs were keyed to English words or phrases, hearing learners might derive an altogether different perception of Sign. For example, it can be shown that several signs are often used by deaf persons to parallel or represent the meaning of a given English word. In effect, these signs function as synonyms or, sometimes, are simply regional variations. Perhaps this could hasten the day when hearing Pidgin Sign English users would cease arguing which is the "right" sign for a given English equivalent. Sign "idioms" could be handled similarly.

3. The organizational principles followed in the *Dictionary of American Sign Language on Linguistic Principles* (Stokoe, Casterline & Croneberg, 1965) or the Israeli dictionary by I. M. Schlesinger and his associates (Cohen, Namir, & Schlesinger, 1977) might suggest simple and efficient ways by which individuals can look up English equivalents to signs encountered in daily life.

4. Some of the logic and techniques used in the patterning exercises developed for second language teaching purposes might be transferable. It could be especially helpful in teaching Sign structure or syntax.

5. Sign is **not** simply a succession of individual signs. It is a language of space and time (Bellugi & Fischer, 1972; Stokoe, 1975). Some characteristics of its use of space and time have been described by Fischer, e.g., incorporation of location, number, manner, size and shape, and use of body movements and facial expression. Instructional materials can and should be developed to teach explicitly these aspects of Sign to hearing people.

LEARNING A COMMUNICATION CODE— A LANGUAGE

Given that first languages appear to be learned rather than taught, I would like to suggest the conditions and circumstances under which organized gesture systems should be maximally effective in providing opportunity for the child to learn. Exactly what level of language proficiency will be achieved eventually will be a matter for empirical determination.

An organized gesture system should be used in the home by parents, siblings, or friends as soon as it is known that the child is severely hearing impaired. The sooner the family is facile with the organized system, the better for the child. Obviously, parents who are deaf themselves are most likely to be capable of using an organized system early and well. As noted earlier, however, about 90% of the parents hear. The gesture system made available to parents who hear should therefore be sufficiently simple to enable them to learn and use it quickly. This is the first basis for choosing between Sign, Pidgin Sign English, or Sign English. As previously noted, most deaf parents already know Sign or a Pidgin Sign English close to Sign. Hearing parents, who are the great majority of the parents in question, are more likely to learn Sign English or a Pidgin close to Sign English. Moreover, such parents are much more likely to accept the logic and utility of Sign English than Sign.[7] Given that both speech and language are desired products of educating deaf children, it may be well to discuss further the general problem of two languages paralleling each other in time.

It is part of the basic logic of Sign English that it parallels spoken English on a time basis. This, of course, is not true with Sign, and raises a most interesting question.

Can one sign Sign and speak English simultaneously? The Gallaudet

[7]The enthusiastic reception of the materials produced by the Gallaudet Pre-School Signed English Project lends some support for this point of view.

community includes a sizable number of hearing bilinguals, almost all of whom were born to deaf parents, and an even larger number of late-onset deaf faculty, administrators, and staff. Rather informally, I queried several members of this community as to whether or not they or anyone they knew could sign Sign and speak English simultaneously. With the exception of one late-onset deaf faculty member, they claimed that they were unable to do this for a sustained message. They could sign "phrases" and occasional "sentences" but had to resort to Pidgin Sign English while speaking. Moreover, they doubted that it was possible. A few reported being able to interpret in Sign while remaining mute. After they finished interpreting, however, they could not remember the contents of the interpreted message. Yet Bellugi and Fischer (1972) report rate comparisons for three hearing bilinguals who simultaneously spoke English and signed Sign.[8] I think that these apparently conflicting statements can be resolved by resort to the Pidgin Sign English continuum hypothesis. Apparently, some bilinguals are able to perform somewhat closer to the Sign pole for some material than do others. There even may be a few people who can do both simultaneously. it is a matter more of scientific interest than practical application because the reader should understand that here we are discussing virtuoso performance. There is only a handful of people who can perform in this manner. As far as almost all parents of deaf children are concerned, they are not likely to be able to sign Sign and speak English simultaneously during their child's critical language learning period. Thus, if speech training and speech reading are dependent upon speech paralleling the gesture system, these skills may suffer some retardation if Sign is the child's initial gesture system. How much, of course, is unknown. On the other hand, I know of no logical reason why Sign English should retard speech acquisition or use of residual hearing. To the contrary—Sign English can parallel speech rhythm in songs and poems. Temporal patterns and stress are easily paralleled. If these attributes could be pleasantly incorporated into speech and listening training, it might improve the voice quality and sharpen the hearing skills of deaf children somewhat. There is one songbook (with record) and one book of nursery rhymes presently available (Bornstein et al., 1973–1974). It would not be difficult to produce others. Research in this area could be most fruitful.

When the child moves into the classroom situation, either at the pre-

[8]Bellugi and Fischer (1972) and Stokoe (1975) have obtained estimates of rates of signing and speaking for three hearing and one deaf subject. They disagree on treatment of pauses and, to a degree, on name of language variety. Additionally, Stokoe maintains that a deaf signer signs much more rapidly in Sign to a deaf audience than he would in Pidgin Sign English to a hearing audience.

school or primary level, some reasonable linkage of gestural systems must be effected. Regardless of which gestural system, organized or unorganized, a child brings to the classroom, that communication situation will most likely be very complicated. Children need and want to communicate with each other. Where a sign word is not known to children, they will frequently invent their own sign (Cokely & Gawlik, 1974). At adult levels, this is often done on a temporary basis in the classroom. I have termed such signs "situation bound" (Bornstein & Kannapell, 1969). Such signs should fall into disuse if and when children are exposed to conventional alternatives, i.e., Sign or Sign English.

Since the purpose of Sign English is to represent English, it is not likely to be more effective than Sign or Pidgin Sign English for children who want to communicate with one another. It seems very probable that Sign or Pidgin Sign English will enter into the classroom and will certainly be found outside the classroom. Indeed, the Sign end of the continuum may always be the principal social language of the majority of deaf people.

In any event, it is worse than useless to label some signs as good or bad, or to try to prohibit the use of "bad" signs, or to try to ignore Sign altogether. One of the central tasks that teachers of deaf children must face eventually is that Sign is a language and that it must be dealt with in a constructive way in educating deaf children. In effect, this means that teachers must be aware of the language varieties described in this paper. They must provide the child with consistent code applications and make orderly and unemotional contrasts for the child when and if he confuses codes. For example, when a child is asked to write an English sentence and mistakenly uses "eat" for "food," or vice versa, it is likely that he is offering one of two English alternates for a Sign word, albeit the wrong one. The teacher should contrast English and Sign in this case and then try to teach the child the appropriate usage.

As noted earlier, I believe that it is relatively unlikely that a high proportion of hearing adults, in this case teachers, will become skillful with Sign if their first exposure to it is as adults. However, this is not an impossible situation by any means. First, teachers can be taught that Sign is a language which should be regarded seriously. (Courses on Sign should be incorporated into teacher training programs.) Second, tools for recognizing contrasts between Sign and Sign English can be developed and should be made available to them for their use. Here, as has happened so often in the past, Stokoe and his associates are in the vanguard. They are conducting a contrastive analysis of English and Sign, from which should come valuable information for the teacher (Stokoe, personal communication). Finally, a bilingual person could be added to a faculty to serve as a resource person who could identify code confusions and help the teacher teach the necessary contrasts. This language specialist should have formal linguistics training (Woodward, 1973b).

I recognize that such suggestions may be received with astonishment by many educators of the deaf. Sign stems from a physical handicap. It flourishes among adults who as children required massive special attention and, as a group, achieve poorly in areas that matter greatly to educators. It must seem presumptuous that such individuals could actually create a language. Further, it is a language which has no writing system. It is not "symbolized" on the printed page. Since reading and writing are perhaps the most important skills acquired in school, it will be even more difficult for teachers to consider Sign seriously. Nevertheless, I doubt that effective instruction will take place until this view becomes a commonplace one.

There are still other matters generally related to language acquisition which should be discussed. Organized gesture systems can be "coupled" to speech in a variety of ways and used over a wide range of instructional strategies. I would like briefly to consider some of the consequences of alternate methods without repeating excessively that which is presented in the chapter entitled Contrived Sign Language.

It should be recognized that there are attitudinal consequences which result from the different logics that can be followed in transforming Sign to Sign English. A sign can be used to represent either the sound, spelling, or meaning, or any combination of the three, of a target English word. Since meaning is the essence of Sign, Sign English words designed to represent spelling or sound are likely to be least attractive to users of Sign. Further, even when a Sign English word represents meaning only, it will not have the same meaning as the original sign over the range of contexts in which it is used. These differences in meaning will also be unattractive to users of Sign. Educators should understand that all of this is unavoidable. There is no possible way to use one language to represent another without changing the first language. Moreover, the entire process is replete with arbitrary decisions. All tastes cannot be satisfied and years of habit must be interfered with. A great deal of skill is required of educators to deal with the resentments that are likely to greet any choice among the several Sign English systems which are presently available. Moreover, they should be prepared to justify why they chose to represent spelling or sound or words.

Perhaps more importantly, the different logics followed in transforming Sign to Sign English can affect these other communication parameters: rate of transmission, effectiveness of decoding, and ease of learning Sign English. Essentially, signs are made to represent English words in English context by a compounding or coupling process. Gestures can be assigned to represent each of the following: word form, word root, prefix, suffix, or free or bound morphemes.

By compounding such gestures, a communicator can represent any desired word. A system which represents more spoken word elements manually will necessarily include more compounds. At some point, increased compounding should begin to have negative effects on the communication parameters listed above. To date, all information on this problem is essentially clinically or intuitively derived. An empirically derived trade-off matrix would represent a major advance in this all-important area.

Educators, understandably, find disturbing the fact that different Sign English systems may have different signs for a given English word. As suggested by Figure 9.1, Pidgin Sign English performers near the Sign English pole usually have less facility in handling dialectal variation in Sign than do those near the Sign pole. Most educators are near the Sign English pole. In fact, more than 80% of the signs in two current systems are identical and another 10% are relatively similar (Bornstein, 1973). A third system has substantially the same amount of overlap with both the above systems (Bornstein *et al.*, 1973–1974). At worst, only a few hundred words are involved.

There are two principal reasons for different signs being used for the same English word. First and most important, there are differences in system logic which call for a specific kind of gesture. If a school has decided upon a certain system, it should use the gesture which fits the system logic. The second reason for difference is probably nothing more than taste. Such signs might well be treated as if they were synonyms. The practice of forming a committee to pick signs on the basis of local taste and/or past experience has little to recommend it. After all, schools do not form committees to choose the English words they will use at the school.

An organized gesture system can be fitted into a wide range of instructional strategies. Traditionally, schools for the deaf have attempted to teach language to deaf children through means of highly structured speech exercises. And, of course, unorganized gesture systems were the principal supplements to speech. Apart from the fact that there appears to be no evidence to support a structured approach to first language development for children (Brown, 1973), I believe that this structured approach will undergo radical change with organized gesture systems. I make this prediction because I believe that a great deal of the structure in language teaching is a direct, if not understood, consequence of using unorganized gesture systems. If a communication code is learned through a feedback loop, then it is of considerable importance that the communication signal or message be clear and unambiguous. It is the dominant consideration, however, when a teacher tries to communicate with a child with the kind of speech signal that a deaf child is capable of generating. In order to reduce this ambiguity or error, a teacher of very young deaf children structures the language context so that she can understand the words the child is trying to communicate to her. She then, in turn, is more likely to provide the "correct" model for the child. Often this must be done on an isolated word basis. The central point that should be made about this instructional procedure is that the teacher does this because she must. Somehow, she must reduce the amount of error in her perception of the child's message. In fact, I believe that it is psychologically intolerable for her not to attempt to reduce such error. It seems to me that an organized gesture serves exactly this purpose. It can reduce the amount of error between message sender and receiver and, above all, make the teacher more comfortable.[9] Being more comfortable, she will provide a looser language environment and also provide feedback in a more natural manner by virtue of having gestures for every word in her utterance. This should afford the student a better opportunity to learn the language.

COMMUNICATION

In common with all children, as the deaf child grows older he turns increasingly to his peers for personal growth, approval, and communication "style." It seems fairly clear that, at the present time, the vast majority of profoundly, prelingually deaf do not achieve a really functional skill in speech and speech reading. Those with a lesser degree of hearing impairment and/or with later onset generally exhibit greater proficiency in speech and speech reading. Some do achieve functional skills. Finally, there are those students who become deafened well after they have achieved speech and language skills comparable to hearing children of the same ages. Some unknown proportion of these students appear to be able to assimilate information without undue difficulty in "normal" schools but need the social acceptance and emotional security of being with "like peers."[10]

---

[9]One aspect of a phonetic gesture system such as Cued Speech is troubling. The phonetic cues were developed to complete a full and effective speech system. But a very young deaf child does not speak effectively. It seems to me therefore that the cues when coupled with ineffective vocalization would provide a relatively ambiguous and difficult signal for the teacher.

[10]It is common to find among large groups of adolescent deaf students, clusters of "hard of hearing" students. They are regarded as such by the "deaf" students for a variety of

Still another thing happens. The English they all encounter in their studies becomes increasingly complex as they progress up through the grades. It is the primary medium through which information is filtered in the classroom, in texts, in the larger environment, and sometimes through the student's peers if he and they have achieved a really functional use of English. Today the evidence is very clear (Gentile & DiFrancesca, 1969) that as the majority of deaf children grow older the discrepancy between the level of English that they are able to manage and the level of English used in the information presented to them increases with every year of life. As noted above, it may not be economically feasible to develop materials specifically tailored to their English language needs.

Clearly, the communication problems that at present remain with older deaf children are very complex. And this will continue to be true until the English language skill of older deaf students rises to match the complexity inherent in the material presented to them. Until such happens, if it ever does, I should like to describe present communication problems with older students.

Most current investigators of language development stress that language learning capacity begins to decline after age three. We have, unfortunately, no parameters of slope. It has been stressed here that the main value of Sign English is to provide a model so that a child can learn English. The value or utility of that model should decline approximately as language learning capacity declines. Further, as this occurs, it is probable that deaf adolescents will make greater use of Sign in informal and social settings. Finally, as language learning capacity decreases, we can expect a marked increase in utility for Pidgin Sign English in the classroom and in similar educational settings because that gesture system is simply easier to use. It will be the main carrier for information transfer. Figure 9.2 presents utility curves for all three language varieties with slopes subjectively generated (imagined, if you prefer) for deaf children born of hearing parents. Figure 9.3 provides a counterpart plot for deaf children born of deaf parents who know and use Sign.

Pidgin Sign English is not a homogeneous language variety but, as has been noted earlier, a very heterogeneous group of language varieties. I suspect therefore that the single curve used for Pidgin Sign English in Figures 9.2 and 9.3 would be better depicted by a class of curves. Those Pidgins that are close to Sign English would have a much steeper slope,

---

reasons, e.g., their ability to "speak," their ability to "hear" (as demonstrated by the use of a hearing aid), their lack of proficiency with Sign, the friends they keep, and so on. The sociology of such peer groupings is a really fertile field for investigation but is beyond the scope of this chapter.

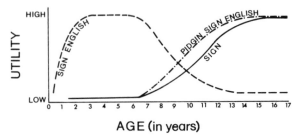

Figure 9.2. Hypothetical utility curves for Sign, Sign English, and Pidgin Sign English in education for children born of hearing parents.

i.e., greater utility in the classroom with increasing age, than those Pidgins that are closer to Sign.

If utility curves such as those in Figures 9.2 and 9.3 could be empirically devised, it should be possible to predict the eventual language competence of a child given knowledge of: (*a*) age at which he was introduced to a given language variety; (*b*) the effectiveness or quality of the language environment for that variety; (*c*) the quality of the linkage or carryover from home to school; and (*d*) the degree to which the different language varieties are consistently used and contrasted in the school setting.

At the present time, the vast majority of adolescent and adult deaf students receive instruction from instructors who sign for themselves and/or through interpreters who sign for the instructors. The deaf students usually are the "class" or sit in on "hearing classes." It is relatively infrequent that the dominant audience is not clearly established. Interpreters are almost always used for guest or outside lecturers and for the "hearing classes." However similar these instructional settings may seem, they are really very different communication situations.

Let me begin with interpreting as a means of communicating with older deaf students. Interpreters are provided by 25 of the 27 existing post-

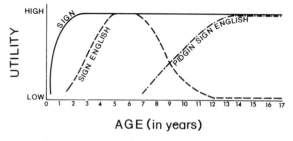

Figure 9.3. Hypothetical utility curves for Sign, Sign English, and Pidgin Sign English in education for children born of deaf parents.

secondary programs for deaf students in America (Stuckless & Delgado, 1973). The National Association of the Deaf has established a Registry of Interpreters for the Deaf which both certifies interpreters and provides information about their availability and use. A model outline of a curriculum for training interpreters has been recently prepared (Sternberg, Tipton, & Schein, 1973). Clearly, the technique and its users are becoming more professional. And there is no doubt that a speaker can communicate effectively with deaf people through an interpreter. There are some limitations to the use of interpreters in educational settings, however, which should be considered.

My comments stem from observations made from 8 years of association with a lecture program at Gallaudet College that employed interpreters generally regarded as among the very best available. Without doubt, the ability of an interpreter to convey information to deaf students is dependent upon the performance of the speaker being interpreted. Leaving aside the question of style,[11] these conditions cause interpreting difficulties:

1. Rapid speech
2. Speech with few pauses or stress on words (no temporal punctuation)
3. Poorly organized speeches
4. Prepared papers which are read
5. Interpolated remarks and digressions
6. Lists of names, places, or things (normally a speaker runs through lists more rapidly than connected passages)
7. Complex sentence structures

Essentially an interpreter can perform at his best with time to group "ideas." The conditions listed above make this more difficult. To keep up with a speaker, and all of the best interpreters are able to do this, they sometimes have to simplify, but more often, are forced to use a Sign English Pidgin which is closer to the Sign English pole than many in their audience are able to comprehend. Here again we have a situation which can be ameliorated when and if students have acquired greater facility with English. Until that happens, it must be reported that there are far too many occasions when deaf students get little information from the interpreter.

Apart from the performance of the speaker, there are other conditions which affect communication. Basically these relate to visibility, e.g., the distance between the interpreter and his audience. Movements of the lips

---

[11]Dull speakers come across as dull.

are the smallest signal, followed by the manual alphabet, and trailed by the largest signal, signs.

Vocabulary, or the limited number of signs for technical vocabulary, causes problems both for interpreters and for instructors who use total or simultaneous communication. However, signs can be invented and are easily learned (Bornstein & Kannapell, 1969; Kannapell, Hamilton, & Bornstein, 1969). At the present time, the National Association of the Deaf is coordinating a joint effort on the part of many postsecondary programs to provide a standardized vocabulary for a variety of important technical subject matters (Pimentel, personal communication).

If we now turn to those classes where the instructor signs while he speaks, it is clear that these circumstances provide the best condition for effective communication. Essentially, all of the parameters of face-to-face communication are under the control of the instructor. He can, within limits, alter his rate of speech, his choice of words and syntax, and the sign language variety he uses. In most class settings where speech is employed, the instructor will probably use a form or variety of Pidgin Sign English. Again it must be recognized that as the material to be communicated involves more complex English, the English language ability of the students acts as a limiting condition. Heterogeneous classes in this regard make for difficult communication even for the very best signers. It should be added, however, that no empirical information on parameters of rate, English complexity, and Pidgin Sign English variety are known.

To this point I have treated Sign in a rather detached fashion. I have been concerned with preparing a deaf student for entry into society at large. There is another point of view. What contributions flow the other way—from Sign and its users to society at large? It takes very little exposure to adult signers before one realizes the expressiveness and power of Sign. It is well suited to drama, and deaf theater groups compete very favorably at university and amateur levels. It is also offered at the professional level by the National Theater of the Deaf. The language variety used by actors depends, of course, upon the production being presented. It usually is closer to Sign than to Sign English. In recent years, Sign has figured in Dance and Rock Gospel productions. These have proved very popular. The Rock Gospel group performs in a Pidgin Sign English which is very graceful and moving. This is another reason that this language variety should not be regarded negatively.[12] Unfortu-

---

[12]It is much easier to parallel the rhythm of songs and poems with Pidgin Sign English than with Sign English because Pidgin Sign English usually does not represent word parts or inflections. As noted earlier, adding word parts requires compounding, which slows rate of transmission.

nately, I can only touch upon the artistic and creative aspects of Sign here. It is a topic worthy of much more extended treatment, however.

Another characteristic of Sign offers an interesting educational application which is possibly less used with deaf than with hearing students. Signers consider mime an important element of style in Sign. Mime, which has no word counterparts, could be used to explain and define many English words to students (deaf or hearing) in terms entirely different from the usual practice of citing English synonyms and English word context. It is an unfortunate consequence of prevailing educational taboos that this form of meaning has not had considerable application in teaching language to very young deaf children.

It is from among the ranks of those who are acquainted with the richness and power of Sign in university life and with adults that one finds the advocates of using Sign for all deaf children as early as possible in a bilingual approach to language learning. For reasons noted throughout this chapter, I believe that a Sign English approach will offer a higher probability of success for more children. I could be wrong.

THE CURRENT STATE OF AFFAIRS

It is still accurate to say that the vast majority of American deaf children of hearing parents are exposed to unorganized gesture systems until they go to school. There they begin to meet with Sign outside the classroom, primarily through contact with their peers. In the absence of adult language models, it is almost a certainty that such children will create, consciously and unconsciously, signs and simple sign structures to communicate with each other. The children in a given school will even devise and use signs not found elsewhere (Cokely & Gawlik, 1974). As these children grow older and increasingly interact with deaf adults, they will adopt "more" of the signs used by adults. How "much more" is a complex question to which we have as yet no clear answers. There is one residue from this situation, however. There has been a strong and abiding desire on the part of many deaf adults to see Sign "standardized" through some mechanism created by such influential organizations as the National Association of the Deaf or Gallaudet College. A direct solution to the problem is simply to permit adult users of Sign to function as models in school settings and to devise Sign English systems for the classroom and home which are as consistent with Sign as possible. The latter course is the announced goal of the more prominent Sign English systems. How well they reach this goal, of course, varies.

In just the last few years, Sign English and Pidgin Sign English have been introduced into the home and into the classroom. The number of schools and day programs using one or another system is growing at a surprisingly rapid rate. It would be nice to report that these systems and language varieties have been selected for use through application of carefully formulated criteria and subjected to empirical evaluation. Nothing could be farther from the truth. They are chosen primarily because of their availability and intuitively assessed worth. It could hardly be otherwise. Children must be educated **now**. Materials and systems are still under development. Formal use of organized gesture systems at early ages has just begun. Goals and expectations are still being formed. It is to be hoped that educators will remain flexible and critical in what must be a very difficult period of change. Progress and techniques must be monitored. Last but not least, educators of the deaf must make use of the resources and professional skills that linguists and scientists can bring to bear on their problems. At present educators often turn to competent signers for advice. It must be stated that facility with Sign endows a person with no more knowledge about how to teach it, modify it for other uses, and evaluate its appropriateness for the classroom than that possessed by native speakers in New York or London or Paris or Moscow for comparable tasks in their languages. Until educators clearly understand the limits to which informants can properly be used, there will continue to arise a variety of wasteful problems caused by variations in habit which detract from the principal job of teaching deaf children as effectively as possible.

SOME FINAL WORDS

I have tried to prepare a review of the role of Sign in the education of the deaf that does some justice to the complexity of the topic. And it is a very complex topic. Consequently, I have had to speculate freely and draw very heavily upon intuition. This is also exactly how I have had to perform over the last few years while directing a project which calls for the development of a Sign English system at the preschool level. This is not an accustomed nor a comfortable position for a scientist, even when the need for change is as compelling as it is in this situation. Taking a position and/or proposing new techniques does serve some useful purposes, however. It is long past time that deaf people receive the benefits of empirical research on matters of importance to them. There are many statements in this chapter which can be supported, refuted, or modified through application of scientific method. It is my hope that persons with appropriate scientific training will undertake work in this area, not only because it will benefit deaf people, but also because there are possible applications for nonverbal hearing retarded children and for some hearing children who may be emotionally disturbed.

ACKNOWLEDGMENTS

I wish to thank John S. Schuchman, James C. Woodward, Jr., Horace N. Reynolds, I. King Jordan, Shirley Stein, and Marianne Collins-Ahlgren for comments on earlier versions of this chapter. My thanks also go to Charles Yeager for a translation of Russian material.

REFERENCES

Anthony, D. A., & Associates (Ed). 1971. *Seeing Essential English*. Educational Services Division, Anaheim Union High School District, P.O. Box 3520, Anaheim, California 98203, 1 and 2.

Battison, R. 1973. Letter to the Editor. *American Annals of the Deaf, 118*, 661–662.

Bellugi, U., & Fischer, S. 1972. A comparison of sign language and spoken language. *Cognition*, 1: 173–200.

Bolton, B. 1971a. Factor analytic studies of communication skills, intelligence, and other psychological abilities of young deaf persons. Paper given in St. Louis, Missouri, Psychometric Society.

Bolton, B. 1971b. A factor analytic study of communication skills and non-verbal abilities of deaf rehabilitation clients. *Multivariate Behavioral Research, 6*, 485–501.

Bolton, B. 1972. Factorial studies of communication skills, non-verbal intelligence, and other psychological abilities of deaf young adults: Validation and refinement. Paper given in Oklahoma City, Oklahoma, Southwestern Psychological Association.

Bonvillian, J., & Charrow, V. 1972. Psycholinguistic implications of deafness: A review. Technical Report No. 188. Stanford, California: Institute for Mathematical Studies in the Social Sciences.

Bornstein, H. 1965. *Reading the manual alphabet*. Washington, D.C.: Gallaudet College Press.

Bornstein, H. 1973. A description of some current sign systems designed to represent English. *American Annals of the Deaf, 118*, 454–470.

Bornstein, H., & Kannapell, B. 1969. *New signs for instructional purposes*. Washington, D.C.: U.S. Office of Education Report 6–1924.

Bornstein, H., Kannapell, B., Saulnier, K., Hamilton, L., & Roy, H. 1973–1974. *Signed English* books: *Little Red Riding Hood, Goldilocks and the three bears, Nursery rhymes from Mother Goose, Hansel and Gretel, The three little pigs, Songs in Signed English* (with record), *The night before Christmas, Three little kittens, Tommy's day, Mealtime at the zoo, I want to be a farmer, Happy birthday Carol, Basic pre-school Signed English dictionary*, Posters: *Rock-a-by-baby, Jack and Jill, Manual alphabet*. Washington, D.C., Gallaudet College Press.

Bornstein, H., Kannapell, B., Saulnier, K., Hamilton, L., & Roy, H. *My toy book, Baby's animal book, A book about me, Count and color, Spring is green, Questions and more questions, Night-day, Sleep-play*. Washington, D.C.: Gallaudet College Press.

Bornstein, H., & Roy, H. 1973. Comment on "Linguistic deficiency and thinking: Research with deaf subjects 1964–69." *Psychological Bulletin, 79*, 211–214.

Brown, R. 1973. Development of the first language in the human species. *American Psychologist, 28*, 97–106.

Cohen, E. L., Namir, L., & Schlesinger, I. M. 1977. *A new dictionary of sign language*. The Hague: Mouton.

Cicourel, A., & Boese, R. 1972. Sign language acquisition and the teaching of deaf children. *American Annals of the Deaf, 117*, 27–33, 403–411.

Cokely, D., & Gawlik, R. 1974. Option II: Childrenese as Pidgin. *Sign Language Studies, 5*, 72–82.

Fant, L. J., Jr. 1972. *Ameslan: An introduction to the American sign language*. Silver Spring, Maryland: National Association of the Deaf.

Ferguson, C. 1959. Diglossia. *Word*, 15, 325–340.

Furth, H. 1971. Linguistic deficiency and thinking: Research with deaf subjects 1964–69. *Psychological Bulletin, 74*, 58–72.

Furth, H. 1973. Further thoughts on thinking and language. *Psychological Bulletin, 79*, 215–216.

Furth, H. 1973b. *Deafness and learning: A psychological approach*. Belmont, California: Wadsworth.

Gentile, A., & DiFrancesca, S. 1969. *Academic achievement test performance of hearing impaired students in the United States: Spring 1969 (Series D, No. 1)*. Washington, D. C.: Office of Demographic Studies, Gallaudet College.

Gustason, G., Pfetzing, D., & Zawolkow, E. 1972. *Signing Exact English*. Rossmoor, California: Modern Signs Press.

Henegar, M., & Cornett, O. 1971. *Cued speech: Handbook for parents*. Washington, D. C.: Gallaudet College Press.

Higgins, E. 1973. An analysis of the comprehensibility of three communication methods used with hearing impaired students. *American Annals of the Deaf, 118*, 46–49.

Kannapell, B., Hamilton, L., & Bornstein, H. 1969. *Signs for instructional purposes*. Washington, D. C.: Gallaudet College Press.

Madsen, W. 1972. *Conversational sign language: An intermediate manual*. Washington, D. C.: Gallaudet College Press.

Meadow, K. 1968. Early communication in relation to the deaf child's intellectual, social and communicative functioning. *American Annals of the Deaf, 113*, 29–41.

Moores, D. 1971. *Recent research on manual communication*. Occasional Paper No. 7. Minneapolis: Univ. of Minnesota Press.

Moores, D. F., McIntyre, C. K., & Weiss, K. L. 1972. *Evaluation of programs for hearing impaired children: Report of 1971–1972*. Research Report 39. Minneapolis: Univ. of Minnesota).

O'Rourke, T. J. (Ed). 1972. *Psycholinguistics and total communication: The state of the art*. Washington, D. C.: American Annals of the Deaf.

O'Rourke, T. (Ed). 1973. *A basic course in manual communication*. Silver Spring, Maryland: National Association of the Deaf.

Quigley, S. 1969. *The influence of fingerspelling on the development of language, communication and educational achievement in deaf children*. Urbana, Illinois: Univ. of Illinois Press.

Quigley, S., & Frisina, D. R. 1961. Institutionalization and psycho-educational development in deaf children, *Council for Exceptional Children*, Monograph No. 3.

Rawlings, B. 1973. *Characteristics of hearing impaired students by hearing status, United*

States: 1970–71 (Series D, Number 10). Washington, D.C.: Office of Demographic Studies, Gallaudet College.

Schlesinger, H., & Meadow, K. 1972. *Sound and sign: Childhood deafness and mental health*. Berkeley, California: Univ. of California Press.

Smith, D. 1972. Language as social adaptation. *George Washington University Working Papers in Linguistics*, No. 5.

Solovjev, I., Shif, Z. H., Rozanova, T., & Yashkova, N. (Ed.) 1971. *The psychology of deaf children*. Moscow: Pedagogica.

Sternberg, M., Tipton, C. & Schein, J. 1973. *Interpreter training: A curriculum guide*. New York: Deafness Research and Training Center.

Stevenson, E. 1964. A study of the educational achievement of deaf children of deaf parents. *California News, 80*, 143.

Stokoe, W. C. 1970. Sign language diglossia. *Studies in Linguistics, 21*, 27–41.

Stokoe, W. C. 1973. Comments on back translation. *Sign Language Studies, 3*, 39–46.

Stokoe, W. C. 1975. Face-to-face interaction: Sign to language. *In organization of behavior: Face to face interaction*. The Hague: Mouton.

Stokoe, W. C. Jr., Casterline, D. C., & Croneberg, C. G. 1965, *A dictionary of American Sign Language on linguistic principles*. Washington, D.C.: Gallaudet College Press.

Stuckless, E. R., & Birch, J. 1966. The influence of early manual communication in relation to the deaf child's intellectual, social and communicative functioning. *American Annals of the Deaf, 111*, 452–462.

Stuckless, E. R., & Delgado, G. 1973. *A guide to college/career programs for deaf students*. Washington, D. C.: Gallaudet College Press.

Tervoort, B., and Verbeck, A. 1967. Analysis of communicative structure patterns in deaf children. V.R.A. Project Report RD-467, 64-65 (Z. W. O. Onderzoek, NR: 585–15). Groningen, The Netherlands.

Tweney, R., & Hoemann, H. 1973a. Back translation: A method for the analysis of manual languages. *Sign Language Studies, 2*, 51–72.

Tweney, R., & Hoemann, H. 1973b. Authors' rejoinder. *Sign Language Studies, 2*, 77–80.

Vernon, M., & Koh, S. 1970. Early communication and deaf children's achievement. *American Annals of the Deaf, 116*, 527–536.

Vernon, M., & Koh, S. 1971. Effects of oral preschool compared to early manual communication in deaf children. *American Annals of the Deaf, 116*, 569–574.

Wampler, D. 1972. *Linguistics of visual English: Morpheme list one, an introduction to the spatial symbol system, questions and answers*. Santa Rosa, California.

Withrow, F. 1973. Education of deaf children in Russia. *Deaf American, 26*, 7–8.

Woodward, J. 1973. Some characteristics of Pidgin Sign English. *Sign Language Studies, 3*, 39–46.

Woodward, J. 1973b. A program to prepare language specialists for work with the deaf. *Sign Language Studies, 2*, 1–8.

Part IV

METHODOLOGICAL PROBLEMS

10

Problems in Sign Language Research

WILLIAM C. STOKOE

EXTRINSIC PROBLEMS

Problems of sign language research come from both within and without. Extrinsic problems may be arbitrary, as when a source of funding discourages or forbids scientific curiosity about signing. But sign language research does take place, as this volume attests, and problems other than those of the data and of explaining it still arise. Such extrinsic problems have either an institutional source—from the nature of educational establishments and those of their subsystems devoted to teaching the deaf—or a popular source—from the ideas, beliefs, and misconceptions that most persons have about gesture and sign language.

Problems intrinsic to sign language research are also of two kinds: Some affect the practice of the research; others are problems of theory. Practical problems may appear troublesome, but they often yield to ingenuity and the passage of time (at least while science and technology are advancing). Theoretical problems will sooner or later frustrate sign language research, but considering them fully may well advance knowledge of things worth knowing.

Educational Systems

Formal systems of public education are instituted by societies for the express purpose of maintaining the structures and value systems of those societies by inculcating them in the young. The institutions are therefore intentionally ethnocentric; and judged in terms of the purposes they serve, it may be well that they are so. Focusing on the values of one culture, they give strength to the social order they serve, and in a relatively stable population they contribute much to cultural integrity. However, when appreciable numbers of young whose cultural, linguistic, or other equipment is different from that of the social norm enter these educational systems, this ethnocentrism, usually unexamined, may destroy instead of build, may shut out instead of lead out.

The impact of such ethnocentrism on sign language research is felt also by other research efforts which must regard cultural diversity. As long as teachers are trained to believe that whatever is in the reading series is right and that proficiency in the received standard of the society is the precious product of all their efforts, sign language research, like Spanish, Indian, and Black American cultural experience will face hostility, or worse, indifference in the schools.

The hostility and indifference of the establishment do not directly affect the undertaking of sign language research, which usually has a university and foundation base, but they do prevent the results of such research from accomplishing what increases in knowledge should do. Another problem for those who would study sign language is that the xenophobia of public education may work to lessen its use. But discouragement of the study and the use of sign language has a long history in the educational subestablishment specifically for the deaf.

Special Education Subsystems

An observer outside the field of special education for the deaf might reasonably suppose that there if anywhere sign language and research into its nature would flourish. This observer would be right if the period of time were between 1760 and 1830. However, the resolution adopted in Milan in 1880 by the International Congress of Educators of the Deaf has been questioned by some but never rejected by the established programs for the deaf in most countries:

> The congress, considering the incontestable superiority of speech over signing in restoring the deaf mute to society, and in giving him a more perfect knowledge of language, declares that the oral method ought to be preferred to that of signs for the education and instruction of the deaf and dumb [quoted in Denmark, 1973].

Research problems multiply when unsupported claims are preferred to scientific knowledge, but institutions **for** the deaf raise further problems, especially when they support research designed to show that sign language is a poor second best to speaking, or that young deaf children may use signs at first but abandon them as they gain proficiency in "grammatical language." Like the general educational establishment, that for the deaf exists to fit every child to the—largely unexamined—norm. Hence it happens that much in print about sign languages comes from teachers of the deaf who give the impression that the signs they describe are only manually expressed code symbols for words (as finger spelling is in fact a code for letters), and that "proper sign language" is the language of these teachers encoded manually. As long as languages differ and educators equate difference with deficit—of vocabulary, of language, of cognition—so long will genuine research into the nature of sign language encounter problems.

Public education and special education for the deaf are both subsumed in governmental programs. These too often hinder sign language research. How native competence in sign language may affect the deaf child's learning of a language like English is just beginning to emerge from research (Mindel & Vernon, 1971; Moores, McIntyre, & Weiss, 1972, 1973; Quigley, 1969; Schlesinger & Meadow, 1972; Stuckless & Birch, 1966). But the Lewis committee in Britain (Lewis, 1968) found no need for the use of "finger spelling and signing in the education of deaf children." Even well-conducted studies by those who have been in schools for the deaf may reflect the built-in bias of the system.

The net effect on policymakers of the usual surveys is likely to be that the system needs support for its attempt to make the deaf better consumers of the official language, and the less said and done about how the deaf communicate with each other the better.

But this attitude must change if sign language research is to continue and to have a proper effect. How the deaf communicate with each other is the crux of sign language research despite official neglect and opposition. Deafness, especially early in life, imposes a communicative situation which, since the species emerged, has resulted in evolution of several highly developed languages with visible instead of vocal transmission systems. A language and a special communicative situation imply a community. A community implies human beings; and if ever a group of human beings needed recognition by the educational establishment of its special situation, that group is the deaf.

Exactly that which official surveys, studies, and commission reports ignore, the sign language used by deaf people interacting, can be the key to improved life chances for those people. Research is now showing how and why the study, use, and official recognition of sign language can lead to better educational achievement, subcultural solidarity, and meaningful integration. It is time that educational establishments stopped their discouragement of research effort and began to benefit by the knowledge it offers. Only by recognizing and respecting the integrity of linguistic and cultural minorities can a modern state win the loyalty and valuable contribution of such minorities to society as a whole.

Misconceptions about Language

What people in general believe about language and about sign language also poses problems. The layman may be willing to admit that physicists and biologists working with subatomic particles or DNA molecules know what they are about, even though their research goes against the grain of common sense and common knowledge. But the layman is not at all willing to admit that a language which has different rules from his own makes sense or that linguists can have anything of importance to say about it. Gleason (1965) shrewdly attributes this attitude to the history of American education:

> Each parent considers himself as good as an expert, most particularly in those segments of the curriculum which have come down from the one-room schools—reading, writing, arithmetic, and grammar. . . . The typical American can hardly conceive of anyone having any special competence in these rudiments—all there is to know is common knowledge [p. 4].

Misconceptions about Sign Languages

This attitude toward grammar and grammarians may grow into suspicion that linguists are charlatans who make simple things hard for their own purposes. Such suspicion threatens not just sign language but all language research. Yet, along with it, many people have completely different ideas about gestures—perhaps because gesture is not in the curriculum. One such popular idea is that "other people" gesticulate when they talk; its holder, of course, supposes that he and his kind are so superior in language, propriety, and ratiocination that they do not need or use gestures. Another idea, hardly compatible with this but often occurring with it, gives gestures universal meanings: Nods, smiles, frowns, headshakes, hand waving, and finger crooking will work any place on the globe where language difference makes speaking useless.

The crudity, slowness, and inaccuracy of such enforced gestural exchanges predisposes many who experience them to suppose that all sign language must be equally unlanguagelike. Nothing could be further from the truth, as Mallery pointed out long ago (1881/1972). But Mallery, zealous in proving that meaningful gestures are a human universal, also pointed out another fact—that many gestures are iconic. Both laymen and many researchers, after Mallery, have joined these two with an undistributed middle so that a serious problem of sign language research today comes from the false syllogism that:

1. All men use gestures.
2. Gestures iconically reveal meaning.
3. "The sign language" is universal.

Add the historical fallacy and the false conclusion is further perverted— sign language is simple. But press the holder of these notions to recall his difficulty getting understood by gesture in a foreign situation, and he may add that "the sign language" he is talking about is used by "primitive tribes," or by "the deaf and dumb," or by people "somewhere else."

INTRINSIC PROBLEMS

No less important than extrinsic problems which need not arise, though they waste much energy and encumber research efforts, are problems intrinsic to sign language research. These latter are, of course, also much more interesting to those who would learn more about sign languages. They will therefore be treated here in more detail.

Whether the researcher comes to sign language from the discipline of anthropology, linguistics, psychology, or sociology, the first need keenly felt is that for means of recording, reducing, and retrieving data. Direct observation of people interacting by means of Sign is a necessary but tantalizing activity. Like listening to hearing persons converse in an utterly foreign language, watching an exchange of signing between two deaf people presents a hopeless variety of phenomena, but at first not a clue to its structure or patterns. However, the student of an exotic spoken language has definite advantages. The principle of alphabetic, i.e., phonemic, writing is ancient; and refinements starting with Panini and continuing through the International Phonetic Alphabet to the *Sound Patterns of English* make the task of phonology more manageable. The task of cherology (analysis of the submorphemic structure of the expressive system of sign language) has no such tradition of helpful studies. Other than the 1960 elucidation that three essential parameters of Sign are *tab, dez,* and *sig*—i.e., location, handshape, and action—there are only suggestions that facial and other visible activity and hand orientation are important.

Technology for Recording Data

To examine sign language scientifically, i.e., to look, judge, look again, test, change the conditions, look again, check, verify, and so on, the researcher needs means of recording data and reproducing it accurately at will. Here again the student of spoken language has technological advantages. Even looking back only a dozen years, we see sound recordings can be made with improved fidelity, at less expense, and with new devices so small that they are both portable to any place data may be found and so easily concealed that their use (however unethical) may be unsuspected by informants.

Technology has advanced in the same period enough so that 8 mm color film and videotape recorders are within the reach of many sign language research programs. However, this technology has not solved all the problems of sign language research.

Film has advantages in definition, videotape in rapidity of replay. Film cameras are also far more portable but usually limited to cartridge-length runs of 5 minutes without a break. The bulkier VTR equipment can at least continue uninterrupted for 30 minutes or more. Both are capable of reproducing real motion slowed for study, but this gets into theoretical problems which will be taken up below. Both are also susceptible to overuse—miles of unanalyzed signing on film or tape constitute an unjustified expense, a gray area in sign language research.

Reduction of Data

There can be no improvement in technology for reducing sign language data until research makes quite clear what is wanted. When all phonologists agree that a bilabial closure followed by release of air, with or without aspiration, but without vocal-fold vibration can be adequately represented by the symbol [p], it is easy enough to find typewriters, teletype machines, and computer on-line printers ready to assist in analysis, in grammar writing, and in lexicography. But sign language research is too new to have evolved one generally accepted system of notation.

Ultimately, deciding what to represent and what to leave unrepresented in sign language notation depends on linguistic theory. This will be discussed further in the section entitled "Theories of Language," but it is useful also to consider the matter from the aspect of technology and graphics.

A first consideration is machine versus human action. For early stages of observation and analysis, symbols which the laboratory or field-worker can draw rapidly may be more necessary than the capability of printing all the symbols with a keyboard machine. But for compiling sign language lexicon and for exchange of information among researchers—especially for the comparative study of diverse sign languages—typewritten or printed notation has advantages. Ideally, a cursive form for rapid field use and a related machine font would both be available.

Second, the number of separate symbols and manner of their use is dictated by the choice of machine. The Vari-typer font designed for the *Dictionary of American Sign Language* (Stokoe, Casterline, Croneberg, 1965/1976) contains up to 90 characters controlled by a 30-position keyboard with two shifts. The newer IBM Selectric system will allow 88 characters from a 44-position keyboard. But a designer of type-character symbols for sign language should consider that a smaller number of primary symbols is preferable. Understandable English can be printed out with 26 characters, a space bar to separate words, and a key to move the paper up for printing a new line. The cost of adding numerals and punctuation marks to this minimum ought to be weighed carefully.

The 55 characters used in the 1965 dictionary were put into more than 55 of the 90 spaces available, because analysis of sig (significant sign action) made it necessary to use more than one character to note a sig. By making sig characters half-height it was possible to stack them vertically to denote simultaneous occurrence (e.g., TD$_\S^\S$), and to repeat them horizontally (e.g., TD^{SS}) to denote sig actions performed in sequence. The capability of printing two characters in the same horizontal space (at the cost of operator time in backspacing or pressing a no-advance key) economizes on the total number of symbols. Thus in the dictionary font, a high curve (⌒) denotes upper head as in signs for *know* or *hat*; a low curve (⌣) denotes mouth or chin as in *eat*; and both vertically aligned (◯) denote the whole head region as in *pretty*.

Another technological economy was achieved by using superscripts and subscripts. In the dictionary, subscripts are used with tab or dez symbols to show orientation; e.g., the signs *school* and *money* are identical except for rotation of the dez hand (B_v in *school*, B_a in *money*). Subscripts or superscripts are also used to indicate placement of the hands relative to each other. Finally, diacritical marks in superscript position indicate repetition, sharply staccato action, alternation, and reversal.

Retrieving Data

This review of some of the technical problems in recording and reducing sign language data does not imply that the problems are solved but does allow more precise definition of practical problems still facing researchers. Retrieving information reduced to notation presents a third problem area and also ground from which to assess other problems.

When all the possible uses to which sign language notation may be put are considered, quite obviously a variety of systems of recording data— i.e., writing sign language—may work adequately. The linguist needs transcriptions narrow enough to allow him to analyze sign phonology (Battison, 1974) and broad enough to allow syntactic analysis without the distraction of differences at the level of transmission. The sociologist or ethnographer needs all the detail about variation that can be observed and recorded. Those interested in physical or behavioral evolution need information about sign language activity which the linguist and sociolinguist may often ignore. Those interested in the relation of signing to dance, in the collection and preservation of folklore texts or conscious Sign art forms, as well as in effective teaching of Sign language and culture require different selectivity in a notation system. It is possible indeed to find notation systems which have been devised to meet the needs of each of these groups.

However, when one looks at the transcription in any of these systems of a stretch of signing and tries to recreate the activity—as is at least partially possible with orthographic, phonetic, or phonemic scripts—the shortcomings of these specialized notation systems become apparent. Perhaps two systems, not one, for recording, reducing, and retrieving sign language should be aimed at: one to enable competent native users of the language to read and write it, the other to enable linguists and other specialists in language to describe for each other observations of activity believed to be significant.

Looked at in this way, the technological problems are seen again to require theoretical foundations to be resolvable; but at least the researcher need not compound difficulty by trying to provide for sign language overnight the whole range of instruments from stylus, brush, and chisel to movable type, keyboards, and light-emitting diodes, nor by trying to straddle the choices among ideograph, syllabary, and alphabet.

The Problem of Significance

Another practical problem for the sign language researcher to face concerns access to significant data. What to look for, where, and how are questions not heretofore given sufficient attention. Caution must be exercised, as was indicated above, in utilizing as data descriptions of signs which state, or tacitly imply, that these are simply manual representations of words. But if the hearing teacher of the deaf is not always a reliable source, neither are the hearing researcher nor the uncritically selected deaf informant. A researcher who was not born deaf cannot easily escape speciocentric assumptions about thought, language, and speech (see Stokoe, 1972, pp. 122–125). A deaf informant may not have native competence in a sign language.

Recent work by Woodward (1973a, 1973b, 1973c) shows that research must take into account not only where signers live and have lived but also such questions as whether their parents also were deaf, their age at first using signs, and their socioeconomic and ethnic background. O'Rourke (1973) also has some negative and ironic criticism that sign language research should heed:

> No one can expect to master a language overnight. It has been said that it takes four or five years to master a language and even then, the individual will not have the skill of a native speaker. One can, however, spend three months studying the language of some primeval tribe and earn a Ph.D. in Linguistics for describing it [p. IX].

Problems of this nature need not vitiate sign language research. If the researcher considers the social nature of language as well as its linguistic nature, data will be sought in real rather than in contrived situations and due attention paid to the function of sign language as well as to its structure. The kind of information that may be elicited from an isolated informant, even if he should be the last surviving native speaker of the language studied, still has its value—if the language is spoken. But an isolated deaf informant among hearing nonsigners may bring them little more of value than would a hearing person dropped into a milieu of none but deaf signers. While a new generation of researchers are being trained from among deaf signers, it is essential that sign language research take full notice of as many social and cultural factors as the state of the art allows.

THEORIES OF LANGUAGE

Remaining problems in sign language research challenge and frustrate the researcher, who may view the present state of language science and linguistic theory and the lack of any scientific theory of man either as severely limiting research scope and relevance or as offering a chance to shape theory. Such a view, of course, does not open from activity intended to show difference in signer and speaker competence by contrasting a sign language with a language in global use. Nevertheless, such activity, sometimes referred to as research, goes on as if it were necessary to prove that those who have only incompletely learned a second language commit errors when they use it. A proper perspective on this kind of activity might be given by transposing it, in imagination, 13 centuries back.

Suppose two groups of subjects in seventh-century England are given scholastic aptitude tests, or any other intelligence tests composed in the language used for education in that time and place. Subjects in Group A are monolingual native speakers of the Anglo-Saxon dialect of their home district, while subjects in Group L are novices or monks engaged in reading and copying manuscripts, i.e., are fluent users of Latin. There can be little doubt of the outcome. In language competence, in general knowledge, and in intelligence, Group L will far surpass Group A. How otherwise when tests and testing are in Language L? As Hewes (1974) writes, "One might have concluded that the vernaculars like Anglo-Saxon had no future as 'real languages'." Sign language researchers need not make problems for themselves by blundering into such conclusions.

The theory of descriptive or structural linguistics seemed to exclude sign languages, but not all structuralists were hostile to sign language research. Sapir (1921/1949) lists sign or gesture languages beginning with Plains Indians and the deaf and moving toward the kind of signaling done at sea or in forests. He then concludes, "The intelligibility of these vague symbolisms can hardly be due to anything but their automatic and silent translation into the terms of a fuller flow of language [1949, p. 21]." Apparently he leaves open the question whether the less vague kinds of gesture systems may have languagelike structure. Bloomfield (1933), without adding justification, goes beyond this position. In words which echo Sapir he briefly discusses and dismisses gesture languages:

> It seems certain that these gesture languages ["lower-class Neapolitan, Trappist, plains Indian, deaf-mute"] are merely developments of ordinary gesture and that any and all complicated or not immediately intelligible gestures are based on the conventions of ordinary speech [1933, p. 39].

Bloomfield limits his linguistic theory further:

> Apparent exceptions [to this dictum that "speech and the manner of speech are our most effective method of signaling"] such as elaborate systems of gesture, deaf-and-dumb language, signaling codes, the use of writing, telegraphy, and so on, turn out, upon inspection, to be merely derivatives of language [1933, p. 144].

Unfortunately, for about 25 years no one did inspect any of these elaborate systems carefully, nor had Bloomfield himself done so, or it would have been discovered that a different theoretical relationship of language, speech, and other signaling methods was needed. Sign language research, ruled out of order by the theoreticians, had no problems in that era.

However, credit and thanks should be given to those second-generation structuralists who, from 1956 onward, encouraged and helped the writer in his first investigations of the "phonology" and morphology of American Sign Language—especially William Austin, Henry Lee Smith, Jr., and George L. Trager. Their position was not that Sign must be language but a true scientific willingness to let evidence that it might be come into court, as Bloomfield would not.

Since Chomsky (1957), linguistic theory is too protean to capsulize; however, one of its manifestations might well be a manifesto for sign language researchers. If important linguistic processes operate to make the surface appear quite unlike what is theorized to be the deep or abstract structure of language, then one might suppose that the language faculty lies so deep within (silent as well as motionless) human cognition that its expression may be indifferently vocal or gestural. In fact, however, few first- or second-generation transformationalists have found much to interest them in sign languages. One reason may be that sign languages, like American Indian languages, have more going on inside the sign or word and less going on in the rearrangements, deletions, and other transformations of the strings of words, than do the languages most often studied (Abbott, 1975). Another reason may be that sign languages, like Chinese (Wang, 1973; Woodward, 1972), do not have the inflectional class systems of Indo-European and related languages which take up a large part of transformational grammars. Though the term "language universals" seems to deny it, much theory which is derived ultimately from its developers' competence in English raises problems for sign language research in the form of shibboleths.

However, enough time seems to have elapsed and theoretical positions to have evolved so that younger scholars can deal with portions of sign language systems in acceptably formal ways (see particularly Battison, 1974; Frishberg 1974; Frishberg & Gough, 1973a, 1973b).

Nevertheless, problems of theory still arise to trouble sign language researchers. Features and constraints have been formally described to show a systematic "phonology" of ASL hand configurations (Battison, 1975; Battison, Markowicz, & Woodward, 1974; Woodward, 1973b). Sign phonology thus appears to belong to the same genus as any systematic phonology. The rules governing sign locations and sign motions seem to be more recalcitrant but should be describable in time. A deeper problem applies as much to any language study as to sign language research: Can we be sure just those features or phenomena now accounted for in current phonologies are the lot? In terms of speech, were linguists correct in excluding paralinguistic phenomena from phonology proper? Among others, Yngve (1975) says no. And what of gestures and other nonverbal communicative behavior? Has it no direct, formal relation to language? Sarles (1975) argues that all this may be "louder"—i.e., more effective methods of signaling than Bloomfield and many others think. In sign language research, the question that haunts the researcher concerns what the eyes, the face, the head, the rest of the body are doing while the hands are working according to their rules.

There are no answers to the questions yet, but developing linguistic theory may enable researchers to cope better with them. Also significant to sign language research is recent work in discourse analysis, the ethnography of communication, semiotics, pragmatics, etc. Conversely, what is discovered about the relation of the expressive system of Sign to the more general language faculty may make significant contributions to theories of language and behavior.

A Theory of Man—A Desideratum

When discussion turns to the adequacy of linguistic theory to explain human communication, human cognition, and the functioning of language in social structures and processes, it becomes obvious that the shortcomings are not solely those of linguistics. Psychological, physiological, and social theory and all their branches fail also to answer important questions. If man emerged by long, slow evolution from the primate line, then so too did his language, and what do all our sciences know about it, for sure? If speech and language came all at once, by a sudden mutation perhaps, then what was the state of affairs just before it and immediately afterward?

Sign language research needs answers, but it also may be of some use in the quest. Other animals use vocal signals. Other animals use visual displays—"gesture" could be applied to more than primate activity. Man's use of voice and man's language are unique, and seemingly inseparable, now. But as pre-man became bipedal, erect, dependent more on noninstinctive reaction than on natural weapons, he made and used tools. While he was using hands and teeth and brain to make tools and weapons, was he not developing symbolic behavior as well? Premack's experiments (1970, 1971) and those of the Gardners (Gardner & Gardner, 1971) show at least that in a nonhuman species there is an unsuspectedly large potential for symbolic behavior. Hewes' suggestion (1973a, 1973b, 1974) that gestures could have played an important role in developing language and in evolving the neurological basis for language points to a direction not taken by previous research. But the future of sign language research will depend much on how soon the physical and the social, the biological, and the cultural sciences can evolve a unified science of man.

REFERENCES

Abbott, C. 1975. Encodedness and sign language. *Sign Language Studies, 7,* 109–120.

Battison, R. 1974. Phonological deletion in American Sign Language. *Sign Language Studies, 5.* 1–19.

Battison, R., Markowicz, H., & Woodward, J. C. 1974. A good rule of thumb: Variable phonology in ASL. In R. W. Shuy (Ed.), *New ways of analyzing variation in English.* Washington, D.C.: Georgetown Univ. Press.

Bloomfield, L. 1933. *Language.* New York: Holt.

Chomsky, N. 1957. *Syntactic structures.* The Hague: Mouton.

Denmark, J. 1973. The education of deaf children. *Hearing, 28,* 284–293.

Frishberg, N. 1974. Arbitrariness and iconicity. Paper delivered at Linguistic Society of America Meetings, San Diego, Dec. 1973.

Frishberg, N., & Gough, B. 1973a. Morphology in American Sign Language. Salk Institute Working Paper, San Diego, California.

Frishberg, N., & Gough, B. 1973b. Time on our hands. Paper delivered at the 3rd California Linguistics Association Meeting, Stanford.

Gardner, B., & Gardner, R. A. 1971. Two-way communication with an infant chimpanzee. In A. Schrier & F. Stollnitz (Eds.), *Behavior of nonhuman primates.* New York: Academic Press. Pp. 117–183.

Gleason, H. A., Jr. 1965. *Linguistics and English grammar.* New York: Holt.

Hewes, G. W. 1973a. An explicit formulation of the relationship between tool-using, tool-making, and the emergence of language. *Visible Language, 7,* 101–127.

Hewes, G. W. 1973b. Primate communication and the gestural origin of language. *Current Anthropology, 14,* 5–24.

Hewes, G. W. 1974. Gesture language in culture contact. *Sign Language Studies, 4,* 1–34.

Lewis, M. M. (Ed.) 1968. *Education of deaf children. The possible place of finger spelling and signing.* London: Her Majesty's Stationery Office.

Mallery, D. G. 1972. *Sign language among North American Indians.* The Hague: Mouton. [Originally published 1881.]

Mindel, E. D., & Vernon, M. 1971. *They grow in silence.* Silver Spring, Maryland: National Association of the Deaf.

Moores, D. F., McIntyre, C. K., & Weiss, K. 1972. Evaluation of programs for hearing impaired children. Minneapolis, RDD Center, Univ. of Minnesota, *Report #39.*

Moores, D. F., McIntyre, C. K., & Weiss, K. 1973. Gestures, signs, and speech in the evaluation of programs. *Sign Language Studies, 3,* 9–28.

O'Rourke, T. J. 1973. *A basic course in manual communication.* (rev. ed.) Silver Spring, Maryland: National Association of the Deaf.

Premack, D. 1970. The education of Sarah. *Psychology Today, 4.4,* 55–58.

Premack, D. 1971. Language in a chimpanzee? *Science, 172,* 808–822.

Quigley, S. P. 1969. *The influence of fingerspelling on the development of language, communication, and educational achievement in deaf children.* Urbana: Univ. of Illinois Press.

Sapir, E. 1949. *Language: An introduction to the study of speech.* New York: Harcourt. [Originally published 1921.]

Sarles, H. 1975. A human ethological approach to communication. In Kendon, Harris, & Key (Eds.) *The organization of behavior in face-to-face communication*. The Hague: Mouton. Pp. 19–45.

Schlesinger, H. S., & Meadow, K. P. 1972. *Sound and sign: Childhood deafness and mental health*. Berkeley: Univ. of California Press.

Stokoe, W. C. 1960. *Sign language structure*. *Studies in Linguistics: Occasional Paper 8* (repr. Silver Spring, Maryland: Linstok Press).

Stokoe, W. C., Casterline, D. C., Croneberg, C. G. 1965/1974. *A dictionary of American Sign Language on linguistic principles*. Washington D.C.: Gallaudet College Press; rev. ed. Silver Spring, MD: Linstok Press.

Stokoe, W. C., Jr. 1972. *Semiotics and human sign languages*. The Hague: Mouton.

Stokoe, W. C., Jr. 1973. Comments on "back translation". *Sign Language Studies, 3,* 73–76.

Stuckless, E. R., & Birch, J. W. 1966. The influence of early manual communication on the linguistic development of deaf children. *American Annals of the Deaf, 111*, 452–560.

Wang, W. S-Y., Chan, S. W., & T'Sou, B. K. 1973. Chinese linguistics and the computer. *Linguistics, 118*, 89–117.

Winnom, W. 1973. Linguistic hybridization. In D. Hymes (Ed.), *Pidginization and creolization of languages*. New York: Cambridge Univ. Press.

Woodward, J. C., Jr. 1972. A transformational approach to the syntax of American Sign Language. In W. C. Stokoe, *Semiotics and human sign languages*. The Hague: Mouton. Pp. 131–151.

Woodward, J. C., Jr. 1973a. Implicational lects on the deaf diglossic continuum. Unpublished Ph.D. dissertation, Georgetown Univ.

Woodward, J. C., Jr. 1973b. Some characteristics of Pidgin Sign English. *Sign Language Studies, 3*, 39–46.

Woodward, J. C., Jr. 1973c. Inter-rule implication in American Sign Language. *Sign Language Studies, 3*, 47–56.

Yngve, V. 1975. Human linguistics and face to face interaction. In Kendon, Harris, & Key (Eds.), *The organization of behavior in face-to-face communication*. The Hague: Mouton. Pp. 47–62.

Index

A
B
C 8
D 9
E 0
F 1
G 2
H 3
I 4
J 5